W9-CEP-065

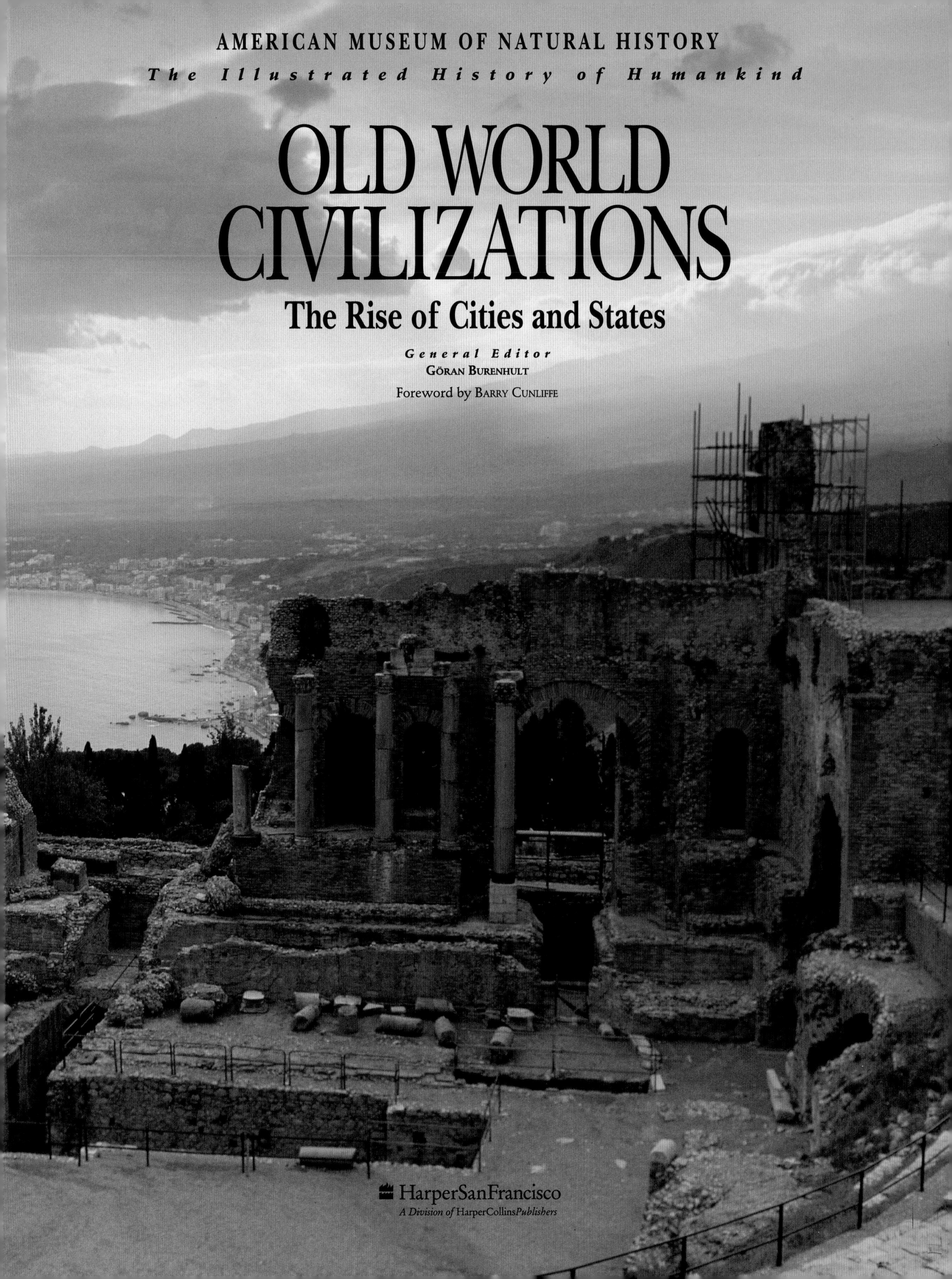

AMERICAN MUSEUM OF NATURAL HISTORY

The Illustrated History of Humankind

OLD WORLD CIVILIZATIONS

The Rise of Cities and States

General Editor

GÖRAN BURENHULT

Foreword by BARRY CUNLIFFE

HarperSanFrancisco

A Division of HarperCollinsPublishers

OLD WORLD CIVILIZATIONS: *The Illustrated History of Humankind.*
Copyright © 1994 by Weldon Owen Pty Limited/Bra Böcker AB.

All rights reserved. No part of this book may be used or reproduced in any manner
whatsoever without written permission except in the case of brief quotations
embodied in critical articles and reviews. For information address HarperCollins
Publishers, 10 East 53rd Street, New York, NY 10022.

FIRST EDITION

Conceived and produced by
Weldon Owen Pty Limited
43 Victoria Street, McMahons Point NSW 2060, Australia
Fax 61 2 929 8352

and

Bra Böcker AB
S–263 80 Höganäs
Sweden
Fax 46 42 330504

The Illustrated History of Humankind
Publisher: Sheena Coupe
Series Coordinator: Annette Carter
Volume Coordinator: Dawn Titmus
Copy Editors: Glenda Downing, Margaret McPhee,
Margaret Olds, Bruce Semler
Editorial Assistant: Vesna Radojcic
Picture Research Coordinator: Jenny Mills
Picture Editors: Karen Burgess, Annette Crueger, Kathy Gerrard
Index: Garry Cousins
Art Director: Sue Burk
Design: Denese Cunningham, Janet Marando, Mark Nichols,
David Roffey, Michele Wiener
Design Assistants: Denny Allnutt and Andrée Dysart
Cartographic Assistants: Peter Barker and Dianne Regtop
Airbrushed shadows: David Wood
Production Director: Mick Bagnato
Production Coordinator: Simone Perryman

Weldon Owen Pty Limited
Chairman: Kevin Weldon
President: John Owen
General Manager: Stuart Laurence
Coeditions Director: Derek Barton

Bra Böcker AB
Publisher: Anders Janson
Editorial Director: Claes Göran Green
Editor: Christina Christoffersson

Library of Congress Cataloging-in-Publication Data

Old World civilizations / Göran Burenhult, general editor.--1st ed.
      p. cm. -- (The Illustrated history of humankind : v. 3)
   Includes index.
   ISBN 0-06-250270-0
   1. Civilization, Ancient -- History. I. Burenhult, Göran.
II. Series.
GN303. I4 1994 vol. 3
[C8311]
900 s -- dc20
[930]   93-38350
                                                  CIP

94 95 96 97 98 WOHK 10 9 8 7 6 5 4 3 2 1

Manufactured by Mandarin Offset
Printed in Hong Kong

A WELDON OWEN PRODUCTION

Endpapers
A painting in the Etruscan Tomb of the
Shields, at Tarquinia, in Italy, showing
people enjoying a meal, accompanied
by musicians.
SCALA

Page 1
This gold death-mask of a king from
Mycenae, thought by German archaeologist
Heinrich Schliemann to be Agamemnon,
dates from the sixteenth century BC.
C.M. DIXON/PHOTO RESOURCES

Pages 2–3
A ruined Greek theatre at Taormina, in the
Messina province of eastern Sicily, Italy.
SANDRO PRATO/BRUCE COLEMAN LTD

Page 240
A detail of the Gundestrup cauldron, a
huge silver vessel of Celtic origin dating
from about 100 BC, which was found in
a bog in Jutland, Denmark.
NATIONAL MUSEUM OF DENMARK

General Editor

Dr Göran Burenhult
Associate Professor of Archaeology
University of Stockholm, Sweden

Editorial Board

Dr Peter Rowley-Conwy
Lecturer
Department of Archaeology
University of Durham, UK

Dr David Hurst Thomas
Curator of Anthropology
American Museum of Natural History
New York, USA

Dr Wulf Schiefenhövel
Professor
Research Institute for Human Ethology
Max Planck Society
Andechs, Germany

Dr J. Peter White
Reader
School of Archaeology, Classics
and Ancient History
University of Sydney, Australia

Contributors

P.J. Casey
Reader in Archaeology
Department of Archaeology
University of Durham, UK

Dr Peter Damerow
Center for Development and Socialization
Max Planck Institute for
Human Development and Education
Berlin, Germany

Corinne Duhig
Research student
Faculty of Oriental Studies
University of Cambridge, UK

Dr Christopher Fyfe
Former Reader in African History
Centre of African Studies
University of Edinburgh, UK

Dr Ian C. Glover
Senior Lecturer
Department of Prehistoric Archaeology
University College London, UK

Dr Helena F. Hamerow
Lecturer in Early Medieval Archaeology
Department of Archaeology
University of Durham, UK

Dr Richard J. Harrison
Reader in Archaeology
Department of Classics and Archaeology
University of Bristol, UK

Dr Pontus Hellström
Professor of Classical Archaeology
and Ancient History
University of Uppsala, Sweden

Dr Cho-yun Hsu
University Professor of History
University of Pittsburgh, USA

Graham Joyner
Lecturer in History
School of History, Philosophy, and Politics
Macquarie University
Sydney, Australia

Barry Kemp
Reader in Egyptology
Faculty of Oriental Studies
University of Cambridge, UK

Dr Katheryn M. Linduff
Professor
Department of Fine Arts
Department of Anthropology
University of Pittsburgh, USA

J.G. Macqueen
Former Reader in Classics and Ancient
Middle Eastern Studies
Department of Classics and Archaeology
University of Bristol, UK

Dr Elizabeth H. Moore
Lecturer
Department of Art and Archaeology
School of Oriental and African Studies
University of London, UK

Dr Robert G. Morkot
Department of Egyptology
University College London, UK

Dr Boyo G. Ockinga
Senior Lecturer in History
School of History, Philosophy, and Politics
Macquarie University
Sydney, Australia

Dr Susan Pollock
Assistant Professor of Anthropology
State University of New York
at Binghamton, USA

Dr Himanshu Prabha Ray
Assistant Professor
Centre for Historical Studies
Jawaharlal Nehru University
New Delhi, India

Dr Charles L. Redman
Professor of Anthropology
Arizona State University, USA

David Ridgway
Reader
Department of Classics
University of Edinburgh, UK

Dr Charlotte Scheffer
Senior Lecturer
Department of Classical Archaeology
and Ancient History
University of Stockholm, Sweden

Dr I.M. Stead
Deputy Keeper
Department of Prehistoric
and Romano-British Antiquities
British Museum, London, UK

Håkan Wahlquist
Curator of Asian Anthropology
National Museum of Ethnography
Stockholm, Sweden

Dr Peter Warren
Professor of Ancient History
and Classical Archaeology
University of Bristol, UK

Dr Charlotte Wikander
Lecturer
Department of Classical Archaeology
and Ancient History
University of Gothenburg, Sweden

Dr Örjan Wikander
Associate Professor
Department of Classics
Lund University, Sweden

CONTENTS

SYLVAIN GRANDADAM/EXPLORER/AUSCAPE

F O R E W O R D

THE MOST ENDURING, and in many ways the most remarkable, characteristic of human society is its capacity for change. Sometimes, and in some places, that change was imperceptible; at other times, it was astonishing in its rapidity.

Over a vast span of time, human societies throughout the world saw little modification: they lived in small bands as hunters and gatherers. Then, about 10,000 BC, the pace of change began to accelerate. Over the next few millennia, in the "fertile crescent" of the Middle East, in the foothills of the Afghan–Iranian Plateau, and in the valleys of the Nile and the Yellow River, communities developed a capacity for producing their own food by cultivating wild grasses and domesticating certain indigenous animals. As these innovative communities became more sedentary, the population began to grow. Thus, the scene was set for the next, amazing leap forward—the development of urban-based societies and the emergence of state systems of government.

Reviewing, as we do in this magnificent book, the full sweep of ancient civilizations in the Old World —Asia, Europe, and Africa—it is difficult, even for the professional archaeologist, not to be staggered by the immense scale of human achievement. In less than 4,000 years, humankind moved from those first, faltering experiments to the huge megacity of Rome, the center of a sprawling empire.

The rise of civilization is a story fascinating in its complexity. On the one hand, the sheer variety of human inventiveness dazzles; on the other, our growing awareness of the similarities apparent between the different manifestations of the urban idea across widely separated territories suddenly brings into focus fundamental questions about the constants that control human social behavior. The kaleidoscope is vivid in its individual elements, but underlying them is a pattern.

For many archaeologists, the questions of origins hold the greatest fascination, and who can help but be intrigued by the emergence of urban states in the great river valleys of the Tigris and Euphrates, the Nile and the Indus—processes that began about 3500 BC and reached early maturity by 2500 BC. The similarities between the environments in which these momentous events were enacted, and the broad synchronism of the developments, might suggest direct influences from one to another. And yet, years of painstaking archaeological research suggest that in each of these valley locations, the momentum that led communities to band together in increasingly large social groups came from within. Only later, as the social and economic systems became more complex, did patterns of exchange, tenuous at first, begin to create links between them. The emergence of the earliest Chinese state system in the Yellow River valley, at the end of the Xia dynasty, is sufficiently isolated from developments in the Near East and India to add further weight to the view that all these early manifestations are likely to have been *sui generis*.

Once under way, the move towards urban-based systems and state structures was inexorable. Regions on the periphery of early centers became innovative centers in their own right—and so "civilization" spread, the core areas often being reinvigorated as, phoenix-like, new configurations arose from the ashes of the old. The human story of the last 6,000 years makes compulsive reading— it races forward with all the excitement of a richly textured adventure. It also makes us think deeply, not only about our past, but about the present … and the future.

Barry Cunliffe
Professor of European Archaeology
Institute of Archaeology
University of Oxford

◄● The front view of the colossal seated figures of Ramses II at the Great Temple of Abu Simbel, in Lower Nubia, Egypt.

MICHAEL FREEMAN

IN THIS, THE THIRD VOLUME of *The Illustrated History of Humankind*, we run squarely into one of the great debates in history and archaeology. Should the major events of world history be attributed to the extraordinary accomplishments of a few individual geniuses? Or are the geniuses of the past merely products of their time, the logical consequences of history's irresistible forces?

What is it that propels one village rather than another to take the lead in the formation of urban life? Why did writing develop when it did? Does progress take place in times of plenty or times of deprivation? Significant innovations—writing, legal codes, the wheel, the plow, metallurgy, mathematics, principles of advanced engineering, the "urban revolution", and the emergence of social classes—can operate singly or in union to launch a society into an era of unprecedented change and creativity. Are such inventions and innovations the result of human genius?

Some would say Yes. This is why the controversial discovery of "Philip's Tomb" has been hailed by some as this century's most important find in Classical archaeology. After all, the argument goes, without Philip II, his son—Alexander the Great—never could have conquered Greece or spread Greek culture into Egypt, Turkey, and Iraq. But thanks to recent discoveries in archaeology, osteology, and forensics, we can all look into the face of one of the greatest figures of human history. We can see what Philip II actually looked like— gruesome eye injury and all.

Why are we fascinated with individuals like Philip II, Alexander the Great, Queen Cleopatra, and the other Hellenistic superstars? Were these personalities so exceptional that they galvanized the momentous events of world history?

Many would respond that the abilities and achievements of an Alexander or an Aristotle must be viewed only as a product of their time, a synthesis of already existing cultural information, an assimilation of newer elements into the pre-existing culture. What if these "universal geniuses" had died in infancy? Would our world be a different place? Had Pythagoras never figured out the triangle, would our world be forever bound by squares and circles?

As you read through this and other volumes of *The Illustrated History of Humankind*, keep in mind this distinction between the global evolution of culture and the specific way in which the history of each region has been played out.

Historical events were heavily conditioned by chance and circumstance. Surely no one could have predicted that King Azana of Aksum would have converted to Christianity in the mid-fourth century AD, nor could anyone have predicted that Emperor Qin Shi Huang would build a "Great Wall" to protect the northern Chinese states. History is a sequence of time-specific events, and individuals such as King Azana and Emperor Qin were enormously important. The world would not have been the same without them.

But in an evolutionary sense, the overall course of humankind is indeed highly determinable, even predictable. This is why plants and animals were domesticated independently in many different places at different times in human history; why cities arose around the globe; why pottery, metallurgy, writing, and mathematics have developed time and time again. This is why the best ideas must be seen as largely independent of the individuals who proposed them. As Leslie White, the distinguished archaeologist and historian of science, once wrote, "The goose who saved Rome was more significant historically than many an emperor who ruled it."

◄● The twelfth-century AD Khmer temple of Prasat Phanom Rung, in northeastern Thailand.

David Hurst Thomas

D millennia BC, the world's first civilizations developed. They did so quite independently of each other, in a number of different places widespread throughout the world. What may seem surprising at first glance is that these revolutionary developments within human societies often did not take place in areas rich in food and other natural resources, but in regions that had successively dried up and turned into deserts and semideserts following the climatic changes of the last Ice Age, some 12,000 years ago.

But when we look more closely at these developments, it becomes evident that it is no mere coincidence that many of these early civilizations developed in riverine areas surrounded by parched lands, which could only be made fertile through the implementation of large-scale irrigation systems. The Nile Valley, the land between the Euphrates and Tigris rivers, and the Indus are classic examples.

With the need to control the forces of nature came a need to harness human resources, in the form of labor, on a hitherto unknown scale. For the first time, labor had to be organized along specialist lines, and this encouraged craft specialization. Around this time, certain groups of people took control of trade, and it was as a method of recording and controlling trade transactions that the earliest writing systems developed. Established religions and a full-time priesthood also made their first appearance—all

explosion of artistic and architectural creativity. Civilization, as we know it, was born.

Old World Civilizations, the third volume of *The Illustrated History of Humankind*, offers a unique insight into this fascinating phase of our past, when, with the birth of written language, our ancestors took the momentous leap from unwritten prehistory to recorded history. From that time on, researchers are no longer wholly dependent on their silent, archaeological find material, but often have a wealth of historically recorded information at their disposal. For the first time, we can read personal accounts of past events written by individuals. These stories are often colored by the author's personal bias, of course, but they nevertheless provide an intriguing glimpse into a previously unknown world of thinking.

"Mesopotamia and the First Cities" traces the development of the earliest urban communities on the Mesopotamian plain, beginning about 4000 BC and ending with the growth of the first empires in Southwest Asia. "The Civilization of Ancient Egypt" recounts the fascinating cultural development that took place along the Nile Valley from 5000 BC, leading to the magnificence of the Old, Middle, and New Kingdoms. "Civilizations in Southern Asia" looks at the growth of cities and states on the remarkably diverse Indian subcontinent from about 3000 BC to the middle of the first millennium AD. "Civilizations of Southeast

using societies in mainland and island Southeast Asia, and the subsequent blending of cultural impulses from other regions in Asia—notably India and China—which have left deep marks on this part of the world. "Dynasties in China" relates the growth of civilization in China from the legendary royal dynasty of the Xia through to the collapse of the Han dynasty in AD 220.

"Emerging Mediterranean Civilizations" describes the first palace cultures to emerge in Europe, including the Minoan culture, in Crete, and the Mycenaean culture, on the Greek mainland. It also traces the development of the Hittite kingdom in Asia Minor and of metal-using societies on the Iberian peninsula. "The Age of Ancient Greece" gives an account of Greek society from the time of the first city-states to the Hellenistic Age, which ended about 31 BC. "The Rise and Fall of Rome" follows Roman civilization from its infancy to the ultimate collapse of this immensely influential empire about AD 500. "The Iron Age in Europe" covers the period from the advent of iron-working in central Europe, with the momentous social changes this set in train, to the subsequent cultural developments that culminated in the formation of states, beginning about 800 BC and ending with the Viking Age. Finally, "The Development of African States" looks at the growth of diverse kingdoms on the African continent between 3000 BC and AD 1500.

Göran Burenhult

BRITISH MUSEUM

◄Θ A Viking Age silver hoard from Cuerdale, in Lancashire, England, dating from the beginning of the tenth century AD.

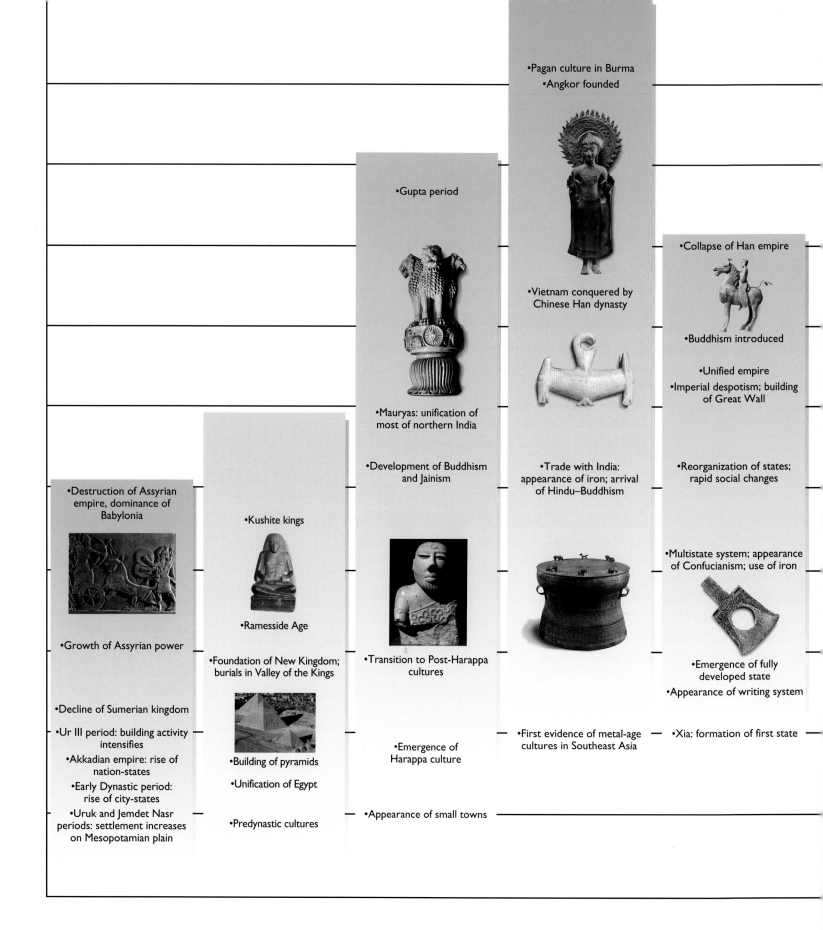

•Pagan culture in Burma

•Angkor founded

•Gupta period

•Collapse of Han empire

•Vietnam conquered by Chinese Han dynasty

•Buddhism introduced

•Unified empire

•Imperial despotism; building of Great Wall

•Mauryas: unification of most of northern India

•Destruction of Assyrian empire, dominance of Babylonia

•Development of Buddhism and Jainism

•Trade with India: appearance of iron; arrival of Hindu–Buddhism

•Reorganization of states; rapid social changes

•Kushite kings

•Growth of Assyrian power

•Ramesside Age

•Multistate system; appearance of Confucianism; use of iron

•Decline of Sumerian kingdom

•Foundation of New Kingdom; burials in Valley of the Kings

•Transition to Post-Harappa cultures

•Ur III period: building activity intensifies

•Akkadian empire: rise of nation-states

•Early Dynastic period: rise of city-states

•Building of pyramids

•Emergence of fully developed state

•Appearance of writing system

•Uruk and Jemdet Nasr periods: settlement increases on Mesopotamian plain

•Unification of Egypt

•Emergence of Harappa culture

•First evidence of metal-age cultures in Southeast Asia

•Xia: formation of first state

•Predynastic cultures

•Appearance of small towns

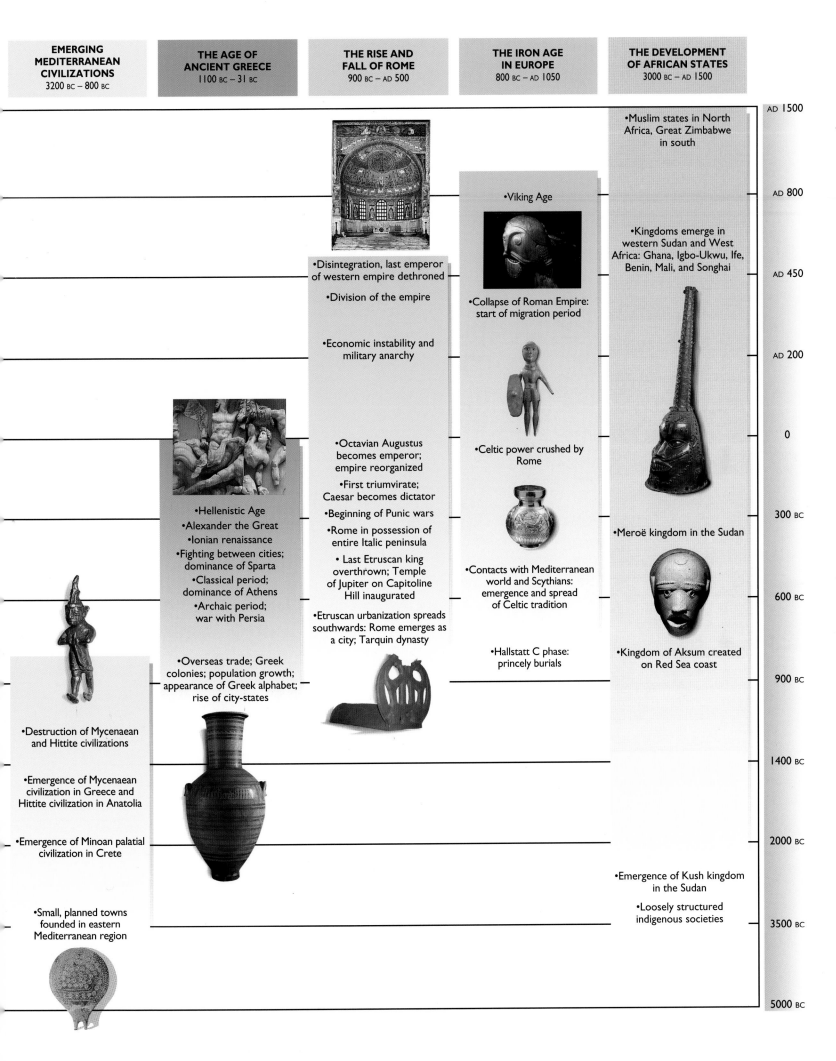

EMERGING MEDITERRANEAN CIVILIZATIONS 3200 BC – 800 BC	THE AGE OF ANCIENT GREECE 1100 BC – 31 BC	THE RISE AND FALL OF ROME 900 BC – AD 500	THE IRON AGE IN EUROPE 800 BC – AD 1050	THE DEVELOPMENT OF AFRICAN STATES 3000 BC – AD 1500

• Muslim states in North Africa, Great Zimbabwe in south

AD 1500

• Viking Age

AD 800

• Kingdoms emerge in western Sudan and West Africa: Ghana, Igbo-Ukwu, Ife, Benin, Mali, and Songhai

• Disintegration, last emperor of western empire dethroned

• Division of the empire

• Collapse of Roman Empire: start of migration period

AD 450

• Economic instability and military anarchy

AD 200

0

• Octavian Augustus becomes emperor; empire reorganized

• Celtic power crushed by Rome

• First triumvirate; Caesar becomes dictator
• Beginning of Punic wars

• Hellenistic Age
• Alexander the Great
• Ionian renaissance
• Fighting between cities; dominance of Sparta
• Classical period; dominance of Athens
• Archaic period; war with Persia

• Rome in possession of entire Italic peninsula
• Last Etruscan king overthrown; Temple of Jupiter on Capitoline Hill inaugurated

• Contacts with Mediterranean world and Scythians: emergence and spread of Celtic tradition

• Meroë kingdom in the Sudan

300 BC

• Etruscan urbanization spreads southwards: Rome emerges as a city; Tarquin dynasty

600 BC

• Overseas trade; Greek colonies; population growth; appearance of Greek alphabet; rise of city-states

• Hallstatt C phase: princely burials

• Kingdom of Aksum created on Red Sea coast

900 BC

• Destruction of Mycenaean and Hittite civilizations

1400 BC

• Emergence of Mycenaean civilization in Greece and Hittite civilization in Anatolia

• Emergence of Minoan palatial civilization in Crete

2000 BC

• Emergence of Kush kingdom in the Sudan

• Loosely structured indigenous societies

• Small, planned towns founded in eastern Mediterranean region

3500 BC

5000 BC

GEORG GERSTER/RAPHO

MESOPOTAMIA AND THE FIRST CITIES

On the Pathway to Urban Society

CHARLES L. REDMAN

ONE OF THE MOST significant milestones in the development of human societies was the growth of the first cities on the Mesopotamian plain. This process, often called "The Urban Revolution", involved much more than just an increase in the size of settlements: it included fundamental changes in the way people interacted, in their relationship to the environment, and in the very way they structured their communities. Processes and institutions that began at this time have continued to evolve, forming the basic structure of urban society today.

Writing, legal codes, the wheel, the plow, metallurgy, mathematics, and engineering principles—all commonplace in our modern world—were first developed in the cities of Sumer (present-day southern Iraq). Despite the vast scope of these technical developments, the most significant changes were those of social organization. There was a quantum leap in the number of inhabitants living in the largest settlements.

◄● The ziggurat of Choga Zambil, on the plain of Khuzistan, in present-day southwestern Iran, dates from about 1250 BC. Ziggurats have a long tradition in Mesopotamia, serving both as raised platforms for important temples and as the focus of public ceremonies.

◔ This clay figurine of a woman holding an infant was excavated in the pre-urban levels of Ur, and dates from about 4000 BC.
THE IRAQ MUSEUM, BAGDAD/SCALA

A s some groups of people acquired access to sources of production—for example, better farmland, more irrigation water, and rare goods traded from other regions—social class became one of the main structures within communities. These communities were organized according to the emerging hierarchical political and administrative systems, which often used written legal codes.

Craft specialization, mass-production industries, and large-scale trade characterized the new economy. Organized warfare, with both massive defensive works and long-distance offensive campaigns, played an increasing role in the survival of societies.

Cities and Their Surrounds

The physical environment of Mesopotamia (present-day Iraq and part of southwestern Iran) and the surrounding regions provided suitable ecological conditions for the early introduction of agriculture and the subsequent growth of the first urban society. An awareness of these conditions is essential to an understanding of the changes that took place.

Mesopotamia is a large, alluvial plain created by two major rivers—the Tigris and the Euphrates—

and is surrounded on two sides by better-watered mountainous zones. The climatic pattern is one of summer drought and winter rainfall, although the lowland plain receives minimal rainfall.

In the south, where the Tigris and Euphrates rivers join and eventually empty into the Persian Gulf, the land is almost flat, and there are many

JONATHON T. WRIGHT/BRUCE COLEMAN LTD

☝ A Babylonian boundary stone, from about 1120 BC, records a gift of land near Edina, in southern Babylonia.
C.M. DIXON/PHOTO RESOURCES

♀ To the north and east of Mesopotamia, many of the mountain river valleys were the scene of early agricultural experiments, and they continued to be important resource zones for the city-states of Mesopotamia.

☝ The Tigris and Euphrates rivers and their tributaries provided the water essential to Mesopotamian agriculture.

ROBERT HARDING PICTURE LIBRARY

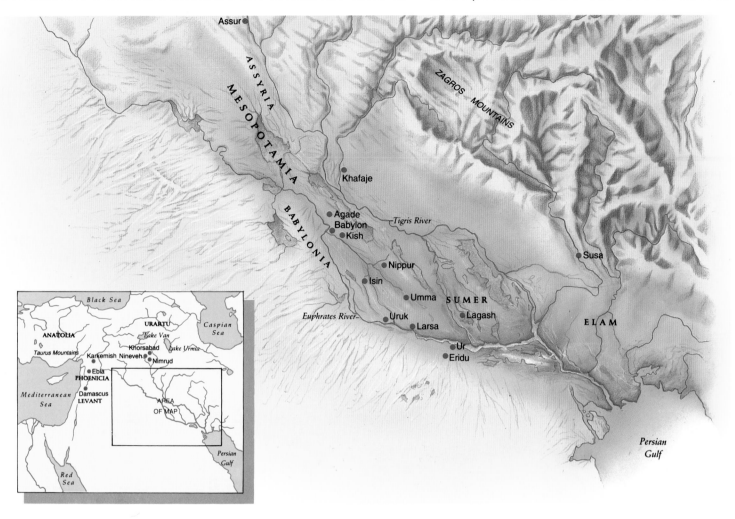

marshy areas. Moving upstream, to the northwest, the slope is small, but it increases perceptibly, giving rise to more clearly defined watercourses surrounded by arid plains. Effective natural levee formation in the southern reaches of the Mesopotamian plain strongly influenced the selection of settlement locations.

Furthest from the rivers were lowland areas that were marshes during the flood season and dry the rest of the year. Some of these lowland areas were saline; others supported natural grasses, which made them useful for grazing animals. Nearer the rivers were farmlands, which, though low-lying, were protected from marshiness by their height above the river. They were within reach of irrigation water, and the closer they were to the river, the greater their productivity. Along the river banks were the levees, which were higher and better drained than the surrounding plain. These were the best locations for intensive cultivation and settlement. The levees had several natural advantages: they were fertile, quickly drained, and least vulnerable to winter frosts. Equally important, as the population density of farmers increased, the levees gave access to river water during years in which the river level was low and all fields could not be adequately watered.

Moving further upstream, to the more northerly areas of the Mesopotamian plain, the gradient increases, the landscape becomes undulating, and the rivers cut into the landscape, making irrigation more difficult. Continuing to the north, the major rivers and their tributaries cut across a series of increasingly high ridges and ultimately reach the Taurus Mountains, to the north, and the Zagros Mountains, to the northeast. Proximity to the uplands and the large tributary rivers provided natural advantages to settlement in the north, such as access to stone and timber for building, while the vast stretches of relatively easily irrigated land facilitated growth in the south.

MESOPOTAMIA

Mesopotamia is a broad, alluvial plain that slopes gently to the southeast, and the Tigris and Euphrates rivers wind their way to the Persian Gulf. To the north and east, the plain steps up into the successively higher, intermontane valleys of the Taurus and Zagros mountains.

CARTOGRAPHY: RAY SIM

ROBERT HARDING PICTURE LIBRARY

◄● Sheep, seen here grazing near the Euphrates River, were among the key resources of the early Mesopotamian cities. They provided meat and milk and their wool was essential to the development of textile production and trade.

GEORG GERSTER/JOHN HILLELSON AGENCY

⬆ Intensively irrigated farmlands along the Shatt-al-Arab River, in extreme southern Mesopotamia (present-day southeastern Iraq). Although this area may not have been farmed in antiquity, it is thought that the areas near the ancient cities of Eridu and Ur that are now desert may have looked like this in the third millennium BC.

👉 A village along the upper Euphrates River in southeastern Anatolia (Turkey). The stone foundations, mudbrick walls, and timber and mud roofs of this village are similar to those of prehistoric villages that have been found all along the upland fringes of Mesopotamia.

Neolithic settlement (8000 BC to 5000 BC) of Southwest Asia had concentrated on the uplands, with only a few settlements around the margin of Mesopotamia in southeastern Turkey, on the Irano-Iraqi borderlands, or along the upper reaches of the major rivers. Researchers have not yet found evidence of any substantial settlement in southern Mesopotamia before about 5500 BC. Between 6000 BC and 4000 BC, however, the area of settlement expanded from the uplands to include more and more of the Mesopotamian plain. This was not a rapid expansion in terms of a single lifetime; it took many generations to learn ways to manage crops and animals in the heat and aridity of the lowlands. At first, expansion was limited to areas of possible, although unreliable, rainfall.

Subsequently, with the aid of primitive irrigation systems, settlers moved into areas that previously could not be cultivated.

Why Did Cities Arise?

The formation of cities and their linking together as one civilization on the Mesopotamian plain was relatively rapid, considering the scope of the social and technological changes involved. Only 2,000 years after the earliest-known occupation of this region, about 5500 BC, cities emerged, and writing and such other traits of urbanism as monumental buildings and craft specialization had appeared. The question of what led to this all-important transformation has challenged scholars for decades. A variety of theories has been advanced to account for the rise of cities, most of which rely on Mesopotamia as their main source of evidence. The rise of cities is not simply the growth of large collections of people—rather, it involves communities that are far more diverse than their predecessors and more interdependent. Specialization in the production of various goods and complex exchange networks are typical of urban societies. Cities are also interdependent with their hinterlands of towns and villages.

Theorists have suggested a variety of factors that could have prompted the growth of cities and the reorganization of society. One of the earliest explanations for the growth of complex society in Mesopotamia and elsewhere, put forward by Karl Wittfogel in the 1950s, was the social reorganization required by large-scale irrigation works. The proposition was that arid alluvial valleys, such as Mesopotamia, would need irrigation to support significant populations, and that the construction, maintenance, and allocation of irrigation works would require a managerial elite. The elite, in turn, would form the core of the complex society.

Another theory, developed by American anthropologist Robert Carneiro in the 1970s, was based on the processes set in motion by an increasing population density. Arable land would "fill up", and conflict would then develop among the settlers and their neighbors. One group would be subdued, forming the lower class for the conquerors, who would assume the role of the elite.

CHARLES L. REDMAN

EARLY MESOPOTAMIAN CITIES AND THE ENVIRONMENT

CHARLES L. REDMAN

Vast stretches of the rich and productive landscape of early Mesopotamia are now unfarmable desert. The conclusion drawn by many is that the climate must have changed dramatically between then and today. Careful research has shown, however, that the climate has changed very little over the past 5,000 years, and so we must look for another cause of this environmental degradation. A comparison of the dissolution of the Ur III state about 2000 BC with the later demise of the Sasanian empire of the early Middle Ages (AD 226 to AD 637), which covered the area of present-day Iran and Iraq, suggests some possible causes.

Centralized Control and Environmental Damage

Paradoxically, it seems that the rapid rise of centralized political control within Ur III society contributed to an era of declining agricultural productivity and environmental damage. Centralized control of the once independent city-states was a logical objective for the Ur III rulers. It gave them access to larger pools of workers, military conscripts, trade goods, and agricultural produce. And, significantly, it helped to maximize the production of food and other goods.

Some of this increased productivity was achieved through increased specialization, but most resulted from the centralized management of the construction and maintenance of the growing irrigation network that fed the Mesopotamian fields and of the allocation of water within it. It was, therefore, a logical decision for Ur III rulers to try to extend the area served by irrigation and to increase the capacity of the existing canal system to carry water to the fields. But the very decisions that brought short-term increases in production— as evidenced by the high population density and the great construction projects of the Ur III period—seem

A view of the mound of Tell Drahem, in southern Mesopotamia. About 2000 BC, according to texts found there, this was an important center for cattle-raising and for preparing meat for shipment to the nearby city of Nippur. Today, the once productive region is largely desert because of the extreme salinization of the soil.

to have rapidly undermined the region's agricultural base.

The people of Ur III appear to have caused their own ultimate downfall through the salinization of their soils. Salinization occurs when salt accumulates near the surface of the soil. In this case, salt from the sedimentary rocks in the mountains was carried by rivers and deposited on the Mesopotamian fields during natural flooding or planned irrigation. In southern Mesopotamia, the natural water table comes to within roughly 2 meters (6 feet) of the surface. Excessive irrigation brings the water table up to within 50 centimeters (18 inches) of the surface. In waterlogged situations, the salt is then carried to the surface, where it kills most plants.

Written records of temple storehouses from the time of the Ur III empire have allowed scholars to reconstruct the relative productivity of fields and the crops planted. There was a long-term decrease in productivity between 2400 BC and 1700 BC. About 2400 BC, wheat was an important crop, accounting for at least 16 percent of the cereals produced. As salinization increased, however, the emphasis gradually shifted to barley, a more salt-tolerant crop. By the end of the Ur III dynasty, wheat accounted for only 2 percent of the cereals grown. By 1700 BC, wheat seems to have been totally abandoned as a crop in southern Mesopotamia. The tail end of this process coincided with a long period without centralized political control.

Many cities were abandoned or reduced to villages, and the emphasis shifted from producing as much as possible for the central rulers to just satisfying the needs of the local populations.

The Sasanian Empire

The decline of the Sasanian empire brings some of these issues into clearer focus. The Sasanians had assembled a truly great "world" empire, spanning most of Iraq and much of Iran. They built large cities and had a very strong central government. Even more than the people of Ur III, they relied on cereal cultivation in irrigated fields and had built a massive system of canals and other facilities to bring water to an ever-increasing area of land. Although it is hard to know for certain, one scholar has estimated that three to four times as much land was farmed during the Sasanian period as in the Ur III epoch. But, as within the Ur III empire, this attempt to maximize production had wide-ranging repercussions. First, the amount of water being brought to the land increased the risk of salinization, even though the Sasanians tried hard to combat this process. Second, the enormous scale of the Sasanian irrigation systems required more comprehensive and more effective management to be successful, allowing little room for errors of judgment. Third, extending cultivation to more marginal lands used yet more water and also swallowed up the fallow lands that

had formerly been used for herding. This third point is particularly important, in that herd-raising had always provided a buffer against bad agricultural years and was also a means of diversifying the diet.

Even the great Sasanian empire could not hold together under these pressures. Scholars believe that diminished productivity was already taking its toll on central control when the region was hit by the plague several times in the sixth and early seventh centuries AD. This further debilitated the system, so that when Muslim armies entered Sasanian territory in AD 637, they were able to topple the Sasanians with surprisingly little resistance.

The Costs of Growth

In these periods of Mesopotamia's past, political stability and economic growth were achieved by centralizing political control and maximizing agricultural production. In fact, this weakened the ability of the agricultural system to react to problems and led ultimately to a decline in productivity.

State ideologies at that time, and probably now as well, assumed that everyone's interests converged in the objectives of a central authority. Yet the objectives may not have been shared by all members of a society, and, indeed, may not have been to the benefit of all. What is less obvious is that the objectives of such ideologies may not even be in the best interests of the central authority in the long term.

⊕ Copper tools and weapons from Tell Sifr, dating from about 1900 BC to 1750 BC. Although all metal ore had to be imported to Mesopotamia, the production of metal implements became quite important in the economy of early cities.

C.M. DIXON/PHOTO RESOURCES

D. BOURBONNAIS/EXPLORER/AUSCAPE

⊗ Although they often focus on the activities of royal personages, later Assyrian bas-reliefs provide graphic illustrations of daily life in Mesopotamia. Hairstyles and dress were often used to portray different ethnic groups, and size was usually employed to denote the importance of the individual.

BAGHDAD MUSEUM/PICTUREPOINT LTD

⊕ A ritual cart in terracotta, found at Khafaje, in northeastern Mesopotamia, dating from about 2600 BC. By Early Dynastic times, it appears that wheeled carts were in use throughout Mesopotamia.

Other theories, including those of Australian prehistorian Vere Gordon Childe and American archaeologist Henry Wright, point towards craft production and exchange as the primary factors in developing the complex Mesopotamian society. With the invention of metallurgy and the various applications for the newly developed wheel, among other technological breakthroughs, it is clear that new industries with specialized workers would emerge. Also, Mesopotamia lacked many natural resources for daily life and some industries, while it appeared to be able to produce surplus goods in other categories. Thus, the efficient organization of manufacturing and the large-scale exchange of products both inside and outside Mesopotamia would promote the rise of a managerial class and specialized producers, both key elements in an urban society.

We know from archaeological findings and somewhat later written records that each of these factors—irrigation, population growth, warfare, specialized production, and large-scale trade— existed in early Mesopotamia, but the actual order of their development is not clear. The key question is whether advances in one or more of these areas preceded cities and were instrumental in leading to urban growth, or whether they followed the formation of cities as a natural outcome of the newly formed urban society. A careful examination of the archaeological evidence by scholars has led to a number of theories that rely on a combination of these and other factors working together to bring about the fundamental changes the urban society implies. In these theories, the importance of irrigation, agriculture, and the exchange of goods is acknowledged as forming the necessary foundation on which a Mesopotamian civilization could be built. But theories such as the multivariate approach of American cultural ecologist Robert McC. Adams look to the changing social relations caused by the increasing numbers of settlements in the Mesopotamian environment. The ideas of the original theorists have not been entirely rejected, but parts of them are used in current theories that focus on the close interrelationship of environment, economics, technology, and changes in social relations.

The Threshold of Civilization

Because of the natural aridity of the lowland parts of the Mesopotamian plain, few people lived there before 5500 BC, when the necessary farming and irrigation techniques were developed. During the next 2,000 years, in a broad period archaeologists have termed the 'Ubaid, advances were slow, but together they laid the foundation for Mesopotamian civilization. Many scholars suggest that the people we now call the Sumerians came to Mesopotamia at this time. During this long period, many of the characteristics of civilization and the Sumerian society itself emerged. However, it was to be another thousand years before true cities and a sophisticated urban network developed.

Sites that date to the 'Ubaid period, and that share many cultural traits, have been discovered throughout Mesopotamia and in the surrounding foothills, on both the Iraqi and Iranian sides of the border. While each site has contributed new detail to the increasingly clear picture of 'Ubaid life, it is one of the first excavated, Eridu, that still seems most informative. Located in the extreme south of the Mesopotamian plain, Eridu, in some ways, may have attained the highest level of development. The original settlement here was probably not much larger than the villages that had dotted the upland mountain valleys for several thousand years, but the people obviously understood the principles of irrigation, and their wheat, barley, sheep, goats, and cattle must have suited the extremes of the Mesopotamian climate. Because there were no natural stands of timber and outcrops of rock, the people relied heavily on clay, not only to make their pots, but to construct their buildings and even to fashion tools, such as sickles and axes, that were made of stone in other regions.

Perhaps the find in Eridu most indicative of things to come was a series of buildings that the excavators interpreted as temples. This inference was based on the layout of the buildings, which had three-part arrangements with exterior buttressing, characteristics duplicated in later Sumerian buildings and identified by written sources as temples. By the time these buildings were being constructed at Eridu, about 3500 BC, the community had grown to cover 10 hectares (about 25 acres) and probably housed at least 2,000 people. The existence of so many people in one settlement implies the evolution of social relations to a new level of integration within the community and a potential reliance on surrounding settlements for some subsistence goods.

ERICH LESSING/MAGNUM

♠ This find of a clay model shows that two-story houses were built in Mesopotamia..

CIVILIZATIONS IN MESOPOTAMIA: 5500 BC – 2000 BC

Date	CULTURES OF MESOPOTAMIA	SOCIAL AND POLITICAL EVENTS	CULTURE AND TECHNOLOGY
2000		Shift in focus of growth and power to central and northern Mesopotamia	Serious salinization in southern Mesopotamia
	Ur III state 2111 BC – 2005 BC		Ur-Nammu began impressive building program 2111 BC
			New language for official business
	Akkadian state 2350 BC – 2150 BC	First nation-state 2350 BC – 2150 BC	Cuneiform writing adopted
2500		Promulgation of earliest legal codes 2350 BC	
		Major period of Ur burials 2600 BC – 2100 BC	
		Earliest Ur burials	Building of palaces
3000	Early Dynastic city-states 2900 BC – 2350 BC	Era of the city-state Major military campaigns	Temple ovals built at some cities
3500	Uruk and Jemdet Nasr period 3500 BC – 2900 BC		Monumental art Sculptures in the round Earliest written script Construction of first ziggurats for temples
4000			Use of the wheel
4500			Development of copper/ bronze metallurgy
			Use of the plow
5000			
5500 BC	'Ubaid period 5500 BC – 3500 BC	First settled villages	Small-scale irrigation

➥ An aerial view of the central part of the great, early city of Uruk (biblical Erech), in southern Mesopotamia. By the end of the Early Dynastic period, Uruk was enclosed by a massive defensive wall, and at its center, there were large temples built atop ziggurats.

GEORG GERSTER/JOHN HILLELSON AGENCY

🜚 This libation jug of stone, with inlaid mosaic, was found at the site of Uruk. It dates from the Jemdat Nasr period, about 3200 BC.

THE IRAQ MUSEUM, BAGHDAD/SCALA

➥ An Assyrian bas-relief, dating from the eighth century BC, shows the importance of boats for moving goods around Mesopotamia and beyond. Boats were most likely used along the major river courses, and probably up and down the coast of the Persian Gulf. Here, timber is being unloaded in northern Mesopotamia.

The City Takes Form

During the following period, the signs of civilization are more abundant, and settlement in the Mesopotamian plain increased significantly. Called the Uruk and Jemdet Nasr periods by archaeologists, this epoch spans roughly 3500 BC to 2900 BC. By then, there were many settlements that probably housed more than a thousand people, both in southern Mesopotamia and also in the north, where recent archaeological research is uncovering large communities along the upper Euphrates and its tributaries. Despite the impressive developments in the north, the focus of urban development appears to have been concentrated in the southern reaches of the Mesopotamian plain.

There was not a revolutionary change in the ways of life of the people of Mesopotamia, but with the growth in community size, agricultural

B. BOURBONNAIS/EXPLORER/AUSCAPE

The most impressive developments in the south are known from the long-term German excavations at the site of Warka (ancient Uruk), not far upstream from Eridu. Here, in a settlement several times the size of the largest of its predecessors from the 'Ubaid period, is evidence of what were clearly temples in the Sumerian tradition. Whereas the largest 'Ubaid period temples at Eridu were only 20 meters by 10 meters (66 feet by 33 feet), several Uruk period temples at Warka were 80 meters by 30 meters (263 feet by 100 feet). Moreover, at Warka, there appears to have been at least one precinct where several temples were adjacent. Some of these impressive structures were built on top of a large platform, or ziggurat, to make them seem even grander. Ziggurats have been uncovered at several sites in southern Mesopotamia from levels dating to the Uruk and Jemdet Nasr periods. These raised temple platforms are the largest examples of Sumerian architectural skill, growing in size and complexity over the next thousand years until they came to dominate the cities.

The following epoch, from 2900 BC to 2350 BC, is now called the Early Dynastic, because we have written records, and actual kings and queens are identified. It is in this period that the cultural identity and language of the Sumerians became distinct and coherently structured.

Whereas in the preceding period there had been a major growth in villages and towns, during the Early Dynastic, much of the population moved into about two dozen cities, a few of which certainly housed tens of thousands of people. More productive farming methods developed to support this population. Although communities still seem to have been established near the banks of the natural watercourses, there is evidence of some major canal construction. Other seed crops were added to the staples of barley and wheat, and orchard fruits, especially dates, became a regular part of the diet.

⚲ The ziggurat at Uruk. It is believed that its now-eroded ramps and stairways were the scene of major rituals, witnessed by the population of the early city.

and craft production appear to have become more organized. Most pottery vessels were made on a wheel or in molds, both processes that allow greater output and standardization of vessels. It has even been suggested that some of these vessels were used to measure standard quantities in a complex trading economy. Metal was more commonly being used to make artifacts, and most important, there is evidence of early efforts at writing on stone and clay. (See the feature *Our Oldest Written Documents*.) Much of this early writing was used for record-keeping, further evidence of the growing sophistication of the Mesopotamian economy. Although not yet completely deciphered, the bulk of the material indicates a continuity with later Sumerian writing and language, and points to the presence of the Sumerians in Mesopotamia during this period, if not earlier.

ROBERT HARDING PICTURE LIBRARY

OUR OLDEST WRITTEN DOCUMENTS

PETER DAMEROW

MESOPOTAMIA WAS THE CENTER of cuneiform writing, a system that was used for about 3,000 years. Usually, the Mesopotamians wrote on tablets of clay, and the signs of the script were produced by impressing a stylus into the smooth surface of the wet clay. This left the wedge-shaped markings typical of the writing system. Cuneiform writing was used in many languages, most of which are now well understood, as the cuneiform script was deciphered in the middle of the nineteenth century.

Archaic Texts

The oldest clay tablets displaying the developed system of cuneiform writing were written about 2500 BC. At the end of the nineteenth century, some older texts were excavated that seemed then to be the precursors of the cuneiform writing system. These were found in Susa, the urban center of a region east of southern Babylonia known in the third millennium as Elam. This pictographic system of writing was thus called "proto-elamite". Drawings of more than 200 of these texts were published in 1905. This system seemed to have many similarities to later cuneiform writing. In particular, it displayed the same kind of number notations impressed vertically or obliquely into the clay using a round stylus.

Only a short time later, however, it was discovered that proto-elamite writing was not the direct precursor of the cuneiform writing systems. Beginning with some tablets unearthed before 1915, more and more clay tablets excavated in the center of southern Mesopotamia showed another system of pictographic writing. It was immediately obvious that this system was the true precursor of the cuneiform script. It is called "proto-cuneiform" writing, and proto-cuneiform and proto-elamite texts are grouped together as "archaic texts".

Archaic writing in this sense covers the period from about 3100 BC to 2800 BC. So far, about 4,500 proto-cuneiform and 1,500 proto-elamite texts or text fragments have been excavated, at several sites in southern Mesopotamia and the highland area of Persia (Iran). They represent our oldest-known writing system. The oldest of these texts are proto-cuneiform texts from Uruk, archaic level 4, where the majority of proto-cuneiform texts have been found. It seems well established now that the proto-elamite writing system, which was used for only a short time, was influenced by this proto-cuneiform script.

Deciphering the Texts

The archaic texts are still only poorly understood, but substantial progress has been made in recent years by the Uruk project in Berlin. Deciphering the texts is mainly based on relationships between the archaic signs and corresponding signs in the developed cuneiform writing system. Cuneiform signs were used both as syllabic signs with phonetic values and as ideograms (pictures that express concepts or objects). As yet, researchers have not been able to identify any archaic signs that were used with phonetic values, but the meaning of several cuneiform ideograms is obviously derived from the meaning of their archaic precursors. Although in most cases the meaning of the cuneiform ideograms had shifted away from the original meaning of the archaic signs, they nevertheless provide valuable hints for reading the archaic signs.

In addition to this, a new technique of analysis has been developed recently, giving a better understanding of the archaic texts. Most of these texts are administrative documents. They record economic activity controlled by the ancient urban centers, such as the allocation of labor, the distribution of rations, and the production of consumables. Most of the texts contain quantitative information arranged in a sophisticated book-keeping system. Hence, by investigating the arithmetic and the system of weights and measures, and the way they are combined, researchers are able to reconstruct the texts.

The Puzzle of Numbers

A major result of this structural analysis is the clarification of the puzzling nature of the numerical notations in the texts. Former attempts to understand these notations were aimed mainly at finding the numerical values of the different signs. The results were contradictory, because they were based on the assumption that these signs represented numbers in the modern sense. But a careful study of the numerical notations has now established beyond doubt that they do not represent anything like abstract numbers. Rather, they predate arithmetic, and their meaning is dependent on the context. Such constructs are well known from preliterate cultures.

The archaic numerical signs were used in different contexts with different meanings and differing numerical values. Fifteen different numerical notation systems have been identified so far. They consist partly of the same signs, but each system has particular numerical relations between the units and a specific area of application. The values of the numerical signs changed with each system, probably because the counting technique suitable in one context needed to be changed for another context. For example, the signs that later assumed the values of 1 and 10 were used in the archaic texts with these values when they were applied to count beer jugs. But the same signs assumed the values 1 and 6 when they were applied to barley measures, and took the values 1 and 18 when they were applied to measures of field areas.

The deciphering of the archaic texts, scanty as it still is, has provided us with the insight that writing was invented to maintain political power and to control property. Some of the most fundamental ideas of humankind, such as the concept of numbers, emerged as a by-product of archaic book-keeping. At the dawn of literacy, humans did not write down their history, their myths, or their religious beliefs. It was another century before people realized that writing could also be used for a purpose quite different from economic control: namely, to represent spoken language in an enduring medium.

☛ A protocuneiform text showing the calculated quantities of raw materials required for several consignments of grain products and beer. This extraordinarily well-preserved tablet is a key document for our understanding of archaic numerical notation systems. Entries relating to various barley products are recorded, followed by figures showing the required quantities of barley groats and malt. Five different numerical notation systems were used to match the different measurement and counting systems applied to different types of goods. A sexagesimal system was used for counting beer jars, a bisexagesimal system for counting barley products and workers' barley rations. There were also three different notation systems for grain measures. The abstract symbols of cuneiform script developed after the scribes had changed the orientation of such tablets by turning them 90 degrees to the left, so that the pictographs appeared sideways (as here). This then became the standard way of writing the symbols. It is not known when this change took place, and so assyriologists orient all tablets to match the way cuneiform script was written in its developed form.
M. NISSEN, BERLIN

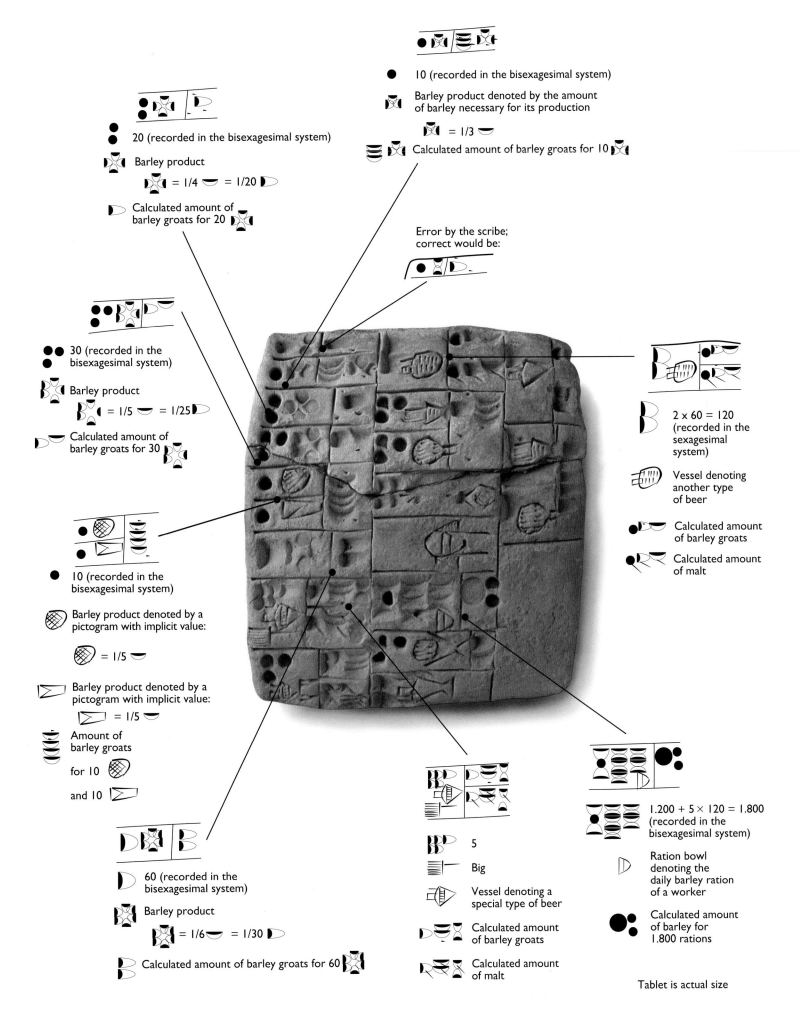

10 (recorded in the bisexagesimal system)

Barley product denoted by the amount of barley necessary for its production

= 1/3

Calculated amount of barley groats for 10

20 (recorded in the bisexagesimal system)

Barley product

= 1/4 = 1/20

Calculated amount of barley groats for 20

Error by the scribe; correct would be:

30 (recorded in the bisexagesimal system)

Barley product

= 1/5 = 1/25

Calculated amount of barley groats for 30

10 (recorded in the bisexagesimal system)

Barley product denoted by a pictogram with implicit value:

= 1/5

Barley product denoted by a pictogram with implicit value:

= 1/5

Amount of barley groats for 10 and 10

60 (recorded in the bisexagesimal system)

Barley product

= 1/6 = 1/30

Calculated amount of barley groats for 60

5

Big

Vessel denoting a special type of beer

Calculated amount of barley groats

Calculated amount of malt

2 × 60 = 120 (recorded in the sexagesimal system)

Vessel denoting another type of beer

Calculated amount of barley groats

Calculated amount of malt

1.200 + 5 × 120 = 1.800 (recorded in the bisexagesimal system)

Ration bowl denoting the daily barley ration of a worker

Calculated amount of barley for 1.800 rations

Tablet is actual size

27

A necklace of gold wire, lapis lazuli, and other semiprecious stones, and a pendant depicting a nude goddess. Dating from the thirteenth century BC, these pieces are an example of the elaborate jewelry that was prized by the elite of the time.

Urban Society in Sumer

Within the new cities, the production of ceramic vessels, metal, and woven goods became more organized, being handled by specialists arranged into industry groups. Stone, wood, metal, ores, and other exotic materials were brought into the lowland cities in ever-increasing quantities. Some of the raw materials were fashioned into goods for the local elites, while other materials and materials were transported back as payment to people in the source areas.

Newly developed products formed an increasingly important part of the local economy. Stone bowls, metal tools and weapons, bitumen for boats, cut stone for temples, and precious metals and gems for ornaments all became essential elements of elite life in the Mesopotamian city. Traders

A bronze figurine of a man on a crouching camel, found at Nineveh, in Mesopotamia. Camels had been domesticated by the middle of the second millennium BC, and it is likely that they expanded the possibility of long-distance trade across the dry regions that border Mesopotamia.

By the end of the third millennium BC, texts were being used to record a wide variety of information. This detailed medical text in cuneiform comes from Nippur.

THE UNIVERSITY MUSEUM, UNIVERSITY OF PENNSYLVANIA

data to more literary, religious, and historical records. Moreover, the original ideographic symbol system, where pictures represented objects or quantities, had evolved into a script where the symbols represented phonetic elements. This greatly simplified Sumerian writing, reducing an original 2,000 symbols to a script with about 600 symbols by

organized by the dynastic leader of the city, and perhaps others operating on their own account, set off in all directions carrying manufactured goods from Mesopotamia to exchange for raw materials from other areas. From written and archaeological evidence, we know that these trade routes extended to the east across the Iranian plateau, to the southeast by boat down the Persian Gulf, and to the northwest to the Anatolian highlands, Syria, and the Levant.

By about 2500 BC, writing had become standardized across the entire Mesopotamian plain, and the variety of texts extended well beyond economic

the end of the Early Dynastic period. The precisely drawn symbols, too, were simplified by using a stylus that produced wedge-shaped marks (or cuneiforms) on the wet clay tablets, replacing actual drawings, and thus making writing and reading less difficult. Hundreds of thousands of tablets of Sumerian texts—perhaps even more—were written in cuneiform. This widely used cuneiform script was so efficient that ultimately it was adopted for use with several later languages, such as the Akkadian and Assyrian languages—distant ancestors of contemporary Semitic tongues—after Sumerian had gone out of common usage.

The cities of the Early Dynastic period began to take on the appearance of ancient urbanism. Dense residential areas made up much of the settlement. Short, twisting streets with multiroomed houses created what must have been a labyrinth for the uninformed visitor. Many of the cities were surrounded by enormous defensive walls. Major areas near the centers of the cities were devoted to massive civic buildings or temples. All of these were

made primarily of sun-dried clay, fired bricks, and wood. Occasionally, stones were used as well.

As was the case throughout most of early Mesopotamian history, the buildings identified as temples and their ziggurat platforms were the largest structures in the cities. Because of this, and evidence from written records, it is now widely believed that much of the political and centralized economic control was associated with the temples. Although it appears that there were city lords and even some who called themselves kings, they seem to have been strongly reliant upon the temple community, at least during the first centuries of the Early Dynastic period. Textual records point towards the association of the temple with long-distance trade and manufacturing as well. A physical sign of this integration of religious, political, and economic activities is the architectural complex called the Temple Oval, which has been excavated in several Early Dynastic cities. The best-known example is from the northern Mesopotamian town of Khafaje. Here, the complex was made up of two

⚲ A cylinder seal and the impression of its design in clay. Termed the "brocade" style by art historians, this is typical of stamps and cylinders used to seal vessels or clay envelopes for texts during the Early Dynastic and later periods.
THE IRAQ MUSEUM, BAGHDAD/SCALA

⚲ The so-called Standard of Ur is one of the magnificent examples of craftsmanship found in the Royal Cemetery at Ur. It demonstrates the way in which representational art was used to portray the social order of the times. The lower register shows goods being transported to the city, while the middle register depicts local people with domestic animals and food in vessels, presumably destined for the elite people shown in the top register (note the larger size), who are seated and being served drinks.
BRITISH MUSEUM/ROBERT HARDING PICTURE LIBRARY

ROBERT HARDING PICTURE LIBRARY

⊙ A view of the partially restored ziggurat of the city of Ur from the site of the earlier Royal Cemetery precinct.

⊙ An alabaster statuette of a Sumerian man. His clean-shaven head and suppliant hand gestures are two typically Sumerian features.
THE LOUVRE/GIRAUDON

concentric ovals of mudbrick walls, enclosing at their center a modestly sized ziggurat surmounted by a temple. Also within the ovals was a series of buildings believed by the excavators to have housed the ruling family, priests, and workers. Outside the oval, the buildings were all of a smaller, more domestic, size and were arranged in what appears to be a labyrinth of twisting alleyways.

A very different building form from the second half of the Early Dynastic period has been excavated at several other, and larger, Early Dynastic sites. Because of their more residential design and massive enclosure walls, they have been identified as palaces. Some scholars have interpreted the palaces as evidence of the growing influence of a secular authority semi-independent of the temple community. Clearly, however, such a dramatic shift in the nature of control in the earliest cities cannot be inferred from the partial excavation of only a fraction of the known cities of the period.

Other evidence of the possible shift in political control comes from the change in distribution of settlements across the landscape from the earliest 'Ubaid settlement through to the end of the Early Dynastic period. In a 1972 survey, Robert McC. Adams and Hans J. Nissen found many communities from

each of these periods in the region surrounding the key southern Mesopotamian city of Uurk. Interestingly, during the first half of the Early Dynastic period, and even before this, there were many settlements scattered along the ancient river courses and in the countryside. Larger centers, such as Uruk, were already apparent, but a significant proportion of the population lived in smaller villages. At least in this region, however, the settlement pattern changed dramatically in the last part of the Early Dynastic period, many of the smaller settlements disappearing and the cities growing rapidly.

The implication is that many rural people moved into the large, and newly fortified, cities such as Uruk. On the evidence of numerous written references and the building of massive city walls, Adams and Nissen have suggested that this may have occurred in response to an increased frequency of intercity warfare, which, in turn, may have been related to the new dominance of a secular-based ruling elite. Although Adams has not found similar settlement shifts in all of the subregions of Mesopotamia he has examined, it seems plausible that the growing power of a militarily based authority could have been a crucial factor in the rise of cities and of state society.

The Growth of City-states

During the Early Dynastic period, these cities continued to grow in number and size as irrigation spread over much of the plain. It is likely that the political entity expanded in many instances to include not just individual cities, but the towns, villages, and countryside immediately around the city. These city-states may still have been ruled in much the same way as in earlier times, but the scale and complexity of political matters must have increased significantly.

By the later part of the Early Dynastic period, there were city-state rulers who identified themselves in texts as kings and warlords. These texts also indicate that some of these warlords were able to conquer several other city-states. For example, Lugalzagesi, ruler of the city of Umma, assumed the title of king of the land and claimed to have ruled a confederation of 50 city-states. Whatever the truth of these claims, political developments during the Early Dynastic period laid the foundation for the subsequent growth of nation-states.

The last Early Dynastic period king of Lagash, a city of growing importance, was Urukagina. About 2350 BC, Urukagina promulgated legal reforms that are preserved in inscriptions on buildings of his time. This code is the earliest-known formal attempt at creating a legal system. It explicitly established rights, delegated authority, and defined punishments. Urukagina claimed that he had a covenant with Ningirsu, the city-god of Lagash, whereby "he would not deliver up the weak and the widowed to the powerful man". Urukagina's intent was to lighten the burdens imposed on the general population by governors and priests, but it may, in fact, also have been an effort to strengthen his position as king. Working-class people were freed from certain taxes and from supervision by an over-expanded officialdom. Protection against the stealing of property and unfair business transactions also benefited the ordinary population. Social injustices involving marriage, divorce, and personal property were corrected. It is interesting to note that efforts to solidify the power of the newly emerged kings were already necessary. The establishment of legal codes, and their enforcement through military might, set the pattern for many episodes in later Mesopotamian history.

By the end of the Early Dynastic period, it is also clear that the more or less egalitarian villages of earlier periods—run primarily along kinship lines—had developed into a hierarchy of towns and cities, with sharply defined social classes among various task-oriented groups, as well as kinship groups. Much of this social stratification was related to the growing specialization of production and the differing access to resources that it entailed.

Sargon and the Rise of Nation-states

The Early Dynastic period came to an end with the ascendancy of Sargon of Agade, a military ruler from central Mesopotamia. Myth surrounds the early years of Sargon, but it is clear that he was a member of a Semitic group, ethnically distinct from the Sumerians. Apparently, Semites had populated much of central Mesopotamia for some time, settling especially in the countryside. Sargon's conquests began with the city of Kish, and spread to the south from there. With him went Semitic culture and language. His successes led to the fall of the last Sumerian rulers and the amalgamation of their cities into the Akkadian empire, centered on the city of Agade. This empire was so integrated that many scholars consider it the first nation-state in world history. The empire lasted from about 2350 BC to 2150 BC.

Although the Akkadian empire seems to have been largely a conglomeration of different groups under a military power, important achievements in the development of state administration are evident. A new language was used for official business, and it gradually became the language of international affairs in ancient Southwest Asia for the next thousand years. Sargon installed local rulers or agents to oversee his interests in newly conquered territories. The appointed officials were supported by military garrisons within the conquered cities. A more integrated system of trade developed, controlled by the palace. There is evidence that

A stone bas-relief from the reign of Ur-Nanshe, during the Early Dynastic period, found at the site of Tello. It apparently depicts a ruler, and perhaps a deity, being attended by less important (smaller) people.
THE LOUVRE/SCALA

This Early Dynastic bas-relief, known as the Stele of the Vultures, provides a detailed illustration of armaments and military formations of the period.
THE LOUVRE/GIRAUDON

♙ A stone statue of Gudea, priest-king of Lagash, dating from about 2150 BC. Gudea is well known from his ambitious construction campaign, and many statues of him have been found in southern Mesopotamia.

THE LOUVRE/ROBERT HARDING PICTURE LIBRARY

♀ The excavations area at the ancient site of Nippur. In Sumerian times, the city had great importance as a ritual center located midway between Sumer and Akkad. It continued to be used as a center periodically for the next 3,000 years.

GEORG GERSTER/COMSTOCK

trade extended as far as the Indus Valley, in present-day Pakistan, both overland and by sea.

The extent of Sargon's empire and the huge scale of his military successes were without precedent. The scribes of his period and those of later times extolled the Akkadian state and held it up as a model for later dynasties. Tribute flowed from the provinces to central Mesopotamia, but, perhaps more important, Sargon had gained control over the sources of raw materials that were sorely needed in the lowland cities: wood was imported from Lebanon, the Taurus Mountains, and the Zagros Mountains; metal (mainly copper) came from Anatolia and Iran; bitumen was obtained from the middle Euphrates; and stone was brought from surrounding upland areas.

In Southwest Asia, there were other important cities and states, which traded with, but were not under the direct control of, Akkad. One of these, Tell Mardikh, identified as ancient Ebla, was a major center on the trade route from the Euphrates to the Mediterranean.

Sargon supported an enormous number of people to carry out the administration of tribute, trade, and militarism in the newly assembled empire. He boasted of feeding 5,400 men at his table every day. The scale of society and administration required a large and growing bureaucracy. The increasing number of functionaries of various kinds itself affected the development of Mesopotamian civilization.

But despite the accomplishments of the Akkadian state, it did not create either a political or an economic system that was to be long-lived. In 2159 BC, less than two centuries after it was founded, the city of Agade was sacked. A series of local revolts culminated in the dissolution of the Akkadian empire nine years later.

Ur III and the Resurgence of Sumer

In the wake of these events, individual city-states re-emerged, each vying with its neighbors for control of more irrigated farmland and traded products. The city of Lagash became very successful, extending its control over an area that included many of its rivals. This was not primarily the re-emergence of a powerful military state, but the growth of an economic empire. The rulers of Lagash attempted to monopolize trade in certain commodities, but this time without a massive military commitment. Their agents traveled throughout Southwest Asia, securing supplies and raw materials. The prosperity of these rulers is amply documented by the number of buildings and works of art they commissioned. Their architectural and artistic legacy shows Akkadian influence, but it can be better understood as a revival of Sumerian ideas and authority.

This revival of Sumerian dominance can be clearly seen in the establishment of the Third Dynasty of Ur, by Ur-Nammu, in 2111 BC. This dynasty was soon to control all of Mesopotamia. The main motivation for this growing empire was, once again, economic, and great strides were made in improving administrative techniques. Legal codes giving clear definitions of authority and appropriate conduct, and written boundary markers showing clearer lines of political control, typified the Ur III state.

The impressive building program carried out by Ur-Nammu and his successors shows their resourcefulness. The canal system was extended, both to increase the amount of farmland that could be irrigated and to improve intercity water transport, which became essential to bring food to the city dwellers. Temples were repaired, and new ones erected. The greatest intensity of building was at Ur, Uruk, and Nippur. The ziggurat of the moon-god Nanna, at Ur, was given its final form by Ur-Nammu. In earlier periods, it had been conceived as a platform for a temple, but it was now transformed into a monument made up of superimposed platforms topped by a shrine. Its design was perfected by Ur III architects. Today, it remains the characteristic building of ancient Mesopotamian civilization.

During the Early Dynastic period, urbanization, especially around Uruk, depopulated the rural countryside. This was not so with the growth of the cities of the Ur III dynasty. Rather, the cities and rural towns and villages all grew at the same rate. This probably reflected an explicit attempt by the rulers to increase the efficiency and total agricultural yield of their lands. The exact extent of the Ur III domain, or that of any other early Mesopotamian state, is difficult to determine with certainty. It is likely that most, if not all, of the Mesopotamian plain and some of the uplands to the north were controlled by the rulers of the Ur III dynasty. The territories were divided into approximately 40 administrative districts. Each

king. Certain important or troublesome districts were run by *shagins* (military governors). The king took precautions to make certain that local *ensis* did not establish hereditary succession. *Ensis* were transferred to unfamiliar districts, and even whole populations are known to have been relocated by the rulers. These early attempts at reducing the potential power of local authorities and groups in order to maintain the strong centralized government increased in subsequent dynasties.

The two major centers of administrative activity in each city were the palace and the temples. The largely autonomous communities of the palace and temples held land, traded, and produced goods. The palace of the king was the main administrative authority, but other productive units existed, although they frequently took orders from the central authority. The palace and temple officials kept detailed written accounts, including daily records of goods brought in by individuals and balance-sheet tallies of receipts and payments. Silver was used as a standard of exchange, although much of the exchange was for other materials. A system of dry volume and weight measures was also employed.

A well-organized transport system overcame the great distances within the realm of Ur III, and kept it closely tied together. River and canal transport was highly developed and tightly controlled. This was especially important for the movement of foodstuffs from the countryside into the large cities, because city dwellers depended on these imports for a large part of their food.

The legal system was another mechanism that held the society together. Legal codes, such as the one established by Ur-Nammu, set standards of behavior and generally upheld the rights of the poorer classes. Courts were established to settle disputes.

A combination of factors seems to have led to the downfall of the Ur III dynasty—the last period of Sumerian dominance. The continual influx of less sedentary groups from the surrounding uplands provided a temporary labor force at some times, but proved to be a threat at others. Local rulers, particularly of the cities of Isin and Larsa, established their own power bases and challenged the central authority in Ur. In addition, the fertility of much of the Mesopotamian plain gradually decreased as a result of intensive irrigation. (See the feature *Early Mesopotamian Cities and the Environment*.) Taken together, these factors created an unstable situation, where even the relatively strong central administrative system of Ur III could not hold the empire together or even defend the capital. It appears that the final blow came during a period of general famine—probably in 2005 BC— when Ishbi-Erra, the local governor of the city of Isin, refused to send needed food to the king and the city of Ur. This led to the break-up of central

control. The isolated and weakened city of Ur was unable to resist an invasion from its former subjects in Elam, to the east, who sacked the city. The great Sumerian empire—the model state for the later ages—came to a tragic end.

❧ A stone head of Gudea, the priest-king of Lagash.
MUSEUM OF FINE ARTS, BOSTON

The Legacy of the Earliest Cities

What is the legacy of the Sumerians and other gifted people who banded together to create the world's earliest cities? Many of their innovations have evolved and become central to modern life. In the realm of technology, the people of Mesopotamia and their neighbors in Southwest Asia appear to have been the first to employ the wheel, the plow, irrigation for agriculture, metallurgy, and a variety of engineering principles. They were also masters of food production, expanding and making more productive the wheat–barley and sheep–goat–cattle farming mix. They also introduced dates, figs, grapes, olives, flax, oats, and a variety of other crops to farming. Equally important, they developed the use of secondary products from domestic animals, such as milk and wool, and began to use animals to pull carts and plows. The manufacturing of textiles, ceramics, and metals developed within the Mesopotamian cities. Trading networks stretched across Southwest Asia and to the further reaches of the known world. Much of this trade was centrally organized for the benefit of the state; by the time of Ur III, and perhaps earlier, there was a class of entrepreneurs who traded on their own behalf as well as for the king.

❧ Dating from about 2100 BC, this bronze statue was used as a votive offering in the foundation of a temple at Nippur, during the reign of Ur-Nammu.
THE IRAQ MUSEUM, BAGDAD/SCALA

SIR LEONARD WOOLLEY'S excavation of the Royal Cemetery of Ur ranks among the most spectacular archaeological discoveries of this century. In five seasons, from 1927 to 1932, he and his co-workers unearthed approximately 2,000 graves, revealing extraordinary wealth and supposed evidence of human sacrifice. Despite more than a century of archaeological work in Mesopotamia, the Royal Cemetery remains in many ways a unique discovery.

This unique gold helmet comes from the richly furnished "private grave" of Meskalamdug. A seal of "Meskalamdug the king" was found in a Royal Tomb, but this may not refer to the same person.
THE IRAQ MUSEUM, BAGHDAD/SCALA

The cemetery was used continuously from approximately 2600 BC to 2100 BC. The earliest graves date to the Early Dynastic period (from 2900 BC to 2350 BC) and include the 16 known as the Royal Tombs. One distinctive characteristic of the tombs is that they include brick or stone-walled chambers with vaulted roofs. In contrast, all other interments—the so-called "private graves"—consisted of simple earthen pits into which the body was placed, occasionally in a coffin, but most commonly wrapped in a reed mat. In addition, most graves in the cemetery were the burial place of a single person. All the Royal Tombs, however, contained multiple burials, ranging from 4 to as many as 75 individuals. Woolley convincingly argued that these did not represent reuse of the tombs but, rather, the burial of a principal person accompanied by a variety of retainers. He considered this to be evidence of human sacrifice.

The Royal Tombs revealed a wealth of grave goods, including elaborate jewelry of gold, silver, copper, lapis lazuli, and carnelian; stone and metal vessels; elaborately decorated musical instruments; and tools and weapons of precious metals. As Woolley was quick to point out, however, great wealth was not exclusive to the occupants of the Royal Tombs: a number of private graves also had rich and abundant grave goods. Indeed, the cemetery included a wide range of burials, from those with no accompanying goods or just a couple of clay pots, to those containing vast wealth and the ultimate offering— other human beings.

BRITISH MUSEUM

Many female retainers in the Royal Tombs were lavishly adorned with necklaces of gold, silver, and semiprecious stone beads, heavy gold earrings, and headdresses of gold ribbon and gold leaves strung on beads, as shown in this reconstruction.

THE IRAQ MUSEUM, BAGHDAD/SCALA

The crushed head of a female retainer from a Royal Tomb, with jewelry in place. Gold ribbon, gold leaves, and beads form a headdress, and strings of lapis lazuli and gold beads were worn around the neck.

◈ One of two similar goat statues found together in a Royal Tomb. The pair may have been part of a larger composition. Goats were among the animals that figured frequently in Sumerian art.

ADAM WOOLRTT/ROBERT HARDING PICTURE LIBRARY

🜂 This lapis lazuli mosaic inlaid with shell and red limestone is part of the Standard of Ur. It depicts people at a banquet, including a musician with an instrument similar to those found in the Royal Tombs.

ANCIENT ART & ARCHITECTURE COLLECTION

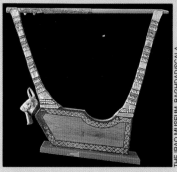

THE IRAQ MUSEUM, BAGHDAD/SCALA

🜂 Several Royal Tombs contained musical instruments such as this lyre. Their recovery was one of Woolley's excavation triumphs, since the wooden frames had long since decayed.

Who, then, were the people buried in the Royal Cemetery? What entitled some to burial in the Royal Tombs? Why did the practice of burying additional people in tombs—"human sacrifice"—die out, and why is there no evidence of similar practices elsewhere in Mesopotamia at this time? These and many other questions have continued to intrigue archaeologists up to the present day.

Woolley identified the people buried in the Royal Tombs as kings and queens, accompanied by members of their courts. He based his argument on finds of inscribed artifacts in some of the tombs that named individuals and also bore the designation "LUGAL", the Sumerian word for king. He believed that the other graves in the cemetery were those of private citizens, some of whom were very wealthy, but none of whom was royalty.

Some scholars, however, have disputed this claim. One difficulty is that none of the inscribed artifacts was found in direct association with the principal occupant of a tomb. The artifacts might, therefore, represent gifts from mourners rather than a possession of the dead person. Second, if all the Royal Tombs were graves of royalty, how do we explain the variation in their size, architecture, and number of occupants? This variation might suggest that there were significant differences among the people buried in the tombs.

Another interpretation of both the Royal Tombs and the private graves is possible if we consider them in a broader context. Documentary sources indicate that the Early Dynastic palaces and temples competed with each other for power and wealth, as well as working to erode the traditional power base of wealthy families. From other sites, we know that Early Dynastic mortuary practices included burial in both cemeteries and houses. The placement of the dead below the house floor implies a close connection to the domestic, family unit. By contrast, burial in a cemetery, removed from direct association with the house, may imply that family ties were weaker. People buried in cemeteries may have been those whose principal ties were to the temples or palace.

According to this interpretation, the people buried in the Royal Cemetery were those whose livelihood was closely tied to the temples and palace of Ur, from those in the highest positions—the high priestesses and priests, kings and queens—to the most menial laborers and the full range of people in between. The variation among the Royal Tombs might, then, be related to the differences between temples and palaces and their personnel.

Reference to the tensions and power struggles in Early Dynastic society may also help to explain the spectacular wealth of some of the burials. Following the argument of prehistorian Vere Gordon Childe, conspicuous consumption in burial practices may characterize periods of great sociopolitical competition. On this view, burial practices are one arena in which competition is played out, with each party vying to mount a more lavish spectacle than anyone else. The vast material wealth and unprecedented evidence for the burial of human retainers in the Royal Cemetery might be just such an indication of competitive display. Whether the competition declined or mortuary practices were no longer part of the struggle for power, the practice of building Royal Tombs and furnishing them with human retainers ceased before the end of the Early Dynastic period, about 2500 BC.

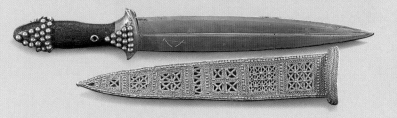

◈ This gold dagger with a lapis lazuli hilt and an intricately worked gold sheath was found in one of the most badly disturbed of the Royal Tombs. The design of the sheath resembles that of sheaths made of plaited reeds or rushes found in less wealthy graves.

THE IRAQ MUSEUM, BAGHDAD/SCALA

♁ The Uruk Vase, a stone beaker with three registers that portray a similar set of activities to the Standard of Ur.
HIRMER FOTOARCHIVE, MUNICH

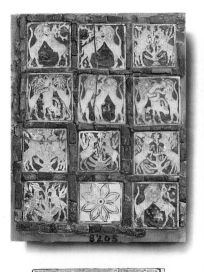

♁ An inlaid table found in the Royal Cemetery at Ur, dating from about 2600 BC. This table and associated pieces are believed to have been used as a board game. Pictorial representations of animals and mythical figures are characteristic of many of the pieces found in the cemetery.
THE IRAQ MUSEUM, BAGHDAD/SCALA

♁ Early Dynastic alabaster statuettes from Tell Asmar, in northeastern Mesopotamia. The woman's dress and the man's curly hair and beard have been interpreted as reflecting the characteristics of a distinctive group that may have populated Akkad (north of Sumer).

Early Mesopotamian society also set the stage for many later developments in religion, law, and ethics. Two major ways of maintaining order in the growing cities of Mesopotamia were organized religion (rituals and sacred beliefs) and legal codes as put forward by secular leaders. According to texts of the time, Sumerian religion was based on a fatalistic theology. The gods established laws that were unchanging. People did not have free will but were governed by the decisions of both the major gods and their own personal intermediary gods. The gods were lords of each of the temples and their estates. In addition, certain gods and goddesses were closely associated with each city. The Sumerian gods were related to life-giving powers in nature, such as water, earth, and air. Humans had been created specifically to relieve the gods of the tedium of work, and the gods appointed human representatives to direct day-to-day activities. At first, these must have been priests within the temple. But with the ascendancy of a secular power base within Sumerian city-states, the gods became associated with the validation of the king's authority as well. Further validation of the superiority of the kings and the relative inferiority of other powers, such as the priests and the landed elite (farm owners), came from the legal codes issued by Sumerian and later kings.

A less obvious, but perhaps an equally powerful, means of expressing and reinforcing the social order comes from the representational art of the early cities. During the Uruk and Jemdet Nasr periods, there was a significant increase in large-scale representational art, and some of it is explicit in its portrayal of what must have been the hierarchical relationships within early Sumerian society. Not surprisingly, this is exactly when writing was developing and moving through its highly representational stage, about 3000 BC. During the following Early Dynastic period, art flourished in many media, and among the many astonishing pieces are some that once again appear to portray a social order and appropriate modes of behavior, such as on the Royal Standard from Ur or the Uruk Vase.

Not all of the developments that accompanied the growth of early cities in Mesopotamia were necessarily good for the majority in all respects. With the growth of social complexity and the need to maintain order, access to productive resources became restricted and was allocated on the basis of class. Instead of being temporary, family or individual wealth became institutionalized into a permanent difference, and an early form of class society developed. Along with these formalized differences between families and broader kin groups, it is likely that the roles of males and females within society further diverged, leading to less social and geographical mobility for women and less access to the centers of civic authority. The factors that caused this process of increased inequality are not clear, but the resulting restrictions placed on females became institutionalized and still affect the choices available to many women.

In the Early Dynastic period, warfare became more frequent and involved larger, more organized groups. It may have been a combination of conflicts over land, irrigation-water access, or outright seeking of booty that began the series of intercity campaigns. These are chronicled in some of the earliest written texts and also attested by the construction of massive defensive walls around most cities.

The formation of the world's first cities on the broad alluvial plain of Mesopotamia initiated one of the great transformations of human history: people learning to live together in large groups for long periods of time. Even as early as about 2000 BC, as much as half the population of lowland Mesopotamia lived in cities, where previously the peoples of the world had known life only in villages and small bands. The concept and development of urbanism swept across the world. Something about urbanism—either its attractions or the coercion of its leaders—was so powerful that today the vast majority of all people throughout the world live in cities that bear a striking resemblance to those of early Mesopotamia.

BABYLONIANS AND ASSYRIANS: STRUGGLING POWERS IN MESOPOTAMIA

GÖRAN BURENHULT

After the decline of the Sumerian kingdom, about 1800 BC, the people of Elam—the Elamites—occupied Mesopotamia, and at the same time, a new Semitic people arrived from the west: the Amorites. The Sumerian cities fell into disrepair, and the Sumerian language became extinct. The subsequent history of the Mesopotamian plain is characterized by a continuous struggle for supremacy between two centers of power: the Babylonian kingdom, in the south, and the Assyrian kingdom, in the north.

An Amorite dynasty made Babylon its capital, and under King Hammurabi (1728 BC to 1686 BC), the old Babylonian kingdom flourished and conquered Assyria, in the north. However, Hammurabi's fame rests mainly on his law-making and organizational skills, such as the large-scale irrigation projects he organized, which created opportunities for a rich material culture to develop. The power of Babylon was crushed about 1530 BC, when the Hittites, from present-day Turkey, conquered and plundered the city.

Towards the middle of the second millennium BC, not only Babylon, but also other early powers of the Near East—such as Egypt and the Hittite empire—collapsed and left behind a vacuum that soon made way for a patch-work of smaller states. Most important of these were Phoenicia, on the Mediterranean coast; Urartu, in present-day Armenia; Karkemish and other Hittite–Hurrite cities, in northern Syria; Damascus, in southern Syria; and the Jewish kingdom, in Palestine.

Between about 1300 BC and 1100 BC, Assyrian power grew rapidly, and from time to time, the country even controlled its arch enemy, the Babylonian kingdom. During this period, nomadic Jewish tribes migrated into Palestine—according to legend, after the exodus

🔥 A scene from the reliefs at the Assyrian king Assurnasirpal II's palace at Nimrud, showing the king on a lion hunt. It dates from the ninth century BC.

from Pharaoh Ramses II's Egypt. Assyria's first true emperor, Tiglat Pilesar I, ascended the throne about 1100 BC, but soon after, a decline occurred, the reasons for which are not known in detail. It was not until the beginning of the eighth century BC that Assyria, under the ruthless King Assurnasirpal (883 BC to 859 BC), regained its powerful position. His successor, Salamanassar III (858 BC to 824 BC), defeated Damascus and received tribute from King Jehu of Israel.

The Rise of Assyria

However, Assyria was still surrounded by rebel vassal states, such as Babylon, Elam, and Urartu, but under Tiglat Pilesar III (745 BC to 727 BC), the country's powerful military forces conquered large areas, among them Urartu. Large-scale deportations were part of the Assyrian rulers' strategy, and the deported populations were replaced by colonists from other countries. Samaria was conquered by Sargon in 722 BC, and the 10 tribes of Israel were exiled. Sargon crushed Urartu once and for all, and the road now lay open for advancing nomadic horsemen, such as the Kimmerians, and later, the Scythians, which was

to prove disastrous for Assyria in 612 BC, when Scythians are thought to have taken part in the destruction of Nineveh. Sargon's son Sanherib (704 BC to 681 BC) leveled Babylon to the ground, and Assarhaddon (680 BC to 669 BC) turned Egypt into an Assyrian vassal state. The Assyrian empire now reached its high point and was the sole ruler of the Near East. Its domains stretched from Egypt and the Mediterranean, in the west, and from Anatolia, in the north, to the Persian Gulf, in the southeast.

Assyria has been called the world's first military power, and rightly so. The strength of the Assyrian war machinery was based partly on the education of an extremely effective organization under well-educated commanders in special branches of the army, and partly on advanced techno-logical knowledge including engineers who constructed roads, bridges, and new weapons, such as battering-rams and catapults. The cavalry was swift and very mobile, and it was supported by both light and heavy infantry, with lances and bows and arrows as the main weapons. Two-wheeled war carts, drawn by two or more horses, were

also part of the military forces. In addition, the development of the siege strategy is attributed to the Assyrians.

The Assyrian empire, one of the world's first imperial structures, was based on an organization of provinces, ruled by powerful governors in local palaces. The royal palaces in the Assyrian capitals, first in Assur and later in Nimrud, Khorsabad, and Nineveh, were filled with detailed reliefs of war and hunting scenes. These are our primary source of knowlege about certain aspects of everyday life in Assyria.

The decline of the Assyrian power had already begun during the reign of the famous emperor Assurbanipal (668 BC to 625 BC). Egypt was abandoned, and the advancing Persians conquered large parts of the country. Nevertheless, it is thanks to Assurbanipal's great interest in art and culture that important information has survived for posterity. For instance, in Babylon, he had copies made of old Babylonian scripts, as well as scientific and religious works, and thereby created the famous library of Nineveh, which, to a great extent, has been recovered.

Babylonia Regains Power

Following the death of Assurbanipal, Babylonia regained its independence under King Nabopalassar, who attacked and destroyed the Assyrian capital, Nineveh, in 612 BC. The Assyrian empire was totally destroyed, and once again, southern Mesopotamia became the center of power. Under Nebuchadnezzar, Babylonia flourished and became great, and the magnificent city of Babylon—with its splendid temples, great ziggurat, and famous hanging gardens—is, essentially, his work. It was not until the Persian invasion of Babylonia when the Persian king Kyros stood outside the town wall of Babylon, in 539 BC, that the cultural hegemony of Mesopotamia came to an end.

EGIZIO MUSEUM, TURIN/SCALA

THE CIVILIZATION OF ANCIENT EGYPT

5 0 0 0 B C – 3 3 2 B C

Life along the Nile

BOYO G. OCKINGA

FEW CULTURES HAVE been so dependent upon and influenced by their natural environment as ancient Egypt. This was already recognized in the fifth century BC by the Greek historian Herodotus, who called Egypt the gift of the Nile. Although there is evidence that Egypt's climate may have been wetter in prehistoric times, from about 3000 BC, it was characterized by excessive aridity, making life totally dependent upon the waters of the Nile.

The Egyptians recognized their reliance on the great river, which distinguished them from other peoples; in his hymn to the sun-god Aten, King Akhenaten praises the god for creating the Nile to keep "humankind" (the Egyptians) alive, and for creating a Nile in the heavens (rain) for foreigners.

A Middle Kingdom hymn calls the Nile: "Bringer of food, rich in provisions, creator of all good things, Lord of awe, sweet of perfume, who satisfies when he comes. Maker of herbage for the cattle, who gives sacrifice for every god. He is in the netherworld, but Heaven and Earth are in his charge, the one who takes possession of the two lands; who fills storerooms, enlarges granaries, and gives goods to the poor."

◆ About 2000 BC, the first hints of a general judgment of the dead appear, involving weighing the heart before the lords of the netherworld. In this eighteenth-dynasty *Book of the Dead* vignette, Khai and his wife, Merit, having passed the test, approach Osiris, king of the netherworld. The papyrus is from their tomb at Deir el-Medina.

◈ Already in predynastic times, Egypt had trade and cultural ties with western Asia. The ivory handle of this finely worked, ripple-flaked, flint knife, found at Gebel el-Arak, near Nag Hammadi, in Upper Egypt, is decorated with a combat scene, and includes two high-prowed boats thought to be of Mesopotamian origin.
THE LOUVRE/ERICH LESSING/MAGNUM

⤷ King Narmer dominates this scene on the Narmer palette. He is depicted smiting a defeated enemy. The falcon-god, Horus, holds the symbol of the defeated marsh region by a leash, and below the king are two other prostrate enemies: the left one represents town-dwellers; the other, nomadic hunters.

CAIRO MUSEUM, EGYPT/ WERNER FORMAN ARCHIVE

♀ The central structure of Djoser's funerary complex at Saqqara, the step-pyramid, is the oldest known building constructed of stone. Originally designed as a mastaba tomb, it underwent six changes of plan before attaining its present form.

attributes the initial unification of Egypt to Menes/ Aha, this distinction more rightly belongs to another historical figure, King Narmer. On his famous palette in the Cairo Museum, he is depicted wearing the two crowns of Upper and Lower Egypt, triumphing over his enemies. Archaeology has shown that soon after the end of the Predynastic period, an advanced culture had emerged with fully developed forms of kingship, religion, art, and script that are distinctly Egyptian in character.

The development of writing in Egypt is a controversial issue. It is generally held that, as in many other cultures, it was connected with the development of administration that occurred here in the Early Dynastic period (2950 BC to 2640 BC). There are, however, indications that it may have come considerably earlier. In the tomb of Hemka, at Saqqara, dated to the reign of Den early in the first dynasty (2950 BC to 2770 BC), a roll of blank, uninscribed papyrus was discovered, and the book roll as a hieroglyphic sign is also known from the first dynasty onwards. Given that papyrus was produced then, writing must have been in wide use considerably earlier in order to stimulate the development of such a sophisticated writing material. It has been suggested that ritual scenes, such as the goddess of writing, Seshat, recording the length of the king's reign on the leaves of the sacred ished-tree of Heliopolis, may reflect an early use of leaves as a writing material. Once the script

ALAIN CHOISNET/THE IMAGE BANK

had been developed and was widely used, its practitioners, the scribes, enjoyed a greatly increased social standing, and the profession became a coveted one. Even the sons of kings were not averse to depicting themselves in the posture of a scribe, and in tomb and later temple reliefs, the scribe is a ubiquitous figure, depicted recording and controlling the activity of others.

Very few written records survive from the Early Dynastic period, but the cultural achievements of this period are considerable, particularly in the minor arts and the development of a central administration. The Old Kingdom began with the third dynasty (about 2640 BC to 2575 BC), and already the second ruler of this period, Djoser, had built a magnificent funerary complex in stone, including the famous step-pyramid at Saqqara. (See the feature *The Quest for Eternity: Temples and Tombs*.) This is the earliest stone building known to history, yet it displays a perfection in skill and form that matches the best that ancient Egypt was to produce. An achievement of this dimension is possible only if a solid cultural base exists upon which its creators can draw.

The Pyramid Builders

The fourth dynasty (2575 BC to 2465 BC) is the age of the great pyramid builders—Snefru, Khufu (Cheops), Khafra (Chephren), and Men-kau-re (Mycerinus). Their massive structures are apt symbols of the Egyptian state, with the king at its apex, his officials (drawn mainly from members of his family) at the higher levels, and the mass of the people forming the bulk of the pyramid.

The fourth dynasty saw a rise in the prominence of the sun-god Re, with the king adopting the title "Son of Re", and the successors of Khufu often including the name of Re in their names. In the fifth dynasty (2465 BC to 2325 BC), most monarchs built a temple in honor of the god. (See the feature *The Sons of Re: The Kings of Egypt*.)

The Old Kingdom is generally held to come to a close shortly after the end of the sixth dynasty (2155 BC). According to Manetho, its last effective ruler, Pepi II, reigned for 94 years; the dynasty ended with a woman, the shadowy Nitocris, who is known only from later records. The reasons for the fall of the Old Kingdom are probably connected with decline in the effectiveness of the administration. There is evidence to show that the size of the bureaucracy continually grew until the state could no longer afford adequately to pay its officials, which no doubt led to inefficiency and corruption, and subsequent collapse under the pressure of a series of low Niles and poor harvests.

During the period of instability known as the First Intermediate period (2135 BC to 2040 BC), a number of rival kingdoms vied for supremacy. Thebes finally won out in Upper Egypt, while Lower Egypt was held by the Herakleopolitans. The movement for reunification emerged from the

ANCIENT EGYPT: 4000 BC – AD 1

Date	DYNASTIES	RULERS	SIGNIFICANT EVENTS
AD 1	Romans	Augustus / Cleopatra	
	Ptolemies	Ptolemy I	Manetho's history of Egypt
	30th	Alexander the Great	
500	27th	Persian domination	Herodotus in Egypt / Circumnavigation of Africa by Egyptian expedition
	26th	Necho II	Greek and Carian mercenaries in Egypt
	25th	Piankhi	Assyrian occupation / Kushite rule
		Sheshonk I	Egypt invades Israel and Judea
1000	21st		Libyan dynasty / The *Story of Wenamun*
	20th	Ramses III	Battle against Sea Peoples
	19th	Ramses II	Egyptian–Hittite treaty / Battle of Kadesh
		Tutankhamun / Akhenaten	Amarna period
	18th	Amenhotep II / Thutmosis III	Consolidation of empire
1500		Hatshepsut	Deir el-Bahri temple
	Hyksos / Second Intermediate period	Kamose	Wars of independence; reunification under Thebes
		Seqenenre Apophis	Hyksos control Egypt
	12th	Amenemhet III / Sesostris I / Amenemhet I	The *Story of Sinuhe* / Reunification under Thebans
2000	11th / First Intermediate period	Mentuhotep III	
	6th	Pepi II / Unas	Collapse of Old Kingdom / Pyramid texts
2500	5th		Rise of cult of Re, construction of sun-temples
	4th	Khufu	Giza pyramids
	3rd	Djoser	Stone architecture: step-pyramid at Saqqara
	2nd		
	1st		
3000		Aha (Menes?)	Unification of Egypt / Narmer palette
		King "Scorpion" / Narmer	
		Naqada III	
		Protodynastic cultures	
3500		Naqada II	
		Naqada I	
4000 BC		Predynastic cultures	

43

⊕ In her temple at Deir el-Bahri, Hatshepsut depicts herself as a traditional Egyptian king. Here, wearing the double crown of Upper and Lower Egypt, she appears in the form of Osiris, god of the dead.

♂ A wooden statue of Sesostris I. It is one of a pair depicting the king wearing the red crown of Lower and (here) the white crown of Upper Egypt.
JUERGEN LIEPE, BERLIN

♀ This ceremonial axe of Ahmose, founder of the eighteenth dynasty, was found in the tomb of his influential mother, Queen Ahhotep.
JUERGEN LIEPE, BERLIN

south, and the energetic Thebans under their king Nebhepetre Mentuhotep II of the eleventh dynasty (2134 BC to 1991 BC) succeeded in gaining control over the north.

During the First Intermediate period, arts and learning declined considerably in the south, which was cut off from the schools of the old royal residence. When the Thebans brought back experts from the north, there was a gradual return to the old standards.

Mentuhotep II built himself a splendid funerary temple and tomb of truly royal quality at Deir el-Bahri, in western Thebes, a building that was to inspire the architect of Hatshepsut's better-known temple. The last king of the eleventh dynasty, Mentuhotep IV, does not seem to have been a legitimate heir to the throne, for he is omitted in later king-lists.

The Feudal Age

Egypt's next ruler was Amenemhet I (1991 BC to 1962 BC), perhaps the vizier (chief minister) of the last king of the eleventh dynasty, although this is not certain. The *Prophecy of Neferti*, a text fictitiously set in the fourth dynasty in the time of Snefru, purports to record a prophecy that, after a period of chaos, the "son of a woman of Nubia", called Ameni, would become king and bring stability back to the land. This was to usher in the Middle Kingdom (2040 BC to 1650 BC), the classical period in Egypt's history. In spite of their southern origins, the rulers of the twelfth dynasty moved their capital to the north, the natural center of gravity of Egypt, at the apex of the delta and the head of the long, narrow Nile Valley.

The Middle Kingdom was a period when the pen was put to work to support the new state. The *Prophecy of Neferti* was clearly propaganda intended to attract support for the new government. The famous *Story of Sinuhe* also belongs to this period. Other texts were specially composed for use in the schools to win young men for the administration, which had to be rebuilt after the First Intermediate period, and to inculcate in them a sense of loyalty towards the new dynasty.

The Middle Kingdom is also known as Egypt's "feudal age", for the provincial overlords held great power. Some even dated events according to their period of office, and they built themselves great tombs, such as those at Beni Hasan. Elements of the old royal funerary practices were adopted—for example, the construction of valley temples. One nomarch, or provincial governor, Djehutihotep of el-Bersheh, proudly records how he had constructed for himself a statue of truly royal proportions; it was more than 6 meters (20 feet) in height, and in his tomb, he depicts how it was transported.

Not until the energetic Sesostris III (1878 BC to 1841 BC) came to the throne was the power of the nomarchs curbed, so strong was the tradition of independence established in the First Intermediate period.

PICTUREPOINT LTD

The last ruler of the twelfth dynasty, as of the sixth, was a woman, Sobekneferu. The thirteenth dynasty (1785 BC to 1650 BC) shows the same characteristics as followed the sixth; there was a rapid succession of rulers and a weakening of central authority, ushering in the Second Intermediate period (1650 BC to 1540 BC). In the eastern delta region, the Asiatic Hyksos, called "rulers of foreign lands" by the Egyptians, took advantage of this situation to wrest control of the area and set up their own kingdom. Although the Hyksos gained influence over most of Egypt, it seems they were content to allow Egyptian dynasts to keep control of their local princedoms as feudal dependencies.

Again, it was from Thebes and the south that the movement for reunification sprang. Sekenenre Ta'a II and his son Kamose, the last two kings of the seventeenth dynasty (about 1650 BC to 1551 BC), began the war of independence against Apophis, the last of the Hyksos. Kamose set up a pair of stelae in Karnak, telling of his glorious deeds of battle. His reign was short, and it was left to Ahmose, his brother and successor, to complete the expulsion of the Hyksos from Egypt.

The Warrior Ethos in the New Kingdom

Ahmose founded a new dynasty, the eighteenth (1540 BC to 1295 BC), and a new age—the New Kingdom (1540 BC to 1070 BC). The warlike events that ushered in the New Kingdom saw the rise of a new warrior ethos in Egypt, and brought about the establishment of a well-organized standing army. Innovations in warfare, influenced by the Hyksos, also appeared: in particular, the use of the horse-drawn chariot as a fighting platform, and new types of weapons, such as the powerful

GUIDO ALBERTO ROSSI/THE IMAGE BANK

The *Story of Sinuhe* was a biography, probably fictitious, of an official who fled Egypt at the death of Amenemhet I, but was encouraged to return by Sesostris I.

I reached the Walls of the Ruler that were built to ward off the Asiatics, to control the Sand-farers. I crouched in a bush for fear of being spotted by the guards on duty at the walls. At night, I set out. By daybreak, I had reached Peten. I rested at the island of Kemwer. Thirst overtook me: I was parched, my throat was dry. I said, 'This is the taste of death.' My spirits lifted, and I pulled myself together when I heard the sound of lowing cattle. I saw Asiatics, and a scout among them— who had been in Egypt—recognized me.

From the *Story of Sinuhe*, translated by Boyo G. Ockinga

composite bow. In the Old Kingdom, armies were raised as required. Since the First Intermediate period, small bands of professional soldiers had been kept by the provincial governors or the king, and these were supplemented by enlistment when needed. In the New Kingdom, a large army of infantry and chariot forces was maintained.

With a few notable exceptions, most rulers of the New Kingdom led their troops into battle, and placed great emphasis on their personal prowess and feats of arms. The most famous of these kings is doubtless Thutmosis III, often called the Napoleon of Egypt. In the course of countless campaigns, he established Egypt's empire in western Asia. His son, Amenhotep II, was an avid sportsman and soldier, who proudly boasted of his martial and sporting achievements. In one of his inscriptions, his outlook on life is succinctly summed up by the description of himself that he places in the mouth of his father, Thutmosis III.

⊕ Hatshepsut placed her funerary temple (in the foreground) to the south of that of her predecessor, Mentuhotep II, using the backdrop of the cliffs of western Thebes to spectacular effect. The now-ruined structure on the platform of Mentuhotep's temple may originally have incorporated a pyramid.

THE ARCHAEOLOGY OF DEATH

CORINNE DUHIG

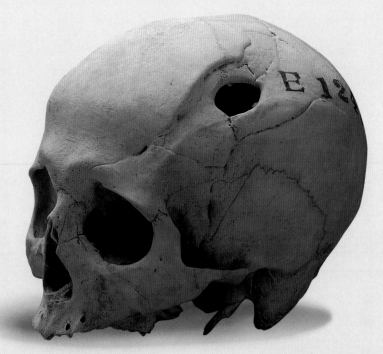

THE ANCIENT EGYPTIANS typically used many methods in an attempt to ensure life after death. Perhaps the best-known is mummification, which aimed to preserve the body as an enduring home for the soul.

This skull from Giza (about the sixth century BC) is of a man who had survived a disabling head wound.
G.J. OWEN/DUCKWORTH COLLECTION, CAMBRIDGE UNIVERSITY

A reconstruction of the priestess Tjentmutengebtiu's head inside its bandages was made using multiple X-ray slices processed by a computer to form a three-dimensional image. Images of the skull revealed that the priestess's brain had been removed, and the chamber stuffed with linen. She died about 900 BC.
ST THOMAS' HOSPITAL (MEDICAL PHYSICS), LONDON

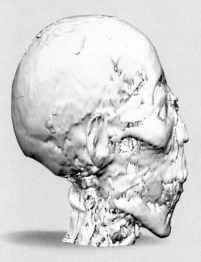

The excavation or plundering of innumerable Egyptian tombs has uncovered huge quantities of human remains. A great deal is poorly preserved, of unknown origin, or even unrecovered—some of the ancient grave-fields are scattered with human bones, mummy fragments, and pieces of bandage. But much is housed in museum collections throughout the world, providing a valuable research resource.

Almost every type of human tissue can be recovered for examination. In special cases, scientific autopsies have been carried out, but the days of "unrolling" mummies from their bandages are now past, and nondestructive methods are preferred. Ingenuity is needed to investigate intact specimens: the use of conventional radiology is a long-established method, but recently, flexible endoscopes have allowed the inside of body cavities to be viewed, and CAT scans have been used to obtain a three-dimensional image of the body.

Marc Armand Ruffer pioneered human paleopathology (the study of ancient diseases) in the nineteenth century. He found bilharzia flatworms (which cause bladder disease) in mummies, examined hardened arteries, and produced a classic description and illustration of spinal tuberculosis. Modern research—using methods including histology (the microscopic study of tissue structure), serology (the study of serums), and various types of electron microscopy—has revealed the disease experience of ancient Egyptians, from pharaohs to commoners. Diseases included parasite infestation, degenerative arthritis, and the most worn and abscessed teeth in the ancient world. Wounds healed well, however, probably because the climate was dry and most people were basically healthy. Syphilis, the scourge of later times, seems to have been absent. Tuberculosis was present from the Predynastic period, but the only evidence for leprosy is from two bodies from a late Nubian cemetery.

Knowledge of ancient diseases is only one aspect, albeit morbidly fascinating, of the study of human remains. Bones and bodies record many aspects of human inheritance and experience. An X-ray survey of the royal mummies in Cairo revealed the skull and facial morphology of several pharaohs from the eighteenth dynasty, revising the identifications made by priests of the twenty-first dynasty. DNA analysis can establish familial relationships: for example, it has confirmed the genetic similarity of Tutankhamun to his supposed grandmother Queen Tiye. Broader projects, using modern measurement and statistical methods, attempt to describe and explain genetic variation in the ancient Nile Valley. Lively academic argument continues as to the composition of the population, and the roles played by migration and interbreeding.

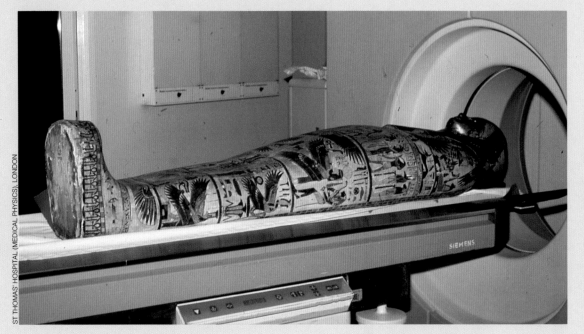

ST THOMAS' HOSPITAL (MEDICAL PHYSICS) LONDON

The priestess Tjentmutengebtiu about to undergo a CAT scan.

"He is not even of an age to engage in military activity and look, he has turned his back on the pleasures of the flesh and chooses strength!"

The famed Queen Hatshepsut (1479 BC to 1457 BC) is best known for her works of peace —her obelisks in Karnak, her funerary temple at Deir el-Bahri, and her expedition to the land of Punt, on the coast of present-day Sudan—but even she kept up the warrior tradition, and depicted herself as a ferocious sphinx trampling down her enemies. Similarly, Amenhotep III, who typifies the pleasure-loving oriental monarch, paid lip service to the warrior ideal. His commemorative scarabs record his hunts against wild bulls and lions, and an inscription reports his campaign in Nubia. His son, the famous Akhenaten, who for so long was idealized as the first pacifist pharaoh, was in fact very traditional in this respect. He, too, set up inscriptions recording his campaign into Nubia and describing himself as a warrior king.

Although the warrior tradition was dominant, New Kingdom Egypt was no Egyptian Sparta. Egypt reached the zenith of material prosperity and imperial power in this period, and art and architecture flourished. In the reign of Hatshepsut, the classical standards of the Middle Kingdom in art, architecture, and the language of royal inscriptions were taken as models. In the age of Amenhotep III (1391 BC to 1353 BC), the art of the New Kingdom reached a climax of sophistication and refinement, exemplified in the reliefs of such tombs as those of Ramose and Kheruef, at Thebes, and the older parts of the temple of Amun, at Luxor. The second king of the eighteenth dynasty, Amenhotep I, established the royal cemetery in the Valley of the Kings, at Thebes.

ROBERT HARDING PICTURE LIBRARY

⚘Almost all that remains of Amenhotep III's once massive funerary temple are these two colossal statues, mistakenly identified by early Greek travelers as belonging to their legendary hero Memnon. The statues flanked the entrance to the temple.

BOYO G. OCKINGA

❦ This relief from Ramses II's temple at Abydos shows the Egyptian infantry and chariotry that formed part of the army he led against the Hittites at Kadesh. Four of the divisions of the army were named after the gods Amun, Re, Seth, and Ptah. A fifth was formed of fresh recruits, the Na'arin, whose timely arrival at Kadesh saved the day for Ramses.

⟐ One of the 401 *ushabti* (worker) figures from the tomb of Tutankhamun, who were to carry out tasks for the king in the other world. He wears the nemes headdress and a diadem with protective vulture and cobra goddesses on his brow, and holds one of the royal insignia, a flywhisk, in his right hand.
SCALA

⟐⟐ An unfinished quarzite head of Akhenaten's queen, Nefertiti. The piece is an exquisite example of late Amarna art, and was found in the workshop of the sculptor Thutmosis, at el-Amarna.
STAATLICHE MUSEEN, AEGYPTISCHES MUSEUM, BERLIN/ ERICH LESSING/MAGNUM

It is also in the New Kingdom that probably the most enigmatic personality of Egyptian history ascended the throne of the pharaohs: Amenhotep IV, better known as Akhenaten, the son of Amenhotep III and his nonroyal queen, Tiye. Akhenaten (1353 BC TO 1338 BC) attempted to introduce a genuine monotheism in Egypt. The old gods, particularly Amun, were mercilessly eradicated. So thorough were the king's servants in their attempt to obliterate the memory of Amun that they climbed to the tops of lofty obelisks to erase his images there, even though they could not be seen from the ground. One of the surest indicators of date in an inscription is the erasure of the name Amun, which proves that it predates the establishment of Akhenaten's new capital at el-Amarna.

Akhenaten's reform naturally failed; his religion was too other-worldly and could not meet the needs of the ordinary people. Its greatest deficiency was probably in the area of funerary practice, where it offered almost nothing compared to the rich traditional rituals.

Akhenaten's two successors, Semenkhkare (1338 BC to 1336 BC) and Tutankhamun (1336 BC

to 1327 BC), were short-lived. With the early death, at about eighteen, of Tutankhamun, who restored the old faith, and won immortality through the chance survival intact of his tomb with its magnificent burial equipment, the royal family of the eighteenth dynasty died out. In the following period, it was the military that was to win control of the country. The immediate successors of Tutankhamun, Ay and Horemheb, were both army commanders, as was the founder of the nineteenth dynasty (1295 BC to 1188 BC), the general Paramessu, who was to become Ramses I.

The military pharaohs were able to stem the tide that was advancing against Egypt in Syria, and reassert Egypt's position there against the encroachments of the Hittites of Asia Minor (present-day Turkey). The most famous Rameside king is doubtless Ramses II (1279 BC to 1213 BC), whose memorials the traveler to Egypt meets at every step. His monuments fill the land—no previous king left so many temples and other works. After a great battle against the Hittites at Kadesh, on the Orontes River, in the fifth year of his rule, the king just escaped with his life, and

ALAIN CHOISNET/THE IMAGE BANK

⟐ A view from the second courtyard of the Ramesseum. Ramses II was the most prolific builder of Egypt's kings. His funerary temple in western Thebes, named after his throne name, Usermaatre, was known in classical antiquity as the "tomb of Ozymandias". A painting of the ruins of the temple inspired Percy Bysshe Shelley's poem "Ozymandias".

only staved off a complete rout thanks to the timely arrival of reinforcements. The Hittites and Egyptians then came to an accommodation in Syria, and eventually formed an alliance that was sealed by the marriage of Ramses with a Hittite princess, given the Egyptian name of Maat-Hor-Neterure. Egypt then enjoyed its last long period of peace and prosperity in the remaining 45 or so years of Ramses's reign.

The last of the strong Ramesside kings was Ramses III, the second ruler of the twentieth dynasty (1186 BC to 1070 BC). He warded off attacks from the Libyans in 1180 BC, and three years later, from the coalition of Sea Peoples, who originated on the east coast of Asia Minor and the Aegean islands. His great funerary temple at Medinet Habu preserves the record of these impressive achievements.

Empire-building in Western Asia

The New Kingdom saw a change in Egypt's relationship with its northern, Asiatic neighbors. Trade contacts had already existed in predynastic times; western Sinai was a coveted source of copper and turquoise, energetically exploited by the Egyptians, who asserted their interests by force of arms when necessary. The coastal city of Byblos (in present-day Lebanon) was also an important trading partner of Egypt in the early period; coniferous timbers, the so-called cedars of Lebanon, were used in first-dynasty tomb construction. The sea route to Byblos was already well established in the Old Kingdom, when the term "Byblos ship" for an ocean-going vessel first appears. The nature of Egypt's relationships with the Levant and Canaan in the Middle Kingdom is disputed. The *Story of Sinuhe*, which speaks of royal messengers regularly traveling through the land, and the numerous finds of Egyptian objects make it clear that they were close. Although it seems unlikely

G. COLLIVA/THE IMAGE BANK

that there was any permanent Egyptian presence in the area, the Egyptians were not averse to using force to exert their will, and mining and trading expeditions were regularly accompanied by soldiers. Yet, on the whole, they relied on trade and the common Bronze Age practice of exchange of gifts between rulers to obtain what they wanted.

In the New Kingdom, the situation changed dramatically. Through the energy of a number of warrior pharaohs—in particular, Thutmosis III— Egypt was able to establish an Asiatic empire in northern Syria and Palestine, organized into three provinces. Imperial rule was loose; each province had an Egyptian governor, and small detachments of troops were stationed in various centers. Day-to-day government was exercised by native city rulers, who were left to their own devices so long as they remained loyal to Egypt and regularly delivered their tribute.

❸ Two of the four colossal, seated, royal statues that flank the entrance to Ramses II's rock-temple at Abu Simbel, in Nubia. Abu Simbel is one of many Egyptian temples built in Nubia to serve as both religious and economic centers.

RIJKSMUSEUM VAN OUDHEDEN, LEIDEN/ERICH LESSING/MAGNUM

◄❍ A detail of a relief in the Saqqara tomb of the general (later king) Horemheb. It depicts Asiatic captives in wooden manacles being led by Egyptian soldiers into the presence of Tutankhamun.

THE QUEST FOR ETERNITY: TEMPLES AND TOMBS

BOYO G. OCKINGA

Ancient Egypt is best known for the brilliance and impressiveness of its monumental art and architecture, which expresses its people's love of life and their search for eternity. The link between monumental architecture and the consciousness of eternity is illustrated by the oldest surviving monumental structures. These are the great mudbrick mastaba tombs and other funerary monuments built at Abydos, in the Early Dynastic period, by the kings for themselves, their families, and retainers, where they were buried, and at Saqqara, where they constructed cenotaphs. The early temples and shrines are smaller and were often built of perishable materials, such as reed and matting. The early tombs were undecorated, for the needs of their occupants were provided for by the institution of a funerary cult conducted by their descendants.

But such cults eventually discontinued, and they were supplemented by inscriptions and reliefs within the tomb showing the requirements of the dead. At first, simple stelae were erected at the offering place, but eventually, the tombs were provided with chapels, whose walls were decorated with scenes of offerings and depictions of the dead ones involved in their favorite activities, showing in fascinating detail the production of the things required for the afterlife.

The earliest stone monument is also a funerary complex, that of King Djoser (2624 BC to 2605 BC) of the third dynasty, at Saqqara, with its dominating step-pyramid. This remarkable group of buildings incorporates the king's tomb, his cenotaph, and his Sed-festival complex. The monument was built by his famous architect, Imhotep, a man later revered as a sage and patron of doctors, and identified by the Greeks with Asclepius.

Djoser's step-pyramid combines two potent symbols—the primeval hill that rose from the waters, the site of the creator god's act of creation; and the pyramidal form, symbol of the greatest of the creator gods, Re, the sun-god of Heliopolis. From the fourth dynasty onwards, the pyramid was to dominate royal funerary architecture, although not all pyramids are as massively built of solid stone as those of Khufu, Khafra, and Men-kau-re, at Giza.

Unlike the tombs of officials, royal pyramids were undecorated until the reign of Unas (2355 BC to 2325 BC), the last ruler of the fifth dynasty. Later Old Kingdom rulers decorated the walls and ceilings of their burial chambers with texts designed to ensure their continued life after death.

Eventually, stone was widely used for temples and tombs, but the dwellings of living mortals continued to be built of less durable mudbrick and wood, for they were needed for only a limited time, whereas the temples and tombs were to last for eternity.

Temples in the New Kingdom

While funerary cults fell into abeyance and the monuments themselves gradually deteriorated, the cults of the gods seemed to endure, and funerary cults became linked with temple organizations and the setting up of statues or stelae in the temples of the gods. A commoner could obtain this only as a favor granted by the monarch, but the monarchs were responsible for building the temples and maintaining their cults, which offered them the opportunity to leave monuments to themselves while gaining the favor of the gods. The result was an explosion of building activity in the New Kingdom. Not only were old mudbrick temples rebuilt in stone, but older structures were expanded. In particular, the temple of Amun, the great state-god of the empire, was added to, resulting in the vast complex that has survived to the present day. With its numerous chapels, halls, pylons, and courts, it was surrounded by a massive wall of mudbrick and covered an area 500 meters by 500 meters (1,640 feet by 1,640 feet).

Plant forms are typical adornments of Egyptian architecture of all periods; in particular, stone columns often represented such plants as papyrus stalks and palms. They had special significance from at least the New Kingdom onwards, when

🔊 A statue of Amenophis, son of Hapu, an influential official of Amenhotep III, depicts him as a scribe with a roll of papyrus on his lap and a scribe's palette —a holder for brush and ink—slung over his left shoulder. The statue stood in the temple of Amun at Karnak, and its inscription addresses visitors, proposing that he act as an intermediary between them and the god in return for an offering. ·
SCALA

temples had a religious, symbolic significance and represented the cosmos. The floor—which the texts say was covered with silver—represented water from which papyrus plants, the columns, grew. The ceiling, painted blue and decorated with stars and birds, represented the sky. The innermost sanctuary, where the image of the god resided, was the primeval hill on which the creator god stood and performed his act of creation.

In the New Kingdom, the increasing importance of the temples for ensuring the immortality of the ruler led to the separation of the royal tomb and the funerary temple. Earlier, the royal funerary temple was attached to the pyramid tomb, but now the tombs were built in the Valley of the Kings, in Thebes. The symbol of the pyramid maintained its significance, however, and chapels of the tombs of commoners

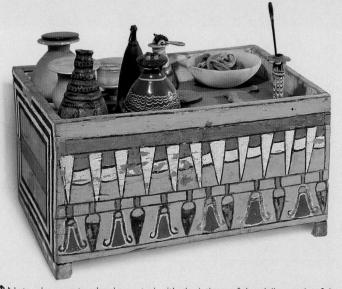

🔊 Not only were tombs decorated with depictions of the daily needs of the deceased, but models of objects used in daily life, or the actual objects themselves, were also placed inside them. This cosmetic chest, with jars of alabaster and colored glass, which belonged to a lady of the eighteenth dynasty named Merit, wife of Khai, was found in the couple's tomb at Deir-el-Medina.
PICTUREPOINT LTD

PHILIPPE ROY/EXPLORER/AUSCAPE

↩ Two statues of Thutmosis III, later usurped by Ramses II, standing in front of the seventh pylon at Karnak. These are two of the countless royal and nonroyal statues set up in the temple. After the second century BC, there were so many that some 800 were cleared from the temple and buried in the courtyard in front of the seventh pylon.

The funerary temples were built where everyone could see them, on the edge of the cultivated land. In fact, they were shrines of the state-god, Amun, incorporating the funerary cult of the ruler, who was also worshiped as a form of the god. Here, just as in the main temples, the deeds of the rulers were recorded in word and image for future generations, thereby securing the rulers' immortality.

The tradition of the ruler as temple builder continued into the Greco-Roman period (332 BC to AD 395); the Ptolemys, in particular, instigated an extensive temple-building program, but the role of the ruler became fossilized. Admittedly, the monarch is still omnipresent, but he or she appears only in the standard religious scenes, performing the temple rituals. No longer do we find anything like the expansive reliefs of the New Kingdom depicting the ruler in a historical situation, doing battle with those symbols of the chaotic, threatening forces of the universe, the foreign foes of Egypt. The individuality of architecture that some of the older temples display is also absent in those of

the Greco-Roman period, which are all built to a standard plan.

What particularly impresses the modern visitor is how completely preserved many of the later temples are, with their numerous rooms, lofty ceilings, stairways leading to the roof, and mysterious subterranean chambers. Some of the Ptolemaic temples, such as the temple of Isis, in its beautiful setting on the island of Philae, capture our imagination, and their architectural detail—in particular, the capitals of columns—is impressive. Although they give a measure of eternity to the rulers who built them, it is the gods who were worshiped in them who are immortalized. The countless inscriptions that cover the walls and pillars preserve for future generations myths about the gods, as well as the words of the sacred rituals that once echoed around their halls.

were usually topped with a small pyramid. It may well be more than coincidence that from certain viewpoints, the highest peak of the mountains in which the royal tombs were excavated has the appearance of a pyramid.

The royal tombs were now also decorated, but not with scenes of daily life. Instead, the walls were covered with the texts and illustrations of various books that describe the netherworld, veritable guidebooks to the hereafter. The central theme of these compositions is the nightly journey of the sun-god through the netherworld. The royal tomb was to be a realization of the underworld, where the dead monarch mystically united with the sun-god and shared his immortality.

Tutankhamun's Tomb of Gold

Although the tombs were built in a well-guarded and secluded valley in the western mountains, already, in antiquity, they were plundered, leaving little of their original movable contents for the modern archaeologist to discover. The great exception to this is the tomb of the young king Tutankhamun. The sensational discovery of his intact tomb, in 1922, by Howard Carter and Lord Carnarvon, made world headlines and captured the imagination of all, even influencing fashions

in clothing, furniture, and architecture at the time. Tutankhamun died unexpectedly, before his royal tomb had been completed, and the body was placed in a smaller tomb intended for another person. But no cost was spared with the equipment that accompanied him into the next world. The tomb was filled to overflowing with objects the king had used in his lifetime—clothing, jewelry, weapons, chariots—as well as things he would need in the afterlife. Many of the items were of gilt or solid gold, and the quantity of gold in the tomb showed the wealth of Egypt at the time, a land where, in the words of the king of Mitanni, Tushratta, gold was as plentiful as the dirt on the ground.

↯ This funerary mask of Tutankhamun is of solid gold, beaten and burnished, and is inlaid with semiprecious and glass-paste imitation stones. It weighs 11 kilograms (24 pounds) and originally covered the head and shoulders of the king's mummy.
EGYPTIAN MUSEUM, CAIRO/PICTUREPOINT LTD

GUIDO ALBERTO ROSSI/THE IMAGE BANK

↩ The three pyramids of Giza belonging to Khufu, Khafra, and Menkau-re. Just as their houses were built around the royal palace, the tombs of the king's officials were built around the royal pyramid. This can be clearly seen in the case of Khufu's tomb, at the top of the photograph.

The Legacy of Egypt

A number of phenomena appearing in the late New Kingdom probably contributed to Egypt's decline. There were indications of widespread corruption and maladministration, with failures in the redistribution system, and consequent economic difficulties. Internal security was weak, and the country was plagued by incursions of marauding Libyans, who penetrated as far south as Thebes. The "warrior ethos" of the early New Kingdom was lost; so, too, it would seem, was the will to defend oneself. Early in the Ramesside period, foreign mercenaries were already being conscripted into the Egyptian army, and their numbers grew after Ramses III, who was followed by a succession of weak kings.

The Libyans, who formed the greater proportion of the mercenaries, eventually established their own, the twenty-second, dynasty.

Today, when Tutankhamun is a household name, it is difficult for us to imagine a time when the only thing most people knew about ancient Egypt was what they read in the Bible. The gradual fading of ancient Egypt from the consciousness of the West began with the early Christianization of the country, in the second and third centuries AD, and was sealed by the fall of Alexandria to the Arabs, in AD 642. The final stage of the language of ancient Egypt survived in the form of the Coptic of Christian Egypt, but since this was written in an alphabet based on the Greek, knowledge of the hieroglyphic script was lost.

In the Renaissance of the fifteenth and sixteenth centuries, when scholars were driven by the desire to return to ancient wisdom, Egypt and its legendary Hermes Trismegistos (the Egyptian god Thoth) were held to be the founts of knowledge. The idea was expressed in the floor mosaic of the cathedral in Siena, in Italy, which depicts the god presenting Egypt with the art of writing and law. Giovanni Bernini's design for the erection of the obelisk in the Piazza della Minerva, in Rome, in 1667, symbolizes the belief in the wisdom of the Egyptians: wisdom, the obelisk, is supported by strength, the elephant.

Not until the eighteenth century did people set about rediscovering ancient Egypt in a spirit of scientific inquiry. Only after Jean-François Champollion succeeded in deciphering the hieroglyphic script, in the first quarter of the nineteenth century, could the ancient inscriptions and writings once again be read. Yet although ancient Egypt had had little direct influence on Western culture before that time, its indirect influence was more significant than is often realized, since it was filtered through the two traditions from which Western culture has largely sprung: the Greco-Roman and the Judeo-Christian. To cite just two examples, Proverbs 22.17–24 parallels the Egyptian *Teaching of Amenemope*, and through such works as Plutarch's *On Isis and Osiris*, Egyptian ideas found their way, via Freemasonry, into Schikaneder's libretto for Mozart's *The Magic Flute*.

♀ Egyptian cultural influence spread far beyond Egypt's borders, as shown by this eighth-century BC Phoenician carving in ivory, found at Nimrud, in Mesopotamia. It depicts a winged Egyptian sphinx wearing the royal headdress and the double crown.
BRITISH MUSEUM/E.T. ARCHIVE/ AUSTRALIAN PICTURE LIBRARY

↪ *Opposite page*: This linen mummy shroud, dating from 180 BC, depicts the deceased standing between the jackal-headed Anubis, god of embalming, and Osiris, lord of the netherworld, who receive him into the next life. The scene well illustrates the symbiosis of Hellenistic and Egyptian culture of the time. Anubis is represented according to the conventions of Egyptian art, with his head shown in profile; while Osiris's iconography is less conventional: he wears an adaptation of his traditional crown, his face is shown frontally, which is very unusual for Egyptian art, and he does not wear his customary ceremonial beard. In contrast, the deceased, who wears a Roman toga, is depicted according to Greco-Roman artistic conventions.
AEGYPTISCHES MUSEUM, BERLIN/ERICH LESSING/MAGNUM

THE FUTURE OF EGYPT'S HERITAGE

BARRY KEMP

T HE DECAY OF THE GREAT SPHINX, publicized when a lump from one shoulder fell off in 1988, has turned what was once a symbol of the enigmatic wisdom of the past into a symbol of its vulnerability. This is, however, only the most public aspect of the dubious future of Egypt's archaeological heritage.

The first detailed European accounts of Egypt, in the late eighteenth and early nineteenth centuries, show the survival of a rich archaeological landscape. This included standing monuments —largely the tombs and temples of Upper Egypt—and mounds representative of ancient settlements spread along the Nile Valley and across the Nile delta alike: a detailed record, spanning thousands of years, of one of humankind's oldest civilizations. The last two centuries have witnessed the devastation of that haunting landscape on a scale that is scarcely believable. No one has tried to measure the loss, but perhaps about 80 percent is not far from the truth.

Three influences from the modern world have largely determined ancient Egypt's fate: economic modernization, population pressure, and the outside world's fascination with pharaonic Egypt. Economic modernization began early in the nineteenth century and quickly hit hard at archaeological sites. A number of lesser ruins became building-stone, but the main damage came through a nationwide move to quarry ancient settlement mounds for agricultural fertilizer, sometimes on an industrial scale. In this way, countless sites were razed. An Egyptian government department to protect antiquities (the Service des Antiquités) was created in 1858, but its vision was long restricted to art treasures and monuments. At the same time, a lust for buried treasure amongst the local population was inflamed by the European passion for collecting Egyptian antiquities. Official agreements led to a number of conspicuous monuments (including

three obelisks) being exported to Europe and North America, but their loss was as nothing compared to the methodical looting of sites, sometimes under official license. Desert cemeteries, where ancient artifacts were often remarkably well preserved, were the prime target.

The theft and export of antiquities, although by no means suppressed, is today no longer a scandal—there is much less to steal. The assault on the ravaged archaeological landscape continues, however, as towns, factories, and farmland expand during the current rapid economic growth and modernization essential for a population that is estimated to double in the next 20 years. A landmark of change was the final step in the total regulation of the waters of the Nile, which came with the completion of the Aswan High Dam in 1971. This hugely increased the volume of water available for agricultural reclamation, which continues relentlessly to eat away the archaeologically rich desert margins. Ground water now stands constantly at a higher level than in the past, impeding archaeological excavation and concentrating salt in the soil, with highly destructive effects as it crystallizes on exposed surfaces of ancient stonework.

☞ A detail of an image of Queen Nefertari from her burial chamber, showing detachment of the plaster layer and damage from surface salts. Recently, the paintings have been cleaned and conserved by the joint efforts of the Getty Conservation Institute and the Egyptian Antiquities Organization.

Archaeologists, too, play a part in the destruction of ancient sites by removing ancient deposits, and the buildings covered by such deposits are frequently left exposed to decay. This is especially the case with buildings of sun-dried mud-brick—the usual building material in ancient Egypt—which tends to disintegrate after exposure to the elements. At many of the less spectacular but still important sites (including Akhenaten's short-lived capital city at el-Amarna and the court cemeteries of the first dynasty at Abydos and Saqqara), mudbrick ruins are almost all that survive. Preservation requires not only painstaking work on a large scale, but also permanent maintenance. Modern remedies only delay disintegration; they do not stop it.

Certain sites, being the focus of mass tourism, face particular problems. Because they are prominent in the public eye, they are safeguarded from outright destruction. Some of them are on so large a scale that they can absorb the daily visits of thousands of people without sustaining damage.

BILL PIERCE/SYGMA/AUSTRAL

The requirement then is for imaginative policies to control tourist access and tourist trade, and for modern facilities to harmonize with the setting. The temples at Karnak and Luxor and the Giza pyramid plateau are sites where successful schemes have been, or are being, introduced. Many tombs, however, including the royal tombs in the Valley of the Kings, are too small to admit the present numbers of tourists without suffering serious deterioration. The painted walls are constantly touched or brushed against, and humidity—up to 9 liters (two gallons) of perspiration per day in the tomb of Tutankhamun—invades the naturally dry air that preserved the paintings for so long. The threat is sufficiently serious to prompt suggestions that replicas of the most visited tombs be made in the vicinity of the real ones. In the meantime, the tomb of Tutankhamun and several other famous tombs remain closed.

Egypt has comprehensive legislation covering all aspects of its ancient heritage, and has, in the Egyptian Antiquities Organization (successor to the Service des Antiquités), a large official agency charged with managing it. All archaeologists, whether Egyptian or foreign, work under its control, and one condition is that all finds remain in the country. Tourism

BARRY KEMP

⬆ The temple of Ptah, at Memphis, dates from the nineteenth dynasty. The floor is beneath the water table, and salts are forming on the stone surface.

↪ A limestone temple of the nineteenth dynasty at Hermopolis (Ashmunein). The building is suffering badly from salts forming on the stone surface.

is a key source of revenue for Egypt, and the condition of major monuments is a matter of political concern. For these reasons, it is likely that the principal monuments will be looked after in ways that will ensure their long-term survival as objects of admiration. It may be, however, that a time will come when these are the only ancient sites left. The real reservoir of future knowledge are the less spectacular archaeological sites away from the main centers. They have become an endangered resource, but, unlike species of wildlife, their stock cannot be replenished.

BARRY KEMP

◄ The ancient city of el-Amarna, showing the Nile, cultivated land, and the remains of ancient walls from the city on the desert land. Cultivated land watered by the Nile is steadily encroaching on ancient desert ruins, such as the city walls of el-Amarna, shown here.

PICTUREPOINT LTD

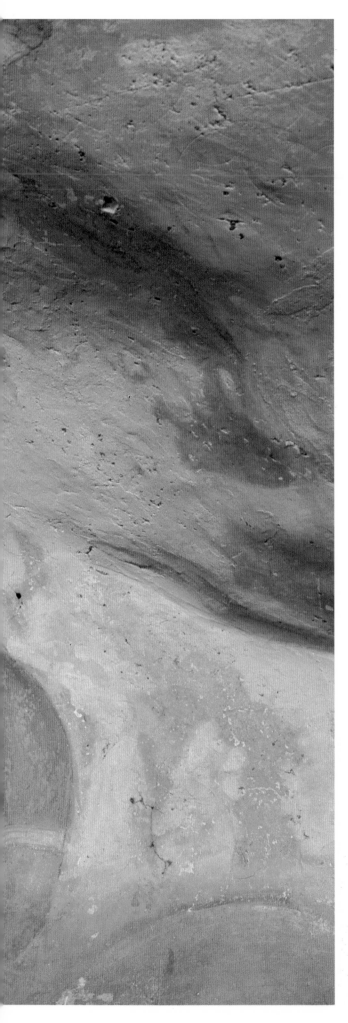

CIVILIZATIONS IN SOUTHERN ASIA

3 0 0 0 B C – A D 5 0 0

The Rise of Kingdoms on the Indian Subcontinent

IAN C. GLOVER AND HIMANSHU PRABHA RAY

T HE GREAT GEOGRAPHICAL and ecological variation found over the Indian subcontinent—with its deserts and lofty mountains, the fertile plains of the Indus and Ganges rivers, eroded hills and plateaus, as well as deep forests—has fostered the rich regional and cultural diversity that distinguishes this part of the world.

When the ruins of Mohenjodaro and Harappa were first uncovered in the 1920s, it was believed that they were simply extensions of the Bronze Age urban civilizations of Mesopotamia. At that stage, there was little evidence of any village or town life on the Indian subcontinent during the preceding Neolithic and Copper ages. Now, some 70 years later, we can see that these first cities of South Asia were the product of some 4,000 years of local cultural development. They owed little to Mesopotamian civilizations, and were quite different in their formal structure and organizational principles. The collapse of the Indus civilization and the later appearance of new ethnic groups from the north paved the way for the growth of a series of lavishly wealthy kingdoms, whose art, architecture, and religion formed the basis of the splendor that was to become India's.

◄⊃ The Sigiriya frescoes are the earliest examples of the Sri Lankan school of painting often described as classical realism. The beauty and elegance of these "celestial maidens" is eulogized in graffiti left by visitors to the site from the sixth to the thirteenth centuries AD.

⊙ A game board (a type of chessboard) found in the excavations at Harappa. Similar specimens made of pottery fragments, brick, and stone have been found at other sites of the Harappan culture, together with a variety of gaming pieces, some with heads of animals.
ROBERT HARDING PICTURE LIBRARY

➷ The foothills of the Afghan-Iranian Plateau, in present-day Afghanistan, were the home of South Asia's first villages. It was from these that the civilizations of the Indus Valley later arose.

THE MACQUITTY COLLECTION

♀ This skull was found in a grave at Mehrgarh, on the Kachi Plain. Large cemeteries from the Aceramic Neolithic phase have been found within the habitation area, some burials containing baskets coated with bitumen and also cakes of red ocher.

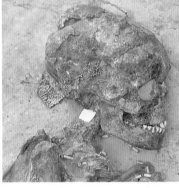

CATHERINE JARRIGE/MAI

♀ Ornaments of local and imported stone, shell, and bone were the other grave goods found during excavations at Mehrgarh. The fine workmanship of many of these beads shows the use of stone microdrills and bow-drills.

CATHERINE JARRIGE/MAI

THE INDUS CIVILIZATION: 6000 BC TO 2400 BC

To understand the civilizations of the Indus Valley, we must look at the settlements from which they arose. The first villages of South Asia appeared in the foothills of the Afghan-Iranian Plateau and on the western margins of tributaries of the Indus River. The earliest and best studied is Mehrgarh, on the Kachi Plain, where the Bolan River has cut 9 meters (30 feet) through the layers of a village known as MR3. Established before 6000 BC and lasting until about 2000 BC, Mehrgarh started out as a collection of small, rectangular, multiroom houses. Stone tools, and grains preserved in mudbricks, indicate that agriculture formed the basis of the villagers'

livelihood. In the early levels, the remains of wild beasts outnumber those of domesticated animals, but later, domesticated sheep, goats, and cattle came to dominate.

The people of Mehrgarh buried their dead with beads made from bone, shell, local stones, and imported turquoise, and sometimes with young goats. The turquoise and shell ornaments show that they participated in exchange networks extending from the coast of the Arabian Sea to the edges of central Asia. We call this phase the "Aceramic Neolithic", since neither pottery nor metal tools supplement the numerous finds of chert knives, arrowheads, bone awls, and polished stone axes. The inhabitants must have known the value of copper, however, for a single bead of rolled native copper was found among the grave goods. Small figurines of unfired clay, resembling finds in western Iran, represent the earliest human images so far known from South Asia.

Small settlements of up to a few hundred people, like Mehrgarh, have been discovered all along the margins of the plateau and in the well-watered valleys that feed the Indus River following the snow-melt in spring. But most sites are deeply buried under later occupation, and have allowed only small excavations. At Mehrgarh, the focus of settlement regularly moved along the banks of the Bolan River; and since the later Neolithic and Copper Age settlements were located a little downstream, quite extensive excavations of the first phase of settled village life in the region have been possible.

Small Neolithic and Copper Age villages proliferated over the next 2,000 years throughout the Indo-Iranian borderlands. The people kept sheep, goats, and humped zebu cattle, and cultivated barley, wheat, cotton, and, possibly, date palms. About 4000 BC, settlements appeared on the plains of the Indus Valley. If any earlier aceramic villages existed near the great river, they

CATHERINE JARRIGE/MAI

♐ The changing course of the Bolan River has eroded a natural section about 9 meters (30 feet) deep through the pre-pottery layers of the earliest village settlement at Mehrgarh.

would have been deeply buried under the silt brought down by the summer floodwaters. Sites such as Amri, where occupation continued after 3000 BC as part of the Indus civilization, were probably founded by migrants from the borderlands moving on to the fertile plains, where there were greater agricultural rewards but also the constant threat of unpredictable floods. Pottery was being made in a variety of local styles, and although flint tools remain in evidence, copper came into regular use in the third millennium BC for simple knives, projectile points, and even axes.

By 3500 BC, some sites had grown into small towns, which were occasionally fortified with stone walls (as at Kot Diji) or mudbrick defenses (as at Mundigak Period 4, and Rachman Dheri, on the Gomal Plain of northern Pakistan). Rachman Dheri, a huge settlement measuring some 22 hectares (54 acres), was laid out on a grid pattern of streets and enclosed by massive walls. With a population of several thousand, its three major periods of occu-pation are identified by changing ceramic styles. Rachman Dheri was inhabited for at least a thousand years, from 3500 BC to 2500 BC. Although it is clearly contemporary with Mohenjodaro, Harappa, and the other great settlements of the Indus civil-ization, the city and its surrounding territory seem always to have stayed outside the "Indus system". Perhaps it was the capital of another Bronze Age polity, contemporary with and rivaling the better-known Indus civilization.

CIVILIZATIONS IN SOUTHERN ASIA: 6000 BC – AD 500

Date	CULTURES AND CIVILIZATIONS	CULTURAL AND POLITICAL EVENTS	CRAFT AND TECHNOLOGY
500			Large bronze religious images cast
	The imperial Guptas AD 319 – AD 450	Hindu religion receives support	
AD 1		Sanskrit as the written language of the elite	
			Trade with the Mediterranean and Southeast Asia
200		Buddhism emerges as dominant religion	
	The Mauryas 321 BC – 185 BC	Mauryan administrative system detailed in the *Arthasastra*	Iron Age flourishes in the south
500	First historic state of northern India	New trade routes opened	Northern Black Polished Ware (NBPW)
		Development of Buddhism and Jainism	Black and Red Pottery
		Introduction of the horse in battle	Painted Gray Ware (PGW)
1000		Vedic epic poetry	
			Ocher-colored Pottery (OCP)
1500	Post-Harappan cultures in western India and Pakistan 1500 BC – 200 BC		Widespread use of copper
		Communities from Iran migrate into far northwest	Light yellow or gray pottery
		Decline in social and political control	Introduction of iron
2000	Late Indus civilization 2000 BC – 1500 BC	Major Harappan sites abandoned	Cemetery H ware
2500	Mature Indus civilization Harappa culture 2400 BC – 2000 BC	Development of Harappan script	Square, inscribed seals and baked bricks
			Faience articles, soapstone seals
3000			Terracotta figurines
			New ceramic styles in the Indus Valley: Kot Diji
3500		Development of small towns	Beginning of copper metallurgy
4000		Settlement on plains of the Indus Valley	Earliest pottery cultures
5000			
6000 BC	Emergence of the Indus civilization 6000 BC – 2400 BC		Aceramic Neolithic period

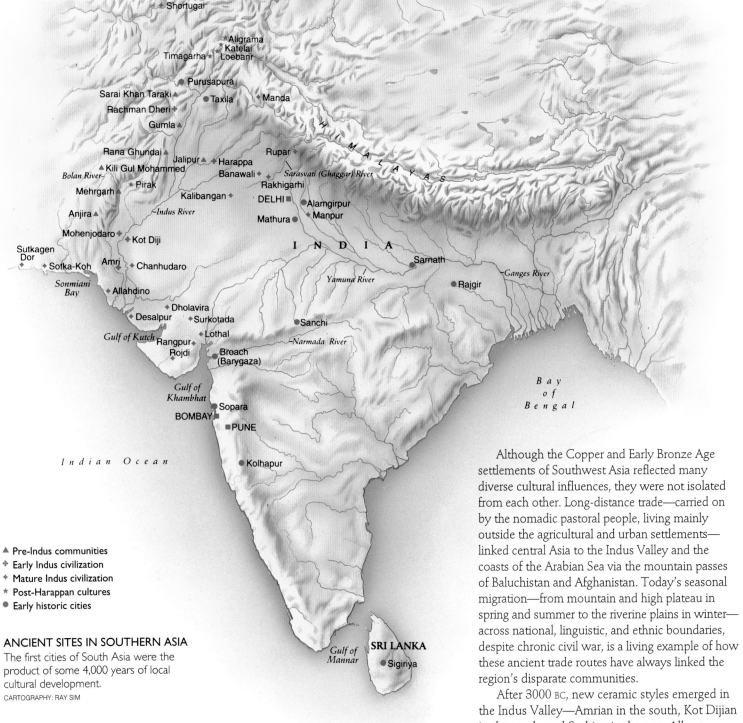

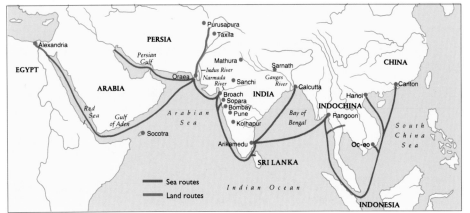

Pre-Indus communities
Early Indus civilization
Mature Indus civilization
Post-Harappan cultures
Early historic cities

ANCIENT SITES IN SOUTHERN ASIA

The first cities of South Asia were the product of some 4,000 years of local cultural development.

CARTOGRAPHY: RAY SIM

EARLY TRADE ROUTES

Although the Copper and Early Bronze Age settlements of Southwest Asia reflected many diverse cultural influences, they were not isolated from each other. Long-distance trade—carried on by the nomadic pastoral people, living mainly outside the agricultural and urban settlements—linked central Asia to the Indus Valley and the coasts of the Arabian Sea via the mountain passes of Baluchistan and Afghanistan. Today's seasonal migration—from mountain and high plateau in spring and summer to the riverine plains in winter—across national, linguistic, and ethnic boundaries, despite chronic civil war, is a living example of how these ancient trade routes have always linked the region's disparate communities.

After 3000 BC, new ceramic styles emerged in the Indus Valley—Amrian in the south, Kot Dijian in the north, and Sothian in the east. All are marked by strong horizontal bands of black paint alternating with rows of linked triangles, chevrons, hatched squares and leaves, or stylized animal horns. At Kot Diji, a distinctive "fish-scale" motif anticipated a design associated with the Mature Indus culture of a few hundred years later; at Kot Diji and Kalibangan, stylized buffalo heads prefigured the *Pasupati* icon (the Hindu god Siva as "Lord of the Animals") found on some Indus seals. Male and female terracotta figurines found at many sites throughout the region suggest the existence of common beliefs and ritual practices. Despite their regional differences, these cultures shared enough common elements to be grouped together as the Early Indus period.

THE HARAPPA CULTURE: 2400 BC TO 2000 BC

About 2400 BC, the diverse cultures of the Early Indus period merged in a distinctive new phase known as the Mature Indus civilization or the Harappa culture. Its emergence was apparently quite sudden, although features such as the mass production of pottery in a few standardized designs, terracotta figurines, and simple metal tools were all associated with some of the Early Indus cultures. What is new in the Harappa culture is the use of writing, particularly on square inscribed seals, and some copperplate inscriptions and graffiti on pottery fragments. Other novel elements include the extensive use of baked bricks

⊕ More than 2,500 soapstone seals have been found at Harappa culture sites, the majority of which have an animal engraved on them and a short inscription. The animal most frequently represented is a humpless bull, earlier referred to as a "unicorn", since only one horn is shown in profile.
KARACHI MUSEUM/THE MACQUITTY COLLECTION

for ordinary houses as well as public buildings, and careful architectural planning. Many sites appear to have been divided into two major areas: a lower, usually eastern, section of domestic buildings, craft workshops, and private shrines; and an elevated, sometimes fortified, area to the west, containing public buildings.

While not all sites within the Greater Indus Valley exhibit the distinctive elements of the Harappa style, there is evidence of some form of central administrative control and trade within the Indus Valley linking the region to Mesopotamia, via the Makran coast of Baluchistan, and to sites in Oman and Bahrain. Nearly a thousand Harappan sites have been identified in Pakistan, India, and Afghanistan within a territory of 1.25 million square kilometers (485,000 square miles)—more

⚲ Terracotta models of bullock carts from Harappa culture sites are similar to carts still used in the region. Cart-tracks found during the excavation of the cities indicate that the wheelspan of the Indus carts has changed little.
KARACHI MUSEUM/ROBERT HARDING PICTURE LIBRARY

⚲ The pottery from Harappa culture sites is frequently plain, but a substantial part is decorated with a red slip and black-painted designs. The painting often has a utilitarian quality, although some pieces show remarkable delicacy of line and artistic freedom. This fragment of a terracotta vase from Mohenjodaro depicts an ibex (wild goat).
KARACHI MUSEUM/SCALA

⚲ A terracotta figurine of the mother-goddess, excavated at Mohenjodaro and dating from 2300 BC to 1750 BC.

NATIONAL MUSEUM OF INDIA, NEW DELHI/THE BRIDGEMAN ART LIBRARY

GEORG HELMES

☝An aerial view of the citadel mound at Mohenjodaro. On the right can be seen the Great Bath, which was probably used for ritual bathing. On the left is the granary.

than for any comparable Old World civilization. The Harappa culture only partly penetrated the northern part of the Indus Valley, and although it had some influence on the Kot Diji and Rachman Dheri cultures, the latter seems to have retained its cultural, and perhaps political, independence for an extensive period. Some Harappan sites have been found in the area, however, notably at Harappa itself (once a Kot Dijian settlement, which was possibly colonized by migrants from the south) and at Shortugai, some 500 kilometers (300 miles) northwest of Harappa on the Oxus River, where a colony was established to keep open the trade routes from central Asia to the Arabian Sea.

East of the Indus River, the Harappa civilization expanded rapidly into present-day India; some 300 sites have been identified along the now-dry bed of the Ghaggar River. Before the headwaters were captured by the Yamuna about 2000 BC, this was a flourishing, well-watered area, and one major site, Kalibangan, has been excavated on a large scale. Harappan settlements, such as Banawali, Rupar,

and Rakhigarhi, were founded in the eastern Punjab, and the culture reached as far as Alamgirpur and Manpur, east of present-day Delhi.

In the south, Harappan settlements spread westwards along the Makran coast towards the Persian border, and the fortified site of Sutkagen Dor provided a staging post for coastal trade to the Persian Gulf. Settlements also extended southeast into the Kutch peninsula, which was probably an offshore island in Harappan times, and south along the Gujarat coast towards Bombay. Two major sites in this region, Lothal and Dholavira, and a fortified village at Rojdi, in Saurashtra, have provided a revealing picture of provincial Harappan society.

Harappan Architecture

Although Harappa was the first site to be excavated, extensive brick robbing by nearby villagers (to build houses and, in the mid-nineteenth century, to provide ballast for the Multan Lahore railway) has destroyed many of the buildings. Harappan architecture is best preserved at Mohenjodaro, which was excavated on

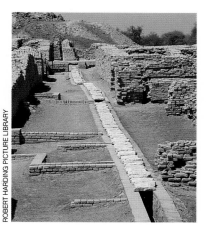

Marshall's team excavated a series of public buildings, the most spectacular of which is the Great Bath. This measures 12 meters by 9 meters (40 feet by 30 feet) and is sunk 2.5 meters (8 feet) below the surrounding pavement. The bath was built from meticulously laid bricks set in gypsum plaster over a waterproof bitumen layer. A nearby well supplied water, which was emptied through a massive corbeled drain.

The lower, eastern part of the city had a grid of streets and lanes roughly oriented north-south and east-west, with blocks of houses entered through narrow lanes. Although the houses varied in size, they all had rooms arranged around a central courtyard, usually with a well in a small room off the court and a bathroom and latrine draining through the wall, either into a soak pit or a covered drain under the street surface. Some houses were of two stories, with brick stairs and tubular drainpipes extending from the upper story. Plumbing installations for the provision of water, bathrooms with polished brick floors, and exterior drains are some of the most remarkable features of the cities of the Indus civilization, and are without parallel in any other prehistoric society.

Although there are public buildings on the citadel mound, no obvious large public temple has been found at either Mohenjodaro or Harappa. Recent architectural analysis of earlier excavations has, however, confirmed a house in the lower town at Mohenjodaro as the possible site of a "Tree Temple". At Kalibangan and Lothal, fire altars were excavated both in private houses and on the "citadel" areas of those towns, which provided space for congregations to assemble. The emphasis on fire and water in ritual activity is central to the two major religions to emerge in this region in historic times—Vedic Hinduism and Zoroastrianism.

☗ A public drain in a street at Mohenjodaro. Among the most remarkable features of cities of the Indus civilization are plumbing systems for supplying water, bathrooms with polished brick floors, and exterior drains.

♀ There is no exact parallel for the Great Bath at Mohenjodaro, with its polished floor tiles sealed with bitumen and its corbeled brick drain to carry the water outside the town walls. It is generally thought to have been used for bathing before worship, a custom found in later Indian religions. Many of the other, larger Harappan towns were equipped with washing facilities in the ceremonial areas. At Lothal, there were 12 bathing places on the highest part of the mound, and Allahdino and Dholavira had large water tanks in the center of the citadel areas.

a large scale from 1922 to 1927 under Sir John Marshall, of the Archaeological Survey of India. Since 1931, a number of archaeological teams have excavated the site. The most recent work has concentrated on completing and correcting the documentation of earlier researchers, and conserving the previously excavated brick buildings, which were suffering badly from salt encrustation caused by the rising water table around Mohenjodaro.

The highest part of the western mound at Mohenjodaro rises 12 meters (40 feet) above the surrounding plain. The earliest and deepest levels of settlement have never been reached, since the Indus floods have raised the plain at least 10 meters (33 feet) over the last 5,000 years. Recently constructed dams and canals have also contributed to raising the water table. It is believed, however, that there are about 30 meters (100 feet) of stratified settlement debris on the site and that the mound was sometimes raised artificially to counter periodic floods. The citadel mound rests on an artificial platform of mud and mudbricks, and is topped by a later Buddhist stupa from the third century AD.

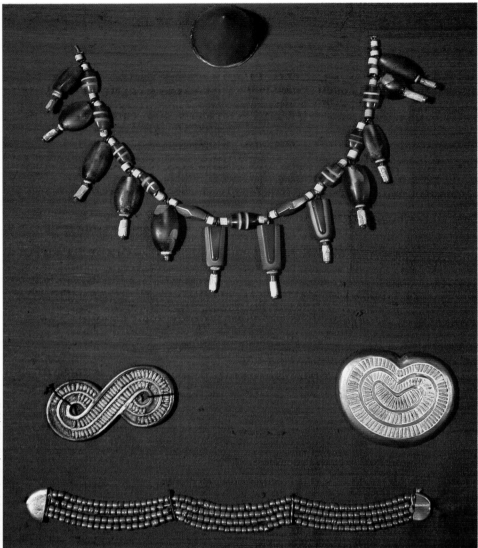

NATIONAL MUSEUM OF INDIA, NEW DELHI/SCALA

blades for reaping crops and probably for most other tasks requiring sharp-edged knives. Chert was quarried from nearby limestone outcrops, and Harappan craftworkers produced some of the finest knapped blades known from any early culture. The same skill was applied to making superb beads from imported agate and carnelian. Indus Valley etched beads provide some of the best evidence we have for long-distance trade between 3000 BC and 2000 BC.

Pottery technology was very advanced, with utilitarian wheel-thrown forms being made at most sites and fired in large kilns. Massive storage jars were also produced, splendidly painted in black on a bright red surface, with parallel designs depicting plants and birds. Pottery sherds of these enable archaeological surveyors to identify Mature Harappan sites with relative ease. Other distinctive pottery forms include tall, cylindrical, pierced strainers and enigmatic triangular pieces of terracotta, which have variously been interpreted as being pot-boilers, sling stones, hearth liners, and abraders for rubbing callouses from workers' feet!

Other significant Harappan crafts include the manufacture of faience (a form of glass) for small ornaments and figurines, and microbeads molded from soapstone paste, a specialty of Chanhudaro. Soapstone, in block form, was also used for making distinctive and beautiful seals, more than 2,500 of which have been found, nearly half at Mohenjodaro. They generally conform to a highly standardized design: square, from 1 to 3 centimeters (three-eighths of an inch to one and a quarter inches) in diameter, with a perforated boss at the back for suspension. The blocks were sawn and polished before being carved with metal or chert gravers, and the finished seals then heated to harden the stone. The surface always bears some characters of the still undeciphered script, above either a single, highly naturalistic animal or, more rarely, a scene depicting animals and people, or semihuman figures, participating in a ceremony.

☝ These examples of jewelry from the Harappa culture were clearly made with superb skill. The necklaces of ground and polished beads of stone (top) and of gold (bottom) show considerable sophistication. The figure-of-eight-shaped piece was perhaps used as a hair ornament, while the round ornament was tied to a fillet worn on the forehead.

Craft Industries

Although we refer to the Indus civilization as a Bronze Age culture, unalloyed copper was used for most artifacts, and only rarely was enough tin available to make bronze. Tools and weapons were simple in form, showing little skill in design or manufacture. They include flat-cast axes and chisels, arrows and small spearheads, small knives, saws and razors, and fishhooks. Nonetheless, craft industries were organized through guilds or associations, and certain areas specialized in specific crafts. Harappan metalworkers were skilled in making beaten copper and silverware. They used modern brassware techniques, such as riveting, and lapped and soldered joints; and made small plates and weights of lead, and gold and silver jewelry of considerable sophistication. Examples of the latter rarely survive, since the Harappans did not bury their dead with the sort of spectacular grave goods found in contemporary Egyptian and Sumerian burials. However, terracotta figurines give some idea of their use of beads, bangles, and necklaces.

As copper knives were rare, and probably not very effective, the Harappans continued to use chert

☝ A copper spearhead from the Harappa culture with a tang for hafting on a wooden shaft. Although the Indus civilization was a Bronze Age culture, most artifacts were made of copper, because of the scarcity of tin to make bronze.
NATIONAL MUSEUM OF INDIA, NEW DELHI/
THE BRIDGEMAN ART LIBRARY

☝ This copper vase from the Harappa culture, dating from about 2300 BC to 1750 BC, is of simple design, like many of the artifacts found from the Indus civilization.
NATIONAL MUSEUM OF INDIA, NEW DELHI/THE BRIDGEMAN ART LIBRARY

The Harappan Script

The language and writing system of the Harappans still defy translation. Although nearly 4,000 inscriptions have now been found, most are very short, with a maximum of 21 characters out of the 419 known to exist. Furthermore, there are no bilingual inscriptions of the sort that enabled scholars to translate Near Eastern cuneiform writing and Egyptian hieroglyphs. Some scholars believe that the Harappan language belonged to the Dravidian family, now found mostly in South India. Others think it is an early Indo-European language and a forerunner of Sanskrit. We do know, however, that both seals and script were used for such administrative purposes as sealing bales of merchandise and even "authenticating" the manufacture of stoneware bangles by sealing shut the saggers, the fireclay boxes that protected them from the great heat of the furnace. It seems likely that the script refers to personal names and official administrative titles.

If writing was widespread—and the occasional graffiti on potsherds, ivories, and bronzes suggests that it was—then it was probably done on some common perishable material such as cloth or palm leaves. This being the case, only the excavation of a waterlogged site with substantial archives will enable the writing system to be definitively translated. In a recent excavation by an Indian archaeologist, R.S. Bisht, at Dholavira, in Gujarat, an inscription 2.8 meters (about 9 feet) long consisting of gypsum characters, 10 centimeters (4 inches) high, was found on a partly preserved wooden board below the main gate to the town. It may have indicated the name of the ancient settlement.

A Classless and Clean Society

We know quite a lot about the Harappans' way of life, trade, craft industries, and religious symbolism, but next to nothing about their social and political system. Unlike contemporary societies in Egypt and Mesopotamia, Harappan culture lacks royal burials, great funerary structures, monumental art, and other symbols of royal or priestly authority. So it would seem that the usual model of a kingdom or empire, headed by a "priest-king" and supported by a royal clan holding authority through dynastic succession, does not apply in this case. There is also little evidence of the strong military influence usually found in Old World empires. The "fortifications" at Harappa, Mohenjodaro, Kalibangan, and some other sites seem to have been intended as much to define social and functional spaces as to protect the citizens from external enemies. The gateways at Harappa show no sign of planning for military defense. However, consistency in the layout of settlements, the use of modular sizes of bricks, and widespread similarities in metal and chert tools, pottery styles, and systems of weights and measures provide strong evidence of firm administrative control over the production and distribution of goods and services.

The pattern of foreign trade also reveals many anomalies when compared with that of other societies. There is evidence for the import of raw materials, exotic stones, gold, copper, tin, and silver, but very few manufactured or prestige goods from outside the Indus culture area have been found. The absence of larger and more ornate houses, exotic luxury goods, and richer than usual burials suggests there was no clearly wealthy class. All these factors suggest the Indus civilization emphasized conformity, lack of personal display, efficient organization of manufacturing and trade, and a concern for sanitation and health without parallel in the past. If we seek a model for the social and political order of the Harappans, it is to be found in the later, Buddhist monasteries of India, or in the Christian West, rather than in the palace and temple society of Ancient Egypt or Mesopotamia.

♀ Few stone sculptures survive from the Harappan period, and they are usually small, crudely made, and badly damaged. An exception is this soapstone image of a bearded man wearing a decorated cloak over one shoulder; a diadem, perhaps once inlaid with a jewel, to tie back his hair; and a similarly decorated armband. Only 18 centimeters (7 inches) high, this powerful but anonymous sculpture from Mohenjodaro is usually called "The Priest King", but this identification is no more than guesswork.

KARACHI MUSEUM/ROBERT HARDING PICTURE LIBRARY

☥ Iron tools and weapons are abundant in South Indian megalithic graves. Shown clockwise from top left are a spearhead, a sickle, and an adze or hoe with iron fastening bands.
C.M. DIXON/PHOTO RESOURCES

♀ The stylized humped bull and peacocks painted on this pottery sherd are characteristic of the so-called Cemetery H culture, which coincided with the end of the Indus civilization at Harappa.
C.M. DIXON/PHOTO RESOURCES

The Harappans in Decline: 2000 BC to 1500 BC

In the central part of the Indus Valley, the Harappa culture seems to have come to a rather abrupt end, although the timing and causes of this are poorly understood and frequently disputed. At Mohenjodaro, administrative control was relaxed after 2000 BC; seals and inscriptions are no longer found in this period, and by about 1800 BC, much of the city seems to have been deserted. Kot Diji, Allahdino, Kalibangan, Rupar, Surkotada, Desalpur, and other Harappan settlements were also virtually deserted at this time. Either the population of the Indus Valley had declined, or the people had returned to a more nomadic pastoral way of life, leaving few traces of this transition for today's archaeologists to find.

Several excavators at Mohenjodaro have reported finding groups of bodies hastily buried or even lying in the streets or where they had tumbled down staircases—evidence of a "final massacre" of the last inhabitants of the once great city. Certainly, natural events had much to do with the end of the Harappan civilization. For instance, there is widespread evidence of earthquake activity, including tectonic uplift along the Makran coast and dramatic changes in the course of the Indus River, resulting in the drying up of the ancient Sarasvati (Ghaggar) river system. It is possible that the Indus totally deserted its ancient riverbed, and with it, the city of Mohenjodaro, which was so dependent on it.

At some sites, such as Chanhudaro, life continued, although building standards declined, as did the manufacture of high-quality soapstone and carnelian beads for export. A range of local pottery styles replaced the relative uniformity typical of Mature Harappan ceramics. At Harappa, too, the later period is typified by flimsy buildings made of reused bricks and a new ceramic style known as Cemetery H ware. Typical Harappan funeral customs changed, from simple burials, sometimes in brick-lined pits, to the placement of bones with other offerings inside large funerary urns. The evidence clearly points to both a complete breakdown of the regional civic administration and the arrival of new ethnic and cultural groups in various parts of the Indus Valley.

Despite the collapse of the Indus civilization, not all was lost. Although the disciplined urban culture of Mohenjodaro, with its sophisticated plumbing, vanished entirely, the traditions and symbols of its religious cults—purification by water and fire, reverence for cattle, tree cults, and the horned deity flanked by animals—were handed on to become integral parts of Brahmanism, Zoroastrianism, and Buddhism.

Post-Harappa Cultures: 1500 BC to 200 BC

Little is known about events in the western part of the Indian subcontinent from 1500 BC. Many villages and towns that had been inhabited over the previous thousand years were deserted, or housed only temporary buildings. After about 1800 BC, communities from Iran migrated into the valleys of the far northwest. Because almost everything known about them is based upon their burial customs, they are called the Gandhara Grave culture.

The main Gandhara sites so far excavated are Katelai, Loebanr, Aligrama, and Timagarha, all situated in the Swat Valley. Their graves usually consist of oblong pits, with dry stone walls covered by roof slabs. The bodies were accompanied by plain, light yellow or gray pottery, highly stylized terracotta figurines, and occasional bronze pins and iron tools. Cremation also became common for the first time in South Asia, the ashes being deposited in urns decorated with carved faces. The discovery of iron artifacts and two horse burials, together with a bronze model horse at Katelai and an iron horse harness at Timagarha, strongly suggests that the Gandhara people were descendants of the iron-using, largely pastoral Indo-European speakers who migrated to northern India from the west in the post-Harappan period. These people are also known to have cultivated wheat, barley, rice, and grapes.

Many settlements in the valleys of Baluchistan also seem to have been deserted. From about 1300 BC, footed goblets and bowls, painted gray, replaced the elaborate Harappan wares, and weapons such as short swords and shaft-hole axes are found in graves at many sites from the Makran coast of Pakistan to northern Afghanistan. In some places, however, settled life continued throughout the period. At Pirak, on the Kachi Plain, after a short break following the Harappan occupation, the village was regularly rebuilt in a consistent style with thick-walled houses incorporating massive wall niches. The inhabitants cultivated rice and sorghum, in addition to wheat and barley, and produced beautiful, multicolored pottery with designs resembling woven textiles.

Ceramic Traditions

In the eastern Punjab and the region of the Yamuna-Ganges Doab, around present-day Delhi, the earliest villages show many elements of the Mature and Late Harappan style. In the southern part of this region, where there are rich copper deposits, we find a ceramic tradition called "Ocher-colored Pottery" (OCP), after the distinctive rusty-red color of its painted surface. This pottery has been found in the earliest levels of village mounds, sometimes associated with hoards of massive, cast-copper tools and weapons. OCP is often discovered in waterlogged deposits or shows evidence of having been immersed in moving water, giving support to ancient Indian traditions of massive flooding in the Doab and the Yamuna River's capture of the waters that once flowed southwest through the ancient Sarasvati (Ghaggar) River into the Arabian Sea. At one time, OCP and its associated copper hoards were regarded as a purely post-Harappan phenomenon. Indian archaeologists now believe, however, that the beginnings of this tradition go back beyond 2000 BC. OCP communities in the Rajasthan copper belt may have provided much of the copper for Harappan metalwork.

About 1200 BC, new ceramic traditions appeared in the Punjab and Rajasthan in the form of Black and Red Pottery, and Painted Gray Ware (PGW). At some sites, PGW is clearly stratified above OCP. In most places, however, the makers of PGW founded new settlements along the rivers flowing east into the Ganges system. It is fairly clear that these new settlements represent the eastward migration of the Gandhara Grave people, encountered a few hundred years earlier in the northwestern valleys of Pakistan. They brought with them iron tools and weapons, the practice of riding horses in battle, prestige exchange, and even sacrifice. This is the period of the later Vedic epic poetry, which, although written down much later, recounts stories of the wars and alliances of the Indo-European tribes, particularly their struggles with the Dasas, the native peoples of the Indus Valley and the Punjab. The Dasas were gradually overwhelmed and reduced to the status of slaves and laborers, the ancestors of the "untouchables" of recent times.

Vedic literature, although difficult to link directly to archaeological evidence, provides a mass of information about the daily life and culture of the times. Ironsmiths rivaled copper workers in importance; wheat, barley, millet, and rice were cultivated; and forests and swamps were cleared for farmland. Houses were simple, circular structures of timber and thatch, with wattle-and-daub walls and partitions, not unlike the dwellings of many present-day tribal peoples of India.

The center of gravity of Indian civilization moved steadily eastwards down the Ganges Valley. By 500 BC, the fertile lands of the areas known today as the states of Uttar Pradesh and Bihar were wealthy enough to support the first historic state of northern India, the Kingdom of Magadha, established in the sixth

century BC at the fortified hilltop site of Rajgir. At this time, PGW, which was already wheel-made from fine clay and fired at high temperatures, was developed into a luxury ware, sometimes painted white, sometimes with metallic crystals on the lustrous, thick black surface. Known as "Northern Black Polished Ware" (NBPW), this pottery matches, both in appearance and technical skill, the contemporary Greek black-painted pottery of the Mediterranean.

Trade and the Spread of Religion

This period, at first dominated by Brahmanical Hinduism, saw the development of two great reforming religions, Buddhism and Jainism, which spread as interregional trade became increasingly more important than agriculture. The NBPW culture moved south along the trade routes linking the upper Ganges to the Narmada Valley and the Arabian coast, where maritime trade linked India to communities in Egypt and the Mediterranean. Money, in the form of silver coins struck by several kingdoms in northern and central India, facilitated this commerce. In the fourth century BC, much of northern India was united into the Mauryan empire by Chandragupta Maurya. At this point, India entered the Western historical tradition when the Macedonian Alexander the Great led his army through the passes of the northwest to confront the Mauryan army on the banks of the Indus. Although victorious, the Greeks withdrew to Bactria, where Alexander's successors maintained trade, cultural, and diplomatic relations with the Mauryan kings, providing the first detailed written accounts of the wealth and brilliant achievements of historical Indian civilization.

Ian C. Glover

⚬ Rice was not cultivated by the Harappans, except in Gujarat, wheat and barley being the main crops in the Harappan period. It was later introduced to the northwestern part of the Indian subcontinent from the Ganges plain.

⚬ This gold coin of the horseman type dates from the time of Chandragupta II, about AD 380 to AD 415. It was under the Guptas that Brahmanical Hinduism re-established itself in South Asia, coinciding with the gradual decline of Buddhism on the Indian subcontinent.
C.M. DIXON/PHOTO RESOURCES

THE MACQUITTY COLLECTION

THE MAURYAS: 321 BC TO 185 BC

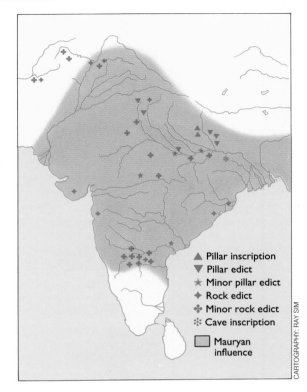

Until the rise of the Mauryas in 321 BC, the Ganges plain was divided into a patchwork of republics and monarchies. It was the Mauryas who unified most of northern India for the first time, establishing themselves in parts of the Deccan peninsula. In the northwest, their domain was bordered by the Seleucid Empire and the Indo-Greek kingdoms; in the south flourished the Iron Age megalithic communities and chiefdoms of the Colas, Ceras, and Pandyas. The most famous Mauryan ruler was Asoka, renowned for his policy of tolerance and *ahimsa*, or nonviolence, by which he renounced all forms of killing, including war and conquest.

By the third century BC, agriculture had become the mainstay of the economy in the north and land tax was the primary source of state income, supplemented by trade revenues and levies on manufactured items. Details of the Mauryan administrative system are contained in the *Arthasastra*, a contemporary treatise on polity and economics. A recurring theme is that the king should take active steps to increase state revenue. The area under cultivation should be increased, either by expanding irrigation facilities or by encouraging peasants living in overpopulated regions to migrate to new areas. Several categories of taxes and land tenures are mentioned: the state-owned, or crown, lands supervised by employees of the king; private land worked by peasants; and communally owned land—a common feature of erstwhile republics.

Asoka publicized his laws throughout the four corners of his empire, having them inscribed on rocks and placed in market centers, at crossroads, and in the cities. His edicts were based on his concept of *dharma*, or piety, a unique idea that the king's duty was to promulgate measures for his subjects' welfare.

While Asoka is credited with the construction of many Buddhist monasteries, or stupas, most of these were enlarged and embellished by later rulers. The finest specimens of Mauryan art are the monolithic stone columns, cut and polished to a shining finish and with finely modeled column heads. The four-lion head of the Asokan column at Sarnath, near Varanasi, has been adopted as the emblem of the present-day Indian republic.

Many historians have associated the policy of nonviolence with the decline of the empire's military strength and its eventual break-up. More recent research indicates that it was rather the Mauryas' failure to expand their resource base that contributed to their decline. Being reliant on localized systems of revenue collection, the empire was ultimately destabilized by regional shortfalls in income.

⚬ The capital of an Asokan pillar from Sarnath, near Varanasi, where the Buddha preached his first sermon. The pillar bore an edict of Asoka, warning Buddhist monks against creating dissension within the Sangha (monastic order).
TETTONI, CASSIO, & ASSOC./PHOTOBANK

THE EXTENT OF MAURYAN INFLUENCE, SHOWING THE LOCATION OF ASOKAN INSCRIPTIONS
Asokan inscriptions were placed in highly visible locations, such as at the entrances to towns, crossroads, and frontier posts. Before being engraved on rocks and pillars, they were orally proclaimed in front of an audience.

▲ Pillar inscription
▼ Pillar edict
★ Minor pillar edict
◆ Rock edict
✤ Minor rock edict
✳ Cave inscription
▨ Mauryan influence

CARTOGRAPHY: RAY SIM

The Satavahanas and the Expansion of Trade

The opening up of new routes under the Mauryas, and official patronage of Buddhism and Jainism, led to an unprecedented expansion of cities and trade networks during the last two centuries BC. Buddhism emerged as the dominant religion of the ruling elite as well as of merchants, traders, and craftspeople.

The northwestern part of the Indian sub-continent faced constant challenges, with frequent incursions of nomadic tribes from central Asia. The first of these were the Sakas, who moved down the Indus Valley and settled in western India. But the most successful were the Yueh-chi tribes, who rose to power in Afghanistan and a large part of northern India, and started the line of Kusana kings. Purusapura, near modern-day Peshawar, in Pakistan, was the capital of the Kusanas, while Mathura, near Delhi, had the status of a secondary capital.

While tribal chiefs continued to rule in the far south and in isolated enclaves in the north, one of the local tribal groups in the Deccan peninsula established the Satavahana dynasty. Land routes through the peninsula were established, and the region was opened up to coastal traffic. Coastal maritime routes linked the west coast port of Broach (Barygaza) to settlements in Sri Lanka and

⚬ An elephant carved out of rock at Dhauli, near Bhubaneshwar, dated to the Mauryan period. Dhauli is also the site of an Asokan inscription.

HIMANSHU PRABHA RAY

➡ This ivory plaque found during archaeological excavations at Begram, near Kabul, formed part of a palace treasure that included Indian ivories, glass and bronze objects of Hellenistic origin, and Chinese lacquer of the early centuries AD.
MUSÉE GUIMET/RMN

✿ A relief from the Buddhist stupa at Goli, in Andhra Pradesh, depicting a cart used for transportation in early India. Bronze models of similar carts have also been found.
HIMANSHU PRABHA RAY

the Persian Gulf. Another prominent destination of transoceanic trading voyages was Suvarnabhumi, the land of gold, sometimes identified with lower Burma (Myanmar).

One of the significant characteristics of this period was the development and spread of an urban way of life. New settlements were planned and constructed, and the quality of life improved. Baked brick and stone were widely used to build fortifications, houses, and large water tanks. Consumer items such as jewelry, ivory objects, fabrics, perfumes, and wine were also in demand. A variety of crafts sprang up, and long-distance trade routes expanded over land and sea.

Broach (Barygaza) and Sopara were only two of a series of ports along the west coast. Commodities such as wheat, rice, cloth, and clarified butter were brought to these ports from centers far inland and exported from them to trading communities on the island of Socotra, at the mouth of the Red Sea. Timber was also exported for shipbuilding in the Persian Gulf. To Alexandria and other towns in Egypt went aromatics, spices, fine cottons, Chinese silk, pearls, diamonds, gems, and pepper. In return, Indian communities received imports of wine, glass,

✿ Gold jewelry found in a hoard near Madras that also contained Roman coins and carnelian intaglios.
HIMANSHU PRABHA RAY

frankincense, dates, coral, metals, and Roman money that had been exchanged at a profit for local currency. While comparatively few Roman coins have been recovered in the Deccan peninsula, they are more common further south.

Archaeological and literary evidence reveals that many nationalities were involved in this maritime trade network, including Arabs and Egyptian Greeks, as well as Indian seafarers. The trade with Southeast Asia is not nearly so well documented, although objects of Indian origin have frequently been found in archaeological excavations in this region. Findings include beads, pendants, carnelian seals with inscriptions in Brahmi (an ancient Indian script), ivory objects, and Indian pottery. These clay vessels were either used as containers or traded as such, and some sherds carry the owners' names, indicating the place of origin. Commodities from Southeast Asia and the Indonesian archipelago that were in demand in India included cinnamon, cassia, cloves, sandalwood, and, perhaps, tin. Many of these items were shipped on from Indian ports to Roman Egypt.

Buddhism and Trade

Historians have debated whether trading links in antiquity helped to spread cultural influences, especially between India and Southeast Asia. Trade was conducted by peddlers with low caste status in Brahmanical society. Such people, it was argued, could hardly be regarded as likely carriers of cultural change. However, recent research shows that until the Gupta period, Buddhism was the paramount religion on the Indian subcontinent, and it actively promoted trading activities.

Writing was used to record the many donations made to Buddhist monasteries by the ruling elite, traders, and craftspeople. Monasteries were the most significant monuments of the period. They consisted of *viharas*, or residences for the monks, and *caityas*, or places of congregation and worship. The image of the Buddha developed along the lines of two distinct schools of art: the Gandhara, in the northwest, which was influenced by the Hellenistic tradition, and the local Mathura style.

Some Buddhist monuments, such as those at Taxila or Sanchi, in central India, were embellished with stone railings depicting scenes from the life of the Buddha and incidents from his previous births. Others were carved out of rock, and more than 800 of these caves survive in the hills of western India. The construction of these monuments was supported by donations from the ruling elite and other devotees drawn from trades such as jewelers, ironsmiths, merchants, and gardeners. One of the reasons for Buddhism's wide appeal among these occupational groups was its tolerant view of society. While Buddhism did not oppose the Brahmanical caste system, it promoted the concept of a social hierarchy determined by moral values rather than caste.

HIMANSHU PRABHA RAY

◉ A typical Satavahana terracotta figure from Ter, in Maharashtra, made in a double mold. The use of a double mold for the production of terracottas is typical of the Satavahana period.

HIMANSHU PRABHA RAY

◉ The interior of a rock-cut *caitya* at Bedsa, near Bombay. The resources for the construction of these Buddhist monuments were donated by traders, merchants, and *yavanas* (foreigners).

➲ An image of the Buddha of the Mathura school of art, carved in red sandstone, with an inscription on the pedestal dated to the thirty-second year of the Kusana era, corresponding to the first century AD.

NATIONAL MUSEUM OF INDIA, NEW DELHI/
THE BRIDGEMAN ART LIBRARY

◄⊙ The original stupa at Sanchi, built on a hill by Asoka, is the sole surviving example from that period. The brick structure was later enlarged and enclosed by a stone railing, to which richly carved stone gateways were added in the first century BC.

⊙ This exquisite metal sculpture depicting the marriage of the god Siva with Parvati was made during the Cola period (AD 900 to AD 1300), well known for the development of the lost-wax method of bronze casting.

♀ A head of the Buddha carved in the Gandharan style, the characteristic features being wavy hair and a moustache.
NATIONAL MUSEUM OF ORIENTAL ART, ROME/SCALA

TETTONI, CASSIO, & ASSOC./PHOTOBANK

J.L. NOU/EXPLORER/AUSCAPE

The ascendancy of Buddhism did not continue unchallenged for long. Strong contenders emerged from among the different sects of the Brahmanical religion, including Saivism and Vaisnavism. Images of Hindu gods such as Siva and Vishnu were worshiped in simple shrines and received patronage and support from the later Gupta dynasty. It was, however, from the seventh and eighth centuries AD onwards that the Brahmanical temple attained monumental proportions and emerged as the religious focal point of society.

One group that sought acceptance within the Buddhist trading network was the *yavanas*, or foreigners. The term *yavana* initially referred to an Ionian Greek, but by the beginning of the Christian era, it was used to refer to any alien. Gifts from *yavanas* are recorded in the Buddhist monasteries of central India and the Deccan. Many *yavanas* adopted Buddhist names, and according to early Tamil sources, those living further south took up other occupations as well as trade, some working as royal palace guards.

of the fifth century AD, the Huns had broken into northern India, and the rule of the Guptas had given way to fragmented principalities and kingdoms.

Land grants to *brahmanas*, as members of the Brahman caste were known, were common practice under the Guptas. A way of ensuring that land under cultivation increased, the practice can be traced back to the Satavahanas, who donated land and villages both to Buddhist monasteries and to *brahmanas*. From the Gupta period onwards, these grants included inhabited villages, with rulers waiving their right to governance and revenue. This led to the growth of *brahmana* feudal territories that were autonomously administered.

Under the Guptas, fine arts and literature reached their peak. Specialized treatises on mathematics, astronomy, law, medicine, and philosophy were written in Sanskrit, the language of the elite.

Images of the deity evolved as the focus of devotional worship among the Hindus, and began to take the form of gods in human form with multiple arms. The symbols held in each of these arms represented the god's diverse powers. Buddhism maintained its position, although it was gradually losing its distinct identity from Brahmanism. This was one of the factors that led to its eventual decline in India, even though it continued to flourish unchallenged in other parts of Asia.

Himanshu Prabha Ray

❧ This stone sculpture of Skanda, son of Siva and Parvati, dates to the Gupta period, when the proportions of images and their attributes were fixed in accordance with the Brahmanical tradition.
C.M. DIXON/PHOTO RESOURCES

❧ A silver coin cast by the Huns in imitation of those of the Guptas, whom they defeated in the fifth century AD.
C.M. DIXON/PHOTO RESOURCES

THE IMPERIAL GUPTAS: AD 319 TO AD 450

The Gupta period has often been referred to as the "golden age" of Indian history. It was during this time that Brahmanical social and religious values and culture were firmly established. However, this was true only in the northern part of India. In the Deccan peninsula and in the south, civilization reached its high-water mark about AD 800. Unlike the vast plains of the north, peninsular India was handicapped by the scattered nature of its agricultural lands. Rival groups were constantly at loggerheads for control of fertile tracts of land.

Although the Gupta era is generally dated from the accession of Chandragupta I, about AD 319, to AD 320, the origins of the Guptas are obscure. The dynasty continued its rule until the fifth century AD, when the first invasions of the Huns threatened the Guptas' hold on the north-western part of the subcontinent. By the end

❧ An image of Vishnu from Udaigiri, 7 kilometers (4 miles) northeast of Sanchi. Twenty Brahmanical caves were carved in these sandstone hills, not far from the ancient city of Vidisa, during the reign of the Gupta dynasty.

TETTONI, CASSIO, & ASSOC./PHOTOBANK

THE PALACE-FORTRESS OF SIGIRIYA

HIMANSHU PRABHA RAY

SIGIRIYA IS an outstanding example of the planned, moated, and walled urban centers found in South and Southeast Asia. It was the political capital of Sri Lanka for a brief period of about 15 years from AD 477, when Kasyapa I, who believed he was a god-king, moved his court and administration to Sigiriya from Anuradhapura, having seized power from his father. Sigiriya is renowned for the paintings on the west face of the rock, the surviving examples consisting of female figures. Their identity is uncertain, although they have often been described as ladies of Kasyapa's court, or *apsaras,* meaning heavenly maidens.

⏶Flanked by the head, chest, and forepaws of a colossal sphinx-like lion made of timber, brick, and plaster, the lion staircase was a magnificent sight to pilgrims in antiquity, who inscribed poems in praise of it on the so-called "mirror wall".

↩ The royal pleasure gardens of Sigiriya are unique in being the earliest landscaped gardens in Asia with an elaborate drainage system. Marble slabs from the nearby quarries were hauled to the summit of the precipitous rock for the construction of tanks and drainage pipes.

⏶Located on top of the rock are the remains of the fifth-century AD palace, which extends over almost 3 hectares (about 7 acres), while on the plain below are two fortified precincts surrounded by successive earthen ramparts and moats.

↪ Massive natural outcrops were the favored building sites of ancient architects, but the fortified capital of Sigiriya remains unsurpassed for its location on a spectacular natural rock formation 200 meters (650 feet) above the surrounding plain.

MICHAEL FREEMAN

CIVILIZATIONS OF SOUTHEAST ASIA

2 0 0 0   B C   –   A D   1   5   0   0

A Blend of Traditions

IAN C. GLOVER AND ELIZABETH H. MOORE

THE CULTURAL DEVELOPMENT of Southeast Asia after the time of the rice-growing Stone Age communities was characterized by an extraordinarily strong regional diversity, unparalleled elsewhere in the world. The region became a melting pot of cultural impulses from other parts of Asia (mainly India, to the west, and China, to the north)—including technology, art, religion, trade, and politics—which were assimilated by the indigenous cultures. These influences soon triggered the growth of cities and, in time, whole nations. The area also saw large-scale migrations of people. The result of this flourishing cultural exchange and development, which were often intimately linked to Hinduism and Buddhism, is still evident in Southeast Asia today.

The first metal cultures emerged during the earliest phases of the Bronze Age, about 2000 BC, and were almost certainly developed locally. Iron first came into use about 700 BC. The technique of iron-working may have been developed locally, but probably came from India.

◄◙ Each of the perforated stupas on the summit of Borobudur houses an image of the Buddha. The Buddha's tranquil expression reflects the serenity that awaits the pilgrims who reach the monument's upper levels.

◙ A bronze axehead and its casting mold from a grave of the Ban Chiang culture, in northeastern Thailand, dating from about 1500 BC.

TETTONI, CASSIO, & ASSOC./PHOTOBANK

CIVILIZATIONS OF SOUTHEAST ASIA: 2000 BC – AD 1800

	BURMA, THAILAND, AND NORTH VIETNAM	SOUTH VIETNAM AND CAMBODIA	INDONESIA
1800	Buddhist kingdom of Bangkok founded		
1600	Burmese–Thai wars	Christianity introduced to Vietnam	Islam replaces Hinduism and Buddhism in Java / "Religion of the Hindu doctrine" (Bali) developed
1400	Buddhist kingdom of Ayutthaya (Thailand) AD 1300 – AD 1700		Bali colonized
1200	Kingdom of Pagan (central Burma) AD 1000 – AD 1200		
1000	Mon combined with Pyu and Burmese cultures / Stone Buddhas in form of *sema* (boundary) stones		Hindu temple of Prambanan (Java) built / Buddhist temple of Borobudur (Java) built
800		Khmer kings of Angkor (Cambodia) AD 800 – AD 1200 / Stone temples	
600	Mon "kingdom" of Dvaravati AD 600 – AD 1000 / Massive stone *cakra*	Kingdom of Champa (South Vietnam) AD 600 – AD 900 / Kingdom of Chenla (Cambodia) AD 500 – AD 800	Monumental architecture AD 700 – AD 1300 (Java)
400		Hindu–Buddhist influences	
200	Intensification of trade with India		
AD 1	Pyu (Burma) AD 100 – AD 900 / Tibeto-Burman group	Kingdom of Funan (South Vietnam) AD 100 – AD 500	Indo-Roman pottery and glass found in Java and Bali
500	Late Bronze Age to Iron Age Dongson culture 500 BC – AD 200		Spread of metallurgy from the mainland
	Lost-wax casting of large, bronze kettledrums throughout Southeast Asia. Iron appears in certain areas of Southeast Asia. Iron artifacts are made by the "direct" process.		
1000	Middle Bronze Age Go Mun culture 1100 BC – 500 BC	Use of iron in later period of Sa-Huynh culture 1000 BC – AD 100	Megalithic structures at Cipari, in Java
1500	Early Bronze Age Dong Dau culture 1500 BC – 1100 BC		
2000 BC	Use of bronze in Late Neolithic Phung Nguyen culture 2300 BC – 1500 BC		Expansion of Austronesian-speaking agriculturalists

THE BRONZE AGE AND IRON AGE IN SOUTHEAST ASIA: 2000 BC TO AD 400

The first bronze artifacts discovered by Western archaeologists in Southeast Asia are large kettledrums, found from South China to eastern Indonesia. In 1705, naturalist G.E. Rumpf gave a detailed description of a drum from Pejeng, in Bali, and sent another to Europe. Many more drums were discovered in the nineteenth and early twentieth centuries. Where the drums came from was not known until the 1920s, when French customs official Emile Pajot excavated some on the banks of the Ma River, at Dongson, near Than Hoa, in Vietnam.

⚓ Dongson drums, such as the one shown here, were classified in 1902 by the German ethnographer Franz Heger into four main types, now known as Heger types I to IV. This is a Heger type I drum.
RIJKSMUSEUM VOOR VOLKENKUNDE

Origins of Bronze in Southeast Asia

Archaeologists long believed that all bronze artifacts found in Southeast Asia came from a "Dongson civilization", centered on South China and Vietnam, which was thought to have traded drums and other bronze ritual vessels throughout the area. Until the mid-1960s, it was thought that bronze came into use in Southeast Asia between 700 BC and 500 BC, probably through the spread of metallurgical techniques from China, or even from southeastern Europe. Recent excavations, however, have caused this belief to be abandoned: Vietnamese excavations at Dongson and elsewhere show continuity from earlier Neolithic cultures.

In the 1960s, a modern phase of excavation began in Thailand, and in 1966, excavations at Non Nok Tha ("Partridge Mound"), in Northeast Thailand, uncovered a burial ground that included numerous bronze axes, ornaments, and projectile points. More important were casting molds, crucibles, and casting spillage, indicating that the artifacts were manufactured locally.

At about the same time as the Non Nok Tha excavations, rich Bronze Age burials and superbly painted pottery were dug from graves by the villagers of Ban Chiang, just south of the Mekong River and nearly 125 kilometers (80 miles) north of Non Nok Tha. Excavations by Thai archaeologists in 1967 and 1972, and by a joint Thai–American team from 1974 to 1975, yielded a wealth of bronze and pottery provisionally dated to various phases from about 3600 BC to AD 200.

This site was extensively looted by villagers, who readily sold the decorated pottery, bronzes, and stone and glass jewelry for which Ban Chiang is famous. Public and private collections in Thailand and overseas benefited, but the context of the finds was ignored, and much of the evidence of burial and occupation was destroyed.

Later reassessments caused revision of the date for the first appearance of bronze at Non Nok Tha and Ban Chiang to about 2000 BC, roughly contemporary with its earliest use in North China. Virtually all specialists now reject the notion that metallurgical knowledge was introduced into Southeast Asia from outside, thinking it more probable that the indigenous peoples, with abundant and easily accessible copper and tin, developed their own methods of smelting and casting.

Since then, other Bronze Age cemeteries have been excavated, notably at Ban Na Di, 25 kilometers (15 miles) south of Ban Chiang; Non Pa Kluay, near Non Nok Tha; Tha Kae, near Lopburi, in central Thailand; and most recently, at Non Nor, on the eastern side of the Gulf of Thailand. The Bronze Age soil strata at all of these sites can be dated to about 2000 BC to 800 BC.

Since the mid-1980s, investigation has shifted to ancient mines and metal-smelting sites, especially around Phu Lon, on the northern end of the Petchabuan Mountains and just south of the Mekong River, and in the Wong Prachan Valley, in central Thailand. The evidence reveals intensive mining and smelting of both surface and deeper copper ores from just after 2000 BC. An unusual technique of crucible smelting produced copper ingots for transport to the village bronze casters of the Khorat Plateau.

⚱ This drum top found in Indonesia is decorated with frogs. It is thought that drums were used in rain-making ceremonies to summon the frogs that appear in the rice fields just before the monsoon rains begin.
RIJKSMUSEUM VOOR VOLKENKUNDE

⚱ A pedestal bowl from the Late period at Ban Chiang, a site famous for its decorated pottery, bronzes, and stone and glass jewelry.
TETTONI, CASSIO, & ASSOC./PHOTOBANK

⚱ A bronze bracelet, dating from the first millennium BC, excavated in the Ban Chiang region, in northeastern Thailand.
LUCA INVERNIZZI TETTONI/GIRAUDON

⚱ Copper ingots from the Wong Prachan Valley, in central Thailand, dating from the Late Bronze to Early Iron Age.
IAN C. GLOVER

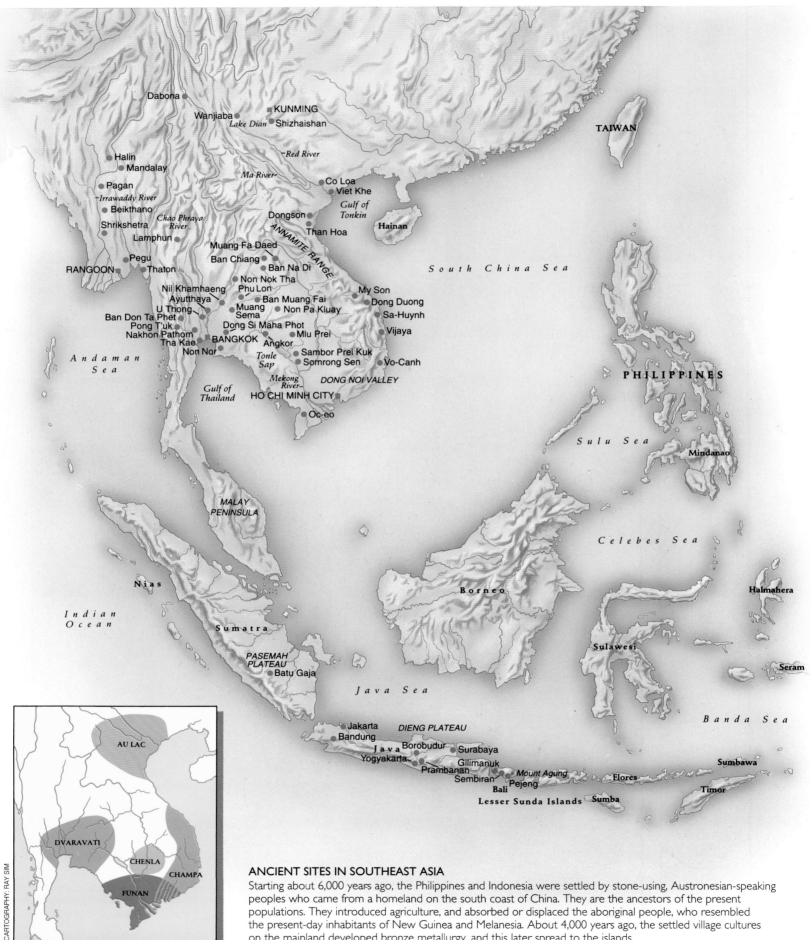

Dabona

Wanjiaba
Lake Dian
KUNMING
Shizhaishan

TAIWAN

Halin
Mandalay

~*Red River*

Ma River~

Co Loa
Viet Khe

Pagan
~*Irrawaddy River*

Beikthano
Shrikshetra

Chao Phraya River

Dongson

Than Hoa

Gulf of Tonkin

Hainan

Lamphun

Pegu

Muang Fa Daed
Ban Chiang
Ban Na Di

S o u t h   C h i n a   S e a

RANGOON
Thaton

Non Nok Tha
Phu Lon

My Son
Dong Duong

Nil Khamhaeng
Ayutthaya
U Thong
Ban Don Ta Phet
Pong T'uk
Nakhon Pathom
Tha Kae
Non Nor

Ban Muang Fai
Muang
Sema
Non Pa Kluay
Dong Si Maha Phot
Mlu Prei
BANGKOK
Angkor
Sambor Prei Kuk
Somrong Sen
Tonle Sap

Sa-Huynh

Vijaya

Vo-Canh

PHILIPPINES

Andaman Sea

Gulf of Thailand

Mekong River~
HO CHI MINH CITY
DONG NOI VALLEY

Oc-eo

S u l u   S e a

Mindanao

MALAY PENINSULA

C e l e b e s   S e a

N i a s

I n d i a n   O c e a n

S u m a t r a

B o r n e o

Halmahera

Sulawesi

Seram

PASEMAH PLATEAU
Batu Gaja

J a v a   S e a

B a n d a   S e a

Jakarta
Bandung

DIENG PLATEAU

Sumbawa

J a v a
Yogyakarta
Borobudur
Prambanan
Surabaya
Gilimanuk
Sembiran
Pejeng
Bali
Lesser Sunda Islands
Mount Agung
Flores
Sumba

Timor

AU LAC

DVARAVATI

CHENLA

CHAMPA

FUNAN

CARTOGRAPHY: RAY SIM

ANCIENT SITES IN SOUTHEAST ASIA

Starting about 6,000 years ago, the Philippines and Indonesia were settled by stone-using, Austronesian-speaking peoples who came from a homeland on the south coast of China. They are the ancestors of the present populations. They introduced agriculture, and absorbed or displaced the aboriginal people, who resembled the present-day inhabitants of New Guinea and Melanesia. About 4,000 years ago, the settled village cultures on the mainland developed bronze metallurgy, and this later spread to the islands.

Trade and Exchange in the Bronze Age

During this period, copper–tin alloys (bronzes) were extensively used in northeastern Thailand and central Thailand east of the Chao Phraya River. In the west, northwest, and south of that country, and throughout the Malay peninsula into Indonesia, there is little evidence of the production and use of metals until much later. Occasional finds of bronze artifacts can better be accounted for by exchange networks along the rivers and coasts, which also carried marine shells and ornaments inland to villages in the far northwest and to the Khorat Plateau.

No doubt, most trade was in organic materials that have not survived in the archaeological record, but enough stone axes from igneous rock deposits, chert and quartz for flaked cutting tools, shells and bronze axes and ornaments have been found to give some indication of Neolithic exchange systems. From about 500 BC, these carried iron, semiprecious stones, and glass jewelry from the west. Later, they carried Indian Hindu–Buddhist ideology and statehood concepts to the most inland parts.

Bronze Metallurgy in Northern Vietnam

With independence in North Vietnam in 1954, and despite war with the French, Americans, and South Vietnamese, numerous surveys and excavations were undertaken in the northern and central provinces. Special attention has been given to the Dongson culture of the Late Bronze to Early Iron Age (about 700 BC to AD 100), which the Vietnamese see as the finest expression of their native genius, before they came under Chinese influence during Vietnam's 900 years as a province of the Chinese Empire.

Vietnamese archaeologists have established a sequence of cultures in the central Red River valley. There, the Late Neolithic Phung Nguyen culture (about 2300 BC to 1500 BC) employed bronze in its final stages. In the Early Bronze Age Dong Dau culture (about 1500 BC to 1100 BC), bronze replaced stone for about 40 percent of edged tools and weapons, rising to about 60 percent in the Middle Bronze Age Go Mun culture (about 1100 BC to 500 BC). Here, there are not only bronze weapons, axes, and personal ornaments, but also sickles and other agricultural tools. In the Late Bronze Age–Iron Age Dongson culture (500 BC to AD 200), bronze accounts for more than 90 percent of tools and weapons, and there are exceptionally rich graves such as that at Viet Khe, where a hollowed log coffin more than 4.5 meters (15 feet) long contained some hundred bronzes, including small drums.

In the Dongson period, a few exceptionally rich cemeteries—the burial places of powerful chiefdoms—contain ritual and personal artifacts such as drums, bucket-shaped ladles, musical instruments, buckles, and ornamented daggers. Towards the end of the period, from about 200 BC, there is an increasing range of imported Han Chinese mirrors, wine vessels, coins, halberds (*ge*), and even a seal such as the Han emperors gave to dependent principalities outside the empire.

Here, Chinese historical texts (the *Shu shu*) and Vietnamese legendary histories come together. Vietnamese scholars identify the Dongson culture in its later stages with Van Lang/Au Lac, traditionally the first unified kingdom of Vietnam, with a ruling royal dynasty, a professional administrative class, and its capital at Co Loa. This fortress, on the northern edge of modern Hanoi, bounded by ramparts extending more than 600 hectares (1,500 acres), was conquered by the Chinese in the first century AD. Much Dongson material has been found around Co Loa, including a huge bronze drum weighing some 70 kilograms (160 pounds) and containing more than 100 socketed bronze hoes or plow shares. Nevertheless, the identification of Co Loa as the capital of an indigenous kingdom remains uncertain.

Dongson bronze weapons and tools, from central Vietnam. Excavations by Vietnamese archaeologists at Dongson and many other sites in the Red and Ma River valleys show continuity between this culture and the earlier Neolithic cultures.
IAN C. GLOVER

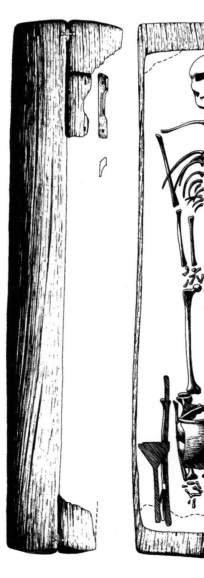

This hollowed log coffin excavated at Chau Can is similar to one found at Viet Khe, in northern Vietnam, dating from the Dongson period. The Viet Khe coffin contained some hundred bronzes, including small drums.
CHARLES HIGHAM

⚲ Designs on Dongson bronze drums depict details of daily and ceremonial life. The upper panel shows armed warriors with a drum on a boat, and the lower panel shows people playing drums in front of a house with outswept gables that is similar to the modern-day houses of the Toraja people, of Sulawesi, in Indonesia.
IAN C. GLOVER

⚲ A Dongson-style drum, from Thailand. Although some Chinese scholars believe that these drums originated in South China from more utilitarian containers, the Vietnamese remain convinced that they developed first in the lower Red River valley and spread northwestwards into China.
TETTONI, CASSIO, & ASSOC./PHOTOBANK

The Drums of Dongson

Several hundred of the great bronze kettledrums of the Dongson culture have been reported; some 150 from Vietnam, 50 from Indonesia, 20 to 30 in Thailand, and many more in South and Southwest China, particularly from Yunnan, Guangxi, Guizhou, and Guangdong provinces. The drums exhibit great skill in the lost-wax casting of large objects—the Co Loa drum would have required the smelting of between 1 and 7 tonnes (1 and 7 tons) of copper ore and the use of up to 10 large casting crucibles at the one time. The pictorial information on the drums' sides illustrates vivid details of daily and ceremonial life. Armed warriors in boats can be seen carrying the very drums on which they are portrayed; there are domestic tasks such as food preparation and the feeding of animals; and music, dance, and religious ceremonies are depicted.

Scholars have argued as to whether the drums were made for religious ceremonies, to rally men for war, or for another secular role. They have been found from China to the borders of Burma (Myanmar) and east to the islands of eastern Indonesia, and it is unlikely that they had the same functions in all communities. Most drums were made in Vietnam and South China, but they were traded to the south and west, and were valued by people with very different cultures. In eastern Java and Bali, a distinctive style of drum developed, taller and narrower with an overhanging tympanum. This is the Pejeng type, first described by Rumpf in 1705, and still in its temple tower at Bedulu, in central Bali.

The Pejeng drums, probably made in the early centuries AD, gave rise to the later and smaller *moko* drums, which were still made in the late nineteenth century. They served as a form of money among certain peoples of eastern Indonesia. In mainland Southeast Asia, too, the early drums were modified and remained in production up to the twentieth century, serving to communicate with the spirit world, for rain-making and shamanist rituals. They were used by many of the mountain hill tribespeoples of Yunnan, in China; Laos; the Annamite Range of Indochina; Northeast Thailand; Burma; and as far west as the northeast frontier provinces of India. They are still made in Laos and Thailand for the tourist trade.

The Dongson drums date to at least the seventh century BC, and probably come from the mountains of far west Yunnan. The earliest known were found at Wanjiba, in a huge wooden tomb from about 600 BC. At Dabona, the "drums", if that is what they are, have a convex end, resembling large cooking cauldrons.

Bronze drums in many shapes and sizes as late as the first century BC have been found among the spectacular royal regalia of the Kingdom of Dian, a powerful multi-ethnic state centered around Lake Dian—south of present-day Kunming, in Yunnan—and outside the Han empire until about 115 BC. Shizhaishan, the royal burial ground on a hill, once an island in the lake, has produced some of the most striking remains in the whole of East Asia. Some drums are clearly of the Dongson style, others are unique to Yunnan; yet others have been adapted as containers for vast numbers of cowrie shells. These have separate lids bearing extraordinary images of war, ritual, musical performances, human sacrifice, and serpent worship, as well as weaving, cooking, and feasting, and village elders in conference with their chiefs.

The Bronze Age in Vietnam and Cambodia

South of the Dongson area, the later prehistory of Vietnam and Cambodia is very poorly known. However, several regionally distinct Bronze Age cultures have been identified, with their own styles of axes, daggers, and ornaments.

The Sa-Huynh culture, for example, is a late prehistoric metal age society on the central coast of the old kingdom of Annam. In 1909, about 200 jar burials were uncovered at Sa-Huynh. Since then, many more have been found, at some 50 sites. Because of the acid soils, these jars seldom contain human bones, but incised pottery, glass and carnelian beads, bronze ornaments, and iron tools and weapons are common. More than 100 examples of a jade ear pendant representing a mythical two-headed beast have been found in Vietnam, with some others in Thailand, the

MICHAEL FREEMAN

Philippines, and Taiwan—evidence of the widespread trading of the Sa-Huynh people.

An early stage of the Sa-Huynh culture, the Long Thanh, is dated a little before 1000 BC. The jars at these sites are egg-shaped; they contain stone tools and ornaments, but no metal. Bronze tools appear in the Binh Chau stage, just after 1000 BC, followed by iron in the Sa-Huynh stage, about 500 BC. Bronze thus appears rather late in central Vietnam, partly perhaps because of the distance from ore sources. As in western Thailand, iron is rather early, quickly replacing bronze.

From about AD 500, the central coast of Vietnam was dominated by the Chams, an Austronesian-speaking people who adopted elements of Indian political and religious culture. Although the first French studies of the Chams did not connect them with earlier cultures, recent Vietnamese work has shown that they are linguistic and cultural descendants of the Sa-Huynh people. There are also many early traces of contact with the west. Indian glass and semiprecious stone beads are abundant, and iron seems to have been used by the Sa-Huynh peoples when their Dongson neighbors were still mostly using bronze.

In Cambodia, rich Bronze Age sites have long been known at Somrong Sen, on the branch of the Mekong River that flows into the "great lake", Tonle Sap, and at Mlu Pre, in the northeast. Conflict in that country stopped all recent archaeological work, and although the prehistoric Cambodian cultures were probably related to those of Thailand and Vietnam, details and chronology before the emergence of the great Khmer towns and temples remain obscure.

⚘ Cham architecture at the Mison temple complex, in central Vietnam, dating from the ninth to eleventh centuries AD. The Chams were an Austronesian-speaking people who have recently been shown to be the linguistic and cultural descendants of the Sa-Huynh people.

⚘ A jade and glass ear pendant from the Sa-Huynh culture, representing a mythical, two-headed beast.
IAN C. GLOVER

⚬ This decorated Cham tile end was excavated from Bui Chau hill, Tra Kieu, in central Vietnam.
IAN C. GLOVER

The Arrival of Iron, and Trade with India

Iron appears in certain areas of Southeast Asia between 700 BC and 500 BC. The earliest evidence comes from copper-mining and smelting sites in the Wong Prachan Valley of central Thailand, especially Nil Khamhaeng, where burials of metalworkers with iron tools and bangles have been dated to 700 BC. By about 500 BC, iron appears in central and northeastern Thailand and the Sa-Huynh sites of central Vietnam. By the early fourth century BC, iron completely replaced bronze for edged weapons and tools at Ban Don Ta Phet, on the western edge of Thailand's central plains.

It was once argued that the technique of manufacturing iron was introduced into Southeast Asia from China. Annals of the Han empire mention that iron was little known there, and specifically forbade its export to the "Southern Barbarians". But recent archaeological work has shown that iron came into use in Southeast Asia as early as in northern and central China, but was made by the "direct" process. Chinese iron-making was dominated by the "indirect" manufacture from cast iron —a technique not adopted in Thailand until the arrival of Chinese iron masters in the eighteenth century AD.

Archaeologists working in Thailand tend to see the development of iron as a local process arising out of the use of iron-rich copper ores. Its early occurrence at the copper-smelting site of Nil Khamhaeng supports this view. On the other hand, we start to get abundant evidence of trade with India in the form of glass, agate, and carnelian beads, including the etched variety, from about 500 BC. Since we know that iron-working spread throughout India from 1000 BC to 700 BC, it is likely that its appearance in Southeast Asia was a consequence of trade.

⚵ An iron spear from Ban Don Ta Phet, in western Thailand, dating from the fourth century BC.
IAN C. GLOVER

⚵ A carnelian lion from Ban Don Ta Phet, a site rich in significant burial deposits.
IAN C. GLOVER

In Indonesia, too, we find at this time many sites with evidence of exchange with India. The cist (slab) graves of Sumatra and Java also contain Indian glass and semiprecious stone beads. (See the feature *Southeast Asian Megaliths.*) Even the form of some of these burial structures may have been influenced by South Indian tombs. In Bali, the Gilimanuk site, from the first century AD, is rich in glass and stone. At the newly discovered trading port of Sembiran, on the north coast of Bali, pieces of Indo-Roman Rouletted Ware occur. This ceramic type of the second century BC to the first century AD is well known from sites in the eastern states of India. One Sembiran fragment has characters in the Indian *Karoshti* script.

Ban Don Ta Phet in Western Thailand

Excavations between 1975 and 1985 at Iron Age Ban Don Ta Phet give the best evidence of the earliest "Indianization". About 100 burial deposits, dated between 390 BC and 360 BC, were found. They contained only a few fragmentary bones, but numerous pottery vessels, and iron tools and weapons; high-tin bronze vessels and ornaments; and more than 3,000 glass beads, and some 500 of agate, carnelian, jade, and rock crystal, including about 50 etched beads of types well known from early Buddhist sites in North and northwestern India. Although the pottery is a locally made low-

◄● Carnelian and agate necklaces from Ban Don Ta Phet, in western Thailand. From about 500 BC, there is abundant evidence of trade with India in the form of glass, agate, and carnelian beads.

TETTONI, CASSIO, & ASSOC./PHOTOBANK

Its success depended on a prior knowledge of the great wealth, prestige, and power of the metropolitan states. Just as archaeological evidence in the form of the cross and fish symbols on the personal jewelry, wall paintings, and mosaics of late Roman Britain testify to the widespread knowledge and partial acceptance of Christianity 400 years before St Augustine's evangelical mission to Britain, so new archaeological data from Southeast Asia are beginning to show that some populations there were familiar with Indian religious ideas long before official Indianization.

Ian C. Glover

◀○ These bronze bowls and bracelets from Ban Don Ta Phet, in western Thailand, date from the fourth century BC. By this time, iron was used for tools and weapons, but high-tin bronzes were valued for their golden color and as prestigious, nontoxic food containers.
TETTONI, CASSIO, & ASSOC./PHOTOBANK

♀ The stone reliefs of Brahma at Pagan, in central Burma, are unique. Shown here are his three faces depicted at Nanpaya temple. Evidence of Hindu worship, however, along with Mahayana Buddhism, is mixed with the predominating Theravadan Buddhism.

fired earthenware, and the iron tools are quite different from forms known at contemporary Indian sites, the bronzes, and glass and stone ornaments can be widely matched in India, and provide evidence not only for trade, but also for the penetration of Indian Buddhism. A conical boss surrounded by inscribed circles appears in the base of some bronze vessels. The symbol is well known on pottery from Indian Buddhist towns such as Sisulpalgarh, in Orissa; on rare high-tin bronze vessels from the Nilgiri Hills and Coimbatore, in southern India; and from a superb carved and polished granite vessel found in an early stupa at Taxila. The date of Ban Don Ta Phet shows that long-held views that Hindu–Buddhist ideas and symbolism affected Southeast Asia only from the second to third centuries AD must now be abandoned.

The Arrival of Hindu–Buddhism in Southeast Asia

By about AD 500, much of Southeast Asia—from central Indonesia to the Sa-Huynh culture of Vietnam—had come under the influence of Hindu–Buddhist civilizations of eastern and southern India. Traditional South Asian histories, such as the *Mahavamsa* of Sri Lanka, record that in the late third century BC to the early second century BC, the Mauryan Emperor Asoka sent three missionaries—Son, Uttara, and Gavtampti —to spread Buddhism in the countries of *Suvanabhumi* (the "Lands of Gold"), in Southeast Asia. From this beginning, the Indianization of Southeast Asia continued.

But, as with St Augustine's mission to the court of King Ethelbert of Kent, England, in AD 597, the official religious conversion followed long-popular routes of communication and exchange.

TETTONI, CASSIO, & ASSOC./PHOTOBANK

☛ This detail of a relief from Borobudur, in Java, Indonesia, shows the type of boat that may have been in use during the ninth century AD. The story is from the *avadanas*, or heroic tales, and recounts the voyage of Hiru to found a new city.

☗ A pre-Angkorean image of the Buddha, 1.5 meters (5 feet) high, probably dating from the sixth to seventh centuries AD. The iconography of this image is strongly influenced by the art of Gupta India, but the symmetry of the arms and the front fold of the robe are also akin to the art of the Dvaravati, in Thailand. Although Angkor was predominantly a Hindu city, Buddhist sects continued to practice. This was particularly true in the pre-Angkorean period (pre-ninth century AD), and again during the reign of Jayavarman VII, at the end of the twelfth century. This second period of Buddhism was Mahayanist, however, whereas pre-Angkorean Buddhism was mostly Theravadan.
TETTONI, CASSIO, & ASSOC./PHOTOBANK

THE RISE OF HINDU AND BUDDHIST STATES IN SOUTHEAST ASIA

During the rise of the Hindu and Buddhist states, foreign and indigenous styles blended to transform Southeast Asian art. For about the first 12 centuries AD, the Indian religions provided a common iconography, but the architecture and sculpture are unique. The impact of Indian culture was profound, and from it stemmed concepts of state and kingship, writing, and legal systems.

A Blending of Styles
Contact with China was the other major influence on Southeast Asia, whose position gave rise to the traditional name "Indochina". Northern Vietnam was conquered by the Chinese Han dynasty in 111 BC, marking the beginning of some 900 years of Chinese rule. Tribute missions to the Chinese court were recorded over many centuries, but it was Indian ideas that were assimilated into Southeast Asian culture, as indicated by the use of Indian-based terms. For example, inscriptions of the Khmer kings of Angkor, in Cambodia, about AD 800 to AD 1200, adopted the suffix *varman*, meaning "protector". The first such uses are much earlier: a Cham inscription at Vo-Canh, Vietnam, has been dated to AD 300, and others in Vietnam go back to the late fourth century AD.

Religion and Trade
Despite the evidence of Indian culture, how it was introduced to Southeast Asia remains a mystery. The archaeological record points to trade. By the first century AD, demand in the West, particularly from Rome, stimulated Indian trade. Voyages from India to Southeast Asian ports were made in accordance with the seasonal monsoons, and ships would often wait many months in port for winds to change. At least 18 months commonly passed between outward and return trips, and traders may well have married locally. Others exploited overland routes, from relatively short distances across the Malay peninsula to longer circuits from Burma into China, or across northeastern Thailand to the valley of the Mekong River.

Scholars have argued that Indian Buddhist missionary activities resulted in Buddhist monasteries and communities being established in Southeast Asia. But peaceful coexistence is characteristic of Hinduism and Buddhism there, as is the blending of both religions with pre-existing ancestral cults.

Indian concepts of state and kingship in Southeast Asia reflect the political power held by religious figures. Native rulers may often have invited Hindus or Buddhists to take positions of

TETTONI, CASSIO, & ASSOC./PHOTOBANK

power in their courts, where Indian ideas of royalty legitimated the rulers' positions.

In the Hindu periods of the kingdom of Angkor, the essence of kingship was expressed in the *devaraja*, a Sanskrit word meaning "god who is king", which consecrated a ruler as an incarnation of a Hindu god such as Vishnu or Siva. Temples and statues dedicated to these and other deities embodied the ruler and expressed his power. On Earth, the *devaraja* established harmony in the human world, between subterranean chaos and the realm of the gods.

The ideal ruler of the Buddhist state was the *cakravartin*. The *cakra*—"disk" or "wheel" in Sanskrit—was set in motion by the Buddha in preaching his first sermon, but it may also be an attribute of the Hindu god Vishnu, and can also symbolize the sun. The *cakravartin* is a righteous and universal emperor whose chariot can roll anywhere without hindrance.

♂ A stone statue of Vishnu, measuring 1.7 meters (5 feet, 8 inches) high, from Surat Thani, in southern Thailand. Somewhat similar statues have been found to the north, including one near Ayutthaya. The dating of all these images is uncertain.

♀ This *dharmacakra,* or "wheel of law", was found near Prachinburi, in south-central Thailand. Other examples have been found in the northeastern part of the country, illustrating the wide geographical area over which sculpture of the Dvaravati style is found.
TETTONI, CASSIO, & ASSOC./PHOTOBANK

Protohistoric Southeast Asia: The Mon of Dvaravati

The Mon "kingdom" of Dvaravati, one of many small polities, was probably located in central and northeastern Thailand, from about AD 600 to AD 1000. Its culture is characterized by massive stone *cakra,* 1 to 2 meters (3 to 6 feet) in diameter. The Indian ruler Asoka is believed to have originated the placing of *cakra* on tall pillars, which may also have occurred in Thailand.

The Thai *cakra* has a central socket, and some scholars suggest that carved stone bas-reliefs—the *panaspati*—were fixed there. The *panaspati* is a mythical creature not seen outside the Dvaravati period. It is a composite of the vehicles of the principal Hindu deities, with the body of Siva's bull Nandi, the beak of Vishnu's Garuda bird, and the wings of Brahma's *hamsa* or goose. The Buddha riding on the *panaspati* signifies the triumph of Buddhism over Hinduism.

Dating from the eighth to ninth centuries AD, this *panaspati* is 37 centimeters (15 inches) high.
TETTONI, CASSIO, & ASSOC./PHOTOBANK

Although the *vitarka*, or "teaching mudra" (symbolic gesture), of the Buddha's hands is known in India, the double *vitarka* of the Dvaravati style is unique.
TETTONI, CASSIO, & ASSOC./PHOTOBANK

Opposite page: The fluidity of Dvaravati stucco work can be seen in this detail of a relief from Chula Pathom Chedi, thought to date from the seventh to ninth centuries AD.

The blending of Hinduism and Buddhism in the *panaspati* typifies Southeast Asia's assimilation of Indian religions. Beikthano, the name of the first to fifth-century AD Buddhist site in central Burma, means "City of Vishnu". In Burma, today renamed Myanmar, spirit worship remains closely interwoven with veneration of the Buddha. This blending of religious ideas and iconographies began during the protohistoric period (the last centuries BC and the early centuries AD).

Written evidence from this period is scant: brief inscriptions on upright stone slabs or columns, references in Chinese dynastic accounts, and inscribed coins. It is from these coins that the name "Dvaravati" was confirmed. A seventh-century AD Chinese traveler referred to a kingdom east of Burma and west of Cambodia as "T'o-lo-po-ti", which in Sanskrit is "Dvaravati". The name is also part of the official titles of two later Thai Buddhist kingdoms: Ayutthaya, AD 1300 to AD 1700; and Bangkok, the present capital, founded in the late eighteenth century AD after the Burmese sacked Ayutthaya. In 1963, the name was firmly substantiated when two silver coins inscribed in Sanskrit with Indian characters, dateable to the seventh-century AD Indian Pallava dynasty, were unearthed at Nakhon Pathom. The characters were translated as "meritorious work of the King of Dvaravati".

Many inscriptions from these sites are in the Mon language rather than Sanskrit, which has led to the identification of Dvaravati with the Mon peoples. The Mon, dating from about AD 500, were found from Burma to the eastern shore of the Gulf of Thailand, across present-day Cambodia, and northeast towards Laos.

The historical record of Dvaravati barely justifies referring to it as a kingdom. It probably included a number of city-states, one of which was Dvaravati. Other sites where Dvaravati objects have been found were U Thong, Pong T'uk, Ku Bua, Dong Si Maha Phot, Muang Fa Daed, Muang Sema, and Ban Muang Fai. Many of these were enclosed by an earthen wall, and sometimes one or several moats. Plans are irregular, each city differing from the others, and there is no obvious religious significance to the shape. Images of the Buddha occur at these and other sites in materials including stone, terracotta, and stucco, and are strikingly similar. Some very fine images are fully rounded, others are bas-reliefs.

The stone Buddhas are in the form of *sema* (boundary) stones. Dated between AD 800 and AD 900, in Thailand, they have been found only in the northeast. The slabs are as much as 2 meters (6 feet) high, carved with scenes from the life of the historical Buddha, as well as with *jatakas*—tales of the Buddha's former lives. The largest collection comes from Muang Fa Daed. Bas-reliefs from the central region of Thailand have been dated as from the seventh to ninth centuries AD. Generally in stucco or terracotta, they are softly modeled and have great charm.

Mon Culture in Buddhist Burma

The kingdom of Pagan, in central Burma, dating from the tenth to the twelfth centuries AD, combined Mon with Pyu and Burmese cultures. The Mon heartland was some 500 kilometers (300 miles) south of Pagan. Many early Mon cities there, such as Thaton and Pegu, have been occupied for more than a thousand years, and dating is difficult, for sacred sites have remained consecrated places. Tantalizing links exist between Thaton and Mon sites in Thailand. A Thai chronicle states that in the eleventh century AD, Mon people migrated to Thaton to escape cholera in their town of Lamphun. At Thaton, they are said to have established Buddhism, displacing Hinduism. Several *sema* stones of that period are still in the Kalyani Sima Pagoda in Thaton. Like the *sema* from northeastern Thailand, they bear scenes from the Buddha's former lives.

From Thaton, the Mon heritage reached Pagan, on the central reaches of the Irrawaddy River. There, the supreme achievement of Buddhist art is found. In Pali, the sacred language of the Theravada ("Way of the Elders") Buddhists, Pagan was "Arimaddanapura", "City of the Enemy Crushers"; the Mons called it "Tattadesa", "Parched

TETTONI, CASSIO, & ASSOC./PHOTOBANK

Many features of this Buddha are typical of Dvaravati images: the downcast eyes, thick lips, large hair-curls, and joined eyebrows. This is a detail of a limestone image, 1.5 meters (4 feet, 10 inches) tall, now in the Bangkok National Museum, in Thailand.

MICHAEL FREEMAN

⚜ The massive Dhammayangyi temple, at Pagan, in central Burma, dates from the twelfth century AD. The graceful tiers of the upper terraces balance the horizontal and vertical elements of the structure.

↪ *Opposite page*: A detail of a mural painting in the Myinkaba Kubyauk-gyi temple, at Pagan, in central Burma, dated to the early twelfth century AD. This guardian figure of a Bodhisattva (savior) protects the entry to the temple. The style is quite different from the *jataka* mural paintings further inside the temple.

Country". Within the region, remains of nearly 5,000 stupas and temples cover an area of about 40 square kilometers (16 square miles). The foundation of Pagan as a cluster of villages is traditionally attributed to the Pyu king Thamudrit. The present moated and walled city was established much later, in AD 849; the kingdom lasted only until AD 1287, when it was sacked by the Mongols.

In AD 1057, King Anawrahta of Pagan invaded Thaton in search of sacred scriptures to purify the religion of Pagan, then said to be in the hands of the Ari, Mahayana Buddhists who worshiped snakes. Thaton also gave access to the sea, vital for trade and contact with Theravadan communities in Sri Lanka. Anawrahta returned to Pagan with 30 elephant-loads of the Tripitaka ("the Three Baskets"), the sacred writings of Theravada Buddhism.

The extent of Mon influence at Pagan is uncertain. Many depictions of *jataka* tales on the temples are bas-reliefs, generally glazed terracotta plaques. These are similar to the bas-reliefs of the Dvaravati Mon. Below each scene, a phrase identifies the life of the Buddha that is pictured. At the earlier temples, these phrases are in Old Mon, and these, according to some, are the only elements at Pagan that are proper to Mon culture. Other authorities describe the temples, single-story and dimly lit, as Mon.

The use of ethnic and linguistic labels for kingdoms and styles makes identification of Pagan's artistic elements difficult. A similar problem surrounds Dvaravati, where the wide distribution of similarly carved Buddhas has led to the conclusion that the artistic spread defined a Buddhist kingdom. At Pagan, the capture of Buddhist scriptures from Thaton resulted in their known dissemination, and analysis has seized upon this to locate elements that may be labeled Mon. The confusion increases when many of the elements called "Mon" in Thailand are called "Pyu" in Burma.

Pyu Culture in Burma

Three major Pyu urban sites are Beikthano (Vishnu City), Srikshetra (Thayekhittaya, near Prome), and Halin (near Shwebo), ranging from about the first to the ninth centuries AD. The Pyu people came from the same Tibeto-Burman group as the Burmese; earlier immigrants than the Burmese, they gradually merged with them. Many Pyu cities were deserted long ago, and have thus preserved some of the earliest Burmese Buddhist remains. Like the Mon, Pyu culture was a crucial model for much classical Pagan architecture.

Buddhist remains at Beikthano include a brick monastery close to two dome-like structures. The building rests on a plinth, measuring 35 meters by

12.5 meters (115 feet by 40 feet); its eight small cells are laid out similarly to contemporary monasteries in South India. The remains at Srikshetra are more complete, including bulbous domes and hollow temples thought to have been prototypes for structures at Pagan. The brick dome of the Bawbawgyi Pagoda, outside the city walls of Srikshetra, rises some 45 meters (150 feet).

The brick wall of Srikshetra is said to have been drawn by Sakra, lord of the devas (gods), using a rope pulled by a serpent, or *naga*. Although the *naga* sheltered the Buddha after his enlightenment, it is rarely seen in the later iconography of Buddhist Burma. One reason may be King Anawrahta's elimination, in the eleventh century AD, of the Ari sect's *naga* worship from Pagan's Buddhist symbolism.

The finds from Srikshetra are primarily Theravadan, but several Mahayanist figures have been recovered, as well as images of Vishnu. The blending of Hindu and Buddhist styles endured at Pagan, and is particularly apparent in the mural paintings.

Technical harmony in royal and religious architecture was achieved at Pagan by the use of brick, stucco, and wood. Stone inscriptions there recount that royal devotees donated palaces for religious use. The combination of the royal and the religious dates back to the historical Gautama Buddha, in the sixth century BC. Born into a royal family, Gautama married but then renounced his princely life. The future incarnation, the Buddha-to-be, can be seen at Pagan in a series of plaques on the Ananda temple, built in AD 1090, where he sits at ease in front of one of the pavilions with roofs of five, seven, and nine tiers.

The Burmese Pyatthat

The tiered roof is known in Burma as a *pyatthat*, from the Sanskrit *prasada*. The word originally referred to any lofty palatial building. The *prasada*, in a Hindu context, is seen in the towering spires of Angkor, in Cambodia; in Burma, it came to denote the multiple roofs of religious or royal buildings. *Pyatthats* were originally constructed in wood, and in Burma, this continued over centuries. Graceful wooden *pyatthats* crown the many entrances of the nineteenth-century AD palace at Mandalay, the last of the Burmese royal capitals before British colonial rule began in 1885.

The wooden *pyatthats* are long gone, but their translation into brick is widely visible in Pagan's architecture. Receding roofs grace the city's temples, from the eleventh-century AD Ananda to later structures, such as the Thatbyinnyu. Another variation crowns the library built by King Anawrahta to house the Buddhist scriptures, the Pitakat-taik; a result of restorations by later Burmese kings, it is further evidence of the continuity of the form. Finally, the tiered roofs of the *pyatthat* appear as decorative window architraves—for example, at the twelfth-century AD Myinkaba Kubyauk-gyi.

Further evidence of combined religious and royal architecture may soon come to light as a result of current excavations at the presumed site of King Kyanzittha's (AD 1084 to AD 1113) palace. An inscription found near the city gates describes the palace as a *pancaprasada*, or "five-fold pavilion"— a central building surrounded by four corner structures. The massive *prasada*, presumably, was once crowned with wooden *pyatthat*.

The Buhpaya temple, at Pagan, has been rebuilt many times, most recently after an earthquake in 1975. Although the present structure is new, its general form dates from about the ninth century AD.

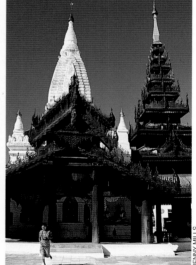

Four "perfume chambers", or *gandhakuti*, are found on the four sides of the Shwezigon stupa, at Pagan. In the background, the tower, or *sikhara*, can be seen. The tiered roof of the rest house in front displays the fine woodworking typical of the Burmese *pyatthat*.

↩ The twelfth-century AD temple of Angkor Wat, in Cambodia, seen from the summit of the nearby hill of Phnom Bakheng.

Cultural Influences at Angkor

Pagan and Angkor have many common architectural elements, including the royal and religious use of the multitiered roof. But although wooden forms certainly existed, all the surviving structures at Angkor are in stone, and for the most part, they crown Hindu temples. The towering roofs are commonly called *prasats*, again from Sanskrit *prasada*.

Angkor was founded north of the "great lake", Tonle Sap, in AD 802, when a Hindu priest consecrated the local ruler King Jayavarman II as "victorious protector". Jayavarman became the first *devaraja*, "god who is king", of Angkor. A settlement already existed, and the natural ecology provided an ideal environment for wet-rice agriculture, the economic basis of the Angkorean empire.

Other kingdoms existed in the region before Angkor, and the Mon Dvaravati certainly played a cultural role in them, but distinguishing Mon elements in Khmer art has proved difficult. For example, of several bronzes cast in the same workshop, one is a Theravadan image considered to be in Mon Dvaravati style, whereas the other is a Mahayana piece thought to be early Angkorean Khmer. They originate from Buri Ram, in northeastern Thailand. Inscriptions indicate this may have been a Buddhist kingdom known as Sri Canasa about the ninth century AD.

Chinese Tribute Missions

The names given by the Chinese to tribute missions from Southeast Asia refer to many small realms in southern Vietnam, Cambodia, and northeastern Thailand early in the first 1,000 years AD. One of these, Funan, was in present-day South Vietnam, on the eastern shore of the Gulf of Thailand; another, Chenla, was probably in northern Cambodia and northeastern Thailand. Some scholars suggest Funan

♀ The enormous moat that surrounds the temple of Angkor Wat symbolizes the cosmic ocean surrounding the sacred temple mountain. The five peaks of the shrine can be seen in the distance, across the 200 meter (650 foot) wide expanse of the moat.

is a Chinese transcription of the Khmer word for mountain, and that the rulers of Funan were "kings of the mountain". Funan's heyday, about the first four centuries AD, appears to precede that of Chenla, from about AD 500 to AD 800.

During the period, China received tribute from all the Southeast Asian kingdoms, and Chinese Buddhist scholars traveled there. In the seventh and eighth centuries AD, particularly, there was considerable Chinese trade along the route to India. Abundant evidence has come from excavations at Oc-eo. Foreign finds were mostly small, highly portable objects, including Indian and Roman medallions, coins, seals, and jewelry.

Chenla was an inland kingdom, the direct predecessor of Angkor, and undoubtedly established many of Angkor's agricultural practices. The irregular moated sites of northeastern Thailand and northern Cambodia exemplify the land and water management that exploited the terrain.

Champa, in Vietnam, was also important in the history of Angkor. Remains at the temple complex of Mison, central Vietnam, date from AD 600 to AD 900, and at Dong Duang is a large Cham Buddhist complex, Quang nam. After the Vietnamese takeover of the north at the end of the tenth century AD, the Cham moved their capital south to Vijaya, in the province of Binh Dinh.

MICHAEL FREEMAN

♠ A detail of a window of the Myinkaba Kubyauk-gyi temple, at Pagan, showing a tiered *pyatthat* roof in relief.

The Khmer Temple: Angkor Wat

The cultures of all the region's kingdoms are blended in the art and architecture of Angkor. Few pre-Angkorean remains are earlier than AD 802, but the prototype of Angkor's temple may be seen at Sambor Prei Kuk, the seventh-century AD capital of Isanavarman I of Chenla. The stone temples were simple cells crowned with a multitiered tower, the *prasat*—often likened to a lotus bud or the summit of a mountain. Interior space gave room only for the priest and an image of the god.

Although Khmer temples of Angkor became highly elaborate, the small interior remained constant. What developed in the ninth to thirteenth centuries AD was the cosmological aspect. The enclosure symbolized the Hindu cosmos, and the temple itself stood for the five peaks of Mount Meru, abode of the gods. The wall and surrounding moat recalled the six concentric rings of land and seven oceans that circled the mountain, the pivot of the world.

The culminating expression of these elements came in Angkor Wat, built by King Suryavarman II (AD 1113 to AD 1150). Although most Khmer Hindu temples are dedicated to Siva, the king chose Vishnu; most Khmer temples face east, but Angkor Wat faces west, Vishnu's direction. The temple was not completed until after Suryavarman's death, perhaps serving as his tomb. The reliefs on the walls of Angkor Wat read counterclockwise, which is often taken to mean that the temple is a tomb.

Architecturally, Angkor Wat is considered the most harmonious of all the Khmer temples. The Khmer did not develop vaulting, which allowed the Burmese at Pagan to erect their towering temples, and this lack meant that large areas could not be roofed. But the Khmers wanted multiple chapels with tiered roofs, and joined tower units with galleries around the central spire of Mount Meru. Overlapping roofs on the galleries and the spire create a sense of scale; the stone roofs are carved to resemble tiles. The three terraces of the temple rise successively: the first is 3.2 meters (11 feet); the next, 6.4 meters (21 feet); and the third, 12.8 meters (42 feet). These vertical units are balanced by the massive horizontal enclosure; the moat is 4 kilometers (2 ½ miles) in circumference. Despite the gargantuan scale, the interior cell is only 4.6 meters by 4.7 meters (15 feet by 16 feet). The power of the temple lies not in its interior space, but in its re-creation of the universe in microcosm.

Hindu cosmology and architecture blended with pre-existing Khmer beliefs. Local ancestral and fertility gods were easily admitted into the new pantheon. Royal power was certainly augmented by the temples, but for the people, they were an expression of long-held beliefs.

♠ The exquisite temple of Banteay Srei, in Cambodia, was built in the tenth century AD. With its diminutive proportions and detailed carvings in deep-pink sandstone, the temple represents a unique moment in Khmer art.

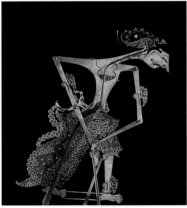

⊕ The overall plan of the ninth-century AD monument of Borobudur, in Java, is best seen from the air: the basement or "hidden foot", the square terraces, and the upper, rounded—but not quite circular—terraces.

⊕ The *wayang*, or shadow puppets, of central Java are used in a wide variety of performances, and continue to be popular today. Although the puppets are highly decorated, lights behind them are used to cast their images upon a screen: it is these shadows that the audience sees during the play.

↪ One of the tiered structures of the tenth-century AD Hindu temple of Prambanan, in Java, known locally as Lara Jonggrang.

Java and Bali

The date and manner in which Hinduism and Buddhism arrived in Indonesia remain uncertain. From the seventh to the thirteenth centuries AD, Java was the center of monumental architecture; as on the mainland, this was a unique adaption of Indian elements. The earliest remains are found on the isolated, volcanic Dieng Plateau. The small shrines there, dedicated to the Hindu god Siva, are called *candi* in Indonesian; the word broadly means any Indianized stone structure with a tower of receding tiers.

The major Buddhist and Hindu remains of Java—Borobudur and Prambanan—are east of the Dieng Plateau, at the foot of the mountain chain forming the island's central spine. Borobudur, the master work of the Mahayana Buddhist Sailendra dynasty, is dated to the ninth century AD. During reconstruction of the temple in the 1970s to 1980s, much was learned about its evolution. The temple may have begun as a Hindu stepped pyramid, similar to temples at Angkor, but doctrinal changes during its construction have resulted in one of Southeast Asia's most complex monuments. (See the feature *Interpretations of Borobudur: Mountain, Stupa, or Mandala?*)

Near Borobudur is Prambanan, known locally as Lara Jonggrang. It is Hindu rather than Buddhist, and was completed later than Borobudur, about AD 900. Whereas Borobudur's cosmic mountain is softly rounded, here the central tower, dedicated to Siva, is more than 40 meters (130 feet) high. It is flanked by buildings dedicated to Brahma and Vishnu, and remains of more than 200 small *candi* surround the central group. The carving on the temple is among the most animated of the classical Javanese period.

Java's most important later monuments are on the eastern end of the island; none of these is on the scale of Borobudur or Prambanan. Developments in sculpture and architecture are reflected today in the arts of the island of Bali, just off the east coast of Java. The naturalistic contours of central Javanese figures became sinuous and elongated, emphasizing silhouettes rather than volumes, in the manner of the popular *wayang* puppet figures. The other major development was in temple plinths and roofs, which became highly elaborated and enlarged.

By the sixteenth century AD, Islam had replaced Hinduism and Buddhism in Java, and ultimately became the religion of all Indonesia except Bali. Bali is thought to have had contact with the central Javanese kingdoms of the eighth to tenth centuries AD, and after the court moved to East Java in the tenth century, links increased. In the fourteenth century, Bali was colonized. When Java became Muslim, Javanese nobles are thought to have fled to Bali, and indigenous ancestor cults blended there with Hinduism, creating *Agama Hindu Dharma* or "Religion of the Hindu doctrine". This unique religion of Bali has continued until today.

Foremost among the symbols of Balinese architecture is the tiered roof, or *meru*. As elsewhere, the tiers are uneven in number; they may honor gods or ancestors within the complex hierarchy of Balinese temples. The largest of these is the great "Mother Temple" of Besakih, on the slopes of Mount Agung—the high mountain that is the center of the Balinese system of orientation. The tiered *meru* are found even in the smallest shrines, living testimony of a 2,000-year-old tradition of religious blending in the far-flung and varied countries of Southeast Asia.

Elizabeth H. Moore

SOUTHEAST ASIAN MEGALITHS

Ian C. Glover

Megaliths are among the most imposing prehistoric structures. Built from massive, largely unshaped stones by people in different parts of the world—who had few or no links with each other—megaliths are particularly common in Atlantic Europe, around the Mediterranean basin, in northern Africa, peninsular India, Indonesia, Melanesia, Korea, Japan, and in parts of South America.

Originally, it was believed that all megaliths were historically related, having been erected by a "megalithic people" who took the building tradition to other parts of the world in their search for metal ores. This simplistic view of megaliths has been discarded, although megaliths found in adjacent regions are sometimes historically related. For example, the great megalithic Iron Age stone circles and graves of peninsular India may be culturally linked with those of Sumatra and Java, in Indonesia.

In the islands of Southeast Asia, megaliths are found principally in south central Sumatra; Java; on the Lesser Sunda Islands east to Timor; in Sarawak and Sabah, in Borneo; in the central highlands of Sulawesi; and in Mindanao, in the southern Philippines. On the mainland, megaliths occur in peninsular Malaya and in the Annamite Mountains of Vietnam; and north to the Plain of Jars, in central Laos. In Thailand and Burma, only one or two megalithic structures have been reported.

To date, no megalith in Southeast Asia has been definitely shown to predate the Iron Age, although a date of about 1000 BC has been claimed for the megalithic structures at Cipari, Java. Appearing about 700 BC, the great megalithic grave structures in South India are the most obvious source of inspiration for megaliths and burial traditions in Southeast Asia, particularly in Sumatra and Java: many details of the design and structure are similar.

Sumatra and Java have the most megaliths and the greatest range.

☝ Megalithic cist (slab) graves from the Pasemah Plateau, in Sumatra.
PETER BELLWOOD/AUSTRALIAN NATIONAL UNIVERSITY

BELINDA SYME

🌱 These huge stone jars were found at the site of Ban Xieng Di, in Xieng Khouang province, Laos, near the better-known site of Ban Ang, also known as the Plain of Jars.

☞ A decorated stone in the late "megalithic" tradition, in honor of the women of the village of Botohosi, in the Nias Islands, off the west coast of Sumatra, Indonesia.

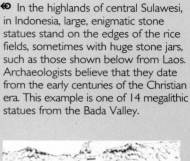

🔗 In the highlands of central Sulawesi, in Indonesia, large, enigmatic stone statues stand on the edges of the rice fields, sometimes with huge stone jars, such as those shown below from Laos. Archaeologists believe that they date from the early centuries of the Christian era. This example is one of 14 megalithic statues from the Bada Valley.

W. MARSCHALL/UNIVERSITÄT BERN

VÉRONIQUE DAUGE/UNESCO, CAMBODIA

They include dolmens (capped standing stones), menhirs (standing stones), stone cist (slab) graves, stone sarcophagi, troughs, mortars, cairns, stone seats, terraced structures, and large statues. In peninsular Malaya, menhirs are most commonly found (singly and aligned in groups), along with cist graves. In Borneo, dolmens as well as menhirs and cist graves predominate. In central Sulawesi, some huge stone urns have been discovered that are remarkably similar to those found in the Plain of Jars, Laos, as well as stone statues and circles. In the Lesser Sunda Islands, stone assembly places, tables, statues, and dolmens are particularly common, some having been built in very recent times.

There have been few technically competent archaeological investigations of Southeast Asian megaliths. Although no single structure has been unequivocally dated, artifacts found with the megaliths suggest that some of them may have been built in the last five centuries BC. For example, iron tools, semi-precious stones, and glass beads were found in cist graves in Java and Sumatra; and glass, iron, bronze, and, occasionally, gold ornaments were found in stone sarcophagi in Java and Bali. Carvings of helmeted warriors, some riding elephants and carrying Dongson-style bronze drums, were found at Batu Gajah (Elephant Rock) and Airpurah, in South Sumatra.

These finds provide evidence of wide-ranging cultural connections: with India in the case of glass and stone jewelry; and with northern Vietnam or South China in the case of the bronze drums.

Recently, Indonesian prehistorians have shown a renewed interest in excavating ancient megalithic sites, and in documenting contemporary megalithic traditions. The most notable recent find has been a series of splendid wall paintings inside cist graves in South Sumatra. These paintings of a tiger, a buffalo, and people carrying Dongson-style drums were discovered in 1990, and are clearly related to those reported in a 1932 study in South Sumatra.

INTERPRETATIONS OF BOROBUDUR: MOUNTAIN, STUPA, OR MANDALA?

ELIZABETH H. MOORE

BOROBUDUR IS a unique Buddhist temple that rises serenely above the Kedu Plain, on the island of Java, in Indonesia. Dated to between about AD 835 and AD 860, it is thought to have been built by the obscure Sailendra dynasty. This area favored settlement, and labor must have been plentiful, for more than a million blocks of stone were cut nearby and transported to the site.

The basement of Borobudur is carved with 160 relief panels. Each panel is 2 meters (6 feet, 6 inches) wide and more than half a meter (1 foot, 8 inches) high. Their motifs are taken from Buddhist ethical texts. During construction, the monument threatened to collapse. The basement was later shored up with a second layer of stone, a wide terrace measuring 113 meters (370 feet) on each side. This covered the reliefs, and even today, only a few, specially uncovered, are exposed for viewing.

From the basement, five square terraces rise in balustraded galleries, representing the world of form above the world of desire. The inner and outer walls at each level are covered with beautifully carved panels, illustrating the path of enlightenment.

The first gallery is 360 meters (1,180 feet) in perimeter; above it, the others progressively diminish in size. The panels are 1 to 2 meters (3 feet, 3 inches to 6 feet, 6 inches) wide by 0.5 to 1 meter (1 foot, 8 inches to 3 feet, 3 inches) high.

Three circular terraces surmount the squares. These are open and simple, representing the realm of formlessness. Seventy-two stone stupas, 3.5 to 3.75 meters (11 feet, 6 inches to 12 feet, 4 inches) high, stand here, all carved in open lattices. The perforations on the first two circles are diamond-shaped, a form said to express change and movement. On the last terrace, they are square, expressing calm stillness. Each stupa shelters a Buddha, which becomes apparent only as the monument is ascended. From a distance, the stupas appear solid.

The temple is crowned with an enormous stupa, some 16 meters (52 feet) in diameter, containing an unfinished Buddha. Some scholars see the Buddha's incomplete state as symbolic of his formlessness;

TETTONI, CASSIO, & ASSOC./PHOTOBANK

GEORG GERSTER

⌖ The wide, lower terrace of Borobudur represents the earthly realm of desire. The reliefs of the square terraces represent the world of form. No reliefs are seen in the formless world of the upper, rounded terraces—only the many images of the Buddha.

On each of the four sides of Borobudur, the images of the Buddha display the same symbolic gesture, or "mudra". In combination with the Buddhas on the uppermost level, these represent the five celestial Buddhas. They were originally set in niches, like those seen in the upper row and in the photograph on the right.

An image of the Buddha on one of the middle terraces. In the center of the niche's arch can be seen the lion-like face of the mythical demon creature known as the *kala,* or *kirtimukha* ("face of glory"), his fearsome expression repelling all evil.

DAVID NICHOLAS GREEN/THE PHOTO LIBRARY, SYDNEY

others take the view that the original statue was stolen and the incomplete one is a replacement.

Borobudur is thought to have served a variety of purposes, being at once a visualization of doctrine for the initiate; a mandala, a design symbolizing the universe and used in meditation; and a sacred and ordered world, a center of ritual activity.

A mandala requires perfect placement of all its elements. The form most commonly identified with Borobudur is the Diamond World mandala, often associated with the Tantric Buddhism practiced in Tibet and Nepal. This interpretation depends largely on the arrangement of the smaller stupas, and the gestures of the Bodhisattva (Buddhist savior) images, but the lack of complete evidence leaves it open to question.

It is more convincing to see Borobudur as a symbolic stupa or mountain. Seen as a stupa, Borobudur represents a continuation of local custom. Stupas were originally earthen mounds topped by pillars of wood. The ashes of the Buddha were later buried under eight such stupas, built in eight of the places important in his life. As a result, the stupa has come to signify any structure that contains relics. It is also credible to interpret Borobudur as a symbolic mountain. The mountain as a sacred place occurs throughout Southeast Asian religious architecture. It may be an expression of Hinduism or Buddhism, or apply to objects of local veneration. The construction of Borobudur on a natural hill, and its blending with the surrounding landscape, confirm this.

Although the precise significance of Borobudur may never be known, some understanding of it comes from seeing the temple itself as the doctrine: Borobudur combines elements of the mountain, the mandala, and the stupa. It is these that comprise the "text".

TETTONI, CASSIO, & ASSOC./PHOTOBANK

TETTONI, CASSIO, & ASSOC./PHOTOBANK

This detail from the side of the panel at left shows three courtiers, each with a slightly different, elaborate coiffeur. The wealth of detail on the reliefs of Borobudur provides an excellent source of information about the customs of Java in the ninth century AD. The soft, naturalistic style of carving is unique to Borobudur. The faces are somewhat rounded, the eyes downcast, and the lips form a slight and gentle smile.

The majority of the relief panels of Borobudur portray episodes from the *Gandhavyuha,* an epic tale of the young Prince Sudhana's search for enlightenment. In this detail, the figure of the prince is sheltered by a royal umbrella. His elaborate headdress also sets him apart from the other figures.

LEO MEIER/AUSTRALIAN PICTURE LIBRARY

DYNASTIES IN CHINA

2 0 0 0 B C – A D 2 2 0

From Early States to Nationhood

CHO-YUN HSU

THE XIA "DYNASTY" is regarded in Chinese legend as the first in a long series of "royal dynasties". In ancient times, the Xia, the Shang and the Zhou were called the Three Dynasties. Together, they are considered to be the fountainhead of Chinese culture known from later history. In modern archaeology, the Xia period is located at the junction of the Late Neolithic period and the Early Bronze Age, about the end of the third millennium BC. Until now, the Xia have not been definitely identified among the numerous Neolithic cultures of the middle reaches of the Yellow River. Since the Xia period is mentioned in the ancient classics so frequently and so consistently, however, it is generally assumed that the Xia people lived along the middle and lower reaches of the Yellow River, especially on the northern bank. This area is a part of the great plain and plateau formed by a thick loess—a fine-grained, fertile soil deposited by wind and water. In this vast stretch of the yellow-earth plain, Neolithic people settled in farming villages. Hundreds of these sites have been excavated, yielding such items as pottery, stone artifacts, and remnants of dwellings and burials.

◄ Fields of crops, with the Chola Mountains, in western Sichuan province, in the background. Numerous Late Neolithic cultures existed in the Sichuan basin, west of the yellow-earth plain.

◊ This bronze wine vessel (*jue*), excavated at Erlitou, in Henan province, was cast in the Yellow River basin in the first half of the second millennium BC for members of a powerful family. Such vessels were used in sacrificial rituals that paid homage to the ancestors, and were then buried with a family member.
METROPOLITAN MUSEUM OF ART

The Yellow River winds through a heavily eroded desert landmark in Ningxia region, in northern China.

A ritual bronze axe (*yue*) dating from the middle Shang period. It was found at Panlongcheng, in Hubei province, far south of the dynastic capital, and was used in the burial ceremony as a beheading instrument.

METROPOLITAN MUSEUM OF ART

CHINA TOURISM PHOTO LIBRARY

The Xia culture, represented in archaeology by the Erlitou culture in Henan province, was only one of the Late Neolithic cultures that spread into the Yellow River floodplain. Beyond the yellow-earth plain, there were other cultures in the coastal area of the east, the Yangtze Valley and the Han River valley in the south, and the Sichuan basin in the west. Further afield were the Neolithic cultures in Manchuria—in the northeast highland regions below the steppe land in the north—and in the vast territory of mountainous regions in the far south and the southwest.

These cultures shared some features with the floodplain cultures, and the speed of cultural evolution was generally consistent across all cultures. Thus, it is quite possible that in a number of regions of China at that time, clusters of villages were being organized into states. However, the best records, both legendary and archaeological, of such organization are found in the middle and lower valleys of the Yellow River. Thus, from what we know, the Xia probably formed the earliest state in China.

The Formation of the First State under the Xia

According to legend, the pre-Xia male leaders were the predominant power and were regarded as "sage-kings" of the ancient "royal court", each one being chosen by his predecessor to succeed to the throne through merit. Once the new king had been installed, his predecessor voluntarily abdicated. Although there are vague references to power struggles among these sage-kings, detailed information is too meager for any conclusion to be drawn about the precise nature of this leadership. However, it is thought that a loose federation of tribes or "nations" was formed by passing the leadership from one individual to another, or from the chiefs of one participating group to those of another.

Legendary sources tell us that the Xia people changed this process. A cultural hero named Yu restored the course of the Yellow River, which had flooded, and was thus chosen to succeed to the throne of the sage-king Shun. Yu then successfully organized a rather more solid confederation of numerous "states". It is said that as many as 800 lords attended great assemblies periodically convened by Yu in various places. Yu's authority was so unchallenged that he could (and did) depose some of these lords, and even occasionally executed the most unruly ones. After Yu died, the successor he had chosen failed to command the lords' support, and the people preferred to make Yu's son the successor to the throne. This was the first "royal dynasty", so it is said, whose ruling house was made up of several generations of father–son successions.

In the case of the Xia, there was, according to legend, a change from the loose federation of participating groups to a state possessing stable and institutionalized authority. The precise extent of Xia territory, however, remains uncertain. Later traditional Chinese history projected a large, unified Chinese empire from the Xia state, and referred to the Xia as overlord of at least the entire northern part of China proper. Modern historical research and archaeology, on the other hand, place the Xia on a much more modest scale, located in the present-day provinces of southern Shanxi and western Henan.

The Xia's heyday would have been from about the end of the third millennium BC to the middle of the second millennium BC. Archaeological research has uncovered bronze tools and artifacts in the Erlitou culture sites in Henan province. Although tools and implements made of bone and shell were more commonly found than bronze pieces, the bronze culture had definitely emerged. The Erlitou culture sites have also yielded remains of large buildings on platformed foundations, and a number of such sites were partly walled in. This indicates that there was some form of urban center with public buildings, which is consistent with the existence of a state.

Cultural Advancement in the Shang Period: 1600 BC to 1100 BC

The Shang, who were part of the Xia federation of ancient "states", were originally located on the lower yellow-earth plain, east of the Xia. A large, dense distribution of Neolithic villages indicates that this area had a substantial population in the Late Neolithic period. The Shang probably founded a state not much later than the Xia,

An oracle bone from the Shang dynasty. Bones of oxen and sheep were used to communicate with the spirits of the ancestors. After a question was asked of the spirits, a hot rod was placed onto the surface of the bone and cracks appeared. These signs were "read" by the ritual leader as the answer from the gods.
BRITISH MUSEUM/ THE BRIDGEMAN ART LIBRARY

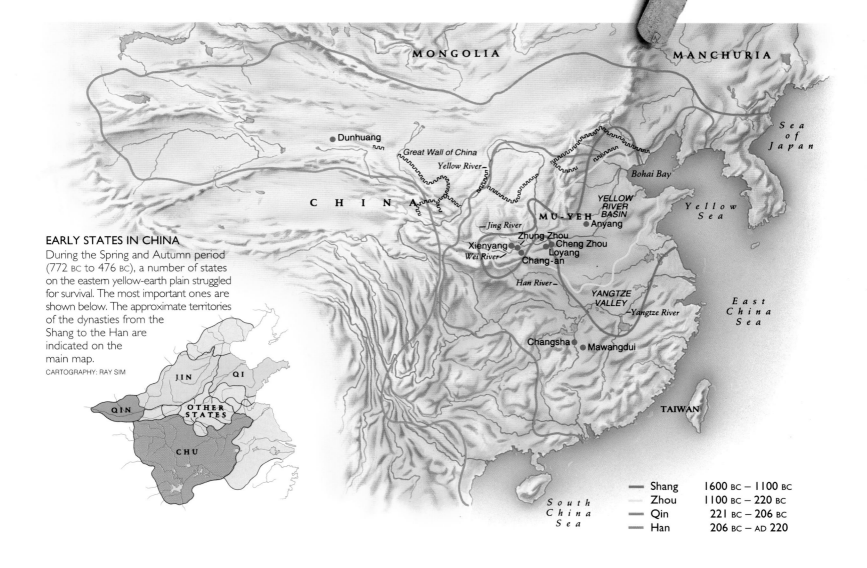

EARLY STATES IN CHINA

During the Spring and Autumn period (772 BC to 476 BC), a number of states on the eastern yellow-earth plain struggled for survival. The most important ones are shown below. The approximate territories of the dynasties from the Shang to the Han are indicated on the main map.
CARTOGRAPHY: RAY SIM

	Shang	1600 BC – 1100 BC
	Zhou	1100 BC – 220 BC
	Qin	221 BC – 206 BC
	Han	206 BC – AD 220

DYNASTIC CHINA: 2500 BC – AD 200

	STATE SOCIETY	INTELLECTUAL ACTIVITIES	CULTURE AND TECHNOLOGY
200	Three kingdoms Development of the South Invasion of foreign tribes	Taoist religion Spread of Buddhism	Advancement of sciences
AD 1	Eastern Han	Imperial Academy established Confucianism challenged Buddhism introduced	Invention of paper
200	Western Han Unified empire Consolidation of China Qin unification	Confucianism as orthodoxy	Civil examinations Silk Road
250	Bureaucratic government Imperial despotism		Great Wall built Highway network constructed
500	Warring States period Reorganization of states	Major schools of thought develop	Rapid social changes: commercialization and urbanization; development of free private land tenure; metal coins appear
800	Eastern Zhou Spring and Autumn period Multistate system	Confucianism Concept of mandate of heaven	Technological improvements in agriculture, irrigation, and manufacturing Use of iron
1000	Feudalism Western Zhou		
1500	Fully developed state Shang		Development of metallurgy Oracle-bone inscriptions Writing system appears
2000	Xia Formation of state		Bronze culture War chariot appears
BC 2500			Late Neolithic cultures

◄● A jade and bronze halberd (*ge*) from the mid-second millennium BC, excavated in 1974 at Panlongchen, in Hubei province. This type of weapon, cast in bronze, was the most characteristic weapon of the Bronze Age. The blade in this example was delicately carved from a single piece of jade, and was too large and fragile for practical use. It was probably used only as a burial object.
RONALD SHERIDAN/ANCIENT ART & ARCHITECTURE COLLECTION

and had been an important power dominating the eastern plain ever since the Xia established their overlordship.

Since the 1920s, archaeologists have excavated several Shang city sites—including one of the capitals, Anyang—and hundreds of settlements and burial sites. The Shang sites were often located in the river valleys on the floodplain. Thanks to abundant archaeological finds from the Shang period —particularly some especially revealing written records from Anyang—we have much more material on the Shang culture than on the Xia. Not only do these records provide more information about Shang life than is available from conventional historical sources; they also confirm many of the legends about Shang history.

The appearance of a developed writing system, by about the seventeenth century BC, is of great historical significance. The Shang records, called oracle-bone inscriptions, consist of predictions about future events recorded on turtle shells or animal bones. The writing system was a prototype of modern written Chinese. The basic units are characters formed from a combination of ideograms (pictures that depict an object or concept) and phonetic elements. There are about 5,000 such characters in the Shang texts, a large number of which can be transcribed into present-day forms and deciphered. The sentence structure found in the Shang texts resembles that of classical Chinese, and is slightly different from the modern structure.

The oracle-bone inscriptions contain a variety of information about the life of the Shang ruling class, including details of ceremonies, rituals, warfare, administration, weather, disease and medicine, hunting, and routine predictions of fortunes every 10 days.

The Shang Take Power

The Shang took over from the Xia as the leading power on the yellow-earth plain in the second millennium BC. The core area of the Shang's dominance seems to have been in the eastern part of today's Henan province and in the southwest of Hebei province. Until the fifteenth century BC, the Shang capital, for some unknown reason, moved from one place to another four times. Finally, Anyang seems to have been the Shang capital for about two centuries. Anyang was certainly the center of the Shang's activities, even though its function was possibly ceremonial and ritualistic rather than political and military.

The Shang state structure appears to have been more complicated than the Xia model. The Shang ruling house was surnamed Zi, and used as its emblem a character resembling an infant with raised arms. There were several branches on the Zi family tree, all of which used a modified version of the principal ruling house's emblem. Thus, the Shang ruling class probably regarded themselves as members of a hierarchically arranged kinship network, sharing the same ancestry and therefore the same identity. The non-Zi people were perhaps subjects of the Zi groups or may even have been in servitude to them. There were also less important lineages, which bore other surnames, and it seems likely that some of these were associated with the Zi through alliances, marriages, or conquest. The Shang state was, therefore, organized by means of a network of various lineages. This type of social structure is characteristic of a chiefdom, consisting of one dominant tribe and a number of lesser groups.

Apart from the fact that their royal authority had yet to be firmly consolidated, the early history of the Shang is by no means clear. After they had settled at Anyang, the state continued to be governed by a hierarchy of social networks. The king and his court resided in the Great City of Shang (Anyang), while other members of the Zi family—headed by generals, princes, or even queens—were scattered within the kingdom of the Shang. As the Shang expanded the territory under their control, other subordinate groups—known as *hou* states (marquisates)—were formed around the Shang people. These groups would respond to the Shang's call for support in their military campaigns against unfriendly states beyond the *hou* territory. Some of these states may have become the Shang's satellites, while others may have continued to resist Shang dominance. Some would no doubt have alternated between these two responses. The Shang retained their supremacy only by periodic displays of force. Their sphere of influence seems to have extended as far as the present-day Shanxi province in the west, the coastal region around Bohai Bay in the east, and the transitional zone between the steppe land in the north and China proper.

Shang royal authority appears to have evolved gradually towards a strong monarchy. By about 1200 BC, the last king of the Shang had even proclaimed himself to be the human counterpart of a supreme god. The kings—who had once been served by royal relatives and domestic servants—now had a government consisting of departments with separate functions, and the former *hou* states were turned into provinces supervised by personnel dispatched from the royal court.

Shang Social Structure

The Shang possessed a sizeable army of archer-warriors, who rode in war chariots accompanied by foot soldiers armed with halberds. The foot soldiers were recruited in the thousands or five thousands from provinces governed by princes and royal agents. It appears that these soldiers were also the farmers who were the mainstay of the Shang farming population. At the lower end of the social scale were the slaves, most likely captured in war from tribes known to the Shang by such descriptions as "the numerous shepherds" and "the numerous horse-breeders".

METROPOLITAN MUSEUM OF ART

♠ A Shang bronze ritual wine vessel (*jue*) dating from the fifteenth to fourteenth centuries BC, found in Anhui province.

♀ This square bronze wine vessel (*fang lei*) from the Anyang period (about 1300 BC to 1100 BC) was cast for the Shang aristocracy. It is decorated with a large *taotie*, or animal mask, on the center of each side, which may signify the Shang clan.

METROPOLITAN MUSEUM OF ART

⬆ A ritual bronze vessel (*ding*) from the Anyang period. This vessel, which is very typical of the period, was used for storing sacrificial meat.

The arrangement of royal tombs vividly reveals the relative status of the various groups. Around the royal coffin, in the central burial chamber, are women and men who were to be the royal companions in the other world. Along the steps of a long ramp is a line of fully armed warriors in a half-kneeling position. Each royal tomb was built upon tightly pounded earthen foundations in which were buried several hundred beheaded bodies of people who had perhaps been used as slaves to build the mausoleum. The entire mausoleum area is surrounded by burial pits in each of which are 10 soldiers and a sergeant. There are also numerous war chariots buried in the pits with horses. Thus, Shang kings obviously had the power of life and death over their subjects.

Shang State Religion

The Shang's faith was shamanism. The *Wu*—who were seers, medicine men, and sorcerers—and their associates—the diviners (people who told fortunes or predicted the future)—were the

mediums between the supernatural world and the human world. They also served as scribes and clerks, ceremonial dancers, musicians, and even high-ranking officials. Moreover, they were proto-type intellectuals, who could not only write and keep accounts, but who were also archivists and historians. Because the cosmos of shamans is full of spirits of all kinds, the Shang state religion was mainly concerned with offering food and entertainment to male and female ancestors of the ruling house; to deceased great men; and to the deities of the mountains, water, rivers, wind, and stars. Since the ceremonies and rituals were of great significance to Shang life, the archaeological finds excavated at the capital at Anyang reflect these functions, rather than administrative ones.

Material Culture

The sophistication of Shang material culture is quite impressive. The long tradition of Neolithic pottery provided the Shang with the foundation for producing pottery fired in kilns. And it was upon that same foundation that the Shang bronze culture was developed. West Asian bronze culture antedates the Shang bronze culture by at least a thousand years, and it may reasonably be assumed that the ancient peoples of China learned

⬆ A bronze ritual vessel, called the Fu Hao *fang ding*, from a tomb of the Anyang period. The deceased was Fu Hao, a consort of the third king at Anyang. Her name is inscribed inside on the base of the vessel.
METROPOLITAN MUSEUM OF ART

➲ A bronze axe (*yue*) from the late Shang period. This kind of weapon was used for beheading at burial ceremonies.
ART RESOURCE

about making bronze alloy in the vast trans-Asian steppe land in North and central Asia. It was there that the technology of the ancient Chinese bronze industry was later developed. Shang bronze vessels are fine, ritualistic pieces that symbolize the authority of the Shang state. The abundance of bronze weapons, tools, and other artifacts discovered in various Shang sites indicates that the Shang had control of, and created, great wealth.

Shang cultural influences seem to have extended far more widely than Shang political power, to areas as far south as the provinces of Guangxi and Guangdong; and Shang-styled pottery and bronzes have been found as far north as western Manchuria.

To their successors, the Zhou, the Shang bequeathed a solid cultural foundation in northern China and political experience that would consolidate the structure of an effective state.

The Zhou Period: 1100 BC to 220 BC

The Zhou were one of the satellite states in the Shang sphere of influence, although the Zhou people were perhaps originally related to the Xia ethnically and culturally. They may have lived initially in the southwest of present-day Shanxi province, the old home of the Xia. Following a rather winding path of migration, the Zhou seem to have been in contact with peoples in the northern steppe land until they finally settled in the valley of the Jing-Wei River, in present-day Shanxi province. In their new home, they established a close relationship with the Chiang people to the west.

From the Jing-Wei River valley, the Zhou gradually expanded eastwards towards the yellow-earth plain, and came into contact with the Shang. The relationship between the two fluctuated between friendly relations and war. The Shang were a major power, and the Zhou were caught in their network of states. During the last 50 years of Shang domination, however, the Zhou maneuvered to build an alliance of lesser states that half surrounded the Shang in the south and the west. In the meantime, the last kings of the Shang had exhausted their resources by engaging in costly foreign wars and expeditions. Their armies no longer had the morale to fight, and they were finally defeated by the Zhou in a showdown at Mu-yeh to which the Zhou had committed their full military might. Thus did a minor neighbor state succeed in destroying the most powerful state in ancient China.

Having inherited the Shang's network of states, the Zhou organized a new interstate order. Princes of the Zhou royal house and their close allies, particularly leaders of the Chiang, were dispatched to set up garrison states on the eastern plain. An eastern capital, Cheng Zhou, was established in Shang territory. Because of a shortage of labor, the Zhou had to seek the collaboration of the Shang people. Consequently,

a Shang prince continued to rule part of the original Shang kingdom, and the Shang troops who had surrendered to the Zhou were stationed alongside the Zhou forces to guard the garrison states. The Zhou feudalistic network was reinforced by matrimonial ties between Zhou–Chiang feudal lords, Shang leaders, and native leaders of the newly conquered land. Similarly, Zhou children were linked together by a bond of kinship that formed a gigantic Zhou lineage system.

E.T. ARCHIVE

♠ A portrait of the beloved King Wu, the founder of the Western Zhou dynasty. He is represented as a statesman, by his hat, and as a scholar, by his robe, denoting the high esteem in which he was held in the early nineteenth century, when this portrait was painted.

♀ The bronze lid of a ritual wine vessel, from the early Western Zhou dynasty (tenth to eleventh centuries BC). On the surface of this piece is the *taotie*, or animal mask—used here, presumably, to pay homage to the already defeated, but honorable, Shang people.

C.M. DIXON

↞ A bronze ritual vessel called a *you*, from the royal tomb at Anyang. This type of wine bucket appeared in the late Shang dynasty and had disappeared by 900 BC. Its tall and slender form suggests that it dates from about 1100 BC.

GIRAUDON/ART RESOURCE

Kinship Networks and Religion

The Zhou thus forged a dual network of both kinship and feudal ties, which encompassed the vast territory of the Yellow River floodplain and formed a much stronger political bloc than the Shang had ever formed. It was the Zhou's open-mindedness, evidenced by a willingness to accept and share power with non-Zhou leaders—even those of their former enemies—that allowed such a network to function. The garrison states became vassal states, and in a typical one, there were often three ethnic and cultural groups—the Zhou nobility, the Shang elites, and the leaders of the people subjugated by the Zhou—all of whom were bound to each other by a network of matrimonial and kinship ties. The Zhou king, with his supremacy as patriarch of the Zhou kinship network and overlord of the feudal pyramid, occupied a pivotal position.

In the Zhou state religion, with its worship of ancestors and a multitude of natural forces, the heavenly god was regarded as the supreme deity. The Zhou believed that they had received the heavenly mandate to rule the world "under heaven", and that this mandate was bestowed upon them—and upon them alone—because they were worthy, the Shang leaders having lost the mandate through their failure to lead a decent life and to behave morally. This was the first time in Chinese history that a supreme god was believed to have passed judgment on human conduct explicitly in accordance with a moral criterion. The Zhou concept of a moral god was a major departure from the notion of a tribal god, and represents a breakthrough that paved the way for the development of the concept of universal moral standards. This new consciousness of a moral god probably provided the Zhou with the legitimacy necessary for developing a claim for universalism; while the coexistence of various groups within the Zhou feudal network helped to create the common identity that was the foundation of a Chinese nation.

The Zhou Are Weakened

In the reigns of at least the first three kings, further feudalization consolidated the Zhou system, and the Zhou continued to expand towards the Yangtze Valley. Their confrontations with northern neighbors along the steppe land, however, were far from successful. Finally, the kingdom of the Zhou, which was directly exposed to the pressure of tribes in the north and the northwest, was lost to the mostly peaceful penetration of non-Zhou peoples, who for several generations had migrated into the core royal domain. The Zhou were weakened not only by defeat in military campaigns against the northern tribes, but also by the heavy burden of maintaining a large defense force recruited from the eastern vassal states, and by the depletion of resources caused by the royal court's continuous parceling out of land to create new vassal states for royal relatives. In 773 BC, the last Zhou king was killed by a coalition of Zhou rebels and non-Zhou tribes within the royal domain. However, the so-called Zhou period proper lasted until 220 BC.

The crown prince of the Zhou fled to Cheng Zhou, the eastern capital, where a new court was established. However, the Eastern Zhou—so named to distinguish them from the court that had reigned in the old royal capital in the west, Zhung Zhou—were never able to hold the original Zhou system together. The Zhou elements of the vassal states, having been localized to their assigned land for centuries, had their own interests to look after. From then on, they merely accorded the Eastern Zhou court nominal recognition of its royal status, while they strove to shape a new multistate system. The centuries that witnessed such a transition are known as the Spring and Autumn period (from 772 BC to 476 BC)—which is named after a chronicle of the early period of the Eastern Zhou—and the Warring States period (from 475 BC to 220 BC)—collectively known as the Eastern Zhou period.

The Spring and Autumn Period

During the Spring and Autumn period, the former vassal states on the eastern yellow-earth plain struggled for survival. Often one state established dominance over the others. The pretext for doing so was to enable the Eastern Zhou states to form an alliance to ward off the threat from the non-Zhou peoples, among whom the most noteworthy was a southern state, Chu, which had developed in the Yangtze Valley during the early Spring and Autumn period. The struggles for supremacy among the states first took place in the central part of the eastern yellow-earth plain. No sooner had the central states exhausted each other, than neighboring states that had much land in which to expand entered the fray. The number of contending states was reduced to no more than four or five major ones, plus a dozen or so minor ones. The most important states were Jin in the north and the central area; Qi on the east coast; Chu in the south—that is, the Yangtze Valley—and Qin in the west, the former Zhou western domain. Cultural exchanges blurred the differences between the Zhou and the non-Zhou: the Chu and Qin became part of the world of Zhou China, while Jin and Qi substantially absorbed non-Zhou elements in the north and east respectively.

◄● *Opposite page:* A bronze ritual vessel called the Qi Hou *yu*, from the Eastern Zhou period (sixth century BC). This large food container bears an inscription inside, suggesting that it was made on the occasion of a marriage contract between Qi and the royal Zhou clan.

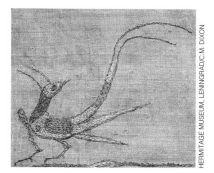

HERMITAGE MUSEUM, LENINGRAD/C.M. DIXON

⚑ A detail of an embroidered tussah silk representing a phoenix, dated to between the fifth and sixth centuries BC.

⚑ This terracotta figure of a kneeling woman from the Qin dynasty was found near the outer wall of the mausoleum of the First Emperor of Qin.

NATIONAL MUSEUM, BEIJING/ERIC LESSING/ART RESOURCE

THE TOMB OF THE FIRST EMPEROR OF THE QIN EMPIRE

KATHERYN M. LINDUFF

The imperial tomb of Qin Shi Huang (259 BC to 210 BC), the first emperor of China and founder of the short-lived Qin dynasty (221 BC to 206 BC), lies 35 kilometers (20 miles) east of the city of Xi'an, in Shaanxi province. The tomb took 36 years to build, and the mausoleum was part of the lavish construction program that characterized the emperor's reign.

Emperor Qin Shi Huang was a man of remarkable talents and achievements. His military conquests were partly the result of a superb mastery of the newest arts of war, such as the use of chariots and mounted soldiers and long spears and swords. He abolished the feudal system, and created a form of centralized, autocratic government, which was essentially maintained until the fall of the last Chinese dynasty in the twentieth century AD. He promulgated a uniform law code. He standardized currency, weights, and measures; the written language; and the axle length of wagons and chariots. He built a vast network of tree-lined roads, 50 paces (about 15 meters/50 feet) wide, radiating from the Qin capital at Xianyang, 30 kilometers (18 miles) northwest of Xi'an. He joined the separate walls created by the earlier northern states, built to deter raiding tribes from the north, into a single 3,000 kilometer (1,850 mile) "Great Wall".

He had a number of elaborate palaces constructed for his own glorification. Although the entire mausoleum is still to be explored and excavated, we know from written records that it was an underground palace complex—the tomb chamber ceiling was a model of the heavens, and the floor was a map of the empire.

In March 1974, the first fragments of what turned out to be terracotta warriors and horses were identified as dating from the Qin dynasty. Three large pits have been excavated to date, and thousands of life-sized clay figures and horses have been unearthed. In December 1980, a pair of bronze four-horse

METROPOLITAN MUSEUM OF ART

JOHN LEE/STOCK HOUSE

🔥 Rows of life-sized, terracotta warriors flanking the tomb of the emperor were revealed in the course of excavations in Lintong, Shaanxi province.

CULTURAL RELICS PUBLISHING HOUSE

🔥 An excavation pit at the tomb of the First Emperor, which contained thousands of terracotta warriors dating from about 210 BC.

◄◘ A painted terracotta warrior from the tomb-pit of the First Emperor of the Qin dynasty, in Lintong, Shaanxi province, dating from about 210 BC. It formed part of the battalion guarding the emperor after his death.

⚲ A painted terracotta charioteer from the area of the tomb of the First Qin Emperor. This life-sized standing figure was found with a total of about 6,000 figures of men and horses, with their chariots, in a pit to the east of the emperor's tomb.
METROPOLITAN MUSEUM OF ART

chariots, each with a charioteer, was found at the same site.

The great underground terracotta army represents the First Emperor's imperial guard, which was stationed to the east of the capital during his lifetime. The entire pit evokes the military might and spirit that secured Qin authority to rule a unified China. The practice of placing clay figures in the tomb replaced the habit of sacrificing people and animals.

There is great variety in the terracotta warriors' dress, facial expressions, hairstyles, headgear, armor, weapons, and vehicles. These detailed, realistic renderings of the military offer graphic evidence of the might and majesty of imperial life in the third century BC, as well as being the first examples of the artistic and cultural values of the emperor.

One of a pair of chariots and charioteers discovered in 1980 in a pit to the west of the tomb of the First Emperor. Made of gilded cast-bronze with silver inlay, they are one-third life size.
CULTURAL RELICS PUBLISHING HOUSE

Life-sized pottery figures of a horse and cavalryman from the tomb-pit of the First Emperor of Qin. Each figure is individually fashioned. The figures and horses were originally painted and outfitted with metal weapons or trappings.

METROPOLITAN MUSEUM OF ART

PHOTOGRAPHIE GIRAUDON

♠ This early nineteenth-century engraving depicts a scene from the life of Confucius (Kung Fu-tzu) and his disciples.

♠ Bronze coins in the shape of a knife (top) from the state of Qi, and a hoe from the state of Zhao, in North China, from the Warring States period. During this period, states developed independently, and coined their own money.

C.M. DIXON

The Warring States Period

The Warring States period witnessed the second phase of the struggle for a new order. The Jin was broken up into three states, while most of the leaders of the other major states were overthrown and replaced by new rulers. None of these states paid even lip service to the remnant of the Zhou royal court, and each of the ruling houses of the principal contending states proclaimed itself the titular king. The major states had by now increased in number, and at least seven engaged in ceaseless wars, forming alliances and counter-alliances. Finally, in the third century BC, the Qin, the least wealthy and least civilized of the seven states, spent about 50 years (the reigns of three kings) defeating the six other states. The king of Qin proclaimed himself emperor in 222 BC.

Although the Spring and Autumn period and the Warring States period were marked by constant warfare, China experienced changes in every aspect of life. The Zhou feudal structure was gradually destroyed. For the purpose of mobilizing resources effectively, the Qin states and the former vassal states were transformed into monarchical states, served by a civilian government bureaucracy and an army of professional soldiers. The aristocracy gave way to bureaucrats recruited from among intellectuals who had been educated by members of the former elite. These intellectuals—among whom were Confucius (Kung Fu-tzu), Mencius (Meng-tzu), Laotzu, Mo-tzu, Chuang-tzu, and Hsun-tzu—not only trained other intellectuals, but, what is more significant, also developed schools of thought that redefined the fundamental premises of Chinese culture. The most important ones were Confucianism, which taught humanism, and Taoism, which taught individualism. Debates on politics and social relationships were common among many intellectuals, and thus, these issues, which had existed since the time of the Eastern Zhou, remained central to Chinese civilization.

During these two periods, bronze was gradually replaced by iron for tools, implements, and weapons. Technological improvements took place in agriculture, irrigation, and manufacturing. A trend towards commercialization and urbanization was evident throughout the Spring and Autumn period and accelerated in the Warring States period, perhaps because of the increasingly frequent communication, and exchange of ideas and materials among the various regions. Free, private land tenure and a monetary economy resulted from all these changes.

The Eastern Zhou period was characterized by dramatic changes, being marked by political turmoil, social mobility—both for members of the feudal system and for commoners—and economic revolution. All these changes occurred rapidly and simultaneously, at a pace that accelerated throughout the 500 years or so of the period. It was a time during which people suffered war and upheaval, yet it also witnessed the most important cultural breakthroughs in Chinese history.

The Rise of the Ancient Empire: 221 BC to AD 220

The Qin's unification of China ushered in a long line of imperial dynasties. The multistate system of the Eastern Zhou period was over, and a single empire, held together by one culture, prevailed for more than 2,000 years. From the Qin, China acquired its name in Western languages.

Under the energetic leadership of the First Emperor of Qin, all the states that existed during the Warring States period were turned into provinces ruled by governors dispatched from the imperial court. A military commandant and an imperial inspector, who supervised officials, were also assigned to each province. Consequently, it was not possible at the provincial level to challenge the supremacy of imperial authority. Laws and writing systems were standardized, and intellectuals were forbidden to criticize policies or to discuss theoretical issues. Only matters of practical value, such as agriculture, horticulture, and medicine, were allowed to be taught by experts; otherwise, the local bureaucrats provided students with the skills and knowledge needed for the civil service.

The Great Wall Is Built

To keep China secure from foreign invasion, the First Emperor ordered the defensive networks built by the individual states in the Warring States period to be linked together into a Great Wall—a long stretch of walls and forts, guarded by 500,000 soldiers. Large numbers of troops were deployed along routes and canals leading to the mountainous region in the south. In addition, a network of highways was built to link all parts of China to the capital, Xianyang, in present-day Shaanxi province, and to each other in order to facilitate deployment of the imperial army. The First Emperor also had an imperial mausoleum built for himself near the capital. It is said that 700,000 conscripted laborers were put to work on making a mound that was filled with treasures guarded by terracotta soldiers. (See the feature *The Tomb of the First Emperor of the Qin Empire*.) All these costly projects demanded

enormous labor power, and the whole country was subjected to heavy demands for unpaid vassal labor. To make matters worse, harsh punishment was meted out to those who failed to report for work or who were late in doing so.

In 210 BC, the First Emperor died. There were rebellions throughout the empire, and after about five years of civil war, the Qin were overthrown. Liu Ban, a commoner who had led peasant rebels against the Qin, then established a new dynasty, the Han, which lasted 400 years.

The Han Empire: 206 BC to AD 220

The Han inherited from the Qin their basic government structure, although they partly restored feudalism by setting up vassal states scattered in the provinces. After rebellions by some of these states, the Han required all vassal states to be governed by appointed officials, and thus, China was once again an empire ruled by one monarch.

In the early Han period, there was a general attitude of laissez-faire, which was a reaction against Qin despotism. As a result, productivity was rapidly restored, the population increased, and China experienced unprecedented prosperity. In early Han burials, as archaeological discoveries testify, even minor aristocrats had astonishingly rich treasures. (See the feature *The Tomb of Lady Dai*.)

The Han not only inherited the Qin government structure, but also made significant adjustments to it. The upper echelons of the Qin government had been an efficient civil service staffed by professional bureaucrats, but there was no mechanism for the recruitment of talent, or for the exchange of information between state and society. Beginning in the second century BC,

⬅ A jade statuette of Laotzu, the reputed founder of Taoism, sitting on a water buffalo.
ANCIENT ART & ARCHITECTURE COLLECTION

⬆ Ritual jade items. From the top: a fish pendant; a *bi*, or ring, symbolizing heaven; a scabbard chape; and a pair of ornaments in the shape of cicadas, which symbolized immortality.
ART RESOURCE

⬅ This ceramic model of a sheep pen dates from the late Eastern Han dynasty. Models of painted clay were often buried with landowners to provide the deceased with wealth beyond death.

BRITISH MUSEUM/E.T. ARCHIVE

D. & J. HEATON/STOCK HOUSE

therefore, the Han gradually developed a system for recruiting intellectuals from the local grass roots into government service. Usually, the role of these recruits was to report to the government on local conditions and to explain government policies to their compatriots.

Meanwhile, Confucianism was made an orthodoxy. Since it was the only subject taught in the Imperial Academy, Confucian ideology dominated the Han bureaucracy. Confucianism is not a religion, however, and so a church–state division did not exist. The Confucian emphasis on humanism, meritocracy, the individual's social responsibility, and collective security—especially solidarity with kinship groups—stabilized the relationship between state and society, and struck a balance between an absolute monarchy and the welfare of the people, while providing a check against wrongdoing by the monarchy.

A ceramic jar from the Eastern Han dynasty. The ceramic industry greatly expanded and diversified during the Han period. This example is of protoporcelain, and prefigures the sophistication of later potters in producing fine, thin-walled porcelains.
SOTHEBY'S LONDON/THE BRIDGEMAN ART LIBRARY

A gilt-bronze lamp from the Western Han dynasty, excavated from the tomb of Empress Dowager Dou, in Mancheng, Hebei province.
METROPOLITAN MUSEUM OF ART

Part of the Great Wall at Baodeling. Long sections of the wall were constructed during the reign of the First Emperor of Qin, in the third century BC. The Qin emperor built the wall in order to set the boundaries of China and to keep the nomads out.

THE TOMB OF LADY DAI

Katheryn M. Linduff

Four kilometers (about 2 miles) east of the city of Changsha, a major city in the central Yangtze Valley, lies a small hill known as Mawangdui. Excavation work at this site began in 1972, when construction of a hospital on the adjacent land revealed evidence of ancient ruins. These were thoroughly investigated, and in what turned out to be a burial ground, archaeologists made some of the most spectacular finds seen in the People's Republic of China in recent years.

The first tomb opened at Mawangdui, now known as Han Tomb no. 1, contained the well-preserved remains of a noblewoman who died some time after the middle of the second century BC, during the period of the Western Han dynasty (from 206 BC to 8 AD). In addition to the corpse, the tomb chamber contained more than a thousand objects, including a large funerary banner of silk painted with multicolored scenes; clothing; food; a large amount of lacquerware retaining its original brilliant coloring; 4 unusually decorated coffins; and more than 100 wooden tomb figures. The identity of the woman is still somewhat uncertain, but she is probably the wife of Li Cang, known as Xin or Xinzhiou, the first Marquis of Dai. Sima Qian, the great historian of the Han dynasty, placed the death of Li Cang at 186 BC. Since Lady Dai's tomb is later than his, she must have died in about 150 BC. Two other tombs have been excavated at the same mound: those of her husband (Tomb no. 2) and her son (Tomb no. 3). All were richly furnished with goods appropriate to a family of noble rank.

Tomb Construction

Tomb no. 1 is located in an oblong pit measuring 20 meters (65 feet) from north to south, and 17.5 meters (about 60 feet) from east to west. The tomb extends for 20 meters (65 feet) from the top of the covering mound to

CULTURAL RELICS PUBLISHING HOUSE

☚ A detail from the funerary banner, or *feiyi*, from Tomb no. 1 at Mawangdui, depicting the land of the immortals. The banner is the earliest polychrome painting on silk known from China. The elaborate design is still quite well preserved.

☙ Two painted and lacquered wooden coffins from Tomb no. 1 at Mawangdui. Four coffins were nested inside the tomb of Lady Dai, the wife of the last Chu governor of the region, Li Cang.
CULTURAL RELICS PUBLISHING HOUSE

the bottom of the shaft. The excavators built four steps to access the crypt; a slanted wall led to the tomb chamber itself. The tomb was oriented towards the north, and arranged so that the corpse would lie with its head to the north.

The crypt contained a tomb chamber constructed of large cypress planks, the largest of which are 5 meters (about 16 feet) long and weigh almost 1,500 kilograms (more than 3 tons). Mortise and tenon construction was used throughout the chamber. Inside lay four coffins, snugly fitted one

inside the other. The compartments between the tomb chamber and the outer wall of the crypt are divided into four sections, and contain most of the tomb furnishings.

The large northern section was draped with silk cloth and contained a considerable number of wooden figures—including several fully attired in ceremonial dress—as well as platters of food. When it was opened, this northern section was found to contain a liquid consisting of mercury and various acidic organic compounds. The purpose of these substances is not clear.

In the western section were plaited bamboo boxes and baskets—containing food, many kinds of herbs, clothing, and bolts of silk and cotton—and musical instruments. The instruments included a type of zither with 25 strings (*sê*); a type of mouth organ with 22 pipes in 2 rows (*yü*); and 12 pitch pipes (*yü lü*), inscribed with the names of the scales of ancient Chinese music.

The eastern section contained more figurines and a complete inventory of the tomb contents written on bamboo strips.

The southern section was filled with lacquer vessels, and the northern section also contained utilitarian implements of all sorts, such as chopsticks and eating bowls, as well as figurines. Some implements were cast-bronze copies of official ritual vessels from previous periods, which were dedicated to ancestors or to officials in commemoration of deeds well done. In accordance with the decrees of Emperor Wen, who reigned from 179 BC to 156 BC, the tomb contained no precious metals, jade, or jewelry.

A layer of charcoal 1.4 to 1.5 meters (4 feet, 7 inches to 5 feet) thick was placed outside the tomb chamber, and the space between the charcoal and the crypt wall was filled with a layer of fine white clay at least a meter (about 3 feet) wide. The marvelous preservation of the tomb and its contents can be attributed to this combination of materials, which kept out moisture and oxygen. The practice of using white clay and charcoal to surround a burial chamber is associated with the local Chu culture. In other parts of China during the Han dynasty, tombs were constructed in a different way. The tombs at Mawangdui clearly point to the continuation of the strong cultural tradition of the Chu state, which had ceased to be a political entity in 223 BC. The early part of the Western Han dynasty was obviously a period when accepted practice in such matters as burial regulations varied widely.

A Flying Garment

The large silk banner found in Tomb no. 1 (a similar example was found in Tomb no. 3) is described in the inventory as a "flying garment" *(feiyi)*. Its placement in the tomb corresponds to the prescribed location for funerary banners *(ming-ching)* displayed during funeral ceremonies and carried in the funeral procession, as described in classical literary sources from the Han period.

The banner from Tomb no. 1 has a painted red field on which an elaborate design was painted in heavy colors, which are still quite well preserved. The cross arm of the T-shaped banner is just under a meter (3 feet) long, the overall height is just over 2 meters (6 feet, 8 inches), and the width at the bottom is 48 centimeters (just under 2 feet). Tassels extend from the four lower corners.

Numerous scholars have tried to decipher the iconography of the scenes depicted on the *feiyi*. It is generally agreed that the scenes represent the conducting of the souls of the dead to the realm of the immortals. The search for immortality was of the utmost concern during the Han dynasty, and this funerary banner is the first example found that illustrates visually, and quite literally, the route of the soul (or souls).

The painting on the banner is divided into three sections. The lower section represents the subterranean region; the middle section, the largest, represents the habitat of human beings on Earth; and the upper section represents the land of the immortals, including the sun and moon. The guiding principles for understanding the painting seem to come from a genuine piece of Chu literature called the *Chuji*, or the *Songs of the South*, which says that the voyage of the souls after death leads in all directions to the four quarters of the universe, as well as above and below. The banner charts that voyage.

At the bottom is the land of the netherworld, a place of water creatures and of darkness below the surface of the Earth, where souls undergo their first metamorphosis. This is the place that the Taoists call the cosmic womb, where the spirit

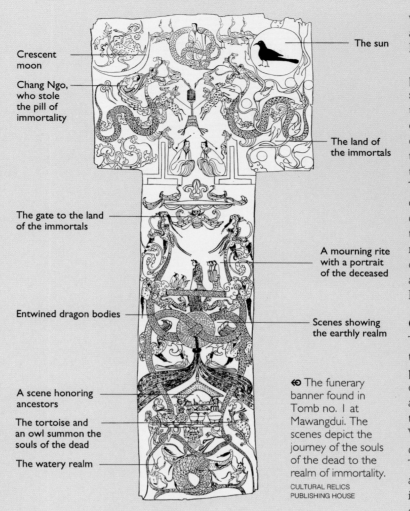

Crescent moon

Chang Ngo, who stole the pill of immortality

The sun

The land of the immortals

The gate to the land of the immortals

A mourning rite with a portrait of the deceased

Entwined dragon bodies

Scenes showing the earthly realm

A scene honoring ancestors

The tortoise and an owl summon the souls of the dead

The watery realm

◄● The funerary banner found in Tomb no. 1 at Mawangdui. The scenes depict the journey of the souls of the dead to the realm of immortality.
CULTURAL RELICS PUBLISHING HOUSE

represented by the *yin* symbols of female creation dwells. It is a place of eternal darkness, with water in its deepest section.

Above the watery realm are depicted two scenes that take place on Earth, both showing mortals acting out their parts in mourning rites. The lower scene depicts a shaman, or holy person, to the left, and a group of attendants seated behind ritual vessels used at sacrifices dedicated to honoring ancestors. Many wooden, lacquered *hu* and *ting* (copies of official vessels cast in bronze in the Shang and Zhou dynasties) were found in the side chambers of the tomb. The shaman's duty was to contact the soul from "below". The upper scene shows another mourning rite, that of welcoming home the soul. The large figure standing in profile in the center is thought to be a portrait of the deceased, and she is shown as if crossing to the "other" world. These two terrestrial scenes represent ritual activities

performed after death. Above and below, the deceased proceeds towards immortality.

The horizontal section at the top of the banner represents the land of the immortals and depicts legendary subjects. The gatekeepers and the bell (whose sound is thought to "penetrate the beyond") are transitional images, standing between heaven and Earth. Above and to the left is the crescent moon, the toad (the symbol of the moon's waxing), and the hare (a symbol of the full moon). The female figure is probably that of Chang Ngo, who stole the pill of immortality from Hou Yi, the archer, and flew off to the moon and caused it to wane. When the pill was returned, the moon waxed. In the center of this section is the figure of Fu Xi, an ancient clan god regarded as the first in the line of legendary rulers—he was the progenitor of the race and the symbol of the essence of everything under heaven. He was thought to be the point from

which *yin* and *yang,* the sun and moon, and heaven and Earth emerged.

The journey of the souls proceeds from death, when the souls separate (one going to the underworld, the other remaining on Earth), through the rites carried out in the earthly realm to "re-join" the souls, to return to the first ancestor of the race and to immortality. The three sections are arranged to correspond to the structure of the cosmos. Upon death, the path of the souls reflects the birth, life, and rebirth as embodied in the nature of ancestor worship, which was already well established in the Han period.

Chu Culture

The tomb of Lady Dai belongs to the Chu cultural tradition. The Chu people inhabited an area southwest of the great north Yellow River basin, and, in historical times, expanded their power into the central Yangtze Valley, encompassing the present-day provinces of Hunan and Hubei. The Chu became one of the largest and strongest contenders for power in the third century BC. They were conquered and destroyed in 223 BC by the generals of the Qin, who went on to unify China in 221 BC. After the fall of the Qin, the Chu again became a very powerful and vigorous group with their own identity. The revival (or continuation) of their own local tomb customs found at Mawangdui is evidence of their pride in their ethnic heritage.

The Western Han period is one of the great formative periods of Chinese history. It took more than a century to reunify China after the fall of Qin. The burials at Mawangdui show that in the kingdom of Changsha in the first half of the second century BC, the requirements of Han rule were not inimical to the continued existence of the Chu cultural tradition. This changed in the time of Emperor Wu (who reigned from 140 BC to 87 BC), but these tombs offer no clues to those later events. They remain as a monument to the complexity and high degree of skill achieved in the craftwork of the Chu people.

BIBLIOTHÈQUE NATIONALE/THE BRIDGEMAN ART LIBRARY

this time was the conflict with the Xiongnu nomadic empire in the steppe land in central Asia and Mongolia. After suffering repeated defeats, the Han finally managed to drive out some of the Xiongnu, and established their hegemony in East Asia. Contact with peoples in central Asia resulted in the appearance of a trading route for silk, which was also a communication corridor between China and the European world, via the many peoples through whose territory the route passed. (See the feature *The Silk Road*.)

In the Han period, technological advances were made in many fields. The Han Chinese were the first to make paper, to construct machinery driven by water power, and to develop the science of metallurgy for the production of steel. Moreover, their mathematics, astronomy, and chemistry were the most advanced in the world. At the same time, Taoism and other schools of thought took their place alongside Confucianism, which had become a highly sophisticated system of thought, as part of the Chinese frame of reference.

☗ An enameled ritual vessel in the shape known as *fang ding*. This ancient style was revived during the Han dynasty to pay homage to traditions of the past.
C.M. DIXON

☗ An emperor of the Han dynasty with scholars translating classical texts. With the establishment of the Han dynasty, classical texts were rewritten from memory by court scholars, the texts in the royal library having been destroyed during the previous period of the Qin dynasty.

➣ Painted pottery jars in the shape known as *hu*, recovered from burials dating from the Eastern Han dynasty. Vessels of this type were often made of clay rather than the more expensive bronze.

Trade Networks and Technological Advances

During the Han period, a nationwide trade network was formed to distribute commodities produced by intensive farming and by the cottage industry. The cottage industry, which had developed as a way of absorbing the excess labor generated seasonally by intensive farming, produced such commodities as clothing, craftworks, and furniture. The network gradually emerged as population pressure made intensive farming a necessity and, according to some scholars, technological advancement a possibility. The trade network reinforced the stability of the unified empire, and, together with Confucian ideology and the imperial bureaucracy, helped China develop a self-sufficient economic system. Thanks to this system, China has remained unified throughout most of the last 2,000 years.

Han territory expanded considerably beyond the Yellow River and Yangtze River floodplains, reaching the mountainous and coastal areas in the south. The most significant development during

ART RESOURCE

THE IMAGE BANK

The Collapse of the Han Empire

The Han dynasty was interrupted briefly by the reign of Wang Mang (from AD 8 to AD 23), after which a member of the Han imperial family succeeded in restoring the Han. The dynasty that resulted is known as the Late Han (or the Eastern Han), while the Han rule ended by Wang Mang is called the Former Han (or the Western Han). By about AD 170, foreign wars, power struggles at the court, and peasant rebellions led by the followers of folk religions had brought about the collapse of the Han. In AD 189, the Han capital, Chang-an, was sacked by mercenaries, and the Han empire was torn by wars among local warlords. Although the last Han emperor continued to reign over the empire—divided by warlords—until AD 220, Han rule effectively ended in AD 189.

During the Han period, China was consolidated into a state that spanned four centuries, and the Chinese established an identity as a nation. It is for this reason that speakers of the predominant language group in China—Mandarin, which is spoken by 85 percent of the population—including Chinese speakers in Taiwan, Hong Kong, and Hainan, still call themselves the Han people.

⚓ Fishing in Guilin, Guangxi province. With the famous limestone outcroppings that dot the countryside throughout South China, this is a typical southern scene.

◄ A bronze horse and rider from the Eastern Han dynasty. This piece is part of a set of cast-bronze horses and horsemen found in a tomb at Lingtai, in Gansu province. Horses were very highly regarded at this time—the emperor even sent abroad for his saddle and parade horses.

GIRAUDON/ART RESOURCE

THE SILK ROAD

HÅKAN WAHLQUIST

ARCHAEOLOGICAL TREASURES and written documents clearly show that, from the earliest times, different regions of the "Old World" were connected by routes along which contacts were made—contacts of war and of military acquisition and defense, but also of peace, trade, and cultural expansion. The first contacts were between neighboring nations; later, more distant nations were linked. From Greek historians, including Herodotus in the fifth century BC, we know that extensive networks of routes stretched eastwards, and from those who recorded the official annals of the Han dynasty (from 206 BC to AD 220), we know about Chinese penetration to the west. It was by interlocking emerging regional trading systems that political and cultural centers as far apart as China and Rome were connected to one another.

When these systems were tied up, there came into existence the long-distance trading routes that the German geographer von Richthofen (1833–1905) called the "Silk Road", because silk played such a vital role in the commercial transactions along the "road". It is useful, however, to think of the Silk Road not as a single "road", but as a network of routes that, because of political and economic changes in the areas that it linked over the centuries, varied in extent and structure. Certain routes were important during certain periods, with the flow of commerce being diverted to alternative routes during other periods. Two kinds of routes were followed: by sea and by land.

The Sea Route

India and Arabia played valuable intermediary roles in the emerging long-distance maritime trade. For several centuries BC, India and China had already been trading, partly via Burma, but, more importantly, by small ships around Southeast Asia. From India, merchandise was carried by Arab ships to the Red Sea or the Persian Gulf, overland to the Mediterranean, and then to European markets.

The sea routes became more significant as maritime knowledge increased and larger ships were built. With the break-up of the Roman Empire and growing Arab expansion towards central and South Asia, access to traditional caravan routes was upset, and trade tilted even more in favor of the sea passage. The final transfer from caravans to ships, however, did not occur until

ROLAND & SABRINA MICHAUD/THE JOHN HILLELSON AGENCY

☝ The overland routes, connecting the Mediterranean region to China, crossed high mountains and wide deserts through the interior of Asia. Bactrian camels, commonly used to carry people and cargo, are here negotiating the Pamir mountains.

♀ Nowadays, only ruins remain of Bezcklik, once a flourishing settlement on the northern branch of the Silk Road. It was a major Buddhist center east of the Turfan depression, noted for its extensive monasteries and beautiful murals.

WERNER FORMAN ARCHIVE

the end of the fifteenth century AD, when Portuguese explorers gave Europe direct access to South and East Asia by ship around Africa. By then, the ancient overland Silk Road, which had existed for at least 1,500 years, had already lost its dominance. When the Ming dynasty came to power in AD 1368, China entered a period of relative isolation. Moreover, political developments in West Asia severely hampered transit trade.

Routes through Asia

The most important early Western move towards the East was undoubtedly Alexander the Great's "invasion" of Asia in 334 BC, a remarkable undertaking that brought European culture and influence far into the continent. A few centuries later, the Chinese moved westwards in earnest. The Han emperors, worried about their nomadic enemies in the west, expanded across what is today Gansu, and consolidated their empire by extending the Great Wall. A new element was introduced into Han policy after 139 BC, when emissaries were sent far beyond the borders of the empire into the land of potential enemies and allies. As the commercial advantages of establishing contact with these areas became evident, envoys were sent yearly to places such as Parthia (Iran) and India. Diplomatic missions also arrived in the Han capital, bringing tribute and goods for trade. The Silk Road as an artery for commerce had been established.

The old Han capital, Chang-an (today's Xi'an), was the easternmost town along the Silk Road. From there, the road ran westwards via Lanzhou, towards the rim of the Lop and Taklimakan deserts. At Dunhuang and Anxi, it split into several alternative routes. One went north of the deserts, another to the south. A third route went west through the Lop Desert, skirting the Lop Nur lake, to the garrison town of Loulan, from where it joined either the northern or the southern trade roads. This desert route was abandoned in the fourth century AD, when Lop Nur changed its position, or dried up, and Loulan was abandoned.

At Kashgar, at the western end of the Taklimakan Desert, the routes met, only to divide again. One went south into the Indus Valley. From there, travelers either turned west through Afghanistan towards Iran, or continued southeast into the heartland of northern India. The other route carried travelers across the Alai Mountains into West Turkestan and on to Iran. In Mashad, it reunited with the desert route that had come from Afghanistan through eastern Iran. The caravans could then move on through Mesopotamia, passing Baghdad before turning south towards Alexandria, west towards the Mediterranean, or north towards Turkey and Byzantium. Eventually, the westernmost extensions of the Silk Road reached the major cities of Europe.

Travelers and Goods

The people who traveled along these routes were from all the nations and cultures that the Silk Road touched during the several thousand years of its existence: Roman, Greek, and Slavonic; Arabic, Iranian, Turkic, Mongolian, Tibetan, Chinese, and Indian. They were soldiers and robbers; emigrants and refugees; merchants, missionaries, and monks; administrators, artisans, and scholars. They left evidence of their lives in the form of chronicles; accounts of trading trips and pilgrimages; administrative and commercial records; religious texts; merchandise taken from one place to another; secular and sacred monuments, and works of art; and land broken and worked.

Along the Silk Road, people carried ideas, knowledge, and skills, as well as artifacts and trading goods.

ROLAND & SABRINA MICHAUD/THE JOHN HILLELSON AGENCY

CARTOGRAPHY: RAY SIM

WERNER FORMAN ARCHIVE/DEMITSU MUSEUM OF ARTS, TOKYO

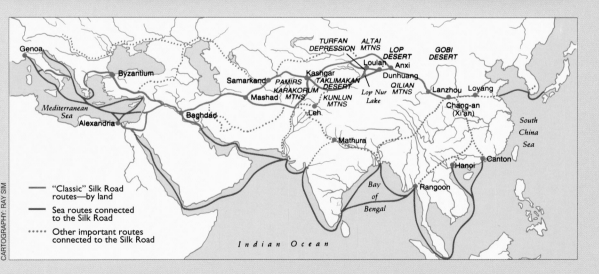

◄● The oasis of Dunhuang is fabled for its caves. These caves were once inhabited by Buddhist monks and pilgrims, such as the one depicted with a tiger on this mural.

♀ Well-preserved and superbly painted and glazed figurines from the Tang dynasty (AD 618 to AD 907) have been found in China. Among other things, they show us that foreign merchants, like this distinctly non-Chinese man, probably from western Asia, frequented the markets in China at that time.

They spread political ideologies, religious faiths, techniques of production, arts, fashions, and material goods. Buddhism was taken from India to central Asia. There, as in China, Korea, Japan, and Mongolia, it was to exert great influence, in confrontation, but also in harmony, with indigenous Chinese philosophies such as Confucianism and Taoism. Islam, emerging in the mid-seventh century AD, spread from Arabia to East Turkestan, taking firm root along the way.

Horses were the first "merchandise" the Chinese desired. Later, when trade extended all the way to Rome, other goods began to arrive: gold, silver, and coins; glassware; textiles; bronze vessels; wine; and papyrus. To the west flowed silk and other luxury goods: skins and furs, household slaves, jewelry, ivory, pearls, tortoise shells, and

THE SILK ROAD

The Silk Road was a network of caravan routes crisscrossing the continent and sea routes connecting the shores of the Yellow Sea with the Indian Ocean and the Mediterranean Sea.

lacquer. In addition, Europeans developed a taste for a host of new spices and dyes: pepper, cinnamon, cardamom, ginger, cloves, indigo, and cochineal.

NATIONAL MUSEUM, ATHENS/SCALA

EMERGING MEDITERRANEAN CIVILIZATIONS

3 2 0 0 B C – 8 0 0 B C

Warlords, Palace Cultures, and the First States in Europe

PETER WARREN, J.G. MACQUEEN, AND RICHARD J. HARRISON

DURING THE SECOND MILLENNIUM BC, Europe's first civilizations developed in the eastern Mediterranean region. The period is characterized by a marked stability, and the rich societies of the Middle Bronze Age were soon transformed into distinctive palace cultures—first came the Minoan culture, on Crete; and later, the Mycenaean culture, on the Greek mainland. These important cultural worlds had complex bureaucratic systems, and developed important trading connections with the central Mediterranean region, with occasional links north of the Alps and to eastern Europe. Europe's first states had been established, and the first writing systems, known as Linear A and Linear B, were developed.

At the same time, an Indo-European-speaking people known as the Hittites established a powerful kingdom in Anatolia (present-day Turkey)—a kingdom that soon expanded in all directions. The Hittites were the first to master the technique of iron-smelting, and they thus began the first Iron Age culture in the world. In contrast to the societies in Crete, mainland Greece, and Anatolia, the local bronze-producing cultures in the Iberian peninsula never developed into true civilizations.

◀◉ Part of a wall painting from the West House at Akrotiri, on Thera, dating from the sixteenth century BC. Shown here is the end of the "Fresco of the Ships". At what is probably the home port of the approaching fleet, crowds of men and women of different social ranks are looking out towards the ships.

◉ A votive figure from the Peak Sanctuary at Petsofa, in Palaikastro, Crete, dating from about 2000 BC to 1700 BC.

RONALD SHERIDAN/ANCIENT ART & ARCHITECTURE COLLECTION

⚥ An embossed gold pendant of a deity holding two waterbirds. Probably made in Crete, it dates from the seventeenth century BC and shows both Cretan and Egyptian influences.
BRITISH MUSEUM/C.M. DIXON/PHOTO RESOURCES

⚥ These pottery vessels from Cyprus, dating from the fourteenth century BC, were found in a Bronze Age wreck off Kas (Ulu Burun), in Turkey.

EARLY AEGEAN CIVILIZATIONS

The Aegean region has been the scene of more than 50,000 years of human development. A high point was reached between 3000 BC and 1000 BC in the sophisticated and splendid civilizations of Crete, the Cyclades, and the Greek mainland. The region is small by global standards: just 600 kilometers (360 miles) from the northern Aegean coast to Crete in the south, and 700 kilometers (420 miles) from the western Ionian islands eastwards to Rhodes. To the west, the Ionian and Adriatic seas offered access to the central Mediterranean, while contacts northwards were made possible by the Axios and Vardar rivers and the Macedonian plains. Although the Rhodope Mountains formed a barrier to the northeast, the Anatolian coastlands (in present-day Turkey) were a critical bridge between the Anatolian plateau and its civilizations, and those of the Aegean island communities. East of Crete lay Cyprus and

the Levant, south lay Egypt—all distant enough to allow Crete a measure of protection from attack, but not so far distant as to prevent the flow of goods and secular and spiritual ideas.

The Aegean is a region of sharp contrasts: the remote mountains and steep, wooded glens of northwestern Greece and Albania, and the fertile plains of eastern Greece, watered in the north by the Balkan mountain rivers. Then there are the islands, located off Greece's western coast; in the northern Aegean Sea; in the central Aegean (the Cyclades); to the south (Crete); and off the Anatolian coast (Lesbos, Chios, Samos, Kos, and Rhodes).

Natural resources were plentiful throughout the region. Timber, limestones, and sandstones for building; clays; and potentially good agricultural land, pasture, edible herbs, and aromatic plants were widely available. But it was the localized concentrations of the raw materials necessary for higher civilization that promoted complex exchange networks and simple strategies of acquisition. Some Cycladic islands and southern Attica had supplies of copper, silver, and lead; gold occurred on Siphnos and in the northern Aegean. Several islands possessed fine white marble. Red marble and porphyritic rock (*lapis Lacedaemonius*) existed only in the southern Peloponnese; black obsidian for tools was acquired from Melos; and volcanic rocks for mortars were available from Melos as well as from Thera and Aigina. Tin, ivory, and exotics such as glass, gemstones, ostrich eggs, alabaster, and rock crystal, and also fine woods and copper, came from bordering regions to the east and south. Interestingly, the major centers of civilization—Crete, Mycenae, and Thebes—had no abundant natural resources of their own, other than fertile land. Like Troy and Poliochni, in the northeastern Aegean, their geographical position was highly significant, and the popularity of their exports ensured a strong supply of further raw materials.

Discovery of the Aegean Past

Our knowledge of early Aegean society and civilization has been gained from archaeological excavations and surveys conducted for just over a hundred years. Heinrich Schliemann cleared the shaft graves of Mycenae, packed with warrior wealth, in 1876, and he uncovered the remains of Troy during the following years. Tombs at Mycenae, at Vapheio, and whole cemeteries in the Cyclades were excavated in the later part of the nineteenth century. From 1896 to 1899, a British team on Melos revealed a major settlement at Phylakope. This was followed by the richest era of discovery in Crete when Arthur Evans, assisted by Duncan Mackenzie, began to uncover the Palace of Knossos on 23 March 1900. American, Italian, and British teams excavated other Cretan sites, and the great Cretan scholar and archaeologist Stephanos Xanthoudides cleared a series of communal tombs dated to before 2000 BC.

BILL CURTSINGER

While valuable finds were made in the 1920s and 1930s, the most significant discoveries have been made only since the Second World War. Probably the most important of all was the decipherment of the Mycenaean Linear B tablets (a script developed from the Minoan Linear A to write an early form of Greek) by Michael Ventris in 1952. This had immense implications for the understanding of the Mycenaean economy and the structure of the state. Meanwhile, the Neolithic tells (mounds) of Thessaly and Macedonia; the palaces of Pylos and Phaistos; the town of Akrotiri, on Thera (the Pompeii of the Aegean); and the finds from the fourteenth-century BC shipwreck off Kas (Ulu Burun), in southern Turkey, all came to light.

Accompanying these and other discoveries at scores of sites explored in recent years have been fundamental, new, scientific approaches to archaeology. Powerful techniques, such as chemical element analyses, enable the origins of objects, chiefly pottery, to be determined. High-resolution microscopy has revealed details of the technology and structures of metalwork. The application of resistivity techniques (an electromagnetic means of showing horizontal planes of structures below ground), ground-penetrating radar (which gives vertical profiles of remains below ground), and digitized computer mapping systems is transforming the recording of sites and terrains in archaeological surveys. Paleobotany has created entirely new levels of understanding of the ancient environment and of food plants; archaeozoology has identified wild and domesticated fauna. Radiocarbon dating has enabled the chronological sequences and time scales of all Aegean societies before about 2000 BC to be determined. After this date, evidence derived from Aegean pottery in Egypt and western Asia, and Egyptian finds in the Aegean, provide the basis for dating periods and developments. Radiocarbon dating offers general confirmation of the sequence of events, although views are divided as to how accurate it is for dating single events such as the Late Bronze Age eruption of the volcano of Thera.

The Beginnings of Aegean Civilization

Aegean society, economy, and culture developed in a series of stages. The idea that historical processes operate at the same time, but at different levels and paces, is useful for understanding the early Aegean in terms of its social, economic, technological, political, and spiritual development. The different levels are: long-term, almost imperceptible human change in relation to the environment; the history of groups, which is measurable across time, as in the rise and maintenance of stable states; and short-term events, such as sudden collapses of stable states or the impact of natural events. There are, of course, constant interactions between these concurrent levels.

ERICH LESSING/MAGNUM

Middle Paleolithic stone artifacts found on the Ionian island of Kephallenia, dated to about 50,000 years ago, provide evidence that sea voyages of at least 20 kilometers (12 miles) between shorelines were made at that time. In nearby Epirus, on the mainland, excavations at cave sites indicate the existence of small groups who migrated according to the seasons along established land routes. They hunted a wide range of animals, including ibex, chamois, beaver, red deer, cave lion, lynx, wolf, pine marten, and badger, according to findings at Klithi (from 17,000 to 10,000 years ago). Mining for red ocher is reported from Thasos at the end of the Paleolithic, when the island formed part of the Thracian plain.

During the final stages of the Paleolithic, continuing through the Mesolithic and Early Neolithic periods, profound developments occurred. At Franchthi, on the Argolid coast, obsidian was being brought a considerable distance by sea from the island of Melos as early as 12,000 years ago. This mastery of land and sea distances by the people of the Paleolithic is the background to the first Neolithic colonies, very probably from Anatolia, between 7000 BC and 6000 BC. Settlements were established on the plains and beside the rivers of Macedonia and Thessaly. The colonization of Crete, however, was their most astonishing achievement, requiring a long sea voyage from southern Anatolia to Knossos, with one or more vessels transporting people, livestock (notably cattle), cereals (especially breadwheat), and provisions such as fresh water.

During this period, agriculture and the domestication of sheep, goats, cattle, and pigs were introduced into mainland Greece and, at a slower pace, into Crete. Exchange networks had also been developed within the Aegean region, since Melian obsidian is found at many sites, and pottery was

⚭ This section of a wall painting from Akrotiri, on Thera, dating from the sixteenth century BC, depicts a coastal town surrounded by rivers and mountains (with deer being pursued by a lion). Standing on the mountains, men and a woman watch departing ships.

⚭ An early Cycladic folded-arm figurine made of white marble, from Naxos, dating from about 2500 BC.
NATIONAL MUSEUM, ATHENS/SCALA

⚡ An early Cycladic pottery "frying pan" figure from Syros. It dates from between about 2500 BC and 2200 BC, and shows a longboat with paddles.
NATIONAL MUSEUM, ATHENS/
C.M. DIXON/PHOTO RESOURCES

⚡ Part of the frieze from the north wall of room 5 of the West House at Akrotiri, on Thera, dating from about 1530 BC. It depicts a seaborne attack and drowning defenders.

NATIONAL ARCHAEOLOGICAL MUSEUM, ATHENS/THE BRIDGEMAN ART LIBRARY

circulated in northern Greece. After 4000 BC, objects of copper, silver, and gold were used in a minor way.

About 3000 BC, further profound social and economic changes occurred. Small, planned towns were founded in the northeastern Aegean region and in northwestern Anatolia, at Besik Tepe, Troy, Poliochni, and Thermi. There is evidence for social ranking and the display of wealth in finds of rich collections of gold jewelry and metal vessels. In Thessaly, the town of Pefkakia had developed as a thriving coastal center with links around the northern Aegean, in contrast with inland Thessalian and Macedonian towns, which were in decline after the richness of their Late Neolithic period. Further south, large settlements were established on virgin ground in Boeotia and Euboea. By 2500 BC, Lerna, on the Argolid coast, once a fortified settlement, had crossed a significant political threshold in becoming an administrative center. Seal impressions on clay found in its main building indicate a system of organized storage.

Meanwhile, on the islands, the farming and maritime villages of the Cyclades reached the zenith of independent achievement. Their production of slender figurines and vessels of finest white marble, and a wide range of copper and bronze tools and silver jewelry, was outstanding. Cultural artifacts

found in Lefkas, in the Ionian islands to the west, have distinct Cycladic links, and island longboats, of which lead models and depictions on pottery survive, prove that sea voyages were undertaken. So, too, does a shipwreck full of pottery at Dhokos, near the island of Hydra. Nearby, mainland Attica had a material culture that was very similar to that of the Cyclades.

The basic food supply, determined by careful investigation at Lerna, comprised einkorn and emmer wheat, barley, oats, brome grass, broad beans, lentils, peas, vetches, figs, grapes, and strawberry tree fruit. This diet may have been typical of the Aegean region, although the absence of olives is a striking exception. The local animals included red fox, hare, boar, red and roe deer, ox, badger, beech marten, otter, and wolf; and domestic cattle, sheep, goats, pigs, dogs, and asses.

On Crete, settlements ranged from small agricultural villages, such as Myrtos (Phournou Koryphe), to coastal sites with Cycladic and Southwest Asian connections, such as Mochlos. The major town of Knossos, with links extending as far as the Greek mainland and Egypt, grew.

Greek mainland and Cycladic island communities suffered severe disruption in the late third millennium BC, probably as a result of migrations from West Anatolia. The impact of these new groups is seen in their architecture, wheel-made pottery, and metalwork, which appeared at several places, from Pefkakia, in Thessaly, to Kastri, on Syros.

Crete, in sharp contrast, maintained its development within a framework of strong cultural continuity. Out of this framework emerged the first monumental buildings or palaces, Phaistos (about 1800 BC) providing the best example. A recently discovered building at Aghia Photia, in eastern Crete, comprises a single small structure of about 500 square meters (600 square yards), with more than 30 rooms arranged around a rectangular court. The monumental approach to architecture probably arrived from western Asia, along with imports of tin and copper. This form of architecture probably coincided with the emergence of a ruling elite.

Early State Society in Crete: 2000 BC to 1500 BC

This was the great age of Minoan palatial civilization (named after the legendary King Minos), with an administration supported by documents in the Cretan hieroglyphic and Linear A scripts (a form of writing using signs for syllables, together with numerals and symbols). Major regional centers, with administrative buildings and storage and production facilities, stood at the head of a network of lesser towns, large country estates, farms, and ports. They also served religious sites on mountain tops, in rural settings, and in caves. Economic links with the mainland, the Cyclades (and as far north as Samothrace); western Anatolia, Cyprus, the Levant, and Egypt were highly developed. At the same time, Minoan settlements were founded in the southern Aegean region (or Minoan elements were added to local cultures).

It is clear that the Minoan rulers exerted control over the import of valuable raw materials—notably, metals, fine stones, and ivory. The distribution of imported goods, however, suggests the existence of at least semi-independent merchants.

In the absence of social information in the written records, the excavated sites themselves can throw some light on Minoan society of this period. Knossos was the largest center (estimated at 75 hectares/ 185 acres), with a population of between 9,000 and 12,000 people. Most other towns had populations of only a few hundred. Taking into account the small population and a short life expectancy (35 years for men, 28 years for women), which allows but a few years for individual achievement, the scale of the total Minoan palatial complex appears all the more remarkable.

The structure of Minoan society remains a mystery, with only a few clues left behind. Collective burials and the compact, cellular settlement plans of the prepalatial period suggest a communal social system. The presence of defined living areas could well indicate the existence of nuclear families or extended family groups. Economic prosperity brought with it differences in status, perhaps already showing up in the Early Bronze Age harbor town of Mochlos, with its very rich communal tombs contrasting with much simpler burials. It has been suggested that powerful families probably occupied the first monumental buildings about 1900 BC to 1800 BC. Soon afterwards, specialized workshops, such as those found at Mallia, could well have been family-based. House sizes in the neopalatial towns suggest that they were family residences, housing about 10 people. The palaces, at least in their final form, were planned on a regular measurement unit, and were divided into functional areas around a great central court. This layout implies a sophisticated organization and administration, but who made the decisions is unknown. A single "ruler" seems likely. In Minoan Crete, as good a case for a female as for a male ruler can be made. Iconography suggests that a female sat on the throne at Knossos—as priestess, ruler, or both. Women were certainly prominent in religion.

The Minoan economy was based on a diversified system of agriculture: different types of wheat and barley, probably oats, pulses, olive oil, wine, figs, honey, edible plants, spices, beef, pork, mutton, venison, and fish, and probably game, milk, and cheese, were staples.

The level of technological achievement across a huge range of activities was astonishing. Buildings were constructed with ashlar masonry (finely dressed on the front face) and large beams of Cretan cypress. Two of the finest examples of construction are the five-story Grand Staircase, in the East Wing of the Knossian palace, and the 35 meter (100 foot) long buildings at the port of Kommos. (See the feature *The Minoan Palace of Knossos*.) Craft products were worked in brilliant stones, including imported speckled obsidian and rock crystal, ivory, faience, gold, silver, and terracotta (including a multitude of brilliantly painted, sometimes eggshell-thin pots). Bronzework sometimes featured the fusion of different metals by heat and pressure, similar to modern-day "Sheffield plate". Delicate, multi-colored wall paintings sympathetically depicting the natural environment were created. Many such crafted items were used in religious rituals or left as offerings in shrines. Others were exported.

Artifacts, excavated sites, and scenes carved in relief on stone vessels or engraved on gold rings and sealstones all demonstrate that religious belief and cult practice played a major role in Minoan life. Rituals included animal and occasionally human sacrifice, food and floral offerings, and the dedication of small votive human and animal figures. Shrines were places where the divine and human worlds interacted. Music, dance, invocation, ecstatic actions with cult stones and trees were the means of attracting the divinity's presence. The purpose of religious activity was to promote the fertility and renewal of the whole environment, including humans and animals, and to avert disease or natural disaster. Whether the Minoans worshiped many divinities equally or a single great female divinity manifesting different aspects, with an entourage of lesser divinities, remains a matter for debate.

At their highest stage of development, in the later fifteenth century BC, the centers of Minoan civilization suffered sudden destruction. Most excavated settlements and estate centers show evidence of fire. The eruption of Thera, the volcano 110 kilometers (65 miles) to the north of Crete, occurred too early to be the cause of the Minoan disaster. Since there is no sign of internal stress in Minoan society (in fact, the opposite is the case), discussion now centers on two possibilities: an invasion by Mycenaean warriors from the Greek mainland; or, with Crete being on the boundary of the African and Aegean tectonic plates, a severe earthquake.

The Emergence of Mycenaean Civilization

After several centuries of peace in the Aegean region, there is evidence that a military elite had begun to emerge about 1600 BC. At Mycenae, quantities of swords have been found in shaft graves, along with pottery, exotic objects from Crete, and about 200 vessels, many of them made of gold. Tombs elsewhere, mostly long since plundered, indicate the growth of wealth and status: at Eleusis, in Attica; at Dendra (Midea), Lerna, and Vapheio; and at Peristeria, in Messenia. It was one or more of these warrior-led communities that either conquered

A dagger of inlaid gold, silver, and copper from Shaft Grave IV at Mycenae. Dating from the sixteenth century BC, it depicts a lion hunt.
RONALD SHERIDAN/ANCIENT
ART & ARCHITECTURE COLLECTION

Knossos in the later fifteenth century BC or filled the vacuum left by natural disaster. This was a pivotal moment in the history of Aegean civilization, as the less sophisticated but powerful and adaptive Mycenaeans quickly learned the structure and centralized administration of a high civilization established centuries earlier by the Minoans.

The Mycenaeans ruled Crete from Knossos for less than a hundred years, before the capital was itself destroyed forever as a palace center (probably no later than about 1350 BC). From this time, palaces were also established on the mainland, at Mycenae, Pylos, Tiryns, Thebes, and, almost certainly, Athens. They were based

on the old megaron, or longhouse, plan, incorporating a porch that led to an anteroom and main room. Long side corridors gave access to smaller rooms and courts. Palaces at Pylos and Tiryns also had secondary, smaller, megaron suites. In addition to their palaces, the Mycenaeans achieved remarkable feats of hydraulic engineering: a dam near Tiryns; an aqueduct to supply Pylos with water; and drainage of the Kopais basin through channels and tunnels, to convert the area surrounding Gla into good agricultural land.

Pylos, Mycenae, Thebes, and Tiryns, the four main palace complexes, were the capitals of their states, and were each headquarters of a centralized,

♀ An aerial view of Mycenae, in the northeastern Peloponnese. Most of the structures date from the thirteenth to fourteenth centuries BC. The palace is the large building in the center.

IRA BLOCK/THE IMAGE BANK

very tightly controlled economy. We know this from translations of contemporary Linear B tablet records, which deal primarily with fiscal matters, including taxation in kind. Raw materials and rations were distributed, and finished products, including agricultural and animal produce, were allocated quotas. Some tablets record contracts of sale of slaves. Large and small estates were owned by individuals, perhaps in return for military service. Some tablets are specifically concerned with military equipment, including armor and weapons. Countless details of technical production, ranging from elaborate inlaid furniture and textiles to chariot parts and scented oils and spices are listed by practitioner or product.

As might be expected from such a controlled economy, society was elaborately ranked, with the king (*wanax*) at the top. Under the king, ranked approximately in the following order, were: the *lawagetas* (second only to the king); *equetai*, or followers; *telestai*, or major landholders; governors and deputy governors of towns or subregions; leaders of craft groups; religious dignitaries; craftspeople; and shepherds and workers (some of whom were slaves), including female textile workers employed in the palace. Farmers are not mentioned, nor are merchants, although the former must have comprised the majority of the population.

As well as the palaces, a number of settlement sites and dozens of cemeteries have been found, including tholos (domed) tombs and chamber tombs. Excavation of palaces or other buildings in palatial towns has yielded inscribed tablets, wall paintings, tens of thousands of pots, carved ivories, stone and metalwork (including multicolored inlaid weapons and cups), and jewelry. Mycenae was an important cult center. Tiryns and the major Cycladic town of Phylakope, on Melos, had shrines that continued to be used after 1200 BC, their location suggesting that their purpose was to ensure divine protection for the walled city.

While most of our information about economic, social, and political matters comes from tablets, these make no mention of trade. The status of trade within the Mycenaean economy is a matter of debate. Although the economy was essentially agricultural, the archaeological evidence is clear: trade (or rather, exchange in its many forms) existed, although it may have involved only the upper ranks of society. Traded items included the fine Mycenaean pottery and the scented oils that originally filled many of the pots found in southern Italy, Sicily, Sardinia, and Spain and at more than a hundred sites from Syria to Egypt. A ship wrecked

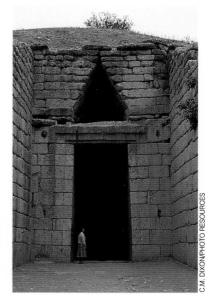

C.M. DIXON/PHOTO RESOURCES

⬆ The entrance to the "Treasury of Atreus", a tholos tomb at Mycenae dating from the fourteenth century BC. The triangular space and the door surrounds were decorated with carved slabs and columns in colored marble.

♀ These items were among those retrieved from a Bronze Age wreck off Kas (Ulu Burun), in Turkey, dating from the fourteenth century BC. As well as a consignment of more than 100 amphoras, the cargo included gold pendants, gold roundels with embossed decoration, and artifacts made of bronze.

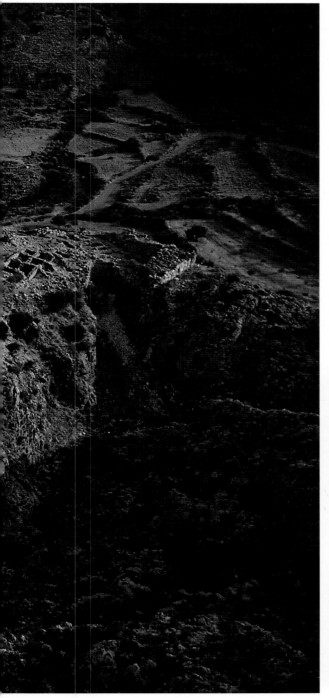

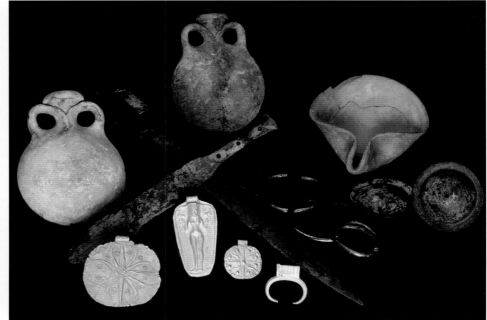

BILL CURTSINGER

THE DEVELOPMENT OF MEDITERRANEAN CIVILIZATIONS

	ANATOLIA	AEGEAN REGION	WEST MEDITERRANEAN REGION
1000			
	Destruction of Hattusas	Mycenaean destructions	
	Battle of Qadesh	Mycenaean palaces	
		Fall of Knossos	
		Linear B script developed	
	Reign of Suppiluliumas	Destructions in Crete	Atlantic Late Bronze Age: contacts with Britain and France
1500			
	Hittite capture of Babylon	Volcano of Thera erupts	Bronze Age expansion in central Spain
		Mycenaean shaft graves	
	Foundation of Hittite kingdom	Linear A script developed	
		Minoan trade to Egypt, the Near East, and Anatolia	
2000	Assyrian merchant colonies	Cretan palaces	Single graves and citadels at Fuente Alamo and El Oficio
			Early Bronze Age
	Troy II and Alaca treasures	Movement from Anatolia to Cycladic islands and Greek mainland	
2500			
		Lerna: early Helladic administration center	Construction of Los Millares and Almizaraque
	Developments in metallurgy	Cretan round tombs	
		Cycladic marble figures	Bell beaker pottery
			Collective tombs and fortified sites
3000	First city of Troy	Early Bronze Age	Copper Age
BC			

off Kas (Ulu Burun), in southern Turkey, carried a cargo of some 357 copper ingots, tin, ivory, cobalt blue glass ingots, spices, ebony, and more than a hundred Canaanite amphoras (two-handled vessels), with nearly 1 tonne (1 ton) of terebinth resin suitable for use in perfumes and incense. In the fourteenth century BC, such a cargo must surely have been destined for a Mycenaean palatial center.

In postpalatial Crete, during the fourteenth and thirteenth centuries BC, Khania, on the north coast, and Kommos, on the south, flourished as port towns with links to western Asia and Italy.

The civilization of the Mycenaeans lasted 200 years at most. In the thirteenth century BC, some rulers built great defensive walls around their citadels and, in some cases, passages beneath the walls to protect water supplies. Athens, Gla, Dendra, Mycenae, and Tiryns are outstanding examples of defensive architecture. A strong wall was built across the Isthmus of Corinth, while Pylos and the Menelaion remained unwalled. All this activity must mean that there was fear of attack by neighbors. The citadels were, in fact, destroyed over a period from about 1250 BC to 1200 BC. Explanations differ: some argue that there were internal conflicts within individual states, as marginal lands and food supplies became scarce; others believe that there was conflict between states (the isthmus wall supporting this view). It must be noted, however, that recent excavators have independently argued that Mycenae, the Menelaion, and Tiryns were destroyed by earthquake.

⚔ Mycenaean armor from Dendra, in the Peloponnese, dating from the fourteenth century BC. This unique find of a bronze cuirass (a piece of armor that protected the torso) and a boar's-tusk helmet has been restored.

NAUPLION MUSEUM/C.M. DIXON/PHOTO RESOURCES

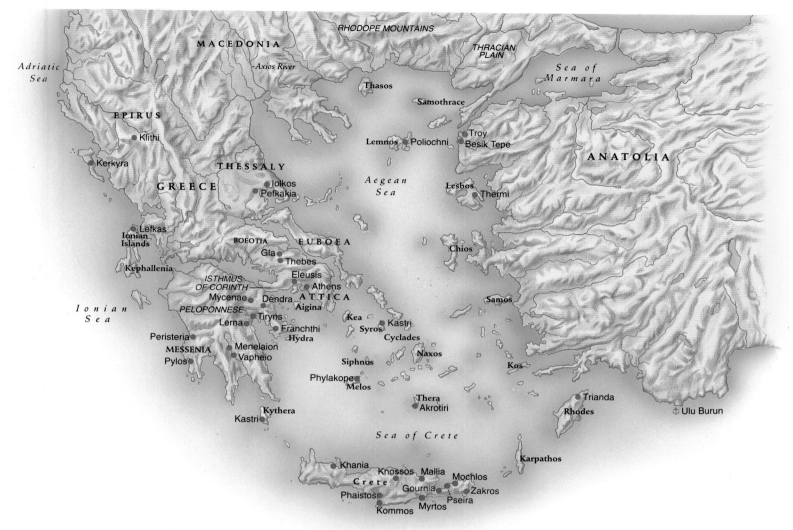

Discontinuities, Survivals, and Continuities

The destructions that culminated about 1200 BC swept away the centralized economies, along with the politically defined kingdoms and complex social systems. Exchange systems, insofar as they were controlled by, and for, the palace rulers, must also have changed radically. Writing stopped. After 1200 BC, there was considerable migration to less densely populated areas—the northwestern Peloponnese and the Ionian islands, in western Greece, and eastern Attica, Euboea, and the Cyclades. There was renewed Mycenaean activity on Crete, and a population shift to naturally defended locations. Mycenaean communities also moved to Tarsus, in southern Anatolia, and to Cyprus and the West Anatolian coast. Iolkos, on the coast of Thessaly, appears to have escaped destruction, and tradition had it that Athens did likewise.

Until recently, it was thought that the migration from the core areas of the northeastern Peloponnese and Boeotia had left these areas severely underpopulated. But discoveries at Mycenae, and especially Tiryns, show that these places remained inhabited, Tiryns being a major town in the twelfth century BC. Its excavator, the late Klaus Kilian, even speculated that the origins of the later Greek polis (city-state) might lie in the twelfth century. New forms of political organization were necessary. Later Greek sources indicate that communities were ruled by kings, or *basileis* (a title that had existed in Mycenaean times, but was then relatively insignificant).

In Crete, new excavation has shown twelfth-century settlement at lowland Knossos, as well as at inaccessible hill sites. Mountain and cave sanctuaries continued to be inhabited, and it was here that much of the religious inheritance of the Bronze Age was preserved and developed in an unbroken line.

Since the tablets of the Mycenaean palaces had already listed many of the later Greek gods and goddesses, continuity of belief was also likely on the mainland. The Greek language also survived. Land use remained the same as it had been for thousands of years, although the control and organization of land, like the political structures, must have changed radically. Although the Homeric poems—largely completed by about 700 BC—might reflect the new social world of the Iron Age, they are even more significant as a record of the Mycenaean Bronze Age past.

Peter Warren

THE AEGEAN REGION

Europe's first civilizations developed in the eastern Mediterranean region during the second millennium BC. The map shows most of the important sites mentioned in the text.

CARTOGRAPHY: RAY SIM

⚓ **Shipwreck**

THE MINOAN PALACE OF KNOSSOS

GRAHAM JOYNER

THE PALACE OF KNOSSOS was a social, economic, administrative, and religious center for a large local population. The original palace, dating from about 1900 BC, probably began as a series of separate buildings with different functions, grouped around a central courtyard. After an earthquake about 1700 BC, these separate, specialized units were rebuilt into one complex structure on several levels, linked by corridors, staircases, and light wells. The palace had a sophisticated plumbing and drainage system and was decorated with frescoes depicting activities of the time. It included storerooms, workrooms, a domestic area, and a multitude of ceremonial rooms, some identified as shrines. Occupied by Mycenaeans about 1450 BC, the palace was destroyed by fire about 1375 BC.

This fresco fragment, dating from about 1400 BC, belongs to a frieze showing at least two large-scale women with several smaller men. Wearing long robes, the men are seated on folding stools and sharing cups. The loop at the back of her neck suggests that the figure known as "La Parisienne" is a goddess or priestess. A ritual is probably in progress, possibly connected with the west side of the palace, where the fresco was found.
ALEX STARKEY/CAMERA PRESS/AUSTRAL INTERNATIONAL

The light well next to the Grand Staircase, on the east side of the courtyard, provides light and access to the domestic area. The left corridor leads to a large hall; on the right are the living quarters. The quality of craftsmanship is revealed in the finely dressed stone, painted cypress beams and columns, and walls decorated with a shield fresco.

ALEX STARKEY/CAMERA PRESS/AUSTRAL INTERNATIONAL

F.H.C. BIRCH/SONIA HALLIDAY PHOTOGRAPHS

AUSTRAL INTERNATIONAL

◂ A suite of rooms near the Grand Staircase identifies the palace's living quarters. They include a "sitting room" looking onto a light well, this bathroom, with its clay tub (emptied by hand), and a flushing lavatory.

⬧ When storerooms were excavated, they were found to contain food storage vessels still in place. Up to 2 meters (7 feet) high, the vessels were hand-formed and decorated with many handles.

◂ A man vaults over a bull's back, and a woman stands behind with outstretched arms. (The woman in front probably does not belong to this scene.) Dating from about 1450 BC, this frieze probably came from public rooms on the east side of the courtyard. Bull-jumping may have been an activity performed in the courtyard, with spectators watching safely from balconies and windows. It remains uncertain whether it was a ritual or a sport.

ALEX STARKEY/CAMERA PRESS/AUSTRAL INTERNATIONAL

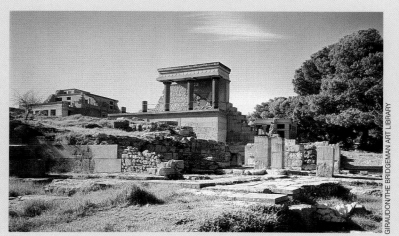

GIRAUDON/THE BRIDGEMAN ART LIBRARY

◂ The ruins of the North Pillar Hall, the palace's northern entrance. An open-air ramp leads up to the courtyard. The galleries above the ramp (shown in a restoration by Sir Arthur Evans) were decorated with relief frescoes. This approach contrasts with the main, formal entrance at the south, whose long, winding corridors were decorated with frescoes showing several hundred large figures in procession.

THE HITTITES: A POWERFUL AND PRACTICAL PEOPLE

⤷ A view over the temple area in the lower city of Hattusas. The principal building (the central courtyard of which is clearly visible) contained shrines dedicated to the sun-goddess of Arinna and the weather-god of Hatti. It was surrounded by rows of long storerooms.

Few people visiting the arid steppe country of what is now central Turkey would guess that the area was once the center of one of the ancient world's great powers. Yet the impressive remains found near the village of Boğazkale (formerly Boğazköy), about 160 kilometers (100 miles) east of Ankara, show that between 1650 BC and 1180 BC, this was Hattusas, the capital of the Hittites. These were a people whose power and influence were at the time equal to those of the better-known kingdoms of Babylon, Assyria, and Egypt.

Dramatic Monuments

The royal palace of Hattusas was built on a great outcrop that juts from the north-facing slope of a rocky ridge, with an almost vertical drop on the northern and eastern sides to a stream bed far below. On the level ground at the foot of the slope, to the west and northwest, lay a "lower city", the site of the principal temple. To the south, a great city wall rose to the top of the ridge, enclosing several lesser "castles" on smaller outcrops, an artificial lake some 90 meters by 60 meters (300 feet by 200 feet) in size, and no fewer than 31 temples. Several surviving gateways are flanked by impressive guardian figures. The total area enclosed within the city wall is more than 160 hectares (400 acres).

Not far from Hattusas, at Yazilikaya, to the northeast, is another dramatic Hittite monument. Here, worn by time and weathering into yet another rocky outcrop, are two natural rock chambers, the walls of which are adorned with low-relief carvings of more than 60 figures. Those in the larger chamber form two processions, one of male and one of female deities, which converge at the inner end, where the principal deities come face to face. Watching the scene from behind the female procession is the figure of a Hittite king. The same king can be seen in the smaller chamber in the protective embrace of his guardian-god. In front of him is carved a huge 3 meter (9 foot) sword, its pommel, or knob, in the form of a god's head, its hilt formed of lions' bodies, and its blade plunged into the rock. On the opposite wall is a frieze of 12 warrior-gods (who also appear at the rear of the male procession in the larger chamber),

⤴ The guardian figure of the King's Gate at Hattusas. He wears only a short kilt and a helmet with flaps to protect his ears and neck, and is armed with a short, curved sword and an elaborate battle-axe.

⤷ The King's Gate in the city wall of Hattusas. The double gateway, of characteristic pointed shape, was flanked by strong towers. Further protection was provided by the carved figure of an armed deity (illustrated above) set against the inner gate-jamb.

moving in menacing formation with their curved swords over their shoulders.

About 35 kilometers (20 miles) to the north of Boğazkale, at the site of Alaca Hüyük, there is further evidence of Hittite architecture and sculpture. Here, the main gate of a small but strongly fortified settlement was guarded by two large sphinxes. The outer walls of the towers flanking the gate were decorated with low reliefs of sacrificial, festive, and hunting scenes.

Who, then, were the Hittites, who left behind these impressive remains? Fortunately for us, their capital has yielded ample documentary evidence that enables us, to a great extent, to reconstruct their history and assess their achievements. They appeared on the political scene about 1650 BC, when their first monarch, Hattusilis I, chose to rebuild Hattusas, which had been destroyed in a local conflict about a century earlier. Intending to use it as a base from which to expand his territory, he eventually controlled central Anatolia, reaching the Mediterranean coast and gaining access to northern Syria, the most important center of trade routes in the ancient Middle East. By about 1600 BC, Aleppo, the main power center of the area, was in Hittite hands, and in 1595 BC, a Hittite army swept far down the Euphrates River to capture Babylon, bringing the dynasty of Hammurabi to an inglorious end.

The Hittites demonstrated both military strength and ambition to achieve status as an international power. But such ambitions are not easily sustained, and it was soon clear that the Anatolian newcomers had overreached themselves. A speedy withdrawal from conquered territories was followed by a series of coups d'etat that quickly reduced the emergent power to its former provincial status. Partial revivals in about 1500 BC, and again in about 1450 BC, promised much, but in the end, achieved little.

The Rise to Power

It was not until about 1380 BC that a young and vigorous king, called Suppiluliumas, was able to re-establish Hittite power on a firm basis throughout central Anatolia. Once again, he conquered northern Syria, thus gaining what was to be lasting control of the vital area between the Euphrates River and the Mediterranean Sea. Final confirmation of Hittite international importance came in about 1352 BC, when the widow of Tutankhamun, the recently deceased pharaoh of Egypt, wrote a passionate letter to Suppiluliumas begging him to save her from being overthrown by sending one of his sons to be her husband and ruler of Egypt. Unfortunately, the king hesitated, giving her opponents time to consolidate their position. When the son was finally dispatched to Egypt, he was murdered before he could be installed as pharaoh. Despite this setback, the Hittites remained one of the major powers of the ancient world, and a series of strong and capable rulers ensured that their power would not be easily lost.

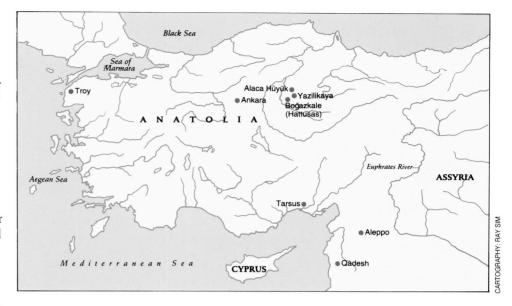

CARTOGRAPHY: RAY SIM

Mursilis II (about 1340 BC to 1306 BC) turned his attention to the west, and successfully extended Hittite control to the Aegean Sea. His successor, Muwatallis (about 1306 BC to 1282 BC), had to face a renewed challenge from Egypt, but when the two powers met in 1286 BC, near the North Syrian town of Qadesh, the Egyptian advance was halted, leaving the Hittites in firm control of this vital area. Even the emergence of a new danger, Assyria, which took advantage of Hittite–Egyptian rivalry to extend its boundaries as far as the eastern bank of the Euphrates and make raids into Hittite territory, did little to diminish Hittite power. Instead, it brought the Hittites and Egyptians into alliance in the face of mutual danger from the east. For 75 years, under Hattusilis III, Tudhaliyas IV, and Suppiluliumas II, the Hittites played an important part in maintaining an international balance of power that provided a period of stability for an insecure world.

At the height of its power, the Hittite state was ruled on feudal lines, with the king at the peak of the social pyramid, supported (or often, not

HITTITE SITES IN ASIA MINOR
Hattusas, the Hittite capital, in central Anatolia, became the center of a feudal state of considerable power.

♀ The 12 warrior-gods from the smaller rock chamber at Yazilikaya, kilted and with sickle-shaped swords at the ready. The sculpture gives a strong impression of relentless, forward movement.

G.T. GARVEY/ANCIENT ART & ARCHITECTURE COLLECTION

🔼 A small gold figurine of a Hittite god. Objects such as this were presumably personal possessions, and had the same protective function as large-scale sculptures such as that on the King's Gate.

RONALD SHERIDAN/ANCIENT ART & ARCHITECTURE COLLECTION

supported!) by aristocratic "barons", who swore an oath of loyalty to him and were rewarded by grants of land. Towards the bottom of the pyramid were the free citizens, most of whom worked either on the land or as craftworkers. The bottom level consisted of slaves, who belonged to individual owners, and deportees from conquered territories, who remained under the control of the state.

The basis of the economy was agriculture, but trade and industry were also important; bronze for weapons and tools, for instance, was vital, and control of metal sources, or of routes that led to them, played a large part in imperial policy.

Local religion was primarily concerned with people's relationship to the great powers of nature. Under the empire, the many local deities were, with difficulty, organized into a state pantheon headed by the sun-goddess of Arinna (who, despite her title, seems to have been a deity of the "mother-goddess" type), and, in a rather subordinate position, the weather-god of Hatti. The king had extensive religious duties, which were regarded as being so vital to the welfare of the state that he sometimes had to return from military campaigns to ensure that the duties were performed at the proper time.

Towards 1200 BC, the situation began to deteriorate. Assyria was becoming increasingly aggressive, while throughout Hittite territory, it became more and more difficult for the king to control his unruly nobles and vassals. About 1235 BC, the Hittite capital itself was temporarily seized by a rival claimant to the throne. Crop failures brought famine conditions in some areas, increasing social instability. In other circumstances, the Hittite kingdom might well have survived this crisis. But far to the west, in the Aegean, and even possibly in the Balkans, a situation was developing over which the Hittites had no control.

Upheaval and Decline

The course of events is impossible to reconstruct with any accuracy. This was a time of social and political upheaval, which resulted in the uprooting of entire communities, and their enforced migration along the coasts of Anatolia and through Syria and Palestine towards the borders of Egypt. Although there is little evidence to suggest that these developments directly affected Hattusas itself, it is clear that the pressure on the western and southern periphery of the already weakened realm was so great that a total collapse followed. Hittite power disintegrated, and the capital was sacked, probably by long-standing enemies from the north. Soon, the very existence of the Hittite Empire was forgotten.

The main area of Hittite interest and influence outside their central Anatolian homeland was, as we have seen, towards the southeast, in northern Syria, where so many of the region's most important trade routes converged. In this area, they must have made contact not only with the other powers of the Middle Eastern world, but also with the Mycenaean Greeks, whose presence is firmly attested to by the abundance of Mycenaean pottery discovered at many coastal sites. It is likely that contacts were also made along the Aegean coast, when Hittite power extended far to the west. Surprisingly, little archaeological evidence for this contact has been discovered in the form of Mycenaean artifacts in central Anatolia or Hittite artifacts at Mycenaean sites. But Hittite texts give ample evidence for relations, both friendly and hostile, with a land known to them as Ahhiyawa. Ahhiyawa can plausibly be equated with the land of the Akhai(w)oi or Achaeans, one of the Homeric names for the Greeks who fought in the Trojan War.

The Hittite Achievement

If we attempt to sum up the Hittite achievement, we have to admit that there were few, if any, ways in which they made a permanent impact on later periods. But while they were at the height of their power, they provided secure and stable government, backed by a humane legal system and a disciplined and efficient army, which never descended to the bloodthirsty ruthlessness displayed by the Assyrian army during the following centuries. If, in comparison to their contemporaries in Egypt, Crete, and Greece, they were lacking in artistic inspiration and achievement, they could at least claim a mastery of large-scale practical architecture, and their sculpture, conventional and repetitive though it is, often has a sense of lively vigor that is in itself attractive. On the whole, however, their achievements were practical rather than intellectual. In that sense, they might be described as the Romans of their age.

J.G. Macqueen

👉 A pair of ritual pottery vessels excavated at Hattusas. They represent the two sacred bulls of the weather-god of Hatti, and are about 1 meter (3 feet) tall. Liquid can be poured in through the funnel-like opening on their backs, flowing through their nostrils when the bulls are tilted.

THE HITTITE MUSEUM, ANKARA/SONIA HALLIDAY PHOTOGRAPHS

FROM BRONZE TO IRON IN THE MEDITERRANEAN REGION

GÖRAN BURENHULT

THE ADVENT OF the Iron Age is closely connected to a period of great economic, social, and political turmoil, and violent changes in the history of southeastern Europe and Southwest Asia. It entailed one of the major technical innovations in the history of humankind, with far-reaching and revolutionary economic, social, and political consequences. One of these consequences was the rapid collapse of Europe's social systems, which had developed in the Stone Age. Iron was accessible to everyone, and power could no longer be based on the control of trade routes for precious materials.

The invention of iron-working has often been attributed to the Hittites of Asia Minor (present-day Turkey), who were thought to have guarded the secrets of this technology for a long time. This, however, is most probably a misinterpretation of Hittite manuscripts, and the identity of the first ironworkers remains uncertain. We do know, however, that the Hittites were the first to master iron-smelting, and thus began the first true Iron Age culture in the world. Although iron objects appeared as early as about 5000 BC, it was not until about 900 BC that the new metal became the dominant raw material for tool-making and weaponry.

Iron technology depends on the knowledge of two processes: carburization (the absorption of carbon by iron to produce steel) and quenching (the rapid cooling of hot metal to produce a much harder final product). Shortage of metal supplies for bronze has been put forward as one of the reasons for the development of iron-working, but this explanation does not apply to most regions in the eastern Mediterranean and Anatolia. An increasing overall demand for metal is more likely to be the main reason for the accelerating use of iron. Furthermore, unlike copper, tin, and zinc, iron was available practically everywhere, a fact that soon led to a rapid change from bronze to iron technology.

After the collapse of the Mycenaean palace societies in Greece, the archaeological record reveals a period of extensive depopulation and complete lack of centralized political power. The time between 1300 BC and 900 BC, called the Submycenaean and the proto-Geometric phases by archaeologists, has been referred to as a period of cultural darkness—the Dark Ages. But it was during this period, from about 1100 BC, that iron became increasingly common in the area. And, successively, archaeological research has bridged the cultural gap between the downfall of the Mycenaean world, about 1300 BC, and the rise of the Greek city-states, in the seventh century BC.

The Geometric period, between 900 BC and 700 BC, got its name from the range of motifs on the pottery—meandering lines, zigzags,

◀◉ A Villanovan burial urn of clay, together with a fibula and a razor.
ARCHAEOLOGICAL MUSEUM, FLORENCE/SCALA

and rhombic shapes. About 800 BC, human figures also appear as decoration, and the high-water mark of Geometric art appears somewhat later with the so-called Dipylon style, manufactured in Athens about 750 BC. Dipylon vases often show burial scenes or processions with chariots and armed warriors—the first depictions of what would become mythological representation in Greek art.

The Villanova Culture

In Italy—mainly in Etruria, the Po Plain, and parts of Campania—the Early Iron Age is called Villanova, after a site outside Bologna. Villanova had its roots in the Urnfield tradition of the Late Bronze Age—the proto-Villanova phase— with close connections to central Europe. Characteristic of this period are fortified settlements, built on the top of high ground. At the beginning of the eighth century BC, the Villanova culture was to develop into the Etruscan civilization under strong influence from Greek and Phoenician seafarers.

The Villanova cemeteries were really urnfields, and the tombs were often pit tombs, dug into the soft, tuffaceous rock. Cremation was practiced, and the burned bones were deposited in biconical urns or in characteristic hut-urns—clay model replicas of the real houses for the living. The graves contain bronze objects, often richly decorated, such as helmets, situlas (bucket-shaped vessels), drinking vessels, and a series of elegant fibulas (brooches and clasps).

Many of the Villanovan settlements show a gradual development into what later were to become Etruscan cities—for example, Tárchuna (Tarquinia), Caere (Cerveteri), Veii (Veio), Felsina (Bologna), Pupluna (Populonia), and Klevsin (Chiusi)— and the same continuity can be shown in the large cemeteries attached to these settlements.

◀◉ A proto-Geometric vase, probably manufactured in Athens during the eleventh century BC. The checkered pattern is typical of the period, whereas the wavy lines may be a remnant of Mycenaean artistic traditions.
BRITISH MUSEUM

A BRONZE AGE MOSAIC IN THE IBERIAN PENINSULA

⚲ A shallow clay bowl with interior decoration from a collective tomb at Los Millares. Ritual objects frequently accompanied richer burials in the third millennium BC.
ARCHAEOLOGICAL MUSEUM, MADRID/SCALA

⚲ The Bronze Age farmstead of El Castillo (center) commands wide views over the fertile valley below. Defense from enemy attacks was an important consideration when selecting places for permanent settlement.

Village life emerged in the Iberian peninsula (present-day Spain and Portugal) about 3200 BC, the same time as the people began to work with copper. The uneven distribution of natural resources and arable land, and big variations in population, meant that different areas of the region developed at different rates—some did not progress at all, while others became centers of innovation. The latter growth was concentrated around the southern and southwestern coasts of Iberia. A major settlement at Los Millares (Almería), in the southeast, extended over 2 hectares (5 acres), and was protected by triple walls of stone and reinforced with towers. An imposing barbican (outer defense) with guard chambers and arrow slits projected from the gateway. Stretching more than 300 meters (980 feet) high above the River Andarax, these defensive ramparts straddle a cemetery containing more than 70 collective tombs. On the nearby hills, 10 or 15 smaller citadels guard the approaches to the village. Inside the walls are a number of modest, round dwellings and a large workshop in which copper was smelted and objects cast in simple molds. Contemporary mines and copper-smelting slags have been found in the Sierra de Alhamilla, less than 20 kilometers (12 miles) to the east.

BRONZE AGE SITES IN THE IBERIAN PENINSULA
Parts of the region developed at different rates: the centers of innovation were clustered around the southern and southwestern coasts of the peninsula.
CARTOGRAPHY: RAY SIM

Metallurgical Knowledge

Advanced metalworking techniques, so widely used throughout southern Iberia, may have been locally developed. However, it is possible that metallurgical know-how circulated quite freely in the prehistoric Mediterranean region, and that the Iberians learned skills discovered elsewhere. The economy was totally based on agriculture; wheat and barley were grown and a range of domestic animals were kept, including cattle, pigs, sheep, and goats. Floodwater was probably all that was available to irrigate river-bottom land in this arid region.

The various objects found in graves at Los Millares, such as cosmetic or perfume vases, copper implements, personal ornaments, and decorated beaker pottery for drinking and feasting, indicate this was a stratified society with marked inequality of wealth. The defensive walls surrounding the settlement and the number of forts suggest the existence of social instability, as well as the raiding and fighting that went with it. This picture is reinforced by similar defended villages found in the western outskirts of Seville and at the Cabezo del Plomo (Murcia), in the east. But it is only in central Portugal that the size of Los Millares can be matched—at Vila Nova de São Pedro and Zambujal. Many Copper Age villages shrank in size or were abandoned by 2000 BC, as Bronze Age settlement shifted to new sites, sometimes only a few hundred meters away. In southeastern Spain, steep hilltops were favored for their inaccessibility.

RICHARD J. HARRISON

Social Differences

Meanwhile, the custom of burying people below the floors of their houses replaced the collective burial practices of the Copper Age societies. Evidence of differences in social standing is very marked at grave sites at settlements such as El Argar and El Oficio (Almería), where the richest women were adorned with a silver diadem or a gold bracelet, while important men were equipped with a bronze sword, axe, and polished pottery. At Fuente Alamo (Almería), the elite lived apart from the rest of the village, in square stone houses with round granaries and a water cistern nearby. Such customs were reflected on a lesser scale in the southern Meseta, where fortified hamlets, known as *motillas,* dominated a flat landscape. In eastern and northern Spain, people did not live in villages at all, but in hamlets such as Moncín, in Zaragoza, or on family farms such as El Castillo (Frías de Albarracin, Teruel). Several hundred of these have been discovered in the mountains behind Valencia. On the other hand, metalworking was in evidence everywhere—first in copper, then in bronze. Metals were obtained through regional exchanges.

Domestic horses became important for the greater mobility they provided, both for riding to distant hunting grounds in search of pelts and furs —for example, at Moncín—or for raiding neighbors. A greater emphasis on hunting as well as dairying meant that small communities could maintain their independence, free from external domination.

In the wetter regions, along the Atlantic coast and Bay of Biscay, small settlements fortified by deep ditches, called *castros,* were established. Here, a flourishing bronze industry developed links with southern Britain and France. The people practiced the same customs of burying hoards of metal tools and weapons. In fact, hoarding metal implements, especially axes, reached a peak in Galicia and northern Portugal between 1000 BC and 700 BC, mirroring similar practices in Brittany and, to a lesser degree, in Britain and Ireland. Scrap was collected for recycling. Deep mining for copper minerals was practiced widely. At El Milagro, Aramo (Asturias), and Riner (Lérida), antler picks and levers abandoned by miners have been found in the underground galleries.

🔸 These decorated gold bracelets from the hoard of Villena were made between 900 BC and 800 BC, probably in southwestern Spain.

◄● Two gold bowls with punched geometric decoration from a dinner service buried in the hoard of Villena. They show the wealth and taste for conspicuous luxury among the ruling aristocracies of the early first millennium BC.

Gold Treasures

Western Iberia has gold treasures, too, such as the ornaments, comb, and cups found at Caldas de Reyes (Pontevedra). Gold became more common after 1100 BC, and a series of massive ornaments has been discovered. Two neckrings from Berzocana (Cáceres) were buried in a bronze bowl made in the eastern Mediterranean about 1100 BC; a collar from Sintra (Portugal) was crafted from three neckrings attached to a base plate; and a 9.75 kilogram (20 pound) treasure from Villena (Alicante) includes a decorated tableware service, and 28 massive gold bracelets, which may have been loot from a raid.

The variety of ways of life and burial customs indicates that Bronze Age Spain formed a social mosaic ranging from tribal villages to much looser associations based on dispersed dwellings. Societies like these were prospering when Phoenician sailors reached southern Spain about 800 BC, opening up a new era of cultural exchange within the Mediterranean region.

Richard J. Harrison

🔸 Deer antler was often selected to haft stone and metal tools, because it absorbed the shocks from heavy blows.
NATIONAL MUSEUM OF ANTIQUITIES, EDINBURGH/ADAM WOOLFITT/ ROBERT HARDING PICTURE LIBRARY

GREEK AND PHOENICIAN COLONIZATION: 800 BC TO 500 BC

GÖRAN BURENHULT

BETWEEN THE SEVENTH and fifth centuries BC, the Mediterranean world was dominated by two far-reaching events that had considerable impact on subsequent cultural developments in the area: Greek and Phoenician colonization. There were several reasons behind this expansion, such as the need for new settlement areas for the rapidly growing populations in the homelands—in Greece, the time of colonization coincides with a period of marked overpopulation—and the ever-increasing need for raw materials and other necessities. To a great extent, both Greece and Phoenicia lacked metal-ore resources, as well as wood for shipbuilding. Later, grain and other foodstuffs played a significant part in the growing trade.

With the exception of parts of present-day Egypt and Libya, Greek expansion largely followed the northern shores of the Mediterranean—the coasts of the Aegean and Adriatic seas, southern Italy, Corsica, southern France, and eastern Spain—as well as the shores of the Black Sea. In contrast, the Phoenicians founded their trading colonies in the south—in North Africa, western Sicily, Sardinia, and southern Spain. The earliest Phoenician colonies were founded in the metal-rich Tartessa region of southern Spain; while the earliest Greek one has been found at Pithekoussai, on the island of Ischia, in Italy. Many trading colonies evolved into important seaports that exist to this day, including Massilia (Marseilles), in France; Neapolis (Naples), in Italy; Carthage (Tunis), in Tunisia; and Syracuse, in Sicily.

GREEK AND PHOENICIAN SITES
The Mediterranean region, showing major Greek colonies and Phoenician cities and colonies.
CARTOGRAPHY: RAY SIM

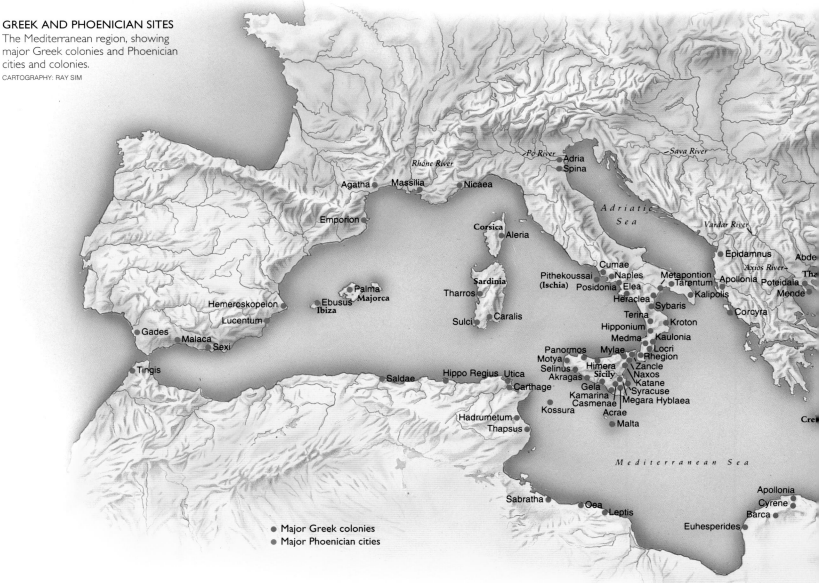

- ● Major Greek colonies
- ● Major Phoenician cities

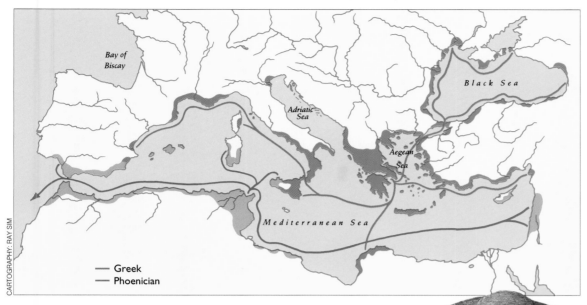

CARTOGRAPHY: RAY SIM

- Greek
- Phoenician

**GREEK AND PHOENICIAN TRADE ROUTES
AND AREAS OF COLONIZATION**

THE LOUVRE/THE BR IDGEMAN ART LIBRARY

☝ This ointment flask (*amphoriskos*)
of sand-core glass was found in
Phoenicia, in the Levant, and
dates from the fifth century BC.
Sand-core glass was made by
winding molten glass strands
around a rod, or core, of clay,
dung, and sand. The core was
removed after the glass
had cooled.

☝ A terracotta mask with negroid
features found in Carthage, in Tunisia,
dating from the seventh or sixth
century BC.

MUSÉE DU BARDO, TUNIS/THE BRIDGEMAN ART LIBRARY

☛ This Phoenician jug was found
in the Greek colony of Ischia (at
Pithekoussai), an island off the coast
of Campania, in southern Italy.

MIKE ANDREWS/ANCIENT
ART & ARCHITECTURE COLLECTION

AUSTRALIAN PICTURE LIBRARY

THE AGE OF ANCIENT GREECE

1 1 0 0   B C   –   3 1   B C

The Birth of Modern Europe

PONTUS HELLSTRÖM

WILD AND FORBIDDING mountains made land contact difficult between settlements in ancient Greece. People living on the numerous coastal or inland plains found waterways the most important means of communication and transport. Overseas connections were common, and not only for those Greeks who had settled on the islands and on the eastern shore of the Aegean Sea.

It is therefore understandable that the ancient Greeks never managed by themselves to form a political unit; the only serious attempt in this direction was the fifth-century BC naval confederacy called the Delian League, led by Athens. Ultimately, unification was imposed on the Greeks, first by Macedonia and later by Rome, but by then, Greece was no longer its own master.

So long as Greece remained independent, it consisted of a large number of separate, self-governing cities, each forming its own city-state. Most of the city-states were small, and consisted of a single settlement surrounded by farmland. The few notable exceptions, such as Athens, Sparta, and Thessaly, were on wide plains, which made larger political units possible.

◖◖ In ancient Greece, the building of marble temples to the gods gave cities prestige. Dating from 447 BC to 438 BC, the Parthenon temple on the Acropolis of Athens is the most perfect of them all. It was built with the use of such subtle refinements as a very slight inwards inclination of the columns, to give an unusual impression of harmony and strength.

♁ A large number of painted marble statues of girls stood on the Acropolis of Athens as gifts to the goddess. This lovely Athenian maiden was one of them. Dating from about 500 BC, she was found by archaeologists a hundred years ago.
ACROPOLIS MUSEUM/SCALA

THE ANCIENT GREEK WORLD

The ancient Greek world included Sicily and southern Italy, to the west, and western Asia Minor and Cyprus, to the east.

CARTOGRAPHY: RAY SIM

After the collapse of the Mycenaean Bronze Age civilization, about 1100 BC, Greece was rather sparsely populated for some centuries. This coincides to a large extent with the so-called Dark Age, which lasted until about 700 BC. Our knowledge of the history of these non-literate centuries is comparatively limited, and is based largely on archaeological finds. For the later history of Greece, we have a literature rich in information of many kinds.

THE AGE OF EXPLORATION: 800 BC TO 600 BC

Greek culture did not regain momentum until about 750 BC. With a fresh interest in overseas trade, Greek colonies were founded both in the west (in Italy) and in the east (on the Levantine coast). (See the features *The Trading Port of Pithekoussai* and *The Greeks in the West*.) In the homeland, there are signs of a growth in population. Overseas connections brought a wide spectrum of cultural influences and foreign inspiration.

This was a time of creativity and invention, in which the Greeks showed themselves to be a highly talented people. In the late eighth century BC, the Greek alphabet came into use, and the oldest preserved Greek literature, by Homer and Hesiod, was written. We also see the beginnings of columnar architecture and sculpture in the round. In vase painting, a number of local schools appeared in various parts of Greece, sometimes showing their apparent pleasure in figured scenes.

Greek society, in this period, was feudal, and we can learn much about it from the works of Homer and Hesiod. Cities were small, and ruled by local aristocracies and chieftains. A new era was rapidly taking over, however—that of the Greek "polis" or city-state.

The Rise of the City-state

A polis can roughly be defined as a small, independent community, with a constitution—either formal or informal—and consisting of male citizens, their families, immigrants, and slaves. It occupied a central

out between Chalkis and Eretria over the Lelantine plain. If so, this was probably the reason for the end of Euboean supremacy. In the following century, trade was taken over to a large extent by Corinth, which had two excellent harbors: Lechaion, on the Corinthian Gulf, for trade to the west; and Kenchreai, on the east coast of the Peloponnese, for the eastern trade. During the seventh century BC, small Corinthian decorated pottery flasks—containers for perfumed oil—were exported throughout the Mediterranean.

In this formative period for Classical Greek civilization, however, the Greek cities in Ionia, on the eastern coast of the Aegean Sea (now Turkey), played an important role. The poet Homer lived on this coast, which was also the home of the earliest Greek philosophy, mathematics, and science. Most of the Greek cities on the northern coast of the Aegean Sea and on the coasts of the Black Sea were founded by colonists sent out from Ionia. Miletus, one of the most important Greek cities in Ionia, allegedly founded 90 colonies.

A so-called *aryballos*, a little pottery bottle produced at Corinth between about 600 BC and 575 BC for the export of perfumed oil. The motifs are of Near Eastern origin, and were probably inspired by imported textiles from the Levant.
MIKE ANDREWS/ANCIENT ART AND ARCHITECTURE COLLECTION

city surrounded by farmland. It was ruled by its male citizens, who met in assembly in the marketplace and elected their own officials—although sometimes the supreme power lay with an unconstitutional ruler. Its army consisted of citizens equipped as foot soldiers (called hoplites), fighting in close formation. Their equipment was cheap enough to be within the means of ordinary citizens, and consisted of corselet, greaves, and helmet; a round shield; a thrusting spear; and a sword.

The Greek city-states were not only on the Greek mainland and Greek islands of today, but also on the eastern coast of the Aegean Sea, in what today is Turkey. By means of colonization, Greek cities were established across the Mediterranean, notably on the coasts of Sicily and southern Italy and on the shores of the Black Sea.

In Dark Age Greece, the cities of Chalkis and Eretria (on Euboea, an island north of Attica) played an important role in overseas trade and colonization. In the late eighth century BC, probably about 720 BC, legend has it that a devastating war broke

This huge clay vase dating from about 750 BC was used as a grave-marker in the cemetery of Athens. It stands 1.55 meters (5 feet) tall. The central part of the painting shows a funeral scene, with the dead lying on a bier, surrounded by mourners.
NATIONAL MUSEUM ATHENS/SCALA

145

☞ The first beauty contest in world history, painted on an Athenian vase. To the left is a procession of the three contestants: Aphrodite, the goddess of love; Athena, goddess of the arts and of orderly warfare, identified by her helmet; and Hera, Mother of the Gods. At the head of the procession is Hermes, the messenger god, and to the right sits the judge, Prince Paris of Troy. Aphrodite won by bribing the judge. In Greek legend, this contest was the origin of the Trojan War. In return for his favorable decision, Paris won the love of Helen, the most beautiful woman on Earth. She followed him to Troy, thereby causing the Greek war of revenge that ended with the destruction of Troy.

ANCIENT ART & ARCHITECTURE COLLECTION

⚨ Athena, goddess of the arts and of orderly warfare. This ancient copy of Phidias's famous gold-and-ivory statue in the Parthenon temple on the Acropolis of Athens, which stood 11 meters (36 feet) tall, dates from the period of emperor Hadrian (AD 117 to AD 138).

RONALD SHERIDAN/ANCIENT ART & ARCHITECTURE COLLECTION

Gods and Heroes

The Greeks had many gods. Their gods had human form, and each had his or her own sphere of influence. Seen from the outside, with Homer as our guide, the gods seem a rather frivolous crowd. This gives an impression that Greek religion was not a very serious matter—a feeling expressed by philosophers of the time.

Homer's stories about immoral behavior among the gods, however, have no connection with the common people's respect for their local deities. By age-old tradition, every village had its own guardian god or goddess. There were also cults of other gods directing specific aspects of life. Thus, cults of Dionysus, for instance, connected with fertility, took place in the appropriate season.

Another characteristic of Greek religion is the hero cult. Many Greek myths are about half-gods, who had a partly human origin. The most famous of these heroes was Hercules, who was worshiped in many places and was of national importance. Other heroes were worshiped only locally—for example, Theseus (worshiped mainly in Attica) and Bellerophon (worshiped at Corinth). The cult of local heroes took its most important step forward in the later Dark Age, when hero cults were created at Bronze Age tombs in the countryside. This can be at least partly explained as a cult of invented ancestors, whereby the landed aristocracy confirmed inherited rights.

The cult of gods of human origin paved the way for a cult of rulers. Such cults had, in a way, begun in the colonization period, when overseas leaders of city-state colonial enterprises received a hero's burial and cult worship in city centers. We also hear of a hero's cult of the still-living Spartan admiral Lysander, which was created in Samos, in the fifth century BC, in gratitude for his having saved the island. This led to a feature of Hellenistic and Roman times, when kings and emperors were the subject of heroic cult worship in their lifetime.

The cult of the gods differed from the heroic cult in the way sacrifices were made. To the gods fell only a part of the sacrifice, and the rest was distributed to those taking part in the rite. The sacrifice to heroes, like that to gods of the underworld, was not to be shared by others; the sacrificed animal was either thrown into a sacrificial pit or completely burned.

The recording in writing of Greek myths was undertaken by the earliest Greek poets, Homer and Hesiod. Homer's *Iliad* and Hesiod's *Theogony* were, however, not holy books like the Bible. The details of the myths could be changed at will, and the texts were not inviolable. When tragedians in the fifth century BC gave alternative versions of older myths, and partly invented new ones according to their dramatic needs, it caused no concern to the audience.

Sacrifice, Creed, and Mystery Cults

The relationship between the Greeks and their gods did not require creed; it required only that proper actions should be taken at the proper times. Taking part in the sacrificial feasts of the gods was one such proper action. It was also important that the sacrifice be performed according to the rules. No creed was involved in the cult of oracular gods—the gods, such as Apollo, who were credited with the power of divine revelation at such sanctuaries as Delphi and Didyma.

It was in the mystery cults that the Greeks came closest to religious feeling and creed. The most sacred mystery cults were those of Demeter and Persephone, at Eleusis, near Athens. There were other famous mystery cults on the islands of Samothrace and Lemnos.

Loosely connected to the mystery cults were some sects based on philosophical ideology. One was founded by the sixth-century BC Samian philosopher Pythagoras, who emigrated to Kroton, in southern Italy, to found a school of philosophy that exerted great influence on philosophical and religious thinking for many centuries. Pythagoras is especially known for his ingenious discovery of the relationship between mathematics and musical harmony, and the consequent theory of the harmony of the spheres. The Pythagoreans believed in reincarnation, and were therefore vegetarians, a custom that brought them into conflict with traditional cult practice requiring citizens to take part in the killing and eating of animals.

♁ A cult-image of Dionysos, god of wine and fertility, surrounded by women celebrating at the festival of flowers known as Anthesteria, held in the month of February, when the new wine was ready for drinking.
MUSEO NAZIONALE, NAPLES/SCALA

ANCIENT GREECE: 1100 BC – 31 BC

AGE	THE GREEK WEST	MAINLAND AND ISLAND GREECE	THE GREEK EAST
HELLENISTIC AGE 323 BC – 31 BC	Rise of Roman Empire	Battle of Actium 31 BC — Romans sack Corinth 146 BC — Rome defeats Macedonia at Pydna 168 BC	End of Ptolemaic rule in Egypt 31 BC — Great altar of Zeus and Athena built at Pergamon c. 180 BC
CLASSICAL GREECE 480 BC – 323 BC		Alexander the Great 356 BC – 323 BC — Demosthenes 384 BC – 322 BC — Philip II 382 BC – 336 BC — Peloponnesian War 431 BC – 404 BC — Delian League 478 BC — Persian War 499 BC – 479 BC — Peisistratos rules Athens 546 BC – 528 BC	Alexandria library built 300 BC — Ptolemy I rules Egypt c. 320 BC – 283 BC — Alexander conquers the Near and Middle East 334 BC – 325 BC — Maussollos governs Caria 377 BC – 352 BC
ARCHAIC GREECE 700 BC – 480 BC	Greek colonization in Sicily and southern Italy c. 750 BC – 580 BC — Euboeans found Pithekoussai c. 750 BC	Draco promulgates legal code in Athens c. 620 BC — Corinth in the lead c. 725 BC – c. 575 BC — Lelantine War c. 720 BC — Euboean expansion c. 750 BC — Rise of the city-state 800 BC – 750 BC — Feudal society c. 840 BC	Sciences and culture flourish in Ionia 700 BC – 500 BC — Homer c. 700 BC
DARK AGE 1100 BC – 700 BC		Collapse of Mycenaean Bronze Age civilization c. 1100 BC	

(Time scale at left: BC 31, 100, 200, 300, 400, 500, 600, 700, 800, 900, 1000, 1100, BC)

THE TRADING PORT OF PITHEKOUSSAI

David Ridgway

Accoriding to the Greek geographer Strabo (63 BC to AD 21), the trading port of Pithekoussai was established by Greeks from Euboea, the large island off the east coast of mainland Greece. At the end of the eighteenth century AD, the site was identified with the modern resort of Lacco Ameno, on the island of Ischia, in the Bay of Naples. It has emerged from Giorgio Buchner's excavations (from 1952 onwards) as the western Greeks' first and most northerly base in Italy, in full working order by about 750 BC. For the next 50 years or so, it seems to have functioned as a major international trading center, of a kind then unique in the west and thus attractive to a wide variety of foreign entrepreneurs. Unlike Euboean Cumae (Kyme), its immediate successor on the adjacent Campanian mainland, Pithekoussai was not a Greek colony in the strict sense.

Craftsmen Welcomed

From the outset, the finds from the well-defined family plots in the Pithekoussai cemetery indicated that the Euboeans welcomed merchants and craftsmen, not only from many other parts of Greece, but also from the Levant, where there is good evidence for a Euboean presence in the multinational "emporium" of Al Mina, at the mouth of the Orontes, in present-day Turkey.

Indeed, knowledge of the potentially profitable sea routes to the west might well have been one of the more valuable commodities acquired in the ninth century BC, when the Euboeans became the first Greeks since the Mycenaeans to establish direct contact with the Cypro-Levantine world. By then, Cyprus, in particular, had long had a special relationship with Sardinia, which, in turn, was already involved in commercial and other exchanges with the area centered on the Colline Metallifere ("metal-bearing hills") in Tuscany.

Buchner's excavations in the cemetery (Valle di San Montano), on the acropolis (Monte di Vico), and in the suburban industrial quarter (Mezzavia) of Pithekoussai have revealed a wide range of activities in the second half of the eighth century BC. Iron (identified as originating from the island of Elba) and the constituent elements of bronze were imported and worked. Bronze was extensively used to make Italian types of fibulas (dress pins)—which suggests interaction, and probably intermarriage, with the native Iron Age communities on the mainland.

Precious metals seem to have been worked, too, perhaps by resident Levantine specialists. If so, a weight from the industrial quarter suggests that the value of the resulting jewelry was assessed on the standard later used for Euboean coinage.

The first Euboean settlers clearly included a number of accomplished potters. They exploited the island's clay beds to produce excellent painted wares in a recognizably Euboean style for local domestic and funerary purposes. Some Pithekoussan ceramic products soon found their way to Sulci, in Sardinia, and to Carthage, in North Africa, while towards the end of the eighth century BC, a few *aryballoi* (small perfume jars) made at Pithekoussai by expatriate Corinthian potters were exported to the Italian mainland.

A locally made crater (wine bowl) from the Pithekoussai cemetery bears a shipwreck scene, and is the oldest-known piece of narrative figured art ever found on Italian soil. A fragment of another example of the same shape from the industrial quarter preserves the earliest-known potter's signature using the *m'epoiese* ("X made me") formula—a kind of advertisement that became familiar throughout the Greek world in later centuries. It was used, for example, on the vases made by the master potters of Classical Athens.

Prosperous People

Pithekoussan literacy is further attested by three lines of verse inscribed (in a Euboean version of the Greek alphabet) on a cup imported from Rhodes and interred in the cemetery about 720 BC: "Nestor had a fine cup, but anyone who drinks from this one will soon be struck with desire for fair-crowned Aphrodite." This witty challenge to King Nestor's drinking cup, a magnificent artifact described in Homer's *Iliad*, is one of the earliest surviving examples of post-Mycenaean Greek writing. Its appearance at Pithekoussai shows that the prosperous community there was cultured enough to produce Europe's first literary allusion.

With the rise of Cumae from the beginning of the seventh century BC, the importance of Pithekoussai inevitably declined. At the same time, it seems that events in Greece blocked continued Euboean participation in east–west commerce.

Other Greeks, especially those from Corinth, were better able to build on the foundations laid by the nameless pioneers from Euboea, and soon established colonies of their own elsewhere in South Italy and in Sicily. Meanwhile, Cumae shrewdly directed the manufacturing skills it had inherited from Pithekoussai towards the lucrative markets offered by the increasingly sophisticated native aristocracies of Campania, Latium, and, above all, Etruria.

◄● The Baia di San Montano, at Lacco Ameno, a small town on the island of Ischia, in the Bay of Naples. This is a perfect natural harbor, and the Euboean pioneers who arrived here, about 750 BC, would have been glad of the shelter it provided for their boats. The beach (left) is at the end of the valley that served as their cemetery. This view is taken from the summit of their acropolis, Monte di Vico, the lower flank of which can be seen on the right.

DAVID RIDGWAY

⚿ The temple of the god Apollo at Corinth. Dating from about 540 BC, this early temple is of limestone, and was originally coated with white stucco to make it look like marble. With their muscular, swelling form, its columns are typical of the early period of Greek architecture.

ARCHAIC GREECE: 600 BC TO 480 BC

The need for formal constitutions followed the rise of the city-state. The motor for change in Greek political life was perhaps the advent of foot-soldier tactics in battle, which required all citizens to fight together in close formation to defend the city. Citizens thus had equal responsibility in battle, and equal expenses for armor. This may have led to a quest for political equality as well. In many cities, the old ruling aristocratic families were overthrown, and new leaders took power. These leaders were called tyrants, a word for "unconstitutional ruler" that carried no connotation of cruelty.

In spite of the rule of tyrants in many city-states, more power came to lie with a widened circle of male citizens, who met in assemblies to elect their magistrates and for other matters. The constitutions created at this time responded, of course, to needs of the day, but they also helped to shape the future. The never-resolved conflict between Athens and Sparta was, to a great extent, caused by their different constitutions. Sparta clung to its old-fashioned, never-changing constitution, whereas the Athenian constitution was repeatedly modernized to meet needs.

Sparta drew up its constitution in the early seventh century BC. Its regulations made Sparta the efficient military machine that, step by step, by force and by diplomacy, subjugated the entire Peloponnese. The heads of state were two kings, one from each of two old families. There were also 5 annually elected ephors (magistrates) and a council of 25 elders, all of whom were ex-ephors. All major decisions of the state were made by these 32 people.

There was an assembly, but it had little real power. It consisted of some 9,000 male members of the aristocracy. Some of the remaining inhabitants were *perioikoi*, "those living around", who were free citizens of surrounding villages with no political rights. The others were helots, the state-owned serfs, who were the indigenous population of the conquered area of Messenia. Helots worked the farms, and presented a constant threat of revolution.

The most important rule in the constitution was that the sons of aristocratic families were taken from their mothers at the age of 5 to begin a training that continued until they turned 30, making them the most professional soldiers Greece ever saw.

The first law code of Athens was drafted by Draco in about 620 BC. We know little more about its rules than that they were severe—"draconian", as we say. Presumably, power lay within a narrow circle of aristocratic families, who elected magistrates and a council of ex-magistrates, called the Areopagus, among themselves. In the early sixth century BC, many farmers had become serfs because of debts to the big landowners. The Athenian politician and poet Solon was assigned to modernize the constitution. The farmers were absolved from their old debts, and a new council was introduced beside the old Areopagus, which thereby lost much of its power. Solon also gave to the assembly the power of a supreme court. These changes sound far from radical, but for the time being, they saved the state from revolution. Solon's was probably the optimum solution—it gave to a wider circle of citizens extended power, but not more than would be yielded by the ruling families.

Feud of the Families

Sixth-century BC Athens was politically dominated by the conflict between two families—the old, Athenian Alcmaeonid family, and the Peisistratid family from Brauron, on the east coast of Attica. Peisistratos ruled as tyrant for several decades, at first intermittently from the late 560s BC, then continuously from 546 BC to 528 BC. After his death, his son Hippias took over. Hippias fell in 510 BC, because of Spartan help to the Alcmaeonids. Athens received a new constitution in 507 BC, drawn up by Kleisthenes, head of the Alcmaeonid family.

The most important innovations in this constitution were a widely extended citizenship and a new administrative grouping of Attica's 139 *demes*, or villages, into 30 blocks: 10 each from the City, the Coast, and the Plain. These were, in turn, grouped into 10 administrative units, called Tribes, each consisting of 3 blocks, one from the City, one from the Coast, and one from the Plain. Each Tribe elected 50 members to the council, and these groups took turns at governing the state, each exercising power for one-tenth of the year. Ten generals were also elected, one by each Tribe. They were military leaders, and were also entrusted with power in certain administrative and financial matters.

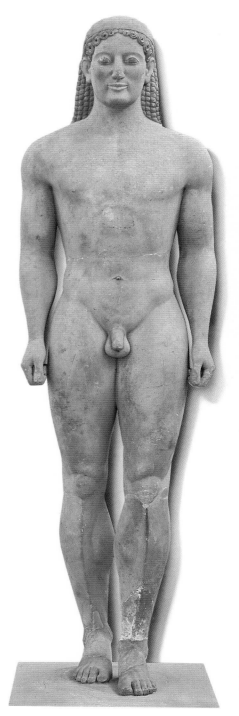

⚿ This marble statue dating from about 530 BC comes from the tomb of Kroisos, a young Athenian who fell in battle. An inscription on the base reads: "Stop and grieve at the tomb of the dead Kroisos, slain by wild Ares in the front rank of the battle."
NATIONAL MUSEUM, ATHENS/SCALA

149

THE GREEKS IN THE WEST

CHARLOTTE WIKANDER

In the *Odyssey*, Homer depicts Sicily as the pastures for the flocks of the sun-god Helios: a wonderful land of plenty, empty of people. The south of Italy and Sicily became an important and well-exploited part of the Greek world, and this mythical imagery of a bountiful nature and a land of plenty played a large part in the Greek view of the west.

From Greek literature, we know of the political and economic prominence of colonial cities such as Syracuse, in Sicily. The impressive ruins of these cities—especially their great temples—have been landmarks for centuries and have attracted travelers from the eighteenth century to our day. But it is only since the Second World War that archaeology has provided more systematic insights into the origins of the colonial enterprises, the life of the Greek colonials, and the relationship between the colonies and the indigenous inhabitants in Italy.

The earliest cities in the west were founded about the middle of the eighth century BC. The first colony was Cumae (Kyme), on the Bay of Naples, shortly before 750 BC. It was followed by the earliest Sicilian colony, Naxos, in 735 BC, and in the following year, by what became the mightiest city in Sicily, Syracuse.

Archaeologists have been able to shed light on the speed of colonization. The presence of Mycenaean Greeks in Italy during the Bronze Age has been shown to be much more extensive than was hitherto believed, and excavations at Pithekoussai, on the island of Ischia, in the Bay of Naples, have proved that a group of settled Greeks and Phoenicians was already trading from there to Etruria by 750 BC. (See the feature *The Trading Port of Pithekoussai*.) Cumae lies on the mainland directly opposite Ischia, and was thus an extension of an already existing settlement. This early Greek presence in Italy also explains some of the rapidity with which the colonies spread. This was not completely unknown land; it had been explored for at least a generation.

DENNIS STOCK/MAGNUM PHOTOS

A view of the volcano Etna from the Roman theater of Taormina, on Sicily. Taormina is the site of the original Greek colony, called Tauromenion by the Greeks.

Trade and Farming

What, then, motivated this massive colonial expansion? Two reasons seem obvious from our sources: trade and farming. Of these, trade was the earlier motivation. Greece is notoriously poor in natural resources, particularly metal, and the magnet that attracted traders to Italy was the rich ores of copper and iron in Tuscany, Etruria. The inhabitants of Iron Age Etruria were, however, obviously able to defend their resources. No Greek colonies were founded north of the Bay of Naples, and the archaeological finds in Etruria amply demonstrate the enormous quantities of goods traded by the Greeks and Phoenicians in exchange for the coveted metals.

In keeping with their trading concerns, the earliest colonies were established at good and easily defended harbor sites, Syracuse being a prime example. Two protected harbors and an island, Ortygia—offering a settlement site for the arrivals—made this a perfect location for such an enterprise.

Syracuse's mother city, Corinth, became the dominant trading power with Italy in the seventh century BC. The main trading competitors were at first Chalcidians (inhabitants of Chalcis) from Euboea, the island just off the coast of Attica. They took control of the trade passages by founding twin cities on each side of the Strait of Messina: Rhegion and Zancle.

Greece was also poor in arable land. According to various commentators, including the Greek historian Herodotus and the Greek poet Hesiod, there was increasing social tension and conflict during the late eighth and the seventh century BC, one reason apparently being overcrowding and competition for farmland. The extensive areas available for farming in the west were an obvious remedy to the situation. Colonial cities based on agriculture were founded along the coastline of southern Italy and on the southern seaboard of Sicily.

A Community Enterprise

A colonial venture was not conceived as an individual enterprise. A Greek city-state let it be known that it intended to found a colony. In some cases, we know that citizen families were required to send one adult son; otherwise, impoverished farmers, whose lots were no longer adequate to support them, set out together under the aegis of the mother city. A leader for the project, the *oikist*, was appointed by the mother city, and the site was chosen in advance with the approval of Apollo's oracle at Delphi.

When the settlers arrived, the new town and its hinterland were carefully divided into lots for habitation and cultivation, with space allotted for public use: the marketplace (*agora*) and buildings functioned as the venue for political organization and religious life. The colonies' prosperity is nowhere so clearly shown as in the massive resources put into the building of sanctuaries, which were obviously a source of civic pride as well as serving a religious function.

Indigenous People

Nevertheless, the areas occupied by Greeks were not empty on their arrival. What of the indigenous people? Did they accept this massive influx of strangers, dividing the land between them? Seemingly, they did, to a surprising extent. Mentions of conflict are practically nonexistent in the early colonial period. The archaeological evidence suggests some of the reasons behind this quiet: excavation of indigenous tombs and sites has shown how extensively native populations took advantage of Greek technology and raised their own standard of living through imports of such foreign luxuries as high-quality pottery and perfumed oils.

Only after about 300 years is there evidence of a changed attitude. The local people of southern Italy—Messapians, Lucanians, and, most of all, the Samnites—put the Greek cities under increasing military pressure from the late fifth century BC onwards. In the end, the proud colonial cities had to apply to the motherland for help, but to little avail: the greediest Italic state, Rome, finally subdued them all. Nevertheless, the colonial cities kept their Greek cultural identity for a long time, and by their profound influence on the culture of Rome, contributed towards the creation of a Hellenized culture throughout western Europe.

In this way, all parts of Attica, however distant from Athens, received equal political rights, and at the same time, the old groupings based on loyalties and geographical proximity lost much of their influence. By creating a completely new administrative structure and giving all Athenian male citizens equal rights, Kleisthenes united Attica, and gave it a modern constitution that was the most democratic of its time. That this constitution excluded women, immigrants, and slaves is only a reflection of the age in which it was created.

Greek Architecture

Greek monumental architecture, in the form of temples surrounded by wooden colonnades, was born about 650 BC. The transformation into stone followed by the end of the century. The temples' columns were of two kinds, or "orders"—the Doric, on the mainland, and the Ionic, on the eastern Aegean coast and the Aegean islands. The most obvious difference between the orders lay in the shape of their capitals, or column heads, but each order also had its own set of proportions and details, especially for the superstructure, or entablature.

Ancient theoreticians compared the Doric column to the male form because of its stout, muscular proportions and severe shape. The Ionic, with its more slender proportions and floral style, was likened to the female form—indeed, the spiral coils of the Ionic scrolled column head do resemble a coiffure.

The earliest Doric temples, surrounded by columns on all sides, were built in the northeastern Peloponnese. The earliest Ionic temples were erected on the island of Samos and at Ephesus, on the eastern Aegean coast. These were big temples, built to glorify the ruling tyrants in these cities.

War with Persia

The Archaic period ended with the Great War against Persia (from 499 BC to 479 BC), which was a successful defensive war, and which brought Greece, and especially Athens, enormous confidence. Between 550 BC and 500 BC, the Persian empire had been steadily growing, and everything indicated that the future would bring either a confrontation with Greek city-states or an unconditional Greek surrender. By the end of the century, all of Asia Minor (present-day Turkey) and Cyprus; all of the eastern and northern Aegean coasts; the entire eastern coast of the Mediterranean; Egypt; and Libya, as far as Cyrenaica, were under Persian rule.

In 499 BC, the Ionian city of Miletus asked the Greek mainland to support an uprising of many Greek cities on the eastern Aegean coast, but the reaction was hesitant. In the end, only Athens and Eretria sent a small force each, 25 ships in all. The Persians crushed the revolt in 494 BC, and turned for revenge on the two Greek cities. The Greek response was prodigious: 10,000 Athenians, with only 192 casualties, crushed a vastly larger Persian army on the plain of Marathon in 490 BC. The Greek navy of 280 ships, led by Athens, outdid a Persian navy three times as big at Salamis in 480 BC; and the Spartans defeated the Persians on the battlefield of Plataiai, in 479 BC, with some 35,000 to 40,000 troops against a far greater army.

The Greeks' strength was partly psychological. The very idea of trying to stop a Persian army perhaps 200,000 strong with a force of only 7,000 (as the Greeks nearly succeeded in doing at Thermopylae in 480 BC) is against all reason. But, of course, the final Greek victory depended very much on superior strategy, on making fewer mistakes than the enemy, and on the efficiency of foot-soldier warfare.

⚅ The heroic general Leonidas, commemorated in this statue in the acropolis of Sparta, fell in battle against the Persians at the mountain pass of Thermopylae in 480 BC, but succeeded in securing the safe retreat of his fellow Greeks.
SPARTA MUSEUM/SONIA HALLIDAY PHOTOGRAPHS

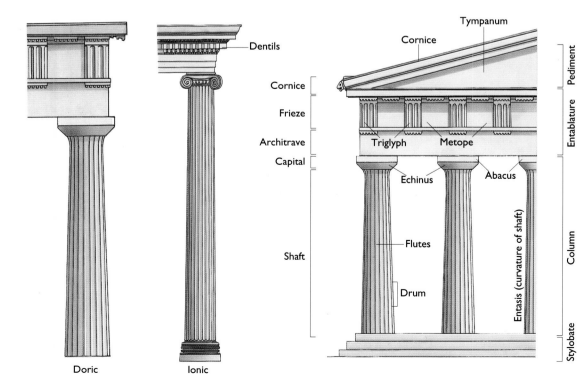

Doric

Ionic

Dentils
Cornice
Frieze
Architrave
Capital
Shaft

Tympanum
Cornice
Pediment
Triglyph
Metope
Echinus
Abacus
Entablature
Flutes
Entasis (curvature of shaft)
Column
Drum
Stylobate

◄⦿ The Doric capital (column head) was quite simple, and consisted of a circular cushion (the echinus), under a square plinth (the abacus). In the Doric entablature, the most conspicuous detail was the frieze with alternating triglyphs and metopes. The Ionic column had more elegant proportions than the Doric, and was set on a molded base. The capital had its origin in plant forms, and consisted of a scroll-like member rolling into a spiral on each side of the column top. Above the architrave beam were the so-called dentils, which imitated the ends of close-set rafters. In later Ionic, the dentils were sometimes exchanged for a figured continuous frieze running round the building on all sides.
ILLUSTRATION: MIKE LAMBLE

151

MICHAEL FREEMAN/BRUCE COLEMAN LTD

❂ The Acropolis of Athens was the religious center of the Athenian empire in the fifth century BC. To the left is the Parthenon, the largest building of the sanctuary, built between 447 BC and 438 BC and richly decorated with marble sculptures. To the right is the Erechtheion, the main cult building, with its old wooden statue of Athena, the city goddess. In the background is the Propylaia, the monumental entrance building of the Acropolis.

CLASSICAL GREECE: 480 BC TO 323 BC

If our sources for reconstructing the history of Greece in the fifth century BC had been purely archaeological, one of the two main military powers would easily have escaped notice. Thanks to our rich literary sources, however, we know that the fifth century saw constant confrontation between Athens and Sparta. Sparta won in the end, but its triumph is not archaeologically visible, because it did not use its resources to erect lasting monuments, like the temples on the Athenian Acropolis.

After the Persian War, which ended with Greek victories on land and at sea, there was relative peace in Greece for almost 50 years. This brought population growth, and by the middle of the century, Athens, the largest city of the world, and the countryside of Attica surrounding it, had about 250,000 inhabitants. Some 75,000 of these lived within the city walls. The male citizens may have numbered about 40,000; the slaves, 100,000. The rest were women, children, and immigrants.

Athens had taken the lead both politically and culturally. Politically, Athens had, in 478 BC, created a naval confederacy as a defense against Persian threats. This was the Delian League, which consisted of some 170 Greek city-states, almost all of them situated on the islands and the coast of the Aegean Sea. The formal seat of the league was the sanc-

tuary of Apollo, on the island of Delos. The league's treasury was kept there until 454 BC, when it was moved to the Athenian Acropolis, ostensibly for safety, but actually to be within easy reach when needed by Athens. In reality, the league was an Athenian empire, with all power centered in the capital of Athens. On several occasions, member-states that wanted to quit the league were brutally forced by Athens to remain in it.

In this period, Athenian democracy saw some small but important adjustments. In 462 BC, jury members in the courts were selected by lot and paid for their work, which made even male citizens who were not very rich eligible. Pay for council members on active duty and for participation in the festivals followed. In the last years of the century came pay for attending the assembly. Thus, there were no economic restrictions on any male citizen wishing to take an active part in politics. That magistrates should be selected by lot and paid was a basic principle of fifth-century BC Athenian democracy. However, the 10 generals remained elected to their position, and since there was a certain doubt about the ability of citizens chosen by lot, the generals came to be the most powerful magistrates of the city. Pericles, who in reality was the ruler of Athens from 451 BC until his death in 429 BC, held the position of one of the 10 annually elected generals for 15 consecutive years.

Athens at Its Peak

Athenian culture was at its height in the fifth century BC. It was created not only by Athenians, but also by intellectuals from other cities, especially from Ionia, where the political climate had changed for the worse after the Persian War. Among such immigrants were the town planner Hippodamos of Miletus; the Ionian philosophers Anaxagoras of Klazomenai and Aspasia of Miletus; and the historian Herodotus of Halikarnassos.

Thanks to its military successes, the young democracy of Athens was enormously confident, and its confidence was reflected in literature, philosophy, art, and architecture. It is still manifest in the remains of the huge building project on the Acropolis, which used the resources of the Delian League, and was under the supervision of Phidias, the most famous sculptor of antiquity, and Pericles, the great statesman and orator. It is also reflected in the painted vases produced in the flourishing pottery district of Kerameikos, in Athens, that can now be seen in major museums. (See the feature *Vase Painting of Ancient Greece*.)

Athens' confidence is even more manifest in literature. This was the period of the great tragedians Aeschylus, Sophocles, and Euripides; of the comedy writer Aristophanes; and of the historians Herodotus and Thucydides. The writings of such philosophers as Plato and Aristotle came in the next century, but followed on from the intellectual climate of fifth-century BC Athens.

In architecture, the Doric and Ionic orders had from the beginning been geographically separated: Ionic on the Aegean islands and eastern Aegean coast, Doric on the mainland. In the fifth century BC, the two orders were used side by side in the great Acropolis project—both within the same buildings and as the orders of different buildings. We can assume that they were seen as representative of their respective cultural districts. Their mixture in the most important and central sanctuary of the empire had seemingly political overtones.

Ever since the Persian War, a cold war had been going on between Athens and Sparta, with their respective allies. There were minor conflicts, but as yet, no major conflict had erupted. Now and then, a truce was declared to give peace a better chance. In the late 430s BC, however, an acute conflict between Athens and Corinth prompted Corinth to appeal to Sparta to put a stop to Athenian oppression. Finally, Sparta decided to take action, and from this evolved the great Peloponnesian War, which lasted from 431 BC to 404 BC, and in which almost all Greek states took part. Sparta emerged victorious, but both sides were so exhausted by the fighting that neither ever completely recovered.

THE FOURTH CENTURY BC

The political history of Greece in the fourth century BC, after the Peloponnesian War, is a story of fighting between cities now weaker than ever—a situation that invited foreign powers to enter the scene. Sparta dominated Greece, and Athens played a secondary role. Athens recovered enough to create a new naval league in 377 BC, but it lasted only until 355 BC.

In the last years of the fifth century BC, an expeditionary force of 10,000 foot soldiers, mostly Spartan mercenaries, was hired by Prince Kyros of Persia to help in overthrowing his brother, the king of the Persian Empire, Artaxerxes. The Greeks did not succeed, but managed to return (the famous "retreat of the ten thousand") with the lesson that Persia was not invincible. Nor was Sparta, as it turned out: in the 370s BC, Thebes, under the general Epaminondas, managed briefly to become the strongest military power in Greece, inflicting a heavy defeat on Sparta at Leuktra, in central Greece, in 371 BC. With the death of Epaminondas in 362 BC, at the battle of Mantineia, in the Peloponnese, the dominance of Thebes came to an abrupt end.

Athenian lawyer and politician Demosthenes (384 BC to 322 BC), the most famous orator of antiquity. He desperately but in vain tried to stop Philip II of Macedonia from conquering the rest of Greece.

Three goddesses: on the right is Aphrodite, the goddess of love. These marble sculptures from the east pediment of the Parthenon on the Athenian Acropolis were made between 437 BC and 432 BC by Phidias, the most famous sculptor of ancient Greece.
BRITISH MUSEUM/SCALA

153

THE RIDDLE OF "PHILIP'S TOMB"

PONTUS HELLSTRÖM

IN NOVEMBER 1977, Manolis Andronikos, of the University of Thessaloniki, made the extraordinary find of an unlooted, very rich, fourth-century BC tomb at Vergina, in Macedonia. The discovery was the most widely publicized archaeological find in Greece in the 1970s, and is a strong candidate to be named the find of the century in Classical archaeology. Its importance lies primarily in the identification of the tomb as that of Philip II. This gives it a very special historical interest, not only because Philip was the father of Alexander the Great, but also because he was a powerful ruler, without whose conquest of Greece Alexander could not have conquered the East.

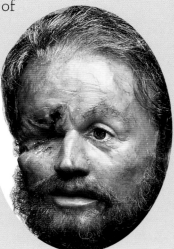

A waxwork reconstruction of the skull found in the tomb, made by a new technique using surviving cranial bones. The eye wound appears to confirm the identification with Philip II, who lost an eye in battle. More recent research by the British team, however, indicates that Philip's eye injury was well treated and left little scarring. If this were Philip's head, and not that of an unknown, one-eyed Macedonian prince, the wound would have looked less nasty. The question then remains: how many one-eyed noblemen were there in warlike Macedonia in the fourth century BC?
UNIVERSITY OF MANCHESTER/LAMBRAKIS PRESS

Vergina is doubtless the ancient Macedonian capital Aigai, where the royal cemetery was situated. Since the tomb was in the biggest mound on the site, it seemed probable that the occupant was a Macedonian king. The tomb contained the cremated remains of two people, each deposited in a heavy, beautifully worked golden chest. In the main chamber, a man aged 40 to 50 years was buried with a rich assortment of weapons and other prestigious grave goods. In the anteroom were the remains of a woman aged 20 to 30 years.

The approximate date of the tomb was established via pottery vases dating from about 350 BC to 325 BC. The only two Macedonian kings from this time and shortly afterwards were Philip II, who died in 336 BC, and Philip III Arrhidaios, Alexander's half-brother and successor, who died in 317 BC and was not a very famous king. Alexander himself was excluded, because we know that he was buried at Alexandria, in Egypt, having died at Persepolis in 323 BC.

All kinds of evidence indicated to Andronikos that the man buried in the main chamber was Philip II, but none of the evidence was conclusive. Other scholars were skeptical and argued for a different interpretation. They asked, for example, who the woman in the anteroom was, and why Philip III should be ruled out.

ARCHAEOLOGICAL MUSEUM OF THESSALONIKI/EKDOTIKE ATHENON SA

The front of the unlooted tomb at Vergina, which contained about 20 kilograms (45 pounds) of gold objects. If the tomb belonged to Philip II, the grave goods were only a small part of his wealth: he received more than 20 tonnes (20 tons) of gold annually from the gold mines of Mount Pangaion, in Macedonia, alone.

The debate was not resolved until 1983, when surprising evidence emerged from scientific research on the cremated remains. A British team consisting of specialists in archaeology, osteology, and criminology—John Prag, Jonathan Musgrave, and Richard Neave—produced a reconstruction of the dead man's head, using cranial bones that had escaped destruction in the funeral pyre. The reconstruction revealed a serious injury to one eye. Since it is known from literary sources that Philip II lost an eye during the siege of Methone, in Macedonia, some years before he was assassinated, the new evidence made many skeptics change their mind and consider the case proved in favor of Philip II.

Moreover, the evidence against Philip III Arrhidaios is overwhelming. In particular, there is evidence that the bodies in the tomb were buried at different times. This is apparent from the fact that the wall plastering in the main chamber was unfinished —indicating that the burial was performed in haste—whereas the plastering in the anteroom, containing the second burial, was finished. We know from written sources, however, that Philip III and his queen, Eurydice, were buried together.

But there is another possibility: the body in the main chamber may have belonged to some other member of the Macedonian royal family. The only evidence that the tomb is a king's, apart from the royal splendor of the grave goods, is the presence of a royal diadem, which, it is thought, could not have been part of a prince's grave goods. Such diadems were, however, used not only by kings, but also by poets and priests.

Philip II of Macedonia then entered the scene. In 359 BC, at the age of 24, he became the ruler of Macedonia. Step by step, he expanded Macedonian territory in all directions. In the west, he reached the Adriatic at Epiros. To the east, he took Amphipolis from Athens in 357 BC, and with it, the very rich gold mines of Pangaion, on the northern shore of the Aegean. He continued east and north, conquered Thrace in a series of campaigns, held all the north coast of the Aegean, and seized a large part of what is now Bulgaria, reaching the shore of the Black Sea.

To the south, he conquered Thessaly in 352 BC, and so acquired a seat in the Delphic council of Greek states. On the pretext of defending the rights of the Delphic council, he took part, with his army, in Greek internal affairs. After having infiltrated territory further south, he was opposed by Athens and Thebes, but it was too late. At the final battle at Chaironeia, in 338 BC, all remaining Greek opposition was decisively defeated, and Greece became part of Macedonia. In 337 BC, Philip declared war on Persia, a war of revenge for the Persian devastation of Greece in 480 BC, but in the following year, before the war had started, Philip was assassinated.

Considering this gloomy background of fourth-century BC political history, it is understandable that art, architecture, and cultural life did not reach the same level of splendor as in the preceding century. The main exception was philosophy, with its giants Plato and Aristotle. Aristotle introduced true scientific inquiry, which was the basis of Hellenistic scholarship and science, as in Alexandria. From the fourth century BC, the center of cultural life started moving away from mainland Greece.

The Ionian Renaissance: 360 BC to 330 BC

Before the Persian War, architecture, sculpture, philosophy, and the sciences had flourished in the Greek cities on the eastern shore of the Aegean. This era ended abruptly with the unsuccessful revolt against the Persians from 499 BC to 494 BC. The succeeding fifth century was a dark age for culture and the arts in Ionia. In architecture, it is a blank: official building all but ceased.

A new era opened in the fourth century BC. Mainland Greece and the Persian Empire were in decline, but the climate improved along the eastern Aegean. In 377 BC, a local prince named Maussollos succeeded his father, Hekatomnos, as satrap (governor) in the new Persian province of Caria, in present-day Turkey. He was the oldest of three brothers and two sisters, the so-called Hekatomnids, who were all to succeed him in turn. Maussollos remained in power for almost 25 years, until 352 BC. From his actions, we can conclude that he was actively working towards the establishment of a kingdom of his own, and like his contemporary Philip II, he apparently had far-reaching ambitions.

Maussollos and His Ambitions

Maussollos's old capital was Mylasa, in the Carian inland. Soon after his ascension to power, in the year the second Athenian confederacy was formed, Maussollos moved his capital to Halikarnassos (present-day Bodrum), a city with an important strategic position on the seafront and an excellent double harbor. There, he kept a fleet of 100 ships, which was put to good use. His policy, unlike the Persians', was anti-Athenian, and he managed to install garrisons in some Greek cities previously belonging to the Athenian confederacy, such as Kos, Chios, and Klazomenai. He systematically enlarged the area over which he ruled on the Asiatic mainland to include Lycia, to the east, and perhaps as far as Smyrna, to the north. His ambitions may have extended even further. He took part in the great satraps' revolt against the king of the Persian Empire, Artaxerxes II, and escaped unhurt.

⚲ The temple of Athena at Priene was built after 350 BC by the architect Pytheos, who also wrote a book about its architecture. According to an inscription on the temple, Alexander the Great gave the temple to the goddess (meaning that he paid for it).

ADAM WOOLFITT/ROBERT HARDING PICTURE LIBRARY

↩ The sanctuary of Labraynda, in Caria, Southwest Asia Minor, as it would have looked in the middle of the fourth century BC. On the upper terrace is the temple of Zeus, surrounded by columns. To the left and on the terrace below are two banqueting halls, with two columns at the front.

ILLUSTRATION: OLIVER RENNERT

↥ Maussollos, the ruler of Caria (377 BC to 352 BC). This portrait comes from his tomb, the huge mausoleum at Halikarnassos, one of the seven wonders of the ancient world.

RONALD SHERIDAN/ANCIENT ART & ARCHITECTURE COLLECTION

Maussollos used the best available Greek architects and artists to work on his most famous building project—his own tomb, the mausoleum at Halikarnassos—which had a podium base, a colonnade, and a pyramidal roof. Because of its sheer size—it was some 50 meters (165 feet) high—and its unusually rich sculptural decoration, it became known as one of the seven wonders of the world. It was in the heart of the city, and was obviously intended to be seen as a monument to a city founder, which means that Maussollos planned for himself the status, and no doubt the sacrifices, of a hero or demigod.

In this period, beginning with the reign of Maussollos, a score of temples and other sacred buildings were built at Carian sanctuaries. The biggest building project apart from the mausoleum was at the mountain sanctuary of Labraynda. Several temples were also built in Ionian cities under Hekatomnid influence. One of them was the temple of Athena, at Priene, which Alexander the Great paid for, but which was begun before his conquest of the district in 334 BC. Another is the huge temple of Artemis, at Ephesus, another of the seven wonders of the world.

These buildings reveal a common source of inspiration in the forms of the Archaic Ionic temples. This architectural style is, therefore, called the "Ionic Renaissance". Considering Maussollos's fight against the Athenian empire, it was natural that his architects should return to old local Ionic forms, rather than use the more recent Athenian style. This was a means of expressing cultural identity against the political power of Athens.

Glorifying the Ruler

At the main Carian sanctuary of Labraynda, in the solitary mountains of the inland, Maussollos launched a major architectural project, which was finished by his brother and successor, Idrieus, who ruled from 351 BC to 344 BC. Swedish excavations at the site since 1948 have revealed an Ionic temple dedicated

however, preceded by a Hellenism by peaceful contacts along the border between East and West. Perhaps the most notable example of such pre-Alexander Hellenism can be seen in the architecture of Hekatomnid Caria of the mid-fourth century BC, especially at the sanctuary of Labraynda. Maussollos and the Hekatomnids did not reach their political goals, but their buildings made a lasting contribution to the history of architecture.

Alexander the Great

When his father, Philip II, was assassinated in 336 BC, Alexander was 19 years old and full of energy and ambition. As soon as it was feasible, he launched the great campaign against Persia that Philip had planned. In 334 BC, he pushed into Asia Minor (present-day Turkey), most of which he subdued, twice defeating the Persian army. After a time-consuming but strategically necessary siege of Tyre, on the Levantine coast, he advanced to Egypt, where he founded the metropolis-to-be Alexandria, one of the many cities that were to carry his name.

In 331 BC, after turning east again, he decisively defeated the Persian king at Gaugamela, on the Tigris, in what today is northern Iraq. After this victory, the Persian Empire fell into his hands. He continued eastwards to India, and by 325 BC, had overcome all resistance up to the Indus River. In 323 BC, only two years after returning to Mesopotamia, he died of a fever. He was 33 years old.

Alexander's military genius brought him a series of astonishing victories on the battlefield. His conquests would probably have had little impact on history, however, had he not founded a large number of cities with Greek and Macedonian settlers. As it was, his empire split into several smaller kingdoms almost immediately after his death. The same fate would no doubt have fallen upon the Hellenistic culture had Alexander not seen how to consolidate his victories. One wonders how much this degree of foresight came from the early training he received from Aristotle. We can probably see Aristotle's influence behind Alexander's decision to include scholars and scientists on his staff. That later conquerors have done the same is no doubt due to Alexander's influence.

to Zeus, the father of the gods, and a number of other buildings with marble fronts, all erected within some 15 years in the middle of the fourth century.

The first structure to be built was a monumental, temple-like banqueting hall (called an *andron*, or "men's hall"), intended to be used for ritual meals during an annual five-day sacrificial feast. At the back of the main room was a large rectangular niche for statues of the rulers. This type of building was a new architectural creation, inspired by the urge to glorify the Hekatomnid dynasty. Its combination of ritual banqueting and glorification of the ruler makes it a forerunner of Hellenistic and Roman rulers' cult buildings.

It is generally considered that the Hellenistic period began with Alexander the Great, and his conquest of the East to the Indus River (in present-day Pakistan), which opened up the East to Greek cultural influence. Hellenism by conquest was,

ARCHAEOLOGY MUSEUM, ISTANBUL/ROBERT HARDING PICTURE LIBRARY

⚓ This marble portrait of Alexander the Great was found at Pergamon, in present-day Turkey. Born in 356 BC, he was the king of Macedonia from 336 BC until 323 BC, when he died at the young age of 33.

THE EMPIRE OF ALEXANDER THE GREAT

In 334 BC, Alexander started the great war against the Persian Empire. The route of his army is shown in red. By 325 BC, he had conquered not only Persia but all of the Near and Middle East, as far as the Indus River.

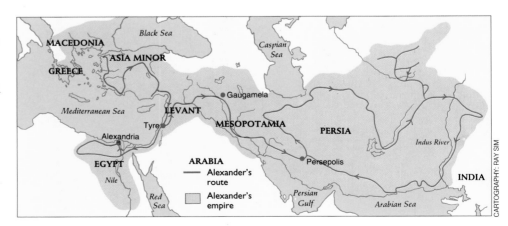

CARTOGRAPHY: RAY SIM

VASE PAINTING OF ANCIENT GREECE

CHARLOTTE SCHEFFER

GRECIAN URNS ARE indeed things of beauty, but they are also practical articles of long durability and transmitters of meaning from times long past. The technique—black figures on a red background from the seventh century BC, replaced in the late sixth century BC by red figures surrounded by black—consisted of "painting" the vases with different kinds of clay, and firing them in three stages with varying levels of oxygen in the kiln. Corinth and, from the sixth century BC, Athens were the leading places of manufacture.

Many different painters have been distinguished, some of them known by name from their signatures. The motifs are at the same time pure decoration, pious stories from the myths, pictures of reality, and ideological statements on the proper behavior of Greek men and women.

➥ Kirke, a sorceress known from the *Odyssey*, leaves her loom to welcome Ulysses, but her "proper" female conduct is false: the potion she is mixing will turn his men into pigs. Perplexed at such deceit, Ulysses turns to us, his viewers, for help. Comic vases such as this one were made in the fourth century BC in Boeotia.
ASHMOLEAN MUSEUM, OXFORD

➥ Attacked by Etruscan pirates, the god of wine, Dionysos, performs a miracle by making his mast sprout leaves like a vine and turning the terrorized pirates into dolphins. The cup, dating from about 540 BC, was painted by Exekias, the foremost of the Athenian painters working in the black-figure technique.
STAATLICHE ANTIKENSAMMLUNGEN UND GLYPTOTHEK, MUNICH

➥ An oil flask in the shape of a charming little owl. Such exquisitely stylized works were already turned out by Corinthian vase painters by the middle of the seventh century BC.
ERICH LESSING/ MAGNUM PHOTOS

NATIONAL MUSEUM OF VILLA GIULIA, ROME/SCALA

➥ Greek foot soldiers engaging in battle to flute music. This small-scale painting with its sharp, precise details has rightly made Corinthian vase painting of the seventh century BC famous.

⚲ Unlike the vases painted in the black and red-figure techniques, this Athenian oil flask with a muse playing her lyre was painted with many different colors on a white background after firing, giving us an idea of what the large-scale painting of the time was like. It dates from about 440 BC.
STAATLICHE ANTIKENSAMMLUNGEN UND GLYPTOTHEK, MUNICH

⚱ Supervised by Hermes, Death and his brother Sleep, all with their names inscribed, are about to carry a Homeric hero to his last rest. Dating from about 515 BC, this large bowl was painted by the famous Athenian red-figure painter Euphronios.
METROPOLITAN MUSEUM OF ART

H. LEWANDOWSKI/THE LOUVRE/RMN

⚱ Satyrs cavorting and doing the things that Greek men normally could not do—this was a favorite motif and suitably so, considering that many of the vases were intended for the men's symposia (banquets). This vase is a wine-cooler, painted by the Athenian Douris, and dates from about 480 BC.
BRITISH MUSEUM

⚱ Ganymedes, still a beautiful young boy playing with his hoop, is pursued by Zeus, who appears on the other side of the vase. The cock is a gift of love from the enamored god. Dating from about 470 BC, it was painted by the Berlin painter, an Athenian, who was named after the location of his most famous vase.

ROBERT HARDING PICTURE LIBRARY

THE HELLENISTIC AGE: 323 BC TO 31 BC

With Alexander's death in 323 BC, his vast empire was divided up between his generals and successors. After a period of utter confusion, three of these kingdoms proved to be of longer duration than just a generation or two. One was Egypt, where Ptolemy established himself and his family so securely at Alexandria that the dynasty continued to rule the country for 300 years, until the battle of Actium, in 31 BC, and the Age of Augustus. The dynasty's last ruler was Queen Cleopatra.

The second kingdom to endure was the Seleucid, which took over the old Persian Empire and Alexander's eastern conquests. This was a vast country, which lost most of its territory when the Romans conquered Greece and Asia Minor in the second century BC, and the Parthian kingdom rose in the east.

The third lasting kingdom was the old Macedonian kingdom, the capital of which was Pella. It was defeated by Rome in the battle at Pydna, in 168 BC.

Apart from Ptolemaic Egypt, none of the Hellenistic kingdoms survived more than 150 years. From the mid-second century BC, Rome was the undisputed ruler of the eastern Mediterranean. It confirmed this fact by its ruthless destruction of Corinth, in 146 BC, and the sale of all survivors into slavery. Greek cities throughout the Hellenistic world were, to a large extent, left to rule themselves. Most had democratic constitutions insofar as all male citizens made up the assembly to elect their magistrates. The rules for nomination, however, made it easy for those in power to manipulate the election procedure. Of course, no city under the rule of a Hellenistic kingdom, or under Rome, could make decisions concerning foreign policy.

Although not a political power, Greece continued to play an important role throughout this era. Hellenism's cultural basis was strictly Greek. Throughout the Hellenistic world, the language was Greek, literature and art were Greek, and political and cultural life were in accordance with Greek customs. Barbarians (non-Greeks) who wanted to take part in Hellenistic culture had to Hellenize by learning the Greek language and by adopting Greek customs. To an extent, even Rome conformed to this rule, once it had extended its influence into the Hellenistic world.

In one field of culture, Athens remained the focal point. In philosophy, two new schools rose to fame with philosophers who had moved to Athens. These were the school of Epicurus of Samos, who moved to Athens in 307 BC, and the Stoic school, founded in 310 BC by Zeno of Kition. The philosophical schools provided teaching of a high order, and Athens remained the most important university city until the Roman emperor Justinian ordered the schools to be closed in AD 529, a date that marks the end of antiquity, and the final victory of the Christian faith.

A coin portrait of Ptolemy I (305 BC to 283 BC), one of Alexander's companions and the founder of the Ptolemaic dynasty, which ruled Egypt for 300 years. At Alexandria, he built the largest library of the ancient world.
C.M. DIXON

The colossal temple of the Olympian Zeus at Athens, built in the Corinthian order by the Roman architect Cossutius from 174 BC, was not finished until AD 132.

☞ Reliefs from the Pergamon altar (181 BC to 159 BC). The sea god Triton (left), son of Poseidon, the ruler of the sea, fights together with his mother Amphitrite (right) against three giants. Triton is a creature with a human chest, wings, a fishtail, and a horse's leg.

Scientific and Architectural Achievements

In the Hellenistic post-Aristotelian age, philosophy and science went separate ways. Science was not a field of interest for the philosophic schools of Hellenistic Athens. The major scientific institution of the period was the library of Alexandria. There, literary scholarship flourished, thanks to its collection of some 500,000 books. The library also became the world's foremost research institute in the fields of mathematics, astronomy, geography, and medicine.

Among scientists who worked at Alexandria was Euclid, the author of *Elements*, the systematic presentation of mathematical theorems that is still valid. Another scientist was Eratosthenes, who managed to calculate the circumference of the Earth with an error of only about 300 kilometers (180 miles). This calculation would, of course, not have been possible without the knowledge, later forgotten, that the Earth is a sphere. The ancient world believed, however, that the Earth was the center of the universe, although Aristarchos of Samos, a third-century BC astronomer, had suggested that the Earth revolved round the sun. His treatise is lost, so we do not know his arguments and evidence.

The Hellenistic age witnessed some imposing architectural achievements. Builders used retaining walls to construct rising sequences of terraces, surrounded by colonnades and connected by monumental processional stairs. Examples of this style can be seen in city planning, as at Pergamon, and in the layout of sanctuaries, such as that of Asclepius, on Cos, off the coast of Asia Minor. In Italy, the sanctuary of Fortuna, at Praeneste, is a striking example of this tendency. These achievements were inspired by the architecture of fourth-century BC Caria.

Classical sculptors had shown much restraint in movement and feeling; in the Hellenistic period,

such restraint was discarded. The most outstanding piece of Hellenistic art clearly illustrates this point: it is the frieze of the great altar of the gods Zeus and Athena at Pergamon, probably built about 181 BC to 159 BC to commemorate the victory over the Galatians—three warlike Celtic tribes that had immigrated to Asia Minor (around present-day Ankara) in the third century BC. There, the Hellenistic baroque style finds its most eloquent expression in sculpture, depicting a battle between gods and giants, which is, of course, an allusion to the Pergamene royal victory over the Galatian barbarians. The many fighting bodies obscure the background, so that the colonnaded altar of Zeus and Athena seems to float above the uproar of the cosmic battle.

☞ The open-air theater at Epidauros, built from about 360 BC by the architect Polykleitos. The acoustics of this theater, which could seat some 12,300 spectators, are remarkable.

The Greek Heritage

Classical Greece was the most important source of European culture, and continues to exert its influence on the rest of the world in many ways, good and bad. This is not only a question of quite naturally transferred, and sometimes superficial, traditions—for example, the tradition that coins should be flat and round with impressed texts and symbols on both sides. Nor is Classical inspiration for modern architecture more than an interesting feature of contemporary society: the influence of heritage is not very strong in this case. Columnar architecture is, however, definitely a Greek gift of importance to world architecture, although Egyptian columns are older. This is not just a question of borrowed forms: Greek columns were bearers of meaning, and so are columns of later epochs. Even if the meaning has changed, the columns remain symbols of power.

Much of the Greek heritage is abstract—for example, democracy. There is certainly no direct line of tradition from Classical Greece to the modern world, but Athenian democracy, however imperfect (and however different from today's imperfect democracies), gave the world a new idea to work on.

Another idea from Classical Greece is the appreciation of individuality and creativity. It is easy to forget that these qualities are products of culture, and are not inherited. Closely attached to the cult of individuality is admiration for the fighter, the invincible hero. This admiration appeared in early Greek fiction, in Homer's histories of Odysseus, the adventurer. Odysseus was the first European or, if one prefers, the first modern man in the European sense—inventive, creative, and selfish, for good and for bad. One wonders whether the ancient Greek obsession with war and violence is not also a bequest to the world, spread by European thinking.

In the field of science also, the modern world owes a great debt to Greece, and especially to that universal genius Aristotle. His analytic work in many fields was directed towards the creation of a coherent, encyclopedic conception of the world. Through the ages, he has had an enormous influence on scientific thinking, from the time of medieval Arabic scholars to that of later European scientists.

Aeschylus, Sophocles, and Euripides—the three major tragedians of fifth-century BC Athens—have exerted a lasting influence. By using ancient myths to illustrate contemporary human conflicts, they created drama that would remain up to date through the ages. The inflammability and never-ceasing topicality of some of the issues dramatized by these tragedians become only too apparent whenever a modern dictatorship bans Sophocles' *Antigone*. The classical dramas have been a constant source of inspiration to poets, novelists, painters, composers, dramatists, and film-makers.

Greece gave the Western world an alphabet containing both consonants and vowels, the first of its kind, in the late eighth century BC. Several local alphabets soon developed in Greece, with slightly different signs used from place to place. It is because Cumae (Kyme), one of the earliest Greek colonies in Italy, was founded by settlers from the island of Euboea, and because early Rome was in close contact with Cumae, that the Euboean set of letters came to form the Roman alphabet. The Greeks today use letters different from those in our Latin alphabet, because theirs are of Athenian origin, not Euboean.

♠A posthumous bronze portrait of Aristotle (384 BC to 322 BC), the most influential of the philosophers of ancient Greece.
NATIONAL MUSEUM, NAPLES/SCALA

♀This early representation of the famous Wooden Horse dates from about 675 BC. In Greek legend, the siege of Troy lasted for 10 years. Pretending to give up, the Greeks left by sea, leaving a wooden horse behind, filled with warriors. When the Trojans pulled the horse into the city, the soldiers came out at night and opened the city gates to the Greek army. In many languages, a wooden horse or Trojan horse has ever since been an expression used to describe the infiltration of enemy troops or agents.

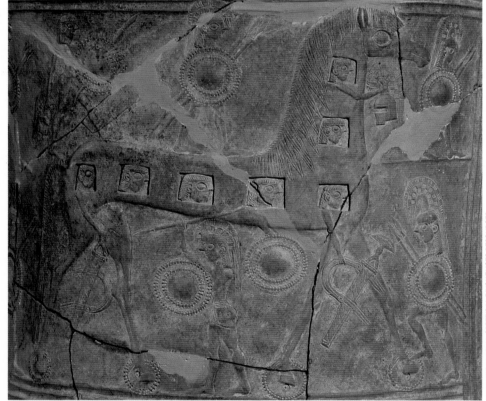

MYKONOS MUSEUM, CRETE/C.M. DIXON/PHOTO RESOURCES

D. & J. HEATON/AUSTRALIAN PICTURE LIBRARY

THE RISE AND FALL OF ROME

9 0 0 B C — A D 5 0 0

From City-state to Worldwide Empire

ÖRJAN WIKANDER

THE PREHISTORY OF ITALY was very much a product of Italy's geographical position. The peoples of southern Italy and Sicily were influenced by cultures in the eastern Mediterranean area, particularly those of Greece; whereas the peoples of northern Italy had strong contacts, through the alpine passes, with the metal-producing cultures in central Europe. Towards the end of the Bronze Age, between the fourteenth and twelfth centuries BC, there is ample evidence of Mycenaean trade, and possibly settlements, along the Italian coasts as far north as southern Etruria. At the same time, traits typical of the central European Urnfield cultures spread deep into northern and central Italy, with some examples found further south and even in Sicily. New metalworking techniques appeared, and the discoveries of new funerary rituals—with cremation and inhumation of ashes in biconical urns (hence the term "Urnfield")—suggest immigration. From the north came the skill of beating bronze into sheet form, and warriors were able to be equipped with heavy armor: helmets, corselets, and circular shields, giving rise to a new, armored fighting technique.

◄o The "Pont du Gard", a Roman aqueduct near Nîmes, in southern France, was built about 20 BC to carry water across the river valley. One of the most impressive of its kind, it is 49 meters (160 feet) high and 270 meters (885 feet) long.

⚭ This inscribed sheet of gold, dating from about 500 BC, was found at Pyrgi, the main port of Cerveteri. The dedication inscriptions—to the Etruscan goddess Uni (Juno) and her Phoenician equivalent, Astarte—are in both Punic (the language of ancient Carthage) and Etruscan, indicating close trading contacts between the Carthaginians and Etruscans.
NATIONAL MUSEUM OF VILLA GIULIA, ROME/SCALA

The change from the Bronze Age to the Iron Age at the beginning of the last millennium BC was gradual. Contacts between the Italic peoples and the Greek peoples were interrupted, but central European influences, particularly from the Hallstatt culture (in modern Austria), remained important.

The Iron Age and the Italic Peoples

A number of Italic Iron Age cultures have been identified, and they are often presented in two main groups according to their burial customs: cremation in the northwest; inhumation (the burial of unburned bodies) in the southeast. In various parts of the peninsula, Iron Age cultures persisted for centuries with few changes—in some cases, up to the Roman conquest in the last centuries BC.

In southern Italy and in the western part of central Italy, the arrival of eastern merchants in the eighth century BC and the ensuing Greek colonization greatly affected the lives of the Italic peoples. Traditional forms of Italic art and crafts took completely new directions; local social and economic structures changed rapidly.

Perhaps the most interesting change is the adoption of the Greek alphabet. Ancient Italy had a number of languages and dialects—most of them were Indo-European, the major family of the languages of Europe. These Italic languages can now be defined, and a historical map of languages and peoples may be juxtaposed with an archaeologically based map of cultures. The two correspond only in parts; for instance, the people of the Estè culture apparently spoke Venetic.

⚲ Dating from the early seventh century BC, this oriental-style bronze cauldron on a conical stand was recovered from the Barberini Tomb at Praeneste (Palestrina). It is decorated with four lion and griffin heads.
NATIONAL MUSEUM OF VILLA GIULIA, ROME/SCALA

⚲ One of the *Tabulae Iguvinae*, seven bronze tablets discovered in AD 1444 at Gubbio, in Umbria. In the third or second century BC, they were inscribed with religious regulations in Umbrian, an Italic language distantly related to Latin.
PALAZZO DEI PRIORI, GUBBIO/SCALA

The Etruscans

Particular interest has been devoted to the relationship between the Iron Age Villanova culture and the highly advanced Etruscan culture. Today, when few scholars would see the Early Archaic (seventh century BC) culture of central Italy as a phenomenon caused by recent Etruscan immigration from Asia Minor, we are rather inclined to trace its gradual development from the Villanova culture under strong Greek influences.

The copper mines of Etruria were one of the few mining resources in Italy. In the eighth century BC, there was evidence of growing social classes among the Etruscans. In among common graves—in which such items as a bronze razor or a bracelet and a few fibulas (clasps or brooches) and pins were found—a

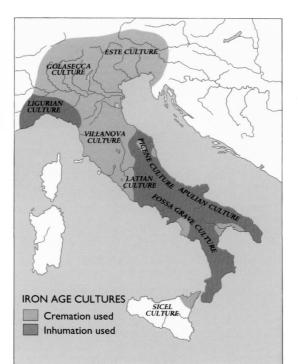

⚲ A reconstruction of an Iron Age hut (*capanna*) from the Palatine hill in Rome. These huts have been dated to the eighth century BC.

ANCIENT ITALY

As the maps show, culture and language areas correspond only in part; for instance, the people of the Estè culture apparently spoke Venetic.

IRON AGE CULTURES
- Cremation used
- Inhumation used

ESTE CULTURE
GOLASECCA CULTURE
LIGURIAN CULTURE
VILLANOVA CULTURE
LATIAN CULTURE
PICENE CULTURE
APULIAN CULTURE
FOSSA GRAVE CULTURE
SICEL CULTURE

EARLY ITALIC LANGUAGES
- Western languages
- Adriatic languages
- Umbro-Sabellic languages
- Non-Italic languages

RAETIC
VENETIC
LIGURIAN
ETRUSCAN
PICENE
LATIN
UMBRIAN SABELLIC OSCAN
MESSAPIAN
SICEL

CARTOGRAPHY: RAY SIM

small number of richer graves have also been found. In these, there are items of pottery, bronze vessels, axes, swords, and horse bits. From these finds, it appears that an aristocratic, warrior class may have been emerging.

Between 725 BC and 650 BC, there is more evidence of wealth in a few extremely rich tombs at several major sites along the Tyrrhenian (Etruscan) coast: at Populonia, Vetulonia, Tarquinia, Cerveteri, and inland Praeneste. There, the grave goods include gold, ivory, and bronze show-pieces—imports from the east. These Early Archaic tombs could have been those of local chieftains, enriched by trading Etruscan metal to the Greeks, at Greek colonies at Pithekoussai and Cumae (Kyme), in southern Italy. The growth of local aristocracies was largely a result of the rapid accumulation of wealth through successful trade. It was also certainly promoted and influenced by contacts with Greek aristocratic ideology. Some Greek nobles visited and settled in Etruria; at Tarquinia, for instance. It is possible that the use of horses and two-wheeled carriages may have been introduced from the north, but the practices of drinking wine and holding symposia (banquets) among the aristocracy doubtless reflect Greek influences. After about 650 BC, noble families buried their dead in huge, circular mounds (tumuli). (See the feature *Death in Etruria*.) Towards the end of that century, Etruscan inscriptions provide us with the first examples of particular inherited family names. From then on, the material wealth of the aristocracy was coupled with class consciousness and pride.

Changes in Society

The emergence of a central Italic aristocracy is not isolated. It is closely linked with an extraordinary transformation of Italic society. There was the creation of a substantial class of craftsmen, including bronze smiths and potters, and increasing urbanization. Pottery became a specialized craft with the break-through of the fast-spinning potter's wheel, imported from the Greek world. In later Roman tradition, King Numa (of the early seventh century BC) instituted eight craftsmen's guilds—including the guilds for bronze smiths and potters—for goldsmiths, carpenters, dyers, tanners, leather-workers, and flute-players.

C.M. DIXON/PHOTO RESOURCES

The increasing specialization of labor led to greater population concentrations, such as in Tarquinia. From the middle of the seventh century BC, settlements that were virtual cities were estab-lished on the Tyrrhenian coast and even in the hinterland of Etruria—along the river valleys, connecting inland areas with the seaboard.

As Etruscan settlements became larger, there was a rapid change from huts with thatched roofs to sturdy, rectangular buildings with tiled roofs. Roof tiles were a recent innovation imported from Greece, but their general use on private buildings in the growing towns was a central Italic achieve-ment. It was not until several centuries later that they were used this way in the Greek world. Terra-cotta tiling proved to be an efficient roof-cover. A simple module system, it also offered rich possibilities for architectural decoration. Painted and relief-molded roof terracottas remained an Etruscan specialty for more than 500 years. Technical progress has its drawbacks, however: Etruscan metalworking and the firing of tiles and pottery are largely to blame for the deforestation of central Italy.

☝ Part of the Banditaccia necropolis outside Cerveteri. The circular tombs (known as tumuli) were built by aristocratic families in the sixth century BC.

☝ An Etruscan ridge tile from Acquarossa, about 1 meter (3 feet) long, with an acroterion (gable decoration) in the shape of two mythical animals. It dates from about 600 BC.
ÖRJAN WIKANDER

◄● This reconstructed Etruscan roof from a private house at Acquarossa, dating from about 550 BC, consists of flat pantiles, semicylindrical cover tiles, and ridge tiles covering the ridgepole.
ÖRJAN WIKANDER

SCALA

DEATH IN ETRURIA

CHARLOTTE SCHEFFER

T HE TOMBS OF THE ETRUSCAN dead are more impressive
than the dwellings of the living. Research and
archaeological excavation have concentrated on the
Etruscans' funeral culture, and our knowledge of that
civilization is largely based on the cities of the dead,
because the extensive writings of the Etruscans are lost.

Etruscan civilization has been
approximately dated to the period
from the end of the eighth century BC
to the end of the first century BC. Even
though the Etruscan language does not
belong to any known language group,
it is fairly easy to read, being written
in the Greek alphabet. Before that time,
a people who were probably their
ancestors—members of the Iron Age
Villanova culture—cremated their dead
and buried the ashes in simple tombs
with, at most, some fibulas (clasps and
brooches), bronze weapons, and, occasionally, a lid in the shape of a helmet.

The Villanovan necropolises give
little or no indication of differences
in social status.

Towards the end of the eighth
century BC, there is evidence that this
society was gradually transformed as
a result of contact with Greek and
Phoenician civilizations. In the seventh
century BC, inhumation (the burial of
unburned bodies) replaced cremation
as the dominant funerary form. From
that time, large separate tombs,
expensively furnished with imported
luxury goods, were built to house the
remains of single families.

⚱The Tomb of the Reliefs, in
Cerveteri, dates from about 300 BC.
On the walls are hung all the para-
phernalia the dead would require in
their new life. The beds are prepared
with plumped-up cushions, and the
slippers stand ready.

An Elegant Society

The great centuries in Etruscan
history are the seventh and sixth BC.
At this time, the Etruscans dominated most of central Italy, including
Rome, and also spread into northern
Italy and Campania. Having grown
rich through trade with the Greeks,
the Etruscan noble families who
lived in the southern Etrurian cities
spent lavishly on both their tombs
and funerals.

The wall paintings in underground
chamber tombs in Tarquinia depict
an elegant society that appreciated
good living. They are painted in
bright colors with no shading, the
central activity being the drinking
of wine, a custom the Etruscans
learned from the Greeks. However,
the Greeks drank in male groups,

⚱A terracotta figure from the Tomb of
the Five Seats, in Cerveteri, dating from
about 600 BC. Male and female figures
were seated on chairs carved from the
living rock. They probably represent
ancestors of the tomb's occupants.
RONALD SHERIDAN/
ANCIENT ART & ARCHITECTURE COLLECTION

mainly for political reasons, whereas Etruscans drinkers are usually depicted as husband and wife—master and mistress of a great house.

Although the members of the drinking parties look very much alive, it may be that what we see is not of this life but rather the owners of the tomb in the company of their dead forebears. The shadow of death rarely falls over these painted scenes—an occasional empty couch, closed door, gesture of mourning providing the only hint. The essential meaning eludes us.

Belief in an Afterlife

The Etruscans filled their tombs not only with furniture and textiles, but also with food and drink, weapons, and cooking utensils, which seems to indicate that they believed in an afterlife, although they did not embalm their dead. Tombs were furnished as houses, with all that a living person needed. Ash urns could depict human features or be made in the shape of a house. In a tomb in Cerveteri, dating from about 600 BC, a row of seated terracotta figures represents ancestors awaiting the latest arrival. Although the scene is ambiguous, the existence of such

A husband and wife on the lid of a sarcophagus from Cerveteri, dating from about 525 BC. The couple is shown taking part in a symposium (banquet), reclining on a couch in the oriental way made fashionable by the Greeks.

figures, and the care extended to dead forebears, probably indicate ancestor worship.

Towards the end of the fifth century BC, the wall-painting motifs become more somber, the colors are darker, and shading occurs frequently. The borrowed Greek myths often involve fighting, bloodshed, and killing. From earliest times, the shedding of blood was probably connected with funerals and the continuing existence of a dead person. Not surprisingly, the Etruscans are believed to have originated gladiatorial games.

Motifs depicting scenes of traveling and the presence of monstrous figures have led some scholars to conclude that the Etruscan concept of a happy afterlife changed to a belief in an underworld, where the shades of the dead await punishment for their former sins. There is, however, no evidence for such an interpretation. The Greek

motifs are superficial borrowings, and the monstrous figures and winged females are included to suggest the funerary content of the scenes rather than as active participants in them.

From the fourth century BC, Etruscans gradually became part of the Roman world. The symposium lost its significance as a status symbol; the

banqueter is alone on his or her couch with an offering bowl. Status at that time was to be a magistrate from a family of magistrates. The facades of tombs became more important than their interiors. Visible from afar in cliff faces, they surrounded the cities of the living.

The Etruscan attitude to death—their belief in a continued, reasonably happy existence, and their view of the funeral and tomb as proper for the display of family unity and position in society—appears to be consistent throughout the changing forms of expression. Like many ancient peoples, the Etruscans probably believed that time was not linear but cyclic, so that after a cycle of time (*saeculum*), all returned to the beginning and the start of a new *saeculum*. In the same way, generation followed upon generation. Their world was preordained and regulated by the gods, who revealed their divine will in omens. The human world was intimately interwoven with that of the gods and of the dead: all were part of the great plan revolving through the *saecula*.

A wall painting from the Tomb of the Augurs (interpreters of bird flight), in Tarquinia, dating from about 510 BC. Two mourners salute a large, painted door. The door may represent the dead person's house or may be a symbolic barrier separating the living and the dead.

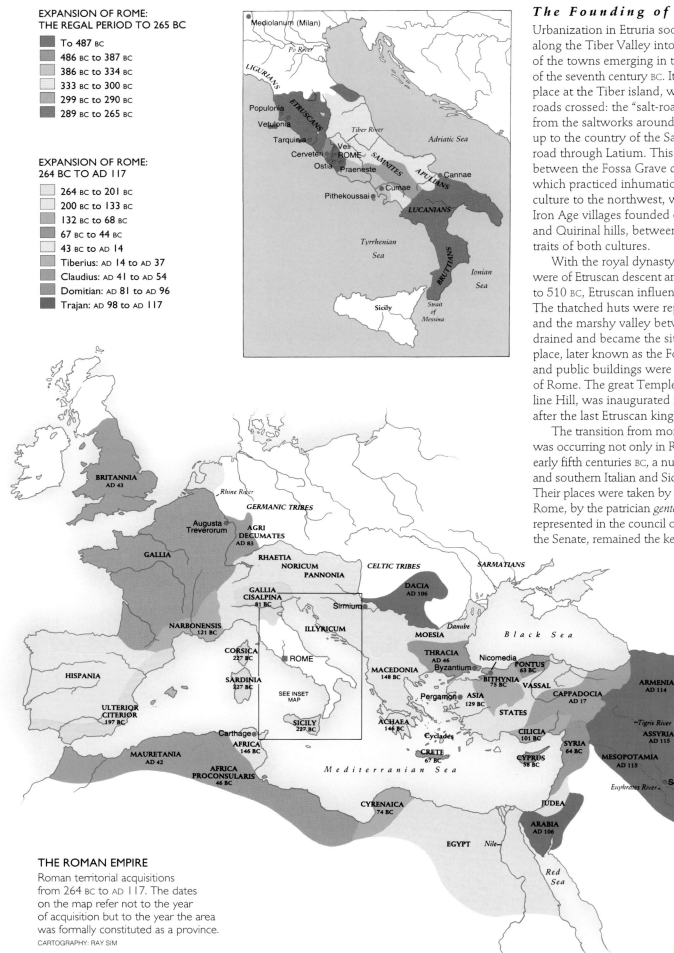

**EXPANSION OF ROME:
THE REGAL PERIOD TO 265 BC**

- To 487 BC
- 486 BC to 387 BC
- 386 BC to 334 BC
- 333 BC to 300 BC
- 299 BC to 290 BC
- 289 BC to 265 BC

**EXPANSION OF ROME:
264 BC TO AD 117**

- 264 BC to 201 BC
- 200 BC to 133 BC
- 132 BC to 68 BC
- 67 BC to 44 BC
- 43 BC to AD 14
- Tiberius: AD 14 to AD 37
- Claudius: AD 41 to AD 54
- Domitian: AD 81 to AD 96
- Trajan: AD 98 to AD 117

THE ROMAN EMPIRE

Roman territorial acquisitions
from 264 BC to AD 117. The dates
on the map refer not to the year
of acquisition but to the year the area
was formally constituted as a province.

CARTOGRAPHY: RAY SIM

The Founding of Rome

Urbanization in Etruria soon spread southwards
along the Tiber Valley into Latium. Rome was one
of the towns emerging in that area towards the end
of the seventh century BC. It was situated in a fordable
place at the Tiber island, where two important
roads crossed: the "salt-road" (*Via Salaria*)—leading
from the saltworks around the mouth of the Tiber
up to the country of the Sabines—and the inland
road through Latium. This was also the border
between the Fossa Grave culture to the southeast,
which practiced inhumation, and the Villanova
culture to the northwest, which cremated its dead.
Iron Age villages founded on the Palatine, Esquiline,
and Quirinal hills, between 900 BC and 700 BC, have
traits of both cultures.

With the royal dynasty of the Tarquins, who
were of Etruscan descent and ruled from about 616 BC
to 510 BC, Etruscan influence grew strong in Rome.
The thatched huts were replaced by tiled buildings,
and the marshy valley between the main hills was
drained and became the site of a central marketplace, later known as the Forum Romanum. Temples
and public buildings were erected in various parts
of Rome. The great Temple of Jupiter, on the Capitoline Hill, was inaugurated in 509 BC, immediately
after the last Etruscan king was overthrown.

The transition from monarchical to republican rule
was occurring not only in Rome. In the late sixth and
early fifth centuries BC, a number of Etruscan kings
and southern Italian and Sicilian tyrants were toppled.
Their places were taken by aristocratic cliques: in
Rome, by the patrician *gentes* (nobles), families once
represented in the council of the kings. This council,
the Senate, remained the kernel of government.

The Social and Political Structure

The Senate delegated executive powers to annual magistrates, to two consuls (chief magistrates) in particular. The consuls retained supreme power in war and peace, but a series of new magistracies was created eventually to take over various functions of a growing administrative structure. The censors were responsible for the census registration; the praetors for the jurisdiction; the aediles for the maintenance of temples and public buildings; and the quaestors for revenue and public finance. In cases of emergency, particularly in wartime, the supreme command was entrusted to a dictator, governing alone, for a period of no more than six months.

Other than the patrician inhabitants of Rome, there were clients (followers of the nobles), free-born plebeians (commoners), and a growing number of slaves and freed people. In later records, the first centuries of the republic of Rome are seen as dominated by class struggles between patricians and plebeians. The accounts are confused, however, by the insertion of material about the history of the Late Republic, several centuries later. Led by the powerful and sacrosanct "tribunes of the people" (*tribuni plebis*), the plebeians eventually enforced equal rights with the patricians. In 445 BC, plebeians obtained *conubium*, the right of intermarriage with patricians; in the next century, accordingly, a growing number of plebeian leaders could claim patrician descent on their mother's side. In 366 BC, the consular lists mention the first plebeian consul, Lucius Sextius Lateranus. In 300 BC, the plebeians won access to the most important religious offices, and in 287 BC, the struggle was brought to an end when plebiscites passed by the assembly of the plebs (*concilium plebis*) were accepted as valid for the whole people—that is, as public laws.

Roman Expansion

Even during the period of the kings (about 700 BC to 510 BC), the people of Rome started to expand the city boundaries by subduing their closest Latin neighbors, including the city of Alba Longa, in the Alban hills, about 20 kilometers (12 miles) southeast of Rome, and the saltworks by the mouth of the Tiber. Involved in continuous fights with other neighboring tribes—Etruscans, Sabines, Aequi, Volsci, and Hernici—in the fifth century BC, Rome became the leader of the Latin League, a confederation of city-states in Latium.

The climax of this development was the conquest of Veii, the southernmost Etruscan metropolis, 17 kilometers (10 miles) north of Rome. The capture of Rome by Senonian Gauls (who had crossed the Alps from the north), in 390 BC, was a temporary setback, as Rome soon regained its position as leader. In 338 BC, the Latin League was dissolved after a war between Rome and other Latin cities, and shortly afterwards, Rome came into conflict with the powerful Samnites, in the

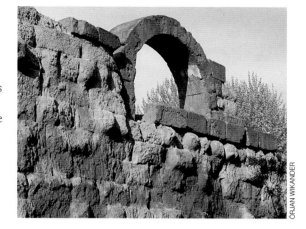

mountainous hinterland of central Italy. The Samnites were finally subdued in 295 BC, and within 25 years, Rome was in possession of the entire Italic peninsula. Etruscans, Gauls, and the Greeks of Magna Graecia (Greater Greece) yielded to the superior force of Roman armies.

The Hellenistic Period and the Roman Empire: 323 BC to AD 395

Rome's capture by the Gauls is the first event in Roman history mentioned in a contemporary Greek source, but 200 years later, Rome was a political power of importance all over the Greek world. The fourth and third centuries BC gave rise to states larger than city-states in both the western and the eastern Mediterranean area. In 334 BC, Alexander the Great started his campaign against the king of Persia, Darius; and Alexander's uncle, Alexander of Epirus, embarked upon an adventure in the West, allegedly to help Greek colonies in southern Italy against increasing attacks from native tribes. He had more far-reaching ambitions, but failed. So did his successor, Pyrrhos, in about 275 BC, even though he temporarily controlled considerable parts of southern Italy and Sicily.

◄ The so-called Servian Wall at the Aventine hill, in Rome, was originally built between 378 BC and 353 BC. The upper arch shown here, intended for catapults (*ballistae*), was a later addition, dating from 87 BC.

♀ The sarcophagus of a Roman patrician, Lucius Cornelius Scipio Barbatus, consul in 298 BC. It was cut about 280 BC and clearly shows the influence of contemporary Greek art in southern Italy and Sicily.
MUSEO PIO-CLEMENTINO, VATICANO/SCALA

HERCULANEUM: A BURIED TOWN

Örjan Wikander

THE MOST FAMOUS eruption of the volcano Vesuvius, which began on 24 August in AD 79, buried more than the city of Pompeii. It also buried a number of smaller towns and villages. Herculaneum was one of these. Situated 14 kilometers (9 miles) southeast of Pompeii, it was hit not only by the fine ash-rain that buried Pompeii, but also by a stream of mud-mixed lava, which hardened to form a layer of tufa more than 20 meters (65 feet) thick.

♀ These apartment blocks for poorer people, on the so-called Cardo IV, were built in a half-timbered style, a cheaper building method that was not unusual in Roman towns.

☞ Private houses in the southern part of the town. To the right of center is the "atrium" of the Casa del Rilievo di Telefo. Most of these houses are more advanced architecturally than Pompeii houses.

The town possessed a theater, a large gymnasium (or palaestra), and at least two public baths. The gymnasium, shown here, took the form of a large courtyard, its northwestern portico almost 90 meters (300 feet) long. The end of the excavated area can be seen in the background, with the houses of the modern-day village of Resina above.

The mud-lava that buried the town has helped to preserve organic material, such as this charred wooden bed frame. Even a library with books of papyrus was preserved.

A grocery store on the *Decumanus inferior*, one of the main streets of the town. In and behind the marble-covered counter, there are eight large storage jars (*dolia*) for grain and vegetables. The presence of a cooking stove suggests that the shop may also have been a *thermopolium*, supplying hot meals to customers.

Regular excavations began only in 1927, and over the years since, substantial areas of the town have been revealed and restored. Apparently much smaller than Pompeii, Herculaneum had fewer than 5,000 inhabitants. The Forum has not been found, and only one temple has been uncovered. Most buildings, both public and private, were erected during the last century of the town's life. The most impressive, upper-class, houses have been discovered in the southwest. Shown here is the Casa del mosaico di Nettuno e Anfitrite.

⊙ A Roman bridge over a deep gorge at Ronda, in Spain.

LUIS CASTANEDA/THE IMAGE BANK

ÖRJAN WIKANDER

⊙ These two well-preserved Republican temples in the Forum Boarium, in Rome, date from the late second century BC. The round temple on the left is one of the earliest surviving Roman buildings erected in marble.

⊙ The large harbor depicted in this wall painting from Stabiae, near Pompeii, dating from the first century AD, may be the one at Puteoli. Puteoli was Rome's most important port until Trajan's harbor was constructed at Ostia some time after AD 100.

NATIONAL MUSEUM, NAPLES/SCALA

The final victory fell to Rome, which did not halt at the Strait of Messina. Long-standing, peaceful contacts with the other great power in the West, Carthage, came to an end in 264 BC, when a conflict about Carthage's influence in Sicily led to the three Punic Wars. These lasted a little more than a century, and the victory led to complete Roman dominance in the western Mediterranean.

The first Punic War (264 BC to 241 BC) gave the Romans their first provinces: Sicily, Sardinia, and Corsica. The second, known as the Hannibalic War (218 BC to 201 BC), gave Rome eastern and southern Spain. The third Punic War (149 BC to 146 BC) caused the total destruction of Carthage, and the division of its African territory between a native vassal king and a new Roman province. The Spanish hinterland remained a military problem for 200 years, but the main parts of the Iberian peninsula were subdued during devastating wars in 154 BC to 133 BC. A land link from there to Italy was gained by lengthy campaigns against the Ligurians along the Italian Riviera (the Gulf of Genoa) and Celtic tribes in southern Gaul (part of present-day France). In 118 BC, southern Gaul became a Roman province, Gallia Narbonensis, which was of interest for the increasingly important trade into central Gaul.

The first two Punic Wars involved enormous strains upon Rome's economic resources and military capacity. After these victories, however, there was no power left in the Mediterranean world that could match Rome's strength. To follow Rome's gradual move into the Greek East is like watching a cat toying with a mouse. In some parts, the conquest passed almost unnoticed; elsewhere, when necessary, it was conducted with unrestrained, brutal force. Both Macedonia and the Seleucid kingdom were rebuked on several occasions, punished with cession of land, and weakened militarily. For a long time, however, Rome preferred to rule through agents: only in 148 BC was Macedonia turned into a formal province, followed by Achaea, in 146 BC. The year 133 BC was notable in the East, because of the bequeathing of western Asia Minor (present-day Turkey) to Rome by the last king of Pergamon. At that time, both Seleucid Syria and Egypt were, in practice, under Roman control.

The establishment of larger states or empires is, of course, not the sole characteristic of the later Classical Antiquity—the Hellenistic period (323 BC to 31 BC) and the Roman Empire (31 BC to AD 395)— as compared to the preceding Archaic and Classical periods. Indeed, the differences are so great and crucial that it is a matter of doubt whether they should be considered as parts of one and the same historical epoch.

The conquests of Alexander the Great completely changed the foundations of Greek economy and culture. Greek settlements; Greek political organization; and Greek language, literature, and art spread to India, in the East, and Egypt, in the south.

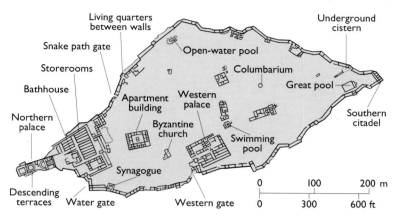

An aerial view of Masada, located about 50 kilometers (30 miles) southeast of Jerusalem, in Israel. The cliff was transformed into a well-defended stronghold by King Herod the Great (37 BC to 4 BC). During the rebellion against the Romans from AD 66 to AD 70, Masada was occupied by 1,000 Zealots, who managed to hold out until AD 73.

ILLUSTRATION: KEN RINKEL

THE PHOTO LIBRARY, SYDNEY

The conquests of the second century BC had immense cultural implications. Greek works of art were stolen and taken to Rome, and the capital attracted Greek artists, philosophers, and writers. Less well known is the fact that, in the same period, Rome and Italy as a whole became strongly influenced by the most recent Greek technology, particularly in agricultural production. The invention of the screw, the crank, and various kinds of gear, at the beginning of the third century BC (or slightly earlier), opened up opportunities for a series of labor-saving devices and machines. The rotary hand mill dramatically increased the volume of grain processed as compared to earlier querns (mills). The principle of the rotary hand mill led to the development of the animal-powered "hourglass" mill (about 200 BC) and the water mill (in the first century BC). By means of other new devices, animals in a capstan could raise water in a geared bucket-chain (*saqyia*), crush olives or metal ore in an edge-runner mill (*trapetum*), or knead dough in the many bakeries that were necessary to supply the growing towns. (See the feature *Cato's Agricultural Machines.*) New modes of production transformed parts of the terracotta industry—for example, roof tiles, brick, and, in particular, fine tableware pottery—into mass production. A constantly growing market in the urban centers throughout the empire, and the emergence of a well-to-do middle class, increased the demand for such commodities to a level never before achieved in the ancient world.

People consumed, production increased, and trade prospered. Larger and better equipped harbors were constructed all over the empire. Archaeological finds, such as stamped storage amphoras (two-handled vessels), help historians to plot the major trade routes. The increase in trade is demonstrated by the discovery of a number of shipwrecks from the period 300 BC to AD 300. These, by far, surpass those from both earlier and later periods.

🔥 Dating from about AD 100, this marble relief from the Tomb of the Haterii, in Rome, shows a crane powered by men in a treadwheel being used in the construction of a temple.
MUSEO GREGORIANO PROFANO, VATICANO/SCALA

With Greek colonization and far-reaching Hellenization already present in the western Mediterranean, Alexander's empire laid the foundations of a new and, at least superficially, uniform world around the Mediterranean. Trade and slave-based production grew rapidly, and so did the many new cities founded in that area.

Even in the fourth century BC, one Greek philosopher had called Rome "a Greek town", but it was only after the conquest of Magna Graecia (282 BC to 270 BC) that the true Hellenization of Rome began. Greek sculptures are mentioned occasionally in Rome, members of the Roman aristocracy started learning Greek, and Romans came into contact with Greek literature. In 216 BC, a Roman noble, Fabius Pictor, led a delegation to the Delphic Oracle following the disastrous defeat suffered against Hannibal at Cannae, and he later composed a Roman history in Greek in order to introduce his country to the Hellenized world.

🔥 A Roman tombstone from Ravenna, in Italy, depicting the shipbuilder Titus Longidienus at work.

CATO'S AGRICULTURAL MACHINES

Örjan Wikander

The agriculture of Hellenistic Italy was transformed not only by the introduction of a large number of technical innovations, but also by a profound structural change. The last two centuries BC witnessed decisive steps towards the establishment of large-scale estates, *latifundia*, which were to play an important role in the course of the empire. Even though the cultivation units remained relatively small for a long period, there was a gradual transition to more extensive farming, largely based on slave labor.

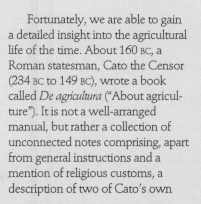

Fortunately, we are able to gain a detailed insight into the agricultural life of the time. About 160 BC, a Roman statesman, Cato the Censor (234 BC to 149 BC), wrote a book called *De agricultura* ("About agriculture"). It is not a well-arranged manual, but rather a collection of unconnected notes comprising, apart from general instructions and a mention of religious customs, a description of two of Cato's own

☝ An edge-runner mill (*trapetum*) from the Athenian Agora (marketplace), dating from the fifth or sixth century AD. Two spherical segments hanging on a horizontal beam were rolled over the olives in order to separate the pulp from the stones.
RABAT MUSEUM, MALTA/C.M. DIXON/PHOTO RESOURCES

estates near the border of Latium and Campania.

One farm—with an extent of 240 *iugera* (about 60 hectares, or 150 acres), managed by 13 people, mainly slaves—specialized in the cultivation of olives. The other specialized in viticulture, occupied 100 *iugera* (about 25 hectares, or 60 acres), and was managed by 16 people. Even though the descriptions refer to these two particular farms, they are doubtless fairly representative of normal cultivation units in Late Republican Italy.

Besides workers and animals, all kinds of tools and equipment are listed, including the precise number of spades, axes, tongs, working tables, and so on used at each farm. As well as this specialized agricultural equipment, Cato describes a series of machines, showing that — in spite of his well-known aversion to everything foreign—he was perfectly aware of the recent achievements of Greek technology.

The olives were crushed in five edge-runner mills (*trapeta*) of various sizes (a recent invention), and the pulp was then transferred to five presses of the most recent models,

☝ A reconstruction of a lever-and-drum press for crushing olives, or grapes for winemaking, in the Villa dei Misteri, at Pompeii, dating from the first century AD. The olive pulp or grapes were placed on the press bed (**a**) and covered with a lid (**b**). The pressing beam (**c**) was drawn down with levers (**e**) and a rope running around a drum (**d**), shown here in the foreground.

at least some of which were provided with block and tackle to hoist the weights. The wine was pressed in similar machines, and there was a series of mills to process grain cultivated for household use: on the olive farm, there was an Olynthian mill, an improved saddle quern, a rotary hand mill (invented about 300 BC), and a donkey mill (a recent invention); in the vineyard, there was one Olynthian mill and three donkey mills.

Cato describes his machines in detail, but they are best illustrated by slightly later archaeological finds—from the cities of Vesuvius, in particular. Variants of the same devices were used throughout the Roman Empire, from Britain and the Rhine frontier to Africa and Southeast Asia. Some of the machines survived in Mediterranean countries well into the twentieth century.

☝ Animal mills are depicted in this relief from a Roman sarcophagus, probably dating from the second or third century AD. The hourglass-shaped upper stone is raised slightly above the conical lower one by means of a wooden construction resting upon a vertical beam inserted into the top of the cone. The grain was placed in the funnel-shaped upper part, passed between the millstones, and ground to flour, which was collected by the man seen on the right.
VATICAN MUSEUM

177

THE ROMAN EMPIRE: 900 BC – AD 500

SIGNIFICANT EVENTS	ART, ARCHITECTURE, AND TECHNOLOGY
500	
The last Roman emperor of the West, Romulus Augustulus, is dethroned AD 476	
Rome sacked AD 455	
400 Rome sacked AD 410	
300 Christian Church officially acknowledged AD 311	Aurelian builds a 19 kilometer (12 mile) wall to protect Rome
Diocletian creates a constitution, the "Tetrarchy" AD 285	
Period of "military anarchy" AD 235 – AD 284	Use of water-powered mill spreads over large parts of the empire
200	
	Public baths, aqueducts, bridges, theaters, amphitheaters, circuses, and libraries are erected all over the empire
100	Hadrian's Wall built in Britain
Eruption of Vesuvius buries Pompeii and Herculaneum AD 79	Fired bricks in use for covering concrete walls
Fire destroys major part of Rome AD 64	*Terra sigillata*
AD 1	Bronze artifacts common in domestic use
	Invention of glass-blowing creates new category of household utensils
Julius Caesar's reign ends the republic 48 BC – 44 BC	
Pompey's victories in the East 67 BC – 62 BC	
Caius Marius crushes barbarian invaders 101 BC	Two large aqueducts constructed
3rd Punic War 149 BC – 146 BC	Greek works of art stolen and taken to Rome
2nd Punic War 218 BC – 201 BC	
1st Punic War 264 BC – 241 BC	
Rome master of the Italic peninsula 270 BC	
Plebeian laws become valid for all people 287 BC	
Etruscans gradually become part of Roman world	Inventions such as the screw, crank, and gear herald technological progress
First plebeian consul 366 BC	
Plebeians gain right of intermarriage with patricians 445 BC	
500	
	Great Temple of Jupiter inaugurated on the Capitoline Hill 509 BC
Royal dynasty of Tarquins 616 BC – 510 BC	
Rise of Rome	
Adoption of Greek alphabet	
Etruscan language used	
Greek colonization of southern Italy and western part of central Italy	King Numa institutes eight craft guilds
Gradual change from use of bronze to iron	
1000 BC	

MAJOR ROMAN EMPERORS

Valentinian III
AD 425 – AD 455

Theodosius II
AD 408 – AD 450

Theodosius I
AD 379 – AD 395

Valens
(eastern empire)
AD 364 – AD 378

Valentinian I
(western empire)
AD 364 – AD 375

Julian
AD 361 – AD 363

Constantine I
AD 306 – AD 337

Diocletian
(eastern empire)
AD 284 – AD 305

Aurelian
AD 270 – AD 275

Gallienus
AD 253 – AD 268

Caracalla
AD 211 – AD 217

Septimius Severus
AD 193 – AD 211

Marcus Aurelius
AD 161 – AD 180

Antoninus Pius
AD 138 – AD 161

Hadrian
AD 117 – AD 138

Trajan
AD 98 – AD 117

Domitian
AD 81 – AD 96

Titus
AD 79 – AD 81

Vespasian
AD 69 – AD 79

Nero
AD 54 – AD 68

Claudius
AD 41 – AD 54

Caligula
AD 37 – AD 41

Tiberius
AD 14 – AD 37

Augustus
31 BC – AD 14

The Hellenization of Rome

Gradually, the attachment of Italy to the Hellenistic Greek economy grew tighter. Trading contacts between the western and eastern Mediterranean had long traditions, and for some time, there were no drastic changes. The Greek colonies in southern Italy, together with occasional representatives of the native Italic population, remained in control of the eastern trade. But the Greek cities were badly afflicted by the devastations of the Hannibalic War and Rome's ruthless postwar policy, from which they never completely recovered. Instead, Campanian and Roman traders took over, extracting great fortunes in a Greek world under increasing political pressure from Rome.

Settling in the East, Romans did business as slave-traders and bankers. We know the names of many such traders, particularly from inscriptions on Delos—a small island among the Cyclades, which became a free port in 166 BC and soon developed into the center of trade in the eastern Mediterranean. Most traders were of the semi-aristocratic class of Roman knights (*equites*). They grew rich from private enterprises or as partners in the powerful companies of *publicani*, who were contracted by the Roman state to collect public revenues and to oversee the work of mines in the newly established provinces. Together, in little more than a century, the aristocracy—as military commanders, plunderers, and robbers—and the *equites*—as profiteers and extortionists—managed to turn the East from prosperity to poverty and destitution.

The second century BC was a period of unbounded Roman success abroad—political, military, and economic—yet the situation in Italy grew continually worse. The Hannibalic War had meant disaster, not only to the Greek colonies, but to considerable parts of central and southern Italy in general. Arable land lay waste, and the Roman policy after the war did not encourage its recultivation by Italic peasantry. Instead, more and more land passed into the possession of members of the Roman aristocracy, while impoverished peasants flocked into the towns. Rome grew rapidly, and to meet the city's increase in population, two large aqueducts were built, in 144 BC and 125 BC. The two older aqueducts, constructed in 312 BC and 272 BC, had been sufficient for more than a hundred years.

Problems in Rome

The growing urban poor could be pacified with food and water, but the problems were not only social and economic. They had even more serious implications for Rome's existence as an imperialistic state: the supply of free men to enroll for the army. Rome's military strength depended on freeholders, and the proletarization of parts of the Italian peasantry made it very difficult to enlist sufficient freeholders for the wars in Spain.

Presumably, this was one of the main reasons why the two Gracchi brothers, who were of aristocratic birth, tried to use the office of tribune of the people—a position intended to defend popular rights—in 133 BC, and in 123 BC to 122 BC, respectively, to accomplish far-reaching changes in Roman society. Both brothers were killed, but as a result of their actions, considerable areas of land were distributed to unpropertied citizens. Although the Gracchi were unsuccessful in their efforts, they recognized the need for reform. In part, they used unconstitutional methods in trying to achieve their goals, and in due time, these methods were instrumental in putting an end to the republic.

Throughout Italic society and the growing empire were contradictions that could no longer be handled, or solved, within a political and social system that had been created for a city-state governed by the representatives of a small, landed aristocracy. The last century of the republic is characterized by the political struggles between the *optimates*—who were nobles basing their actions upon the authority of the Senate—and the *populares*—who followed the example of the Gracchi by appealing directly to the people over the head of the Senators.

The problem of finding men for the army was solved by Caius Marius, a parvenu from the class of knights who had won military successes in Africa. In a national crisis, when Rome was under threat from two barbarian tribes from the north— the Cimbri and Teutoni—which had defeated several consular armies, unpropertied citizens were taken on as paid soldiers. Caius Marius organized new legions that finally crushed the barbarian invaders in 101 BC.

Marius had created a professional army, no less loyal to its generals than to the state. In 83 BC, Sulla, the leading *optimate*, returned from victories in the East and defeated the followers of Marius. He conquered Rome and made himself dictator for life, proscribing and murdering thousands of his enemies, between 82 BC and 79 BC. Pompey won a similar position by impressive victories in the East (67 BC to 62 BC), but he hesitated to draw the formal, political consequences of his position. A coalition between the three most powerful men in Rome—Pompey, Julius Caesar, and Crassus ("the first triumvirate", in 60 BC)—postponed the decision. In the end, a civil war brought death to Pompey, in 48 BC, and dictatorship to Julius Caesar. Four years later, Caesar was murdered by aristocratic followers of the former oligarchic rule.

Augustus and the End of the Roman Republic

Caesar's short reign ended the republic. Through Caesar's highly developed military and organizational skills, and through his open-minded and imaginative analysis of the requirements of Rome and the Roman Empire, he had demonstrated that the republican Senate was incapable of handling the empire's affairs.

After Caesar's death, there was a long struggle for power: first, between his heirs and his murderers;

then, among the heirs—his closest associate, Mark Antony, and Caesar's adoptive son, the future emperor, Octavian Augustus. After his naval victory at Actium, in 31 BC, Augustus remained sole ruler, and in 44 years, he reorganized the Roman Empire. Wisely, he avoided the dictatorship and every formal monarchical title, basing his rule, instead, upon existing republican offices and institutions, which he gradually transformed to suit his personal ambitions. On the whole, this pseudo-republican imperial constitution (the "Principate") was to last for 300 years.

Augustus's reforming zeal intervened at almost all levels and sections of Roman society, but there is little doubt that his most important achievement was the transformation of the haphazard, disorganized Roman Empire into a well-arranged and well-functioning realm, controlled firmly by the hand of the emperor. The conquests of Pompey in Southwest Asia and Caesar in Gaul had added vast territories to the empire. The boundaries of the Asian and African provinces were defined in Rome's favor, owing to the easily defendable Euphrates border, the African desert, and a number of client kingdoms. However, the situation in Europe was less favorable, with an unreasonably long border leaving considerable parts of the Alps and the northern Balkans outside the empire. For the first time in the history of Rome, Augustus made detailed plans for creating a more easily defendable border. During most of his reign, his generals fought fierce mountain tribes in the Alps and the Balkans and even Germanic tribes in the north; by the time of his death, Augustus left an empire neatly bordered by the two great northern rivers, the Rhine and the Danube.

The administration of the provinces changed: the former attitude, which treated them basically as conquered territories, gave way to a new policy in which provinces were rather to be seen as more or less fully integrated parts of a peaceful nation. The military forces were concentrated along the borders, and the former economic extortion was replaced by a new system of collecting revenues. The *Pax Augusta* brought peace to the empire; the provinces and their cities prospered.

A Roman coin with a portrait of Emperor Augustus, struck about 19 BC.
RONALD SHERIDAN/ANCIENT ART & ARCHITECTURE COLLECTION

This marble statue depicting a Roman aristocrat holding portrait busts of his ancestors dates from the late first century BC.
MUSEI CAPITOLINI, ROME/SCALA

❀ A Roman relief dating from the second or third century AD, showing peasants using the *vallus*, a type of harvesting machine driven by a donkey that was in common use in northern Gaul in this period.

❀ These two Roman glass bottles, dating from the second or third century AD, come from Nîmes, in southern France.
C.M. DIXON/PHOTO RESOURCES

♀ A reconstructed wall painting from a tomb outside Rome, dating from the third century AD. A riverboat (the *Isis Giminiana*) is being loaded at the port of Ostia before being towed up the Tiber to Rome.

Technology and Trade

In combination with rich archaeological finds, the agricultural writers Varro and Columella provide a clear and detailed picture of the forms and organization of agrarian production. The large estates (*latifundia*) offered opportunities for extensive farming, based upon slave labor and made more efficient by the adoption of new technical devices. The harrow was taken into general use, the heavy plow was introduced from the north to work the clay soil of the Po Valley, and in Gaul, the grain was reaped with special harvesting machines (*vallus* and *carpentum*). In the second century AD, the use of the water-powered mill had spread over large parts of the empire.

The terracotta industry developed further. Fired bricks became the general covering for concrete walls from the first century AD. The relief-molded *terra sigillata* (clay vessels) offered a method to produce fine pottery cheaply without requiring highly skilled potters and painters. Bronze artifacts became common for domestic use, and the recent invention of glass-blowing, between 50 BC and 20 BC, created a new category of household utensils.

Long-distance trade increased in volume. Grain, wine, olive oil, pottery, marble, and other heavy goods were transported over the Mediterranean, but to the almost exclusive benefit of those living on the coast or navigable watercourses.

In spite of the impressive road system constructed over the empire, land transport remained extremely expensive—50 times as costly as sea transport, according to a convincing estimate. Sea transport was promoted, and lighthouses were built and protected harbors were developed. Rome's port, Ostia, was rebuilt by the emperors Claudius (AD 41 to AD 54) and Trajan (AD 98 to AD 117) to fulfill the needs of the capital.

The appearance of Rome changed considerably. Augustus and his successors erected or rebuilt public buildings. A more complete transformation followed upon the devastating fire in AD 64, which destroyed the major part of the city. Rome, as we know it from most archaeological excavations— with brick-covered house walls and temples shining with marble—was created mainly between the time of the fire and the early fourth century AD. Multistoried residential buildings, up to more than 20 meters (65 feet) high, housed a population of approximately one million people, whose provision with the necessities of life remained a constant challenge to the emperors. A sophisticated organization (*annona*) brought grain from Africa and had it transformed to bread in public bakeries; wine and oil came up the Tiber in barges, with the grain; and impressive amounts of fresh water flowed from the mountains in 11 major aqueducts.

The rest of the empire, comprising Italy and the provinces, was organized around both established and newly founded towns, built according to a more or less uniform plan. The central forum was surrounded with religious and civic public buildings— most important, the Temple of Jupiter ("Capitolium"), the center of official cult, and the meeting place of the local "senate". In the second century AD, building activity was intense: public baths, aqueducts, bridges, theaters, amphitheaters, circuses, and libraries were erected, even in small towns, all over the empire. Together, the investments reached such a level that they strained the economic resources of many communities.

The Efficiency of Roman Emperors

Roman history droops under the load of imperial evil and madness. The importance attached to the eccentricity of certain emperors, in both ancient and modern history-writing, has tended to conceal the fact that most Roman emperors were very competent administrators, who managed the realm far better than did their republican predecessors. For a very long time, the empire prospered. Never before in the history of civilization did such a large proportion of a huge population benefit from peace, material welfare, education, and other human privileges.

A standing army of more than 300,000 men ensured interior stability; it protected the borders from aggression from Germanic tribes in the north and the armies of the Parthian Empire in the east.

⚹ This house facade still standing in the Via Biberatica, a Roman Imperial street near the Forum of Trajan, dates from the second century AD. The ground floor was occupied by shops, while the upper floors contained apartments and lodgings for ordinary citizens.

On the whole, Augustus's borders were maintained, and only in a few cases were new provinces established. Besides four former client kingdoms (Cappadocia, Mauretania, Thracia, and Arabia), three new areas were annexed, all along the northern border: Britannia (Britain), the Agri Decumates (in southern Germany), and Dacia (in modern Romania). (See the feature *The European Frontiers of the Roman Empire.*) Emperor Trajan's attempt to force the Parthians back beyond the Euphrates in AD 114 to AD 115 failed; the new provinces in Mesopotamia and Armenia were given up after a few years.

⚹ The interior of a *thermopolium*, a shop selling hot meals, at the Roman port of Ostia. It dates from the third century AD.

Economic Instability and "Military Anarchy"

The organization of the empire and the comparatively high standard of living among its inhabitants, the impressive building activities, and the great size of the standing army all depended upon the prospering economy. But, apparently, the Romans exploited their resources to the utmost, leaving small margins for economic decline or increasing expenditure. The growing pressure on the northern and eastern borders from AD 160 onwards could only just be met with existing military forces. The situation grew manifestly worse after AD 226, when the faltering Parthian Empire was overthrown by the Persian, Sassanid dynasty. A series of severe wars with Persia followed, and the military crisis was further complicated by Germanic tribes crossing the Rhine and forcing their way through Gaul into Spain and Italy. Economic life collapsed, and the military situation grew critical; it soon became obvious that one supreme leader could no longer manage the defense of the entire empire. Usurpers appeared in numbers: to posterity, the period from AD 235 to AD 284 is known as one of "military anarchy".

It is a sign of Rome's fundamental vigor and strength that the empire survived. After a period of disruption and chaos, the legitimate emperors started recapturing and reorganizing the divided

⚹ A view of the Forum Romanum from the southeast. In the foreground are the podium and three standing columns of the Temple of Castor and Pollux; to the left is the Basilica Iulia; and in the background, the Arch of Septimius Severus and the Curia (the meeting hall of the Senate).

⚹ A wall painting from Pompeii, dating from the first century AD, showing a baker selling bread in his shop.

181

⚘ This Sassanid rock relief at Bishapur, in Iran, commemorates the capture in AD 260 of the Roman Emperor Valerian by King Shapur I.

↪ *Opposite page*: The magnificent apsis of the Basilica of St Apollinare in Classe, in Ravenna, Italy. The walls are covered with polychrome mosaics dating from the first half of the sixth century AD.

↪ A detail of the reliefs on the Column of Trajan, erected in the Emperor's forum to commemorate his victories over the Dacians (in present-day Romania) between AD 101 and AD 106. The reliefs depict a variety of scenes, including battles, Roman soldiers building fortifications, and Trajan addressing his troops.

realm. The most important contribution was made by Aurelian (AD 270 to AD 275), who took control of the entire empire and built a city wall, 19 kilometers (12 miles) long, to protect Rome from future barbarian attacks. He did not live to conclude his restoration of the government, and his achievements were unjustly overshadowed by those of two of his successors, Diocletian (AD 284 to AD 305) and Constantine (AD 306 to AD 337).

The Empire Is Divided

Diocletian created a constitution, the "Tetrarchy", which acknowledged that the empire was too large to be controlled effectively by one ruler. The provinces were split into more than 100 smaller units under 12 dioceses, subordinate in turn to 4 prefectures: 2 in the West and 2 in the East. Four emperors, two *augusti* and two *caesares* (their designated successors), were responsible for these basic parts of the empire, with their new capitals in Augusta Treverorum (Trier), Mediolanum (Milan), Sirmium (near Belgrade), and Nicomedia (at the Marmara Lake). From then on, the city of Rome lost all political importance, although it retained its symbolic value for a very long time. Many emperors favored Rome economically, but few bothered to visit it. The status of Italy no longer differed from that of other provinces: the empire's focus had moved towards its borders.

The immense differences between the Greek East and the Latin West became more pronounced in all respects: economy, politics, warfare, art, religion, and so on. Restoration of military and political authority was the first prerequisite of the renaissance of the empire, but it had no real future without settling the economic anarchy, too. During the Tetrarchy, economic life revived, but debased currency and uncontrolled inflation counteracted the efforts of reorganization. Several monetary reforms failed, and so did the Price Edict of AD 301, an attempt to stop inflation by freezing the prices of goods and services.

The Tetrarchy collapsed only a few years after Diocletian's abdication. In AD 324, one of his successors, Constantine, assembled the entire empire under his rule and established a parallel seat of government in Byzantium (Constantinople), in the East—the door to the trade between Europe and Asia. Only Constantine succeeded in bringing order to the monetary system by introducing a new gold coin, the solidus. At that time, however, the importance of money was rapidly diminishing. Trade receded, a barter economy prevailed, and the towns were depopulated, their functions being gradually replaced by self-supporting rural estates. The husbandmen, *coloni*, lost their freedom and were gradually transformed into villeins, taking the place of the former rural slaves. In reality, Classical Antiquity as an urban civilization had ceased to exist. After Constantine's death, the empire split again and was ruled by his three sons. It was seldom to be in the hands of a single ruler. The last time was in 394 BC to 395 BC.

For some time, the cities retained their importance as cultural centers, not least for the Christian Church. After centuries of work and struggle, and after grave persecutions (under Decius, AD 249 to AD 251, and Diocletian, AD 303 to AD 305, in particular), the church was officially acknowledged in AD 311. Its power and importance grew constantly until, at the very end of the fourth century AD, it became the sole legally admitted religion in the empire. Paganism survived in the countryside and its small villages (*pagi*), but the towns became centers in the hierarchic organization of the church. Bishops and archbishops built richly decorated cathedrals, and churches and monasteries gradually took over responsibility for the transmission of the cultural heritage of antiquity.

The Roman Empire Disintegrates

While the eastern, Byzantine, part of the empire prospered around its new capital, Constantinople, the western emperors finally lost the struggle against invading barbarians and a collapsing economy. Almost simultaneously, the western Roman Empire disintegrated. In AD 406, Germanic tribes crossed the Rhine and founded a series of new states upon the ruins of the empire—Vandals in Africa, Visigoths in southern Gaul and Spain, Salian Franks in northern Gaul, and so forth. Rome was sacked in AD 410 and in AD 455, and in AD 476, the last emperor of the West, Romulus Augustulus, was dethroned—a symbolic event, but one of little real consequence by this time.

In the East, Roman emperors were to rule for a thousand years more, until Constantinople fell to the Ottoman Turks in AD 1453. In the West, the Christian Church represented continuity, until a new emperor—Charlemagne, king of the Franks—was crowned by the Pope, Leo III, in Rome on Christmas Day, AD 800.

+SANCTVS APOLENARIS

185

LINDOW MAN: A 2,000-YEAR-OLD HUMAN SACRIFICE

I.M. STEAD

LINDOW MAN is the name given to an ancient body found in a bog at Lindow Moss, near Manchester, in England, in 1984. The previous year, workers digging up peat had found the remains of a human head, and so they were not very surprised when a human leg came to light at the same site. They contacted an archaeologist, who located the rest of the body, which was removed, still encased in a large block of peat, and sent to the British Museum for excavation.

The block of peat contained the upper half of a body that had been sliced by the peat-cutting machine; the rest had been ripped apart and scattered. The remaining pieces, including the leg the workers had found, were discovered in the loose peat. Much of the skin was well preserved, being dark brown and leathery, but the body was almost flat, having been compressed by the great weight of the peat. It had been lying face down in a bog pool. Thanks to the presence of a relatively high concentration of humic and fulvic acids in the peat, which acted as antibiotics and attacked any bacteria present, and the absence of oxygen, the body was preserved for posterity.

The dating of Lindow Man posed problems. He was unclothed and had nothing with him, so the body could not be dated by means of associated artifacts. The position of the body, more than 2 meters (6 feet) beneath the original surface, showed that it was ancient. An examination of associated pollen, together with radiocarbon dating of the peat, indicated that he had lived nearly 2,000 years ago. Initial radiocarbon dates from the body itself varied considerably, but the latest results from Oxford University, where 19 dates have now been processed, suggest that he died in the first century AD, or perhaps early in the second century.

Lindow Man was subjected to photogrammetry (taking measurements from photographs), xeroradiography (high definition X-rays), and body scanners (CAT scans and Magnetic Resonance Imaging) before being thoroughly examined by a surgeon. Specialists determined that he had been in his mid-twenties, some 168 centimeters (5 feet, 6 inches) tall, and perhaps 60 kilograms (130 pounds) or more in weight. He had been quite healthy, although some of his vertebrae had Schmorl's nodes (cavities in the end-plates of vertebrae, perhaps related to severe strain) and he had suffered from worms. No DNA had survived, but his blood group was O. His moustache and beard had been cut by shears, and his fingernails were neatly rounded. Nothing remained of his liver, lungs, or heart, but a length of gut was found, which contained digested food. His last meal consisted of griddle cakes made from flour containing a mixture of wheat (spelt and emmer) and barley and cooked over an open fire.

Lindow Man had not drowned in the pool but had been killed before he entered it. A pathology report revealed that a blow from a small axe had stunned him and fractured his skull. He had then been garrotted (the knotted ligature was well preserved) which broke his neck, and his throat had finally been cut. The position of the garrotte would have speeded up blood loss, and this deliberate bleeding suggests ritual slaughter rather than common murder. One slight clue may point to the identity of the murderers: some mistletoe pollen was found in the man's gut, which is a rare occurrence in an archaeological context. Mistletoe was used by the Druids, the philosopher-priests of the Celtic world, who appear to have taken part in human sacrifices. Little is known about them, but Druids were certainly active in Britain in the first century AD.

Once the body had been taken out of the bog, it was in danger of drying, shrinking, and falling to pieces. Decomposition was prevented in the short term by keeping the body cool and damp. Its long-term preservation was achieved by freeze-drying: the body was immersed in polyethylene glycol (water-soluble wax) for 10 weeks, and was then frozen for three days and freeze-dried for three weeks, the ice being converted directly to vapor and removed to a condensor, where the temperature was minus 60 degrees Celsius (minus 76 degrees Fahrenheit). The outcome was successful, with only slight shrinkage, no color change, and no variation in the texture of the skin. The body is now on permanent display at the British Museum.

The body of another adult male was found in the same bog in 1987, but it had been badly mauled by the peat-cutting machinery. It seems likely that the head found in 1983 belongs to this body. The cause of death has not yet been established, but it seems clear that this second body was more or less contemporary with Lindow Man.

BRITISH MUSEUM

◄● The upper part of Lindow Man's body, with the detached leg on the left, on display at the British Museum.

⛨ This house facade still standing in the Via Biberatica, a Roman Imperial street near the Forum of Trajan, dates from the second century AD. The ground floor was occupied by shops, while the upper floors contained apartments and lodgings for ordinary citizens.

⛨ The interior of a *thermopolium*, a shop selling hot meals, at the Roman port of Ostia. It dates from the third century AD.

On the whole, Augustus's borders were maintained, and only in a few cases were new provinces established. Besides four former client kingdoms (Cappadocia, Mauretania, Thracia, and Arabia), three new areas were annexed, all along the northern border: Britannia (Britain), the Agri Decumates (in southern Germany), and Dacia (in modern Romania). (See the feature *The European Frontiers of the Roman Empire.*) Emperor Trajan's attempt to force the Parthians back beyond the Euphrates in AD 114 to AD 115 failed; the new provinces in Mesopotamia and Armenia were given up after a few years.

Economic Instability and "Military Anarchy"

The organization of the empire and the comparatively high standard of living among its inhabitants, the impressive building activities, and the great size of the standing army all depended upon the prospering economy. But, apparently, the Romans exploited their resources to the utmost, leaving small margins for economic decline or increasing expenditure. The growing pressure on the northern and eastern borders from AD 160 onwards could only just be met with existing military forces. The situation grew manifestly worse after AD 226, when the faltering Parthian Empire was overthrown by the Persian, Sassanid dynasty. A series of severe wars with Persia followed, and the military crisis was further complicated by Germanic tribes crossing the Rhine and forcing their way through Gaul into Spain and Italy. Economic life collapsed, and the military situation grew critical; it soon became obvious that one supreme leader could no longer manage the defense of the entire empire. Usurpers appeared in numbers: to posterity, the period from AD 235 to AD 284 is known as one of "military anarchy".

It is a sign of Rome's fundamental vigor and strength that the empire survived. After a period of disruption and chaos, the legitimate emperors started recapturing and reorganizing the divided

⛨ A view of the Forum Romanum from the southeast. In the foreground are the podium and three standing columns of the Temple of Castor and Pollux; to the left is the Basilica Iulia; and in the background, the Arch of Septimius Severus and the Curia (the meeting hall of the Senate).

⛨ A wall painting from Pompeii, dating from the first century AD, showing a baker selling bread in his shop.

181

ROBERT HARDING PICTURE LIBRARY

⬆ This Sassanid rock relief at Bishapur, in Iran, commemorates the capture in AD 260 of the Roman Emperor Valerian by King Shapur I.

↪ *Opposite page*: The magnificent apsis of the Basilica of St Apollinare in Classe, in Ravenna, Italy. The walls are covered with polychrome mosaics dating from the first half of the sixth century AD.

↪ A detail of the reliefs on the Column of Trajan, erected in the Emperor's forum to commemorate his victories over the Dacians (in present-day Romania) between AD 101 and AD 106. The reliefs depict a variety of scenes, including battles, Roman soldiers building fortifications, and Trajan addressing his troops.

realm. The most important contribution was made by Aurelian (AD 270 to AD 275), who took control of the entire empire and built a city wall, 19 kilometers (12 miles) long, to protect Rome from future barbarian attacks. He did not live to conclude his restoration of the government, and his achievements were unjustly overshadowed by those of two of his successors, Diocletian (AD 284 to AD 305) and Constantine (AD 306 to AD 337).

The Empire Is Divided

Diocletian created a constitution, the "Tetrarchy", which acknowledged that the empire was too large to be controlled effectively by one ruler. The provinces were split into more than 100 smaller units under 12 dioceses, subordinate in turn to 4 prefectures: 2 in the West and 2 in the East. Four emperors, two *augusti* and two *caesares* (their designated successors), were responsible for these basic parts of the empire, with their new capitals in Augusta Treverorum (Trier), Mediolanum (Milan), Sirmium (near Belgrade), and Nicomedia (at the Marmara Lake). From then on, the city of Rome lost all political importance, although it retained its symbolic value for a very long time. Many emperors favored Rome economically, but few bothered to visit it. The status of Italy no longer differed from that of other provinces: the empire's focus had moved towards its borders.

The immense differences between the Greek East and the Latin West became more pronounced in all respects: economy, politics, warfare, art, religion, and so on. Restoration of military and political authority was the first prerequisite of the renaissance of the empire, but it had no real future without settling the economic anarchy, too. During the Tetrarchy, economic life revived, but debased currency and uncontrolled inflation counteracted the efforts of reorganization. Several monetary reforms failed, and so did the Price Edict of AD 301, an attempt to stop inflation by freezing the prices of goods and services.

The Tetrarchy collapsed only a few years after Diocletian's abdication. In AD 324, one of his successors, Constantine, assembled the entire empire under his rule and established a parallel seat of government in Byzantium (Constantinople), in the East—the door to the trade between Europe and Asia. Only Constantine succeeded in bringing order to the monetary system by introducing a new gold coin, the solidus. At that time, however, the importance of money was rapidly diminishing. Trade receded, a barter economy prevailed, and the towns were depopulated, their functions being gradually replaced by self-supporting rural estates. The husbandmen, *coloni*, lost their freedom and were gradually transformed into villeins, taking the place of the former rural slaves. In reality, Classical Antiquity as an urban civilization had ceased to exist. After Constantine's death, the empire split again and was ruled by his three sons. It was seldom to be in the hands of a single ruler. The last time was in 394 BC to 395 BC.

For some time, the cities retained their importance as cultural centers, not least for the Christian Church. After centuries of work and struggle, and after grave persecutions (under Decius, AD 249 to AD 251, and Diocletian, AD 303 to AD 305, in particular), the church was officially acknowledged in AD 311. Its power and importance grew constantly until, at the very end of the fourth century AD, it became the sole legally admitted religion in the empire. Paganism survived in the countryside and its small villages (*pagi*), but the towns became centers in the hierarchic organization of the church. Bishops and archbishops built richly decorated cathedrals, and churches and monasteries gradually took over responsibility for the transmission of the cultural heritage of antiquity.

The Roman Empire Disintegrates

While the eastern, Byzantine, part of the empire prospered around its new capital, Constantinople, the western emperors finally lost the struggle against invading barbarians and a collapsing economy. Almost simultaneously, the western Roman Empire disintegrated. In AD 406, Germanic tribes crossed the Rhine and founded a series of new states upon the ruins of the empire—Vandals in Africa, Visigoths in southern Gaul and Spain, Salian Franks in northern Gaul, and so forth. Rome was sacked in AD 410 and in AD 455, and in AD 476, the last emperor of the West, Romulus Augustulus, was dethroned—a symbolic event, but one of little real consequence by this time.

In the East, Roman emperors were to rule for a thousand years more, until Constantinople fell to the Ottoman Turks in AD 1453. In the West, the Christian Church represented continuity, until a new emperor—Charlemagne, king of the Franks—was crowned by the Pope, Leo III, in Rome on Christmas Day, AD 800.

SCALA

THE EUROPEAN FRONTIERS OF THE ROMAN EMPIRE

P.J. CASEY

THE ROMAN EMPEROR AUGUSTUS abandoned ideas of world conquest when the Roman army, invading Germany north of the Elbe, was massacred in AD 9. He established a European empire ending at Germany's borders on the banks of the Rhine and the Danube rivers. Along this line, a system of forts and fortresses protected the provinces and served as bases from which he could conduct punitive campaigns against the barbarians. Flotillas of river-craft prevented incursions by raiders and smugglers.

The emperor Hadrian. A restless traveler within his empire, he ended imperial expansion and formalized the frontiers. Hadrian's Wall is an enduring monument to this policy of consolidation.

A regularly paid army guarded the frontiers of the provinces, and each regiment occupied a fort built to a standard plan. At Chesters, on Hadrian's Wall, the underground strongroom, in which the unit's pay and savings were stored, survives to the present day.

There were minor changes to this grand design. Between the two rivers, various schemes of forts and fortifications—which represented attempts to gain strategic locations—have been identified. Early in the second century AD, Trajan crossed the Danube, adding the province of Dacia (modern Romania) to the empire. Dacia was abandoned in the late third century AD; the Danube was once again the frontier line. Claudius added Britannia (Britain) to the empire in AD 43, but once it was decided to conquer only part of the island, the task of establishing a viable frontier against the northern barbarians presented a major problem.

Frontier Defense Strategy

The strategy of frontier defense was based on the two main elements of the army: the citizen legionaries and the noncitizen auxiliaries. The legionary heavy infantry was usually deployed in units of about 5,500 men; their fortresses provided them with accommodation, workshops, and technical and medical facilities. Auxiliaries were recruited from defeated tribes or enrolled from unenfranchised peoples within the empire. They served for the reward of Roman citizenship, conferred at the end of 25 years' service with the colors. Auxiliary regiments varied in their make-up; most comprised 480 infantrymen or a similar number of cavalry troopers. A minority of regiments comprised 1,000 horse or foot soldiers; some others were a mixture of both. Sensibly, the Roman administration tended to post newly recruited auxiliary units to provinces, distant from their homelands. There, they settled for long periods in garrison, forming liaisons with the community and attracting traders, until a distinctive frontier culture evolved, and a population grew up that depended on the local fort for its livelihood and existence. Some of these civilian settlements grew into substantial towns. From these communities (*vici*), new members of the local regiment were recruited. In time, units with names derived originally from distant tribes were entirely served by locally born *vicani*.

This strategy, and its modification and development, are best demonstrated by Hadrian's Wall in

Frontier forces were accommodated in barrack blocks designed to hold 80 soldiers. Eight men shared a two-room unit in cramped company with their equipment, personal effects, and bedding.

Britain, constructed during the reign of Emperor Hadrian (AD 117 to AD 138). Along its 130 kilometer (80 mile) line were 17 forts, manned by infantry units totalling some 8,400 men. At 1.6 kilometer (1 mile) intervals, fortified gates allowed passage through Hadrian's Wall under military supervision. Towers at 500 meter (1,750 foot) intervals allowed surveillance of the landscape. Approach to Hadrian's Wall from the south was prevented by a vast ditch (the *Vallum*), which followed the wall, up hill, down dale, through bog, and through scrubland, across the width of Britain. For a 130 kilometer (80 mile) deep zone south of the wall, further auxiliary forts protected the rugged uplands of the frontier zone. A full legion at Eburacum (York) reinforced the wall garrisons in case trouble erupted that could not be dealt with by local resources. The *vici* attached to auxiliary forts flourished, especially in the third century AD. After AD 350, most *vici* were abandoned, probably because unit size was reduced to about one-third of the strength in the first century AD. This created accommodation space for soldiers and their families within the forts.

Community Response to Frontiers

The presence of these frontiers had profound effect on the communities living beyond them. Local people adopted different strategies at various times and in various places. The simplest response was attack, but the instances of successful penetration of Roman defenses, before the end of the fourth century AD, were very rare. Hadrian's Wall was crossed in AD 181, but the resulting punitive campaign certainly outweighed any advantages gained by the attackers.

On the Danube, a long campaign was fought by Marcus Aurelius (between AD 161 and AD 181) against the Marcomanni (literally, "people of the frontier"). In the third century AD, attacks launched across the Rhine resulted in devastation in Gaul and the creation of a separatist dynasty of Roman emperors, ruling Germany, Gaul, and Britain. They were devoted to protecting regional defense interests.

Trade across the frontiers was regulated, not discouraged, and access to Roman goods may have been used to create pro-Roman elites among the tribes beyond the frontier. Evidence from Germany suggests that chieftains and leaders with access to such goods used them to reward their followers. Through trade, Rome acquired amber, furs, wild animals, and slaves. Barbarian soldiers also crossed the frontiers to serve in the Roman army.

The Frontier Falls

The collapse of the frontier system was swift in northwestern Europe. In the winter of AD 406, the Rhine froze over, and a mass of refugees—driven west by the expansion of eastern tribes—crossed the river and quickly moved through Gaul and on to Spain. These peoples created their own kingdoms inside the empire, and these eventually superseded the Roman administration.

In Britain, the forts on Hadrian's Wall were probably occupied into the middle of the sixth century AD, perhaps under some sort of local dynastic control. On the Danube, the frontiers crumbled slowly, following the defeat of the East Roman army in AD 378 by the Visigoths at Adrianople. Frontiers had ceased to

be effective barriers; depleted of a labor force and served by inferior troops, they were a minor deterrent. In the event of a major incursion, mobile armies, kept in reserve within the provinces, were rushed in to attack the invaders. This system worked well until the army was reduced in numbers, and as recruiting became more difficult, barbarian armies were hired to fight barbarian invaders.

Frequently, the hired "allies" set up self-ruling barbarian kingdoms in the heartland of the Roman Empire. Moreover, improvements in marine technology brought shiploads of invaders to the coastal regions, and this further stretched the logistic base of the Roman frontier defenses. It was then clear that the tide of history had undermined even the strongest frontier defenses.

Hadrian's Wall extended 120 kilometers (70 miles) across Britain, forming a barrier that, in the words of a Roman source, divided the barbarians from the Romans.

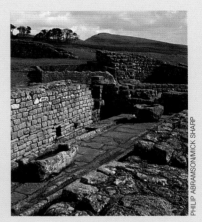

In the fort at Housesteads, on Hadrian's Wall, comforts provided for the troops included bathing facilities and elaborate sanitary arrangements. The lavatory block shown here seated up to 20 men and was flushed by running water.

The fort at Hardknott (Cumbria) guards a high pass through the bleak spine of hills that passes through northern Britain. Forts such as this one ensured the safety of travelers and military convoys in the remote frontier area.

PAT ODEA/BORD FAILTE

186

THE IRON AGE IN EUROPE

8 0 0 B C – A D 1 0 5 0

Horsemen, Ironsmiths, and Vikings

GÖRAN BURENHULT

THE INTRODUCTION OF iron-working in Europe during the eighth century BC was to have truly revolutionary consequences, not the least of which was that it brought about the rapid collapse of the continent's ancient social systems, which had their roots far back in the Stone Age. For the first time, a raw material that could be used to make tools, weapons, and ornaments was accessible to everybody. Power could no longer be based on the control of the trade routes for precious materials, such as copper, tin, and zinc. From about 500 BC, more and more parts of Europe appeared in the limelight of history as a result of intensified contacts with the Mediterranean world. At the same time, the westward thrusts of the nomadic Scythian horsemen from Siberia and the Russian steppes significantly influenced art, clothing, and military strategies in the powerful chiefdoms of central Europe. The rich Hallstatt culture, centered in present-day Austria, became a melting pot of cultural influences from the Scythians, the Etruscans, and the Greeks—giving rise to the Celtic tradition that would soon spread across much of Europe.

◀ Facing the roaring Atlantic, the Celtic Iron Age hill-fort of Dún Aenghus, on the island of Inishmore, off the western coast of Ireland, constantly braves the fury of the elements. This magnificent site once may have been a religious center, but its location and fortifications, in the form of so-called *chevaux de frise* (closely spaced, erect stones), indicate that its function was mainly defensive.

⚔ This miniature bronze cult wagon from a Hallstat burial at Strettweg, in eastern Austria, dates from the seventh century BC. Its frame bears figures of mounted warriors, flanking a large, naked woman, who is thought to be a goddess. It was probably used as a ritual object.

RONALD SHERIDAN/ANCIENT ART & ARCHITECTURE COLLECTION

The Lake Hallstatt area, in the Austrian Alps, was the heartland of the emerging Iron Age. Its rich resources of salt—an important trade item—and copper and iron spurred the development of the first major metal cultures in central Europe.

But while the Mediterranean world and increasingly large parts of central and western Europe now stepped into historic times, the people of the Germanic world in the north were to experience another 1,500 years or so of unwritten prehistory. Nevertheless, contacts with the "civilized" world to the south would leave a deep mark on society on both sides—politically and culturally.

A New Europe

To understand these far-reaching changes, and the subsequent rise of Celtic dominance, we need to look at both the relationship between and the events of the three main cultural phases that characterized the period between about 1200 BC and 400 BC—the Late Bronze Age and what are known as the Hallstatt and La Tène periods—as well as at the important role played by increasing contacts with the Mediterranean area.

The Late Bronze Age societies in central and northern Europe, and their ruling classes in particular, were marked by a high degree of uniformity. New burial practices prevailed in these societies. Bodies were cremated and the remains deposited in clay urns in grave-fields, giving the tradition its name: the Urnfield culture. The Urnfield tradition, which is equivalent to the first two phases of the Hallstatt period (A and B)—so named after an important site in western Austria—between 1200 BC and 800 BC, was notable for the gradual introduction of iron.

During these last phases of the Bronze Age, contacts with the Mediterranean area were intensive. Powerful chiefs lived in heavily fortified settlements strategically situated on high ground. Society was hierarchic, with power based on control over the surplus production of both staple and luxury goods in exchange for the security offered by a strong and successful leader. A desire for prestige and status is reflected in finds of rich hoards and sacrificial offerings.

During the Hallstatt C phase (about 800 BC to 600 BC), some notable changes took place. In many areas, from present-day France in the west to the Czech Republic and the Balkans in the east, inhumation (the burial of unburned bodies) once again became the dominant form of burial. At the same time, a number of remarkably rich, princely burials (burials of the leading elite, or so-called *Fürstengräber*) took place. These usually take the form of timbered chambers containing four-wheeled carts, horse trappings, and exceptionally rich grave goods. Similar burial practices are also found further east—for example, in the so-called Timber Grave culture of the South Russian steppes, where the custom may have originated. These magnificent burials reflect the development of a warrior aristocracy in Europe. An all-embracing political power probably never existed; rather, the many mutually warring tribes were led by their respective chiefs. During this period, contacts with the Mediterranean world appear to have all but ceased.

This bronze Tarquinia sword found in Bavaria, in southern Germany, is a typical weapon of the Urnfield period.

Undoubtedly, the transition from bronze to iron, with the immense social upheavals this brought about, lay behind these changes.

One of the most significant local groups within the Urnfield tradition lived in the Lausitz region, located in present-day Poland, eastern Germany, and the Czech Republic. The Saale River region and the southern shores of the Baltic Sea were also important. The Urnfield period was a time of technological innovation. In particular, an advanced bronze-working technique was developed that allowed the thin metal plates used to make shields, helmets, bronze vessels, and other objects to be embossed with ornamental motifs, often in the form of animals. Alloy and casting techniques were also refined. Glass production, too, was introduced from Egypt, and ceramic technology reached a high level in many areas. Painted pottery appeared in the Hallstatt area, and the Lausitz ceramics influenced pottery-making all over northern Europe. About 1000 BC, iron swords came into use within the Urnfield area; a few centuries later, iron tools and weapons were commonplace throughout central Europe.

Wealth and Turmoil

After 600 BC, the political situation in central Europe changed radically, and the region once again came into direct contact with the Mediterranean world. It was during this period that Greek colonization reached its high point, beginning about 750 BC and culminating in the foundation of Massilia (present-day Marseilles), about 550 BC. In the process, Greek culture spread to large parts of southern France and also to Italy, where it strongly influenced the Etruscan culture. About 500 BC, the Classical Age began in Greece, and a few centuries later, Rome emerged on the scene—an event that was to have a considerable impact on subsequent developments in Europe.

The contacts between the peoples north and south of the Alps were reflected in the import of magnificent luxury items, which have been found in the princely burials of this period. The wagon

grave at Vix, in eastern France, is a particularly important example. But the peoples of central Europe were also inspired to advance their own artistic and technical skills. The architect who designed the fortified settlement of Heuneburg, in Germany, with its walls of clay blocks, was surely influenced by Mediterranean prototypes. Other important fortified settlements of this period have been found at Hohenasperg and Breisach, in Germany; and at Mont Lassois, Château-sur-Salins, and Châtillon-sur-Glâne, in France. Feudal society had appeared in Europe.

Excavation sites such as Heuneburg have shown that this feudal society came to an abrupt end during the last phase of the Hallstatt period, in the sixth century BC. Currently, there is no evidence to suggest that these powerful chiefdoms survived into the La Tène phase of the Early Iron Age in Europe, and this is one of the great problems faced by prehistorians in trying to establish continuity in the history of settlement in the region. Ludwig Pauli of the Bavarian Academy of Science, in Munich, has pointed to a series of fundamental changes that occurred in central Europe during the fifth century BC. The destruction of the fortified settlements coincided with the end of the tradition of princely burials. At the same time, princely burials appeared in new areas that had previously been only sparsely populated—areas in which iron was apparently common. A new kind of princely burial, primarily containing adornments and ritual objects of the early Celtic La Tène type, appeared in many places. Cultural influences from the south and east were manifested in art, handicrafts, and symbols: Greek–Etruscan palmettes (fan-shaped ornaments), Oriental motifs, and Celtic circular motifs. At the same time, the characteristic symbols of the Late Bronze Age and the Hallstatt culture, including solar disks, waterfowl, and horses, disappeared. In fact, Europe was going through its own process of "orientalization": Celtic expansion had begun.

⚓ A reconstructed wagon from the Hallstatt wagon grave of Vix, in eastern France. The grave is that of a woman, and dates from the end of the sixth century BC. Among the imported luxury items it contained were a black-figure cup and a large bronze crater (wine bowl) from Greece, and bronze flagons from Etruria.
RÖMISCH GERMANISCHES ZENTRALMUSEUM

↩ Numerous settlements dating from the Late Bronze Age have been found in Europe. All were situated near water, in the form of rivers, springs, or lakes. In some regions, heavily fortified artificial islands—so-called lake dwellings—were built. Lake dwellings were particularly common in Ireland, where they are known as crannogs, and a large number have been found there. Shown here is a reconstructed crannog at the "Craggaunowen Project", at Quin, in County Clare, Ireland.

GÖRAN BURENHULT

♟ A gold vase from the burial mound (*kurgan*) of Kul-Oba, in the Crimea, depicting a Scythian legend recorded by the Greek author Herodotus.
STATENS HISTORISKA MUSEUM, SWEDEN

THE WIDE WORLD OF THE STEPPE NOMADS

During the Iron Age, tribes of nomadic horsemen roamed the Eurasian steppes, from the Carpathian Mountains, in the west, to the Altai Mountains, in the east. The Scythians, a western group of these horsemen, were to have a significant influence on Europe's cultural development.
CARTOGRAPHY: RAY SIM

Horsemen from the East

It was not only contact with the developing states in Greece and Italy that transformed the feudal societies of central Europe into a uniform Celtic culture. For the first time in the history of Europe, the ancient nomadic horsemen of the South Russian and central Asian steppes made their presence known—the Scythians had begun to move west.

Most of our knowledge of these colorful peoples springs from the Greek author Herodotus, who devoted his fourth book about the Greek struggle against alien tribes to the Scythian wars against the Persian king Darius. As early as the seventh century BC, the Greeks had founded trading ports along the northern shores of the Black Sea, where they came into contact with these mounted nomads. This led to an extensive exchange of goods, and Scythian chiefs also commissioned items from Greek craftworkers and artists, especially goldsmiths, whose products have been found in richly adorned mound burials on the steppes. About 450 BC, Herodotus visited one of these Black Sea trading ports—Olbia, at

the mouth of the Bug River—and came in contact with people who had dealings with the steppe nomads.

The nomadic horsemen had developed an advanced culture that stretched from the Great Wall of China, in the east, to the Danube River, in the west—a distance of more than 7,000 kilometers (4,350 miles). The Scythians, a western nomad group, roamed the area north of the Black and Caspian seas. Over thousands of years, their ancestors had developed a way of life centered on the horse: at Dereivka, in the Dnepr River area, for example, 74 percent of the animal bones excavated were those of horses. The Dereivka finds belong to the Sredny Stog culture, which was followed by the so-called Pit Grave culture, which, in turn, developed into the Catacomb Grave culture. Dating from about 2500 BC, the graves of this latter culture have yielded the world's oldest known examples of wheeled vehicles. The previously mentioned Timber Grave culture emerged about 1900 BC, and it is in the graves of this culture that light, horse-drawn carts are found for the first time. Not until about 1500 BC, when

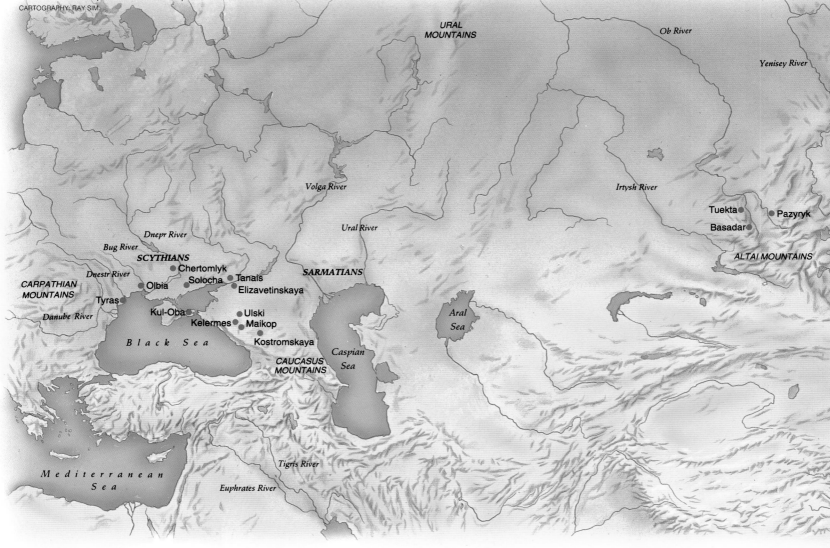

the Andronovo culture first appeared in the same region, did true nomadic societies begin to develop from these hitherto relatively sedentary herding peoples. About 500 BC, the Scythians appeared.

During periods of drought, the nomads traveled beyond their regular migration areas, and their thrusts towards the east, the south, and the west can be distinguished more or less clearly at different times. The oldest parts of the Great Wall were built by the emperor Qin Shi Huang between 221 BC and 210 BC as a defense against attacks from eastern groups of these horsemen. Warlike nomadic horsemen of Scythian origin are also thought to have taken part in the destruction of the Assyrian capital, Nineveh, in 612 BC.

It has been said that the Scythians were the world's foremost light cavalry. What is certainly true is that these master horsemen were largely responsible for introducing horses to European warfare during the Late Bronze Age and Early Iron Age. Because it was easy to subdue crowds of people from horseback, the horse became an important adjunct to the exercise of power. Rich finds of sacrificial offerings of horse

trappings from this period surely reflect this new development.

But it was not only in the ongoing social transformation and in military strategies that Scythian influence was significant. The manners and customs of the nomadic horsemen also left their mark on clothing and ornamental decoration in Celtic and Germanic Europe. Trousers were introduced in Europe, and naturalistic motifs featuring horses, deer, and birds were further elaborated in the Germanic world.

The superior fighting techniques of the Scythians, which included use of the bow and arrow, made them indomitable masters of the steppes for a long time. It was not until the fourth century BC that another tribe, the Sarmatians, managed to shatter their power. It has been suggested that the Sarmatians invented the iron stirrup, which allowed them to carry lances in their saddles, and thereby push their enemies off their horses. It was to be about another thousand years, however, before the iron stirrup came into widespread use in the Germanic world of northern Europe.

⚲ Magnificent burial mounds on the South Russian steppes, so-called *kurgans*, are impressive reminders of the Scythians' heyday. They contain the remains of the most powerful chiefs, along with those of their wives, servants, and horses, who accompanied their masters to the land of the dead.

STATENS HISTORISKA MUSEUM, SWEDEN

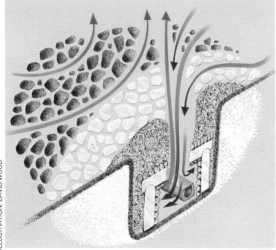

ILLUSTRATION: DAVID WOOD

FROZEN TOMBS IN THE ALTAI
At Pazyryk, in the High Altai, Russian archaeologists have made some sensational discoveries. Stone burial cairns in this region were found to have prevented the soil underneath them from warming up in summer, and allowed frost to penetrate to the bottom of the grave during winter. The permafrost thus formed around the timbered burial chamber has preserved organic materials for posterity, including wood, body tissue, and magnificent textiles. (After L.L. Barkova)

ERICH LESSING/MAGNUM

♙ The site of La Tène, on the shores of Lake Neuchâtel, in western Switzerland, has given its name to the Iron Age phase that succeeded the Hallstatt period, about 500 BC. Votive offerings of bronze, iron, and wooden objects were found here in the shallow waters at the lake's edge.

La Tène and the Celtic Expansion

While the nomadic Scythian culture flourished on the eastern steppes, Celtic tribes in central Europe were spreading out over vast areas from their homeland along the upper reaches of the Rhine River. The reasons behind this expansion are not fully known—overpopulation and internal conflicts have been put forward as probable causes—but the course of events is evident from both classical literary sources and the archaeological record. Herodotus described these "Keltoi" as "living further west than any other European people, except the Kynetians". The latter inhabited the southwestern corner of the Iberian peninsula, in present-day Portugal. Another Greek author, Eforos, classified them as one of the four great barbaric peoples: Celts, Scythians, Persians, and Libyans. Later, during Roman times, the Celts were known by the Romans as Gauls.

Celtic societies grew rapidly and markedly during the fifth and sixth centuries BC, with the rise of a number of warrior societies. These emerged in two main centers in central Europe: the Hunsrück-Eifel region of the central Rhineland, in Germany, and the Champagne district of northeastern France. Both were associated with powerful

Hallstatt chiefdoms: Hunsrück-Eifel with the Hohenasperg complex, and Champagne with the Mont-Lassois complex.

Clearly, trade with Massilia played a decisive role in this process. Products from the north, such as foodstuffs, gold, iron, furs, and slaves, were exchanged for goods from the eastern Mediterranean area and Italy, and the main transport route into the Celtic heartland followed the Rhône River valley. It has been suggested that slaves were the main commodity in this interchange of goods. Celtic warrior societies "collected" slaves in the far north and northwest and sold them to more sedentary Celtic chiefdoms in the western Hallstatt region. These, in turn, had contacts with the Mediterranean area, where Phocaeans (from Phocaea, an ancient Greek city in present-day Turkey) and Etruscans in particular were reputed to be notorious pirates and slave-traders.

Towards the end of the seventh century BC, however, the Celtic warrior societies had forged their own, direct contacts with Massilia, becoming more or less independent of the merchants in the old Hallstatt region. This led to great political changes in central Europe. Beginning about 500 BC, a number of other events in the Mediterranean area also influenced the situation. Widespread Greek

♀ The "Battersea Shield", a splendid example of Celtic craftmanship, was found in the River Thames, in London, in 1857. Dating from the early first century AD, it is made of bronze, has glass inlays, and is decorated with cast-bronze disks featuring bosses and tendril-shaped designs.
C.M. DIXON/PHOTO RESOURCES

present-day France and parts of Belgium, western Germany, and northern Italy), including Alesia, Bibracte, and Avaricum, which became famous in connection with Caesar's campaigns. Manching, in southern Germany, is in a class by itself and is one of the best-studied examples of these city-like settlements.

The Celtic tribes became the first historically known peoples north of the Alps, and their role as intermediaries of eastern, Mediterranean, and Oriental culture was significant. The Celtic world became a melting pot, combining local traditions and the cultural influences of Scythians, Etruscans, and Greeks within its religious, artistic, and social life.

From the fifth century BC, Celtic tribes apparently spread throughout much of Europe, sometimes by means of peaceful colonization, sometimes by war campaigns. About 400 BC, Celts from present-day Switzerland reached Italy. In 386 BC, they defeated a Roman army at the Allia River, and with the exception of the Capitolium, burned the city of Rome to the ground. From there they pushed southwards to Apulia and Sicily. At

NATIONAL MUSEUM, PRAGUE/ERICH LESSING/MAGNUM

colonization, including the foundation of Alalia, in Corsica, meant that Greek merchant fleets could reach Massilia without having to enter Etruscan ports. At the same time, the Greeks' interest in their western colonies waned, following political events in Asia Minor (present-day Turkey), such as the Persian Wars. As a result, these colonies eventually formed an independent, western Mediterranean region. The Greek cities in southern Italy and Sicily, strategically situated in the middle of the Mediterranean, were in a key position. Together, these events resulted in the beginning of the traditional Celtic societies' disintegration, and the consequent spread of their influence far afield. The Celtic peoples of Europe never formed a unified state or even an ethnic group. Many of their dialects were closely related, but they often spoke completely different languages. The different ruling families and chiefs, with their roots in the Hallstatt tradition of the Late Bronze Age, created a great number of independent regions, governed from strategically situated so-called *oppida*. These often consisted of heavily fortified cities built on high ground, but they were also important cultural centers, with skilled craftworkers and flourishing trade. It has been estimated that there were 700 *oppida* in Gaul alone (which covered the area of

◄● This Celtic stone bust from Mšecké Zehrovice, in Bohemia, in the Czech Republic, was found near a ritual site. Possibly representing a god, it dates from between 150 BC and 50 BC.

the same time, Celtic tribes settled in large parts of southern England, including Cornwall, and Wales and Scotland, and soon after, also in Ireland. In the third century BC, other Celtic tribes penetrated into the Balkans, where they were defeated in 279 BC, after having burned down the temple of Delphi. Another group of Celts migrated into Asia Minor, where they founded the state of Galatia.

The Celtic world, however, was centered on an area that includes parts of present-day France and northern Italy. These regions, called "Gallia Narbonensis" and "Gallia Cisalpina" by the Romans,

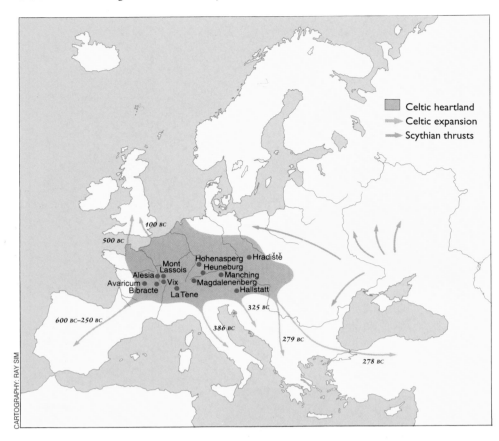

⚱ This large, silver cauldron was found in a bog at Gundestrup, in Vesthimmerland, Jutland, Denmark, in 1891. Manufactured by Celtic craftsmen about 100 BC, possibly in Thrace, in the Balkans, it eventually found its way deep into the Germanic regions of northern Europe.
NATIONAL MUSEUM OF DENMARK

↪ *Opposite page:* This spectacular bronze face was mounted as decoration on the side of a four-wheeled wagon found at Dejbjerg, at Als, in Jutland, Denmark. It dates from the first century BC.

CELTIC EXPANSION

From the fifth century BC, Celtic culture began to spread from its central European homeland to the British Isles, Iberia, Italy, the Balkans, and Asia Minor. At the same time, the nomadic Scythians were thrusting westwards into Europe.

⚱ A Celtic bronze statue of a warrior-god from Saint-Maur-en-Chaussée, in Oise, northern France.
A. LE TOQUIN/EXPLORER/AUSCAPE

were intimately linked to subsequent events in Roman history. In 225 BC, Celtic tribes once again penetrated into the Apennine peninsula, but at Telamon, on the coast of Etruria, they were defeated by joint Roman and Etruscan forces. The Romans then conquered Gallia Cisalpina, and, soon after, turned it into a Roman province.

In 121 BC, Gallia Narbonensis also became a Roman province, although conflicts with rebellious tribes continued there for a long time. The Gauls rose under the leadership of the famous chief Vercingetorix, but the revolt was put down following the siege of Alesia, in 52 BC. Celtic power came to an end, and Caesar conquered the rest of Gaul.

Although the political power of the warlike Celts had been crushed by Caesar's campaigns and the subsequent expansion of the Roman Empire, Celtic culture, art, music, and beliefs were to survive into modern times. This was particularly evident in marginal areas such as Brittany, Wales, and Ireland, where Celtic tribes lived on relatively undisturbed.

It was the Celtic tribes of central Europe who introduced iron-working during Hallstatt times, and this surely accounts for much of their political and economic success. The Hallstatt soon transformed into the La Tène period, after an important site on the shores of Lake Neuchâtel, in Switzerland, and rich chiefly burials dating from this time bear witness to a considerable concentration of power. Skillful artists transformed Scythian, Greek,

and Oriental motifs into vivid, naturalistic compositions with spirals, whirls, and stylized animals. Ornamentation on such items as jewelry, weapons, and drinking vessels included founded (molded) glass pearls and inlays of red enamel. Ceramics were characterized by beautifully painted, thrown pots of high quality. The Celts also struck their own coins on the model of Hellenistic and Greek prototypes. This bears witness to intensive and far-reaching trading contacts, in which metalwork goods served as the basic commodity of exchange.

Several splendid bog finds in northern Europe, notably in Denmark, include objects that originated in Celtic workshops in central Europe and reached the Germanic world through trade, such as a famous silver cauldron from Gundestrup, in Vesthimmerland, and two four-wheeled carts from Dejbjerg, at Als, in Jutland. While these finds most likely represent sacrificial offerings to the gods, the famous and remarkably well-preserved Danish and North German bog bodies dating from this period are probably those of executed criminals. The Roman author Tacitus described how thieves, homosexuals, and traitors were put to death by garrotting, and then were placed in swampy watercourses. Most of the bog bodies show signs of severe ill-treatment, and only a few are fully dressed. (See the feature *Lindow Man: A 2,000-year-old Human Sacrifice*.)

The political developments taking place in the south also involved the Germanic peoples of the north in an extensive interchange of goods—but this time with a totally different power: Rome.

LINDOW MAN: A 2,000-YEAR-OLD HUMAN SACRIFICE

I.M. STEAD

LINDOW MAN is the name given to an ancient body found in a bog at Lindow Moss, near Manchester, in England, in 1984. The previous year, workers digging up peat had found the remains of a human head, and so they were not very surprised when a human leg came to light at the same site. They contacted an archaeologist, who located the rest of the body, which was removed, still encased in a large block of peat, and sent to the British Museum for excavation.

The block of peat contained the upper half of a body that had been sliced by the peat-cutting machine; the rest had been ripped apart and scattered. The remaining pieces, including the leg the workers had found, were discovered in the loose peat. Much of the skin was well preserved, being dark brown and leathery, but the body was almost flat, having been compressed by the great weight of the peat. It had been lying face down in a bog pool. Thanks to the presence of a relatively high concentration of humic and fulvic acids in the peat, which acted as antibiotics and attacked any bacteria present, and the absence of oxygen, the body was preserved for posterity.

The dating of Lindow Man posed problems. He was unclothed and had nothing with him, so the body could not be dated by means of associated artifacts. The position of the body, more than 2 meters (6 feet) beneath the original surface, showed that it was ancient. An examination of associated pollen, together with radiocarbon dating of the peat, indicated that he had lived nearly 2,000 years ago. Initial radiocarbon dates from the body itself varied considerably, but the latest results from Oxford University, where 19 dates have now been processed, suggest that he died in the first century AD, or perhaps early in the second century.

Lindow Man was subjected to photogrammetry (taking measurements from photographs), xeroradiography (high definition X-rays), and body scanners (CAT scans and Magnetic Resonance Imaging) before being thoroughly examined by a surgeon. Specialists determined that he had been in his mid-twenties, some 168 centimeters (5 feet, 6 inches) tall, and perhaps 60 kilograms (130 pounds) or more in weight. He had been quite healthy, although some of his vertebrae had Schmorl's nodes (cavities in the end-plates of vertebrae, perhaps related to severe strain) and he had suffered from worms. No DNA had survived, but his blood group was O. His moustache and beard had been cut by shears, and his fingernails were neatly rounded. Nothing remained of his liver, lungs, or heart, but a length of gut was found, which contained digested food. His last meal consisted of griddle cakes made from flour containing a mixture of wheat (spelt and emmer) and barley and cooked over an open fire.

Lindow Man had not drowned in the pool but had been killed before he entered it. A pathology report revealed that a blow from a small axe had stunned him and fractured his skull. He had then been garrotted (the knotted ligature was well preserved) which broke his neck, and his throat had finally been cut. The position of the garrotte would have speeded up blood loss, and this deliberate bleeding suggests ritual slaughter rather than common murder. One slight clue may point to the identity of the murderers: some mistletoe pollen was found in the man's gut, which is a rare occurrence in an archaeological context. Mistletoe was used by the Druids, the philosopher-priests of the Celtic world, who appear to have taken part in human sacrifices. Little is known about them, but Druids were certainly active in Britain in the first century AD.

Once the body had been taken out of the bog, it was in danger of drying, shrinking, and falling to pieces. Decomposition was prevented in the short term by keeping the body cool and damp. Its long-term preservation was achieved by freeze-drying: the body was immersed in polyethylene glycol (water-soluble wax) for 10 weeks, and was then frozen for three days and freeze-dried for three weeks, the ice being converted directly to vapor and removed to a condensor, where the temperature was minus 60 degrees Celsius (minus 76 degrees Fahrenheit). The outcome was successful, with only slight shrinkage, no color change, and no variation in the texture of the skin. The body is now on permanent display at the British Museum.

The body of another adult male was found in the same bog in 1987, but it had been badly mauled by the peat-cutting machinery. It seems likely that the head found in 1983 belongs to this body. The cause of death has not yet been established, but it seems clear that this second body was more or less contemporary with Lindow Man.

BRITISH MUSEUM

◀◉ The upper part of Lindow Man's body, with the detached leg on the left, on display at the British Museum.

CARTOGRAPHY: RAY SIM

Germanic Peoples and Rome

Following Caesar's pacification of Gaul, the Germanic peoples in northern Europe came in contact with the Roman Empire. The different tribes were now described in detail by Roman historians, and for the first time in history, individual tribes were mentioned by name, giving us a fascinating, contemporary glimpse into prehistoric customs, beliefs, and political conditions. Germanic chiefs were described as skillful commanders, capable of challenging the Roman legions' supremacy. Our knowledge of these historic events comes largely from the brilliant accounts of Tacitus, in his *Annales* and *Germania*, but also from other Roman authors, such as Pliny and Virgil, and the Greek writer Strabo.

During the reign of Caesar Augustus (31 BC to AD 14), the borders of the Roman Empire were consolidated, and for several centuries, peaceful trading with the Germanic tribes in the north alternated with periods of conflict. In northern Europe, the period between the beginning of the first century AD and AD 400 is for this reason called the Roman Iron Age. The borders followed the Rhine and Danube rivers. When, in AD 9, Augustus decided to shift the borders northwards to the River Elbe by annexing large parts of present-day Germany, this attempt came to a sorry end in the Teutoburg Forest. Here, the Roman army, under the command of Publius Quinctilius Varus, was wiped out to the very last man by joint Germanic forces led by the Cherusci chief Arminius. Thereafter, the Roman border, or "Limes", as it was known, largely followed the Rhine River, whose strategically and commercially important mouth was under Roman control. The long border was heavily fortified, and ditches and palisades were constructed from present-day Holland, in the north, to the Balkans, in the south.

The social and economic changes that took place in the Early Iron Age society of northern Europe also resulted in a different system of goods exchange. The circulation of prestige items and "status symbols", which was characteristic of the Bronze Age, was closely linked to the control of the trade routes that carried bronze from central Europe to Scandinavia. Such items were often placed in lakes or marshlands as offerings to the gods, thereby acquiring prestige. During the Late Bronze Age and the Early pre-Roman Iron Age, this traffic ceased; the focus of Europe's interest had switched to the Mediterranean world.

Imported finds once again appear in the archaeological record in the last few centuries BC, but they now reflect a different kind of exchange system. More than ever before, the distribution of luxury items by chiefs and ruling families was probably aimed at securing friendship and loyalty both from other tribes and from within their own tribal group. Rich warrior graves show that men who were capable of bearing arms were more and more closely linked to the political system. At the same time, chiefs seem to have become richer and fewer in number: power was concentrated in a few hands, indicating the beginning of a process of centralization had begun. Luxury items from this period are usually found in rich graves and rarely as sacrificial offerings to the gods. Increasingly, offerings included weapons and other articles of war instead, bearing witness to military events and the emergence of a more solid machinery of power. Centralization was fully consolidated by about AD 100, and a network of trade routes was built up, linking northern Europe with the developing feudal societies and their handicraft centers in the Roman provinces. There are some splendid examples of luxury commodities that reached the Germanic world in this way, including various Roman utensils for wine-drinking, such as bronze situlas (bucket-shaped vessels), wine dippers, strainers, and drinking vessels.

⏴ GERMANIC TRADE ROUTES
As a consequence of their intense trading contacts with the Roman Empire, a number of Germanic tribes living along the northern banks of the Rhine and Danube rivers assimilated aspects of Mediterranean culture and passed them on to the tribes further north. In some cases, goods were transported from craft centers and bronze industries in the motherland, Italy, but more often, the objects that reached northern Europe originated in nearby Roman provinces, such as Gaul. There is also evidence to suggest that Roman fleets, sailing from the mouth of the Rhine, reached as far north as Scandinavia: Augustus's famous temple inscription, *Monumentum Ancyrarum*, at Ankara, in Turkey, tells of voyages to the land of the Cimbri, in present-day Jutland, Denmark.

⚲ The Rhine marked the boundary not only between the Roman Empire and the Germanic domains, but also between written history and unwritten prehistory.

ROBERT HARDING PICTURE LIBRARY

CARL O. LOFMAN/PROMEDIA

⚲ Following the collapse of the Roman Empire in the fifth century AD, huge amounts of gold circulated among the Germanic tribes of northern Europe, much of it finding its way to Scandinavia. This gold hoard from Timboholm, in Sweden, consisted of 2 ingots and 26 spiral rings, with a combined weight of more than 7 kilograms (15 pounds).

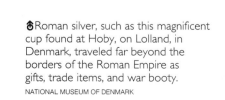

⚲ Roman silver, such as this magnificent cup found at Hoby, on Lolland, in Denmark, traveled far beyond the borders of the Roman Empire as gifts, trade items, and war booty.
NATIONAL MUSEUM OF DENMARK

Clearly, the Germanic tribes in the north must have offered something attractive in return for these luxury goods. Hides and furs were presumably of great importance, the Roman armies requiring enormous amounts of hide for clothing, tents, shields, and harnesses. Rich finds of Roman imports on the Swedish island of Öland, together with evidence of skin-working and large-scale sacrificial offerings of horses, may indicate the large-scale production and export of hides and, possibly, of live horses as well. Iron, amber, beeswax, and wool, and surely also slaves, were other important commodities, while in many southern Germanic areas, salt and copper were the main items of merchandise. Foodstuffs, such as dried meat, fish, and cereals, may also have been exchanged.

During the last pre-Christian century, the sought-after Roman products arrived directly from Italy, including magnificent bronze objects from the major metal industries established at Capua, in Campania. Clay vessels (so-called *terra sigillata*), gold objects, Roman coins, and glass products also made their way via Aquileja, on the Adriatic coast, through the Alpine passes, to the Roman province of Noricum (present-day Austria), and onwards, via Carnuntum and through Bohemia and Moravia, to the Germanic peoples along the coasts of the Baltic Sea. Somewhat later, workshops and trading posts in Gaul supplied the north with industrial products, including *terra sigillata* and glass. The Danish island of Zealand

appears to have been a center of economic and political power within this exchange system.

Peoples on the Move

At the beginning of the second century AD, the Roman Empire had reached its zenith. During the reign of Emperor Hadrian (AD 117 to AD 138), a large, defensive wall was constructed in northern England. Patrolling the long borders of the empire entailed tremendous expense, and economic difficulties in combination with far-reaching internal disintegration had dramatically weakened the empire towards the end of the second century. At the same time, the Germanic peoples had begun to realize that unity meant strength.

Between AD 161 and AD 181, the so-called "Marcomanni Wars" took place when the joint forces of Marcomanni, Quadi, Hermunduri, and Lombards temporarily crossed the Limes for the first time. Then, in AD 260, Saxons, Franks, and Alemanni pushed the borderline south of the Rhine once and for all. This was the prelude to a series of Germanic migrations and military adventures, the reasons for which are not fully known. Gothic tribes left their homeland in northern Poland and conquered Dacia, in present-day Romania, in AD 275. At the same time, the Franks penetrated as far south as the Iberian peninsula. But the definitive starting point of the migration period can be pinpointed to AD 375, when the Huns, a tribe of horsemen from central Asia, pushed into the heart of Europe from the

RURAL SETTLEMENT IN ANGLO-SAXON ENGLAND

HELENA F. HAMEROW

AN INCREASING INTEREST in the history of the English landscape and the origins of the English village has fueled archaeological investigations into the earliest Anglo-Saxon communities of Britain. The buildings, size, layout, and distribution of Anglo-Saxon settlements of the fifth to eighth centuries AD, when the English landscape was overwhelmingly rural, are now the subjects of extensive research. Archaeology, place-name studies, topographic work, and historical documents have all contributed to our understanding of the early English village. Yet archaeological traces of these villages are difficult to detect, and it is only relatively recently, since the 1960s and 1970s, that such villages have been excavated in a systematic way.

The conventional picture of the Anglo-Saxon community is of "Ye Olde English Village": a small, stable community of several extended families, established soon after the migrations, in the fifth and sixth centuries AD, of the ethnically mixed group of Germanic peoples who came to be known as the Anglo-Saxons.

The first early Saxon settlement to be scientifically recorded was excavated in the 1930s. It was not until the 1960s and 1970s, however, that excavations were undertaken on a sufficiently large scale to reveal how these early Anglo-Saxon communities actually functioned. It is now known that the Anglo-Saxons lived in settlements consisting of two main types of buildings: rectangular, post-built timber dwellings with wattle-and-daub walls and thatched roofs, and so-called sunken huts, small constructions with sunken floors, used mostly for storage or as workshops for activities such as weaving. Fifth and sixth-century AD settlements were loosely structured, and had few enclosures or well-defined trackways. No obviously "high-status" settlements incorporating exceptionally large buildings are known from this period, despite the number of burials accompanied by rich grave goods. The size of these settlements varied widely, from just two or three families at West Stow, Suffolk, to a community of up to 100 at Mucking, Essex.

◄● A reconstruction of the largest hall excavated at Cowdery's Down, in Hampshire.
ROYAL ARCHAEOLOGICAL INSTITUTE

Economy and Trade

Just as our knowledge of the size and structure of early English communities has grown, so, too, has our understanding of their economic base. Exceptionally complete assemblages of animal bones, seed remains, and industrial debris found at West Stow, and current excavations at West Heslerton, in North Yorkshire, will add further detail to the picture we already have of mixed arable farming, dominated by barley, oats, rye, and wheat, and animal husbandry, with varying emphasis on rearing cattle, pigs, sheep, or, occasionally, horses.

Despite the traditional view of these communities as "self-sufficient" and rather isolated, long-distance trade continued throughout this period, as evidenced by regular finds of amber, precious metals, crystal, amethyst, coins, and imported ornaments, such as brooches from the continental European homelands of the Anglo-Saxons and from the Mediterranean world. Local and interregional trade in commodities such as iron, scrap bronze, and, perhaps, pottery also played a significant role in these economies.

The excavation of settlements, with their associated burial grounds, such as at Mucking and West Heslerton, should yield still more information about the demographic structure and economy of the earliest English villages. Inevitably, this will raise as many questions as it answers. At Mucking, for example, two cemeteries were excavated that contained a number of rich burials, suggesting social stratification. The settlement, however, consisted of a rather haphazard scattering of between 50 and 60 small timber "halls" and more than 200 sunken huts (not all contemporary), but no large, "high-status" buildings. Could this apparent paradox reflect stratification within, rather than between, families? The rich burials may be of heads of families, buried in a more ostentatious style, rather than of particularly rich members of the community. It certainly appears that until the seventh century AD, at least,

power was relatively fluid, and was not monopolized by certain lineages.

A Social Elite Emerges

The archaeological record reveals that there were a number of interrelated socioeconomic developments in the seventh century AD. The majority of burials were accompanied by only a few grave goods, or none at all, yet a small number of graves were very rich indeed. The most striking example is the presumably royal ship burial at Sutton Hoo, in Suffolk. At the same time, a number of identifiably high-status settlements with large, central buildings and a carefully structured layout appear, such as at Yeavering and Milfield, in Northumberland, and, on a somewhat less grand scale, at Cowdery's Down, in Hampshire. These settlements and burials suggest the emergence of an aristocratic elite. Even in "ordinary" settlements dating from the beginning of the seventh century AD, such as West Stow, enclosures and what appear to be property boundaries were being built.

It is clear that many early Anglo-Saxon settlements were not fixed in one place. In continental Europe, the phenomenon of gradually "wandering" settlements is well known. Abrupt shifts of several hundred meters could occur, but more often, the shifts were gradual, occurring when houses fell into disrepair and were rebuilt on a new site, leaving the old farmyard to be brought under cultivation. Evidence from Anglo-Saxon settlements such as Mucking suggests that this was frequently also the case in England, where truly stable settlements may not have developed for several more centuries.

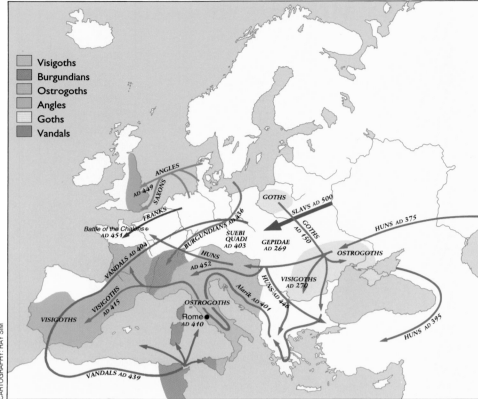

Legend:
- Visigoths
- Burgundians
- Ostrogoths
- Angles
- Goths
- Vandals

CARTOGRAPHY: RAY SIM

CARL O. LÖFMAN/PROMEDIA

⚜ This gold collar was found at Färjestaden, on the island of Öland, in Sweden, and may have been a sacrificial offering. Dating from the migration period, it is one of a series of spectacular jewelry finds and has unparalleled decorations of filigree and granulation.

THE MIGRATION PERIOD

The collapse of the Roman Empire triggered a series of large-scale migrations by Germanic peoples. Several tribes left their northern European homelands and ventured to far-flung places, such as northern Africa, sometimes founding new kingdoms. The Angles and Saxons of southern Jutland and northern Germany crossed the North Sea and established themselves in Britain at this time. The Goths were located on the southern shores of the Baltic in the second century AD, and north of the Black Sea in the third century AD.

South Russian steppes. For a century, they ravaged large parts of central Europe, and the whole Germanic world was stirred into motion.

The Goths had split into two groups, the Ostrogoths and the Visigoths. The former were defeated by the Huns, while the latter penetrated into the Balkans in AD 378 and into Italy in AD 401. In AD 395, Emperor Theodosius split the Roman Empire into two parts, the Western and Eastern empires. In AD 410, the Goths, under the command of Alarik, captured the city of Rome. At about the same time, the Romans left Britain, which soon afterwards was occupied by Angles and Saxons from southern Jutland and northwestern Germany.

Gaul now lay open for the Germanic onrush: about AD 400, the Franks arrived from the north, and in AD 406, Vandals, Suebi, Lombards, Quadi, Gepidae, Heruli, Alemanni, and Burgundians poured in from the east. Their barbaric ravages have been vividly described by contemporary authors. In AD 446, Attila became ruler of the Huns in the east, and in AD 451, he pushed westwards with an enormous army made up of Huns and their allies, including Ostrogoths, Gepidae, and Heruli. Having devastated large parts of northern Gaul, he finally stood face to face with an army consisting of Visigoths, Franks, Burgundians, and Saxons, under the command of Aëtius. The battle took place in the Catalaunian Plains, near the River Seine. Attila and his band were defeated. Soon after,

the Huns disappeared from the European stage. The Germanic peoples had now taken over Rome's role in western Europe, and about AD 500, King Clovis founded the Frankish kingdom, which became the dominating force and the cultural intermediary of western Europe for the next 500 years.

Rising Powers in the North

The Gothic historian Jordanes and the Greek author Procopius both give us a glimpse into the great number of tribes that inhabited Scandinavia around AD 500. Some of these tribes can be quite accurately located on a map, whereas the names of others are probably based on misunderstandings. These writers may well provide the first historical accounts of the Laps (referred to as the Screrefennae, or Skrithifinoi) and the Swedes, who lived further south (referred to as the Suehans, or Suetidi). The former were mobile hunter-gatherers, while the Swedes were said to be a sedentary people. A region referred to as Raumaricicae is probably identical to present-day Romerike, in Norway, and the Rygi people may have inhabited modern-day Rogaland, also in Norway. Obviously, the Dani lived in Denmark, and the Finni in Finland.

In this multitude of Germanic peoples, some areas seem to have been particularly important, and during the course of the Late Iron Age, these regions developed into significant centers. The basin of Lake Malar, in eastern Sweden, the Baltic islands of Öland and Gotland, southern Norway, and Denmark all played an important part in the subsequent formation of states.

A stream of luxury items from the continent continued to reach Scandinavia's central regions. They derived largely from the same countries as during the heyday of the Roman Empire, but now it was Frankish craftsmen who manufactured the glass and bronze products. Large amounts of goods destined for the Scandinavian markets were produced in the Namur and Picardy regions of Belgium and France. The Danish island of Zealand appears to have lost its commercial importance, which was so evident during late Roman times, and Sweden and Norway now traded directly with central Europe. As time went on, a number of trading centers developed, from where goods were distributed across the countryside. At Dankirke, in the Jutland peninsula, in Denmark; and on the island of Helgö, in Lake Malar, veritable business houses were established in the fifth and sixth centuries AD.

Most conspicuous, however, are the rich finds of gold that have caused this period to be called Scandinavia's Golden Age. Evidently, huge amounts of gold circulated among the tribes of northern Europe after the collapse of the Roman Empire. Attila the Hun, for instance, received 432,000 solidi (Roman gold coins) from

NATIONAL MUSEUM OF DENMARK/LENNART LARSEN

Theodosius II, emperor of the Eastern empire, in 443 AD, in exchange for not plundering the country. This is equivalent to about 2 tonnes (2 tons) of solid gold! Large numbers of solidi were imported into Scandinavia. Most were used as ornaments or melted down by local goldsmiths and reshaped into magnificent objects, including collars and necklets. Hidden hoards of these items, which may have been sacrificial offerings, have been found, among other places, at Ålleberg, Storegården, and Möne, in western Sweden, and at Färjestaden, on Öland.

Somewhat later, in the seventh century AD, rich so-called boat graves appeared, possibly representing warrior burials of people close to the king. Members of this warrior aristocracy also owned large farms, and almost certainly played an important part in the formation of the Swedish state. Particularly magnificent are the boat graves at Vendel and Valsgärde, in east central Sweden, where great men were buried with all their possessions: helmets, shields, weapons, household utensils, horses, cattle, dogs, and gyrfalcons. Iron probably played a major part in the development of the land of the Swedes. The abundant supply of this metal apparent from the contents of the boat graves can be explained by extensive trade with continental Europe and the British Isles.

⚜This gold buckle from the boat grave at Sutton Hoo, in Britain, was found next to the purse lid (top right).
BRITISH MUSEUM/C.M. DIXON/PHOTO RESOURCES

One of the boat graves at Sutton Hoo, on the east coast of England, also bears witness to Sweden's long-distance contacts. Boat graves are not found in continental Europe, and the only true parallels of the Sutton Hoo grave are to be found in the grave-fields of Vendel and Valsgärde, in Sweden. The superb helmet from the Sutton Hoo grave was very likely made in Sweden, although it may have been manufactured locally under continental influence, since all the helmets of this period are derived from Roman prototypes. The shield also appears to have been made in Sweden, and it has even been suggested that it was manufactured by the same craftsperson as one of the Vendel shields. The motif, scale, and animal ornamentation are very similar in both cases.

The most obvious link between the two areas is the boat grave itself. With one or two exceptions, this type of grave is not found elsewhere. British archaeologist David Wilson has pointed out, however, that the eighth-century AD heroic

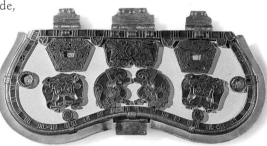

↞ These Danish gold bracteates (thin, ornamental plates) are replicas of Roman emperor medallions (medallions bearing the emperor's face) and date from the migration period.

⚜ The lid of an elegant purse from the boat grave at Sutton Hoo, adorned with gold and cloisonné enamel. The purse contained 37 gold coins, 3 coin blanks, and 2 small gold ingots.
RONALD SHERIDAN/ANCIENT ART & ARCHITECTURE COLLECTION

⚲ The famous helmet from the boat grave at Sutton Hoo (now restored) is very similar to helmets found in eastern Sweden, and may have been made there.
BRITISH MUSEUM/ROBERT HARDING PICTURE LIBRARY

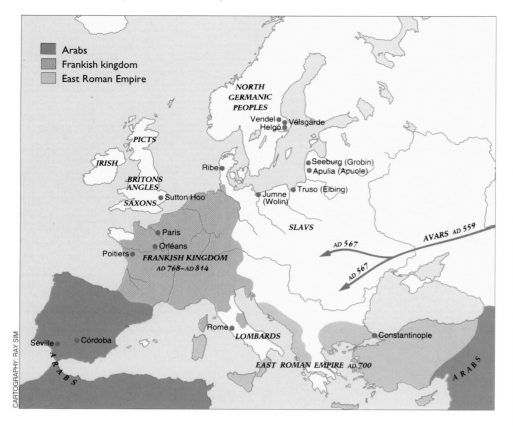

CARTOGRAPHY: RAY SIM

EUROPE: AD 500 TO AD 800
The political situation in Europe towards the end of the Germanic Late Iron Age was dominated by three major powers: the Frankish kingdom, in the west, the East Roman (or Byzantine) Empire, in the eastern Mediterranean area, and the Arabs, in North Africa and the Iberian peninsula.

↷ The style of ornamentation used in Late Iron Age Scandinavia resembles Celtic ornamentation found in England and Ireland during the same period, one example being the famous *Book of Kells*, an illustrated copy of the Bible dating from the early eighth century.

poem *Beowulf* contains an account of the burial of Scyld, who was placed in his boat together with rich treasures. The boat was not buried, but was put out to sea. Such a practice could explain why boat graves are not found along the coasts of the North Sea. The custom of placing the dead in boats may have been much more widespread than is revealed by the archaeological record.

The Viking Age

The period of Scandinavian expansion between AD 800 and AD 1050, usually referred to as the Viking Age, did not follow a single pattern. In reality, different motives lay behind the Vikings' long journeys, which began towards the end of the eighth century. The differences are particularly evident between Denmark–Norway on one hand, and Sweden on the other. In the west, the expansion took the form of straightforward colonization or forays for plunder. In the east, a fine-meshed network of trade routes and colonies was developed, which supplied the Baltic area with large amounts of silver and exotic products, especially from the Abbasid caliphate, an Islamic empire encompassing much of southwestern Asia.

The new conquests in the west are largely reflected in increased levels of settlement, which are clearly visible in the archaeological record. In Denmark and Norway, as the demand for new land exceeded supply, population pressure was channeled to the islands north of Britain—Orkney, Shetland, and the Hebrides. At the same time, the Frankish kingdom in western Europe gained an

increasingly powerful trade position, and important commercial towns developed on the English Channel: Quentowic, in France, and Dorestad, at the mouth of the Rhine. As the Scandinavian communities expanded, northern Europe attracted the interest of the Frankish kingdom.

It is often thought that the dramatic Viking voyages, with constant war expeditions to the east and west, were characteristic of Scandinavian society as a whole, but this was never the case. The people we call Vikings were only a minority of the population; most Scandinavian people of this time were farmers, who had little to do with these undertakings. They cultivated their land as they had done for generations, and it was only at the intersection of different trade routes, where harbor conditions were favorable, that more outward-looking communities developed.

There were two main reasons for the success of the Viking enterprises. First, the political situation in the Frankish kingdom and in Britain alike was characterized by disunion, with internal power struggles and fighting between the many small states. A unified resistance was therefore impossible. Indeed, there are many examples of local rulers allying themselves with the Vikings for their own political ends. Clearly, the Scandinavians made the most of these periods of division.

The second factor was the element of surprise. Thanks to their seaworthy, clinker-built ships (built of overlapping boards), the Vikings were able to carry out rapid surprise attacks on horseback along coasts and rivers. As the boats could be pulled out of the sea onto any beach under the cover of the morning fog, the Vikings' arrival could never be anticipated.

IRISH TOURIST BOARD

Towards the end of the eighth century, Norwegian Vikings had already occupied the Faeroe, Shetland, and Orkney islands. About AD 825, the Irish author Dicuil described how the Christian Picts living on some of these islands were driven off by the Scandinavians—events that are clearly visible in the archaeological record. The Viking Age settlements all postdate those left behind by the Celtic-speaking Picts. In the Hebrides, however, the Celtic population lived side by side with the Scandinavian settlers.

About AD 820, the Scandinavians began to attack the coasts of Ireland. Here, they came into contact with a culturally prosperous area: Celtic art was to exert a great influence on Germanic ornamentation in Scandinavia. Since Ireland was firmly divided between five rival kings and a number of tribes and clans under the leadership of local "chieftains", it fell an easy prey to the Vikings. In AD 840, Turgeis arrived with a large fleet and founded Dublin.

Recently, excavations at Wood Key, in central Dublin, have thrown new light on its early development and the earliest Viking Age houses. Both Irish and Scandinavian kings governed in Dublin till AD 1169, when English conquest of the

PROMEDIA SWEDEN

◄O This magnificently carved wooden head was mounted as decoration on a wagon found on the well-preserved Viking ship excavated at Oseberg, in Norway.

island began. The Scandinavians in Ireland formed some sort of warrior aristocracy, and only a few of them supported themselves peacefully by farming. The Irish entered into alliances with Danish Vikings several times in order to drive off the Norwegians. Finally, however, the heroic Irish king Brian Boru managed to defeat the local Irish kings in AD 1004, and in AD 1014, the Scandinavians were crushed at the battle of Clontarf, outside Dublin. Both Brian Boru and his son, as well as a number of local Irish kings, were killed in the battle, but the victory was a turning point in rebuffing Scandinavian colonization of the island.

THE VIKING WORLD

The red lines indicate the routes of Viking journeys. The expansion in the west by predominantly Danish and Norwegian Vikings took the form of sheer colonization and forays for plunder. In the east, Swedish Vikings built up a network of trade routes and colonies. Leif Eriksson, son of Erik the Red, is usually credited with being the first European to discover America, in AD 1000. Accounts of contacts between Scandinavians and Indians in Vinland (Grass Land), Markland (Wood Land), and Helluland (Flat-stone Land), which have been the subject of vigorous debate for decades, have now been verified.

CARTOGRAPHY: RAY SIM

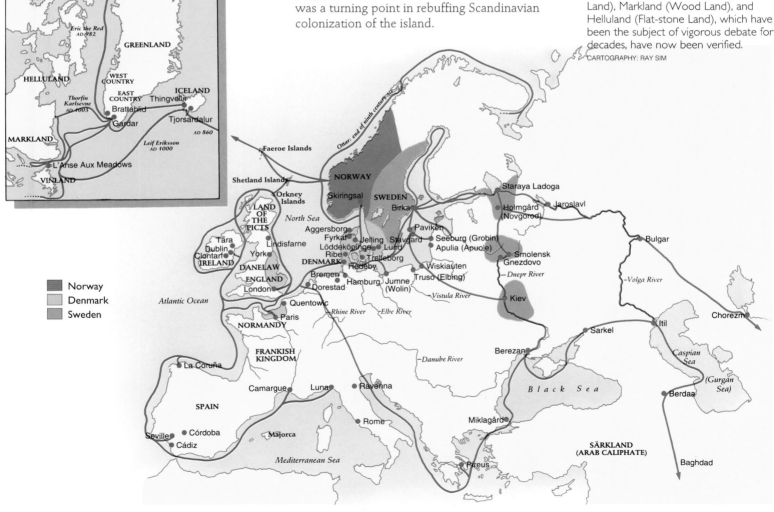

Iceland was colonized quite late. About AD 900, a period of intense settlement took place, and it is estimated that about 30,000 people had made their home on this northerly and previously uninhabited island by the middle of the tenth century AD. Our knowledge of these events comes not only from the archaeological record, but also from the *Book of the Icelanders* and the *Book of Settlements*, dating from the twelfth and thirteenth centuries AD. In many cases, farms and settlements named in these sources have been verified by excavations—for example, Stöng, in Tjórsárdalur, which was destroyed in a volcanic eruption in AD 1104. The political reasons behind the large-scale emigration to Iceland are also touched upon in these early scripts. The *Book of Settlements* tells of "outlawed and political emigrants from Norway", many of whom were probably opponents of King Harald Fairhair, who seized power in Norway towards the end of the ninth century AD. Perhaps it was due to distrust of royal power that Iceland never formed a kingdom, but rather a "republic of chiefs". It seems likely, however, that the settlement of Iceland is at least partly to be explained by the need for new land; a considerable number of people also arrived from Ireland.

In AD 930, the first Althing (legislative assembly), which consisted of 39 of the island's most prominent chiefs, was held at Thingvellir. The country was divided into 12 "thing areas", and the Althing was presided over by three so-called "godar", who were elected from among the most important chiefs.

Large farms dating from the earliest settlement of Iceland, in the tenth century AD, have been excavated in Tjórsárdalur, in the south of Iceland. The buildings shown here are a reconstruction of a farm, known as Stöng, which was destroyed by a volcanic eruption in AD 1104.

The entrance to the main farm building, made of timber and turf, at Stöng, in Iceland.

At its peak, the Scandinavian colony in Greenland is estimated to have had 3,000 inhabitants. The settlement was abandoned in the fifteenth century AD, possibly because the climate became much colder. In the 1960s, the remains of the site of Brattahlid, including a church built by Tjodhilde, Erik the Red's wife, were discovered at Kagssiarssuk.

PARKS CANADA/CANADIAN HERITAGE

◉ The first indisputable Viking settlement in North America has been excavated at L'Anse Aux Meadows, in northern Newfoundland, Canada. Remains of house sites and of iron-working have been found, together with find material that has clearly Scandinavian characteristics. The houses shown here are reconstructions.

Danish Colonization

Whereas the journeys to northern Scotland, Ireland, Iceland, Greenland, and America were predominantly carried out by Norwegian Vikings, the interest of their Danish colleagues was primarily focused on England and the Frankish kingdom. The first major attacks were carried out as early as the 830s, when Danes successfully exploited periods of weakness in these two areas.

The extensive Danish settlement in east central England was subject to Danish law and administration. When William the Conqueror occupied England after the Battle of Hastings, in AD 1066, a register of lands, known as the *Domesday Book*, was established.

Notably, there are many surviving place-names with Scandinavian suffixes—villages and towns with names ending in "by", "thorp", and "toft". More than 700 East English place-names today end in "by". Moreover, the English language still has many Old Danish loan-words, such as "window" and "happy", all of which bear witness to the massive Scandinavian influence on the English community during the tenth century AD.

Swedes in the East

As early as the eighth century AD, growing Swedish interest in eastern trade contacts had led to the establishment of trading colonies on the east coast of the Baltic—for example, at Grobin and Apuole. During the early Viking Age, these contacts resulted in the development of an extensive communication network with the Orient via Russian rivers. Several Scandinavian colonies at posts along the trade routes developed into virtual nations. A number of Swedish rune stones describe voyages to "Gårdarike" (Russia), "Särkland" (the Arab caliphate), and "Miklagård" (Constantinople, capital of the Byzantine empire). Even more important sources of information include Nestor's *Chronicle* (from the twelfth century AD), Constantine VII Porphyrogenitus's *De Administrando Imperio* (a Byzantine work from the tenth century AD),

MAJOR VIKING EVENTS IN THE WEST

AD 793	Vikings destroy the Lindisfarne monastery on Holy Island, off the coast of eastern England.
AD 795	The monastery of Saint Columba on Iona, in the Hebrides, is ravaged.
AD 795	First attacks on the Irish west coast.
AD 812	120 Viking ships are thought to have rounded Ireland and reached the Kerry peninsula.
AD 820	First major Viking attacks on Ireland.
AD 825	The Christian Picts are driven off the islands north of Scotland.
AD 834	Dorestad, in the Frankish kingdom, plundered.
AD 835	First major Viking attacks on England.
AD 840	Turgeis arrives in Ireland and founds Dublin.
AD 841	First attacks along French rivers: Seine, Loire, Garonne.
AD 843	Nantes, in France, plundered.
AD 844	Vikings reach the Iberian peninsula; La Coruña and Lisbon plundered, Cádiz and Seville captured.
AD 845	Viking fleet sails up the River Elbe; Hamburg, in Germany, is burned to the ground.
AD 845	Paris plundered.
AD 850	Viking settlement in France, primarily in Normandy and at river mouths.
AD 859	Vikings reach the Mediterranean and plunder Majorca, off the coast of Spain, as well as Pisa and Luna, in Italy.
AD 865	A large Danish army, under the sons of Lodbrok, arrives in East Anglia, in England; 10 years of war begin.
AD 867	York (Jorvik), in England, attacked and captured.
AD 869	Mercia and Wessex, in England, attacked and occupied.
AD 878	The Danes are beaten by Alfred the Great, king of Wessex, but are awarded Northumberland, East Anglia, half of Mercia, and part of Essex.
AD 896	The Danelaw, one of three judicial ares in England, becomes the unified Danish possession, and Danish settlement is established.
AD 900	Iceland is colonized from Norway.
AD 911	Charles the Simple, king of the Frankish kingdom, gives Normandy to the Vikings under the chief Rollo.
AD 930	The first Althing in Iceland is held at Thingvellir.
AD 980	Greenland is colonized by the outlawed Icelander Erik the Red.
AD 986	Leif Eriksson sails from Greenland to America
AD 988	Sweyn Forkbeard inherits the Danish throne from Harald Bluetooth.
AD 994	Sweyn Forkbeard sails up the Thames with 93 ships and attacks London, together with Olaf Tryggvason, king of Norway.
AD 1002	Torfin Karlsevne from Greenland spends three years in Vinland, in America.
AD 1013	Sweyn Forkbeard occupies all of England and proclaims himself king of the whole country.
AD 1014	Brian Boru crushes a Viking army on 23 April at Clontarf, outside Dublin, in Ireland; Brian Boru and a number of Irish chieftains are killed, but the battle is a turning point in the process of rebuffing Scandinavian colonization.
AD 1016	Sweyn Forkbeard dies and is succeeded by his sons Edmund and Canute.
AD 1017	Edmund dies and Canute the Great, who spends most of his time in England, takes over the whole North Sea kingdom.
AD 1035	Canute the Great dies and the vast Danish kingdom is divided between his sons, Harald Harefoot (England), Hardecanute (Denmark), and Sweyn (Norway).
AD 1047	Harald the Ruthless becomes king of Norway and tries to conquer both Denmark and England.
AD 1066	Harald the Ruthless is killed in the battle at Stamford Bridge, in England.
AD 1066	The Battle of Hastings, on 14 October; the Normans, under William the Conqueror, defeat the English army and become the dominating power in western Europe. This event marked the end of Viking activity in western Europe. The establishment of effective naval forces, which could avert attacks on the open sea, and fortifications along exposed coasts put an end to Viking supremacy.

CARL O. LÖFMAN/PROMEDIA

⚓ During the Late Iron Age, Birka developed as an important trading port on the island of Björkö, in Lake Malar, in eastern Sweden. (Lake Malar was at that time part of the Baltic Sea.) The town was situated on the shore next to a fortified hill known as Borgberget. Recent excavations in the central part of the town, the so-called "Black Earth" (a residential area named after the black color of the soil, indicating human activity), have greatly added to our knowledge of city life, craftwork, subsistence, and trade in the Viking Age.

☙ Thanks to historical accounts and recorded tales, we know a great deal about the pre-Christian religious beliefs of Scandinavians. Thor was the god of war and thunder, and the thunderbolt was represented by his hammer, called Mjollnir or Mjölner. Many protective amulets in the shape of Thor's hammer have been found throughout Scandinavia and other parts of Europe. This one comes from Erikstorp, in Östergötland, Sweden.

and the Arab authors and travelers Ibn Khordabeh and Ibn Fadlan of the ninth and early tenth centuries AD. Their vivid descriptions have given us a unique insight into the everyday life of Vikings in the East —knowledge that also provides a glimpse into the conditions and customs in Scandinavia in that period.

During the ninth century AD, the ar-Rus (the Arab name for the Swedish traders) found their way along two major routes: along the Dnepr River to the Black Sea, and along the Volga River to the Caspian Sea. Towards the end of the ninth century AD and during the tenth century AD, the former became increasingly important. Both routes started at Lake Ladoga, where an important Scandinavian settlement was established early on at Staraya Ladoga, by the Volchov River. Archaeological excavations have revealed a city-like community very similar to Hedeby, in Denmark, and Birka, in Sweden, with a conglomeration of houses and narrow alleys surrounded by a wall.

The Dnepr River was reached via the Dyna, and it was along this route that the Swedish settlements and colonies developed. Although the extent of these settlements is unknown, it is probable that the Scandinavians' primary aim was to control the trade routes. At Smolensk, there was intensive Swedish settlement over a long period, as evidenced by a grave-field outside the city containing more than 4,500 burial mounds. A number of Scandinavian burials have been

CARL O. LÖFMAN/PROMEDIA

excavated here, the finds including sets of weights, "Thor's hammers" (a type of amulet), and women's ornaments of Scandinavian type, as well as a boat grave containing weapons, boat rivets, and ornaments. The find material provides a significant insight into Swedish trade in the East and into the colonies that developed in its wake. A well-organized system of transportation, involving transshipment and reloading, developed at an early stage at junctions such as Staraya

CARL O. LÖFMAN/PROMEDIA

This eastern trade of the Swedish kingdom is reflected in the great amounts of Arabic silver found in Viking Age hoards in Sweden, particularly the island of Gotland. But this represents the final destination of only a very limited part of the interchange—the part that for some reason was taken out of circulation. Viking goods were much sought after by the caliphate: furs of sable, beaver, squirrel, and fox; axes; honey; wax; walrus tusks; and slaves. The Scandinavians received in return silver, bronze vessels, pearls, and Chinese silk. Many of the commodities traded by the Scandinavians originated in the region of Russia—particularly furs and Slavic slaves.

In the first half of the tenth century AD, the importance of the Volga route was greatly diminished, following uprisings among the Kazars and the Volga–Bulgarians. Similarly, the Dnepr route declined in importance as the Slavic kingdoms in Russia grew more powerful. About AD 970, the two routes were abandoned, and all trade with the Byzantine empire now traveled along the rivers of central Europe. This is reflected in the increasing number of western European coins found in Scandinavian silver hoards of this period.

By about AD 1050, the whole of Scandinavia had officially converted to Christianity: the entire continent of Europe had thereby entered historic times, and the Iron Age had come to an end.

◄● A bronze figure from Rällinge, in Södermanland, Sweden, depicting the phallic pagan deity Freyr, also known as Frö. Worshiped mainly in eastern Sweden, Frö was the god of fertility, peace, sunshine, and rain; and phallic cults, fertility rites, and sexual symbolism, relating to such objects as this figure, were linked to him.

♀ A silver hoard found at the Viking Age town of Birka, situated in the Lake Malar basin, in Sweden. Along with different kinds of silver objects, it contained Arab coins, the most recent of which were minted in AD 963 or AD 967. More than 1,100 Viking Age silver hoards have been found in Sweden, most of them on the two Baltic islands of Öland and Gotland. Seven hundred hoards have been found on Gotland alone, yielding more than 130,000 imported silver coins.

Ladoga, Novgorod, and Smolensk. Merchants settled here with their families, under the protection of garrisons stationed in the area. The Scandinavians soon intermixed with the Slavic population, and as a result, an increasingly large number of Slavic objects are found in graves.

Further south, the Dnepr route passed through Kiev, eventually ending up in Berezan, an important reloading station and trading post on the Black Sea coast. From Berezan, Miklagård (Constantinople) and the eastern Mediterranean were reached via the open sea. Regular trading contacts with the capital of the Byzantine empire are reflected in the strict regulations the Scandinavians had to observe when visiting the city: only unarmed men with permits were admitted; the amount of goods that could be exported was limited; and all goods had to be stamped upon departure. On the other hand, the Scandinavians were offered women, baths, food, and drink, indicating that they were coveted trading partners, if not to be trusted.

The major trading post on the other important route, the Volga River, was Bulgar, situated at the center of the Volga–Bulgarian kingdom. It was here that the Scandinavians came in contact with the Silk Road. The Volga route ended at Atil, on the Caspian coast, the capital of the Kazar people. From the Caspian Sea, the Scandinavian traders sailed on to Berdaa and Baghdad, in the Arab caliphate.

STATENS HISTORISKA MUSEUM, SWEDEN

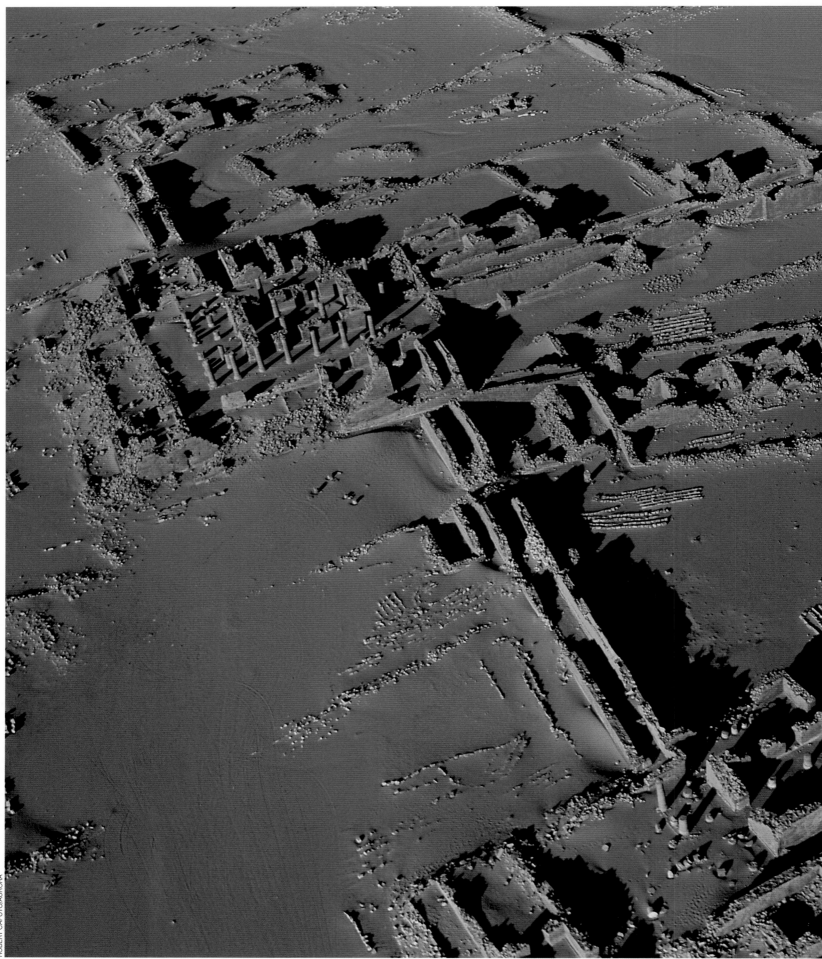

ROBERT CAPUTO/AURORA

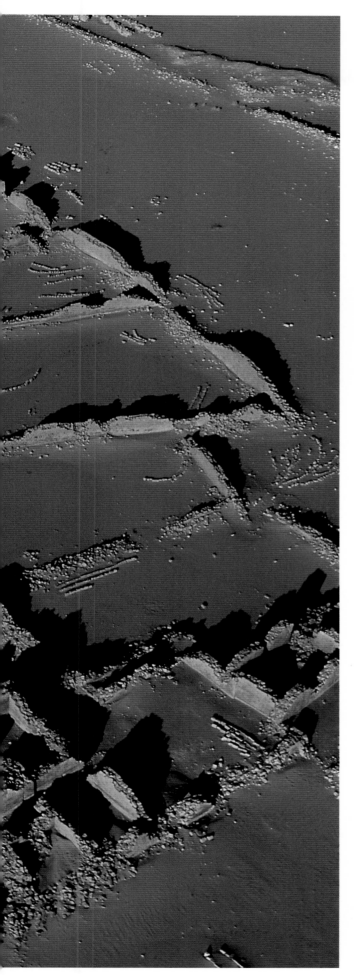

THE DEVELOPMENT OF AFRICAN STATES

3 0 0 0 B C – A D 1 5 0 0

Loosely Organized Political Communities

CHRISTOPHER FYFE

DURING MUCH OF the long period from 3000 BC to AD 1500, most Africans lived in small, loosely organized political communities, without monarchs, hereditary nobles, or permanent officials. Each community had its own distinctive form of government, which enforced rules its members accepted. These forms of government had to be devised and agreed to by individuals, and were based on rational decisions. They did not somehow "evolve" in a notionally organic way.

When and how they were devised and agreed to, we cannot now tell. Nor can we know how they operated. We have no records to enlighten us as to the remote African past. Inevitably, then, historians are tempted to try to infer the past from the present—to take, for instance, what social anthropologists have written about similar communities in our own era and apply it to earlier societies. This is not how historians should operate, however. African societies were not "timeless" (although some people have asserted that they were). Like everything else, they changed over time. When the Sahara began to dry up, in the third millennium BC, the inhabitants' ways of life changed, and so did their political structures. Similarly, the spread of iron-working through Africa, from the middle of the first millennium BC, altered political as well as social arrangements. Africans innovated in all spheres when it suited them—political, economic, and the arts.

◄● A general view of Meroë, in modern-day Sudan. For more than a thousand years, it was one of the major centers of Meroë kingdom. There may have been a major center here, or in the vicinity, as early as the second century BC.

♠ This terracotta head, from the Nok culture of modern-day northern Nigeria, was sculptured during the first millennium BC.

ANCIENT ART & ARCHITECTURE COLLECTION

☞ The headpiece of a ceremonial society mask that covered the whole body, made in the Kuba country, in modern-day Zaire. Constructed of raffia and cloth, it was mounted on a wooden frame and sewn with leather beads and cowrie shells.
PRIVATE COLLECTION/WERNER FORMAN ARCHIVE

🜨 This face mask, made by a society among the Dan people of modern-day Liberia, would originally have been part of a body mask made of raffia or some other fabric that covered the wearer's whole body.
BONHAMS, LONDON/THE BRIDGEMAN ART LIBRARY

PICTUREPOINT LTD

🜨 The people who executed this rock painting found at Kondoa-Iringi, in modern-day Tanzania, would have been members of a loosely organized political community.

H istorians are therefore in a dilemma. If we interpret political behavior in the remote past by reference to similar-looking behavior in the present, we are guilty of "presentism" (looking at the past in terms of the present) and of suggesting falsely that African societies were timeless. If we stick to our normal methods, however, and put down only what we can deduce from verifiable data, we shall be forced to erase from the historical record all reference to many millions of Africans; and that we must try not to do. We should not present the African past in the way historians have regularly presented the past of Europe and Asia—solely as the achievements of highly organized states. We must swallow our principles, however unwillingly, and infer how these loosely organized political communities are likely to have been organized in the past from our knowledge of similar communities in the present.

Such communities are sometimes described as "stateless societies". This is misleading. Though loosely structured, they were, like most structured states, self-governing sovereign entities, each with its own distinctive political constitution. The constitutions varied, but seem to have followed a basic pattern. The community was divided into small groups distinguished by descent, age, or some other feature. Each was separate from the others, but ready to combine with them to resist outside pressure or to solve problems of common concern. No one group was allowed by the others to become too strong, and the rivalry between groups held them together.

Normally, the members of each group carried on their own daily life without reference to the other groups, and groups combined only when common concerns arose. Hence, there was no need for a permanent administration; there were no career officials or judges. Administration was contingent on events, not continuous.

Similarly, no individual within a group was allowed to become too powerful. Those who gained wealth were under strong pressure to redistribute it to others. Among the Igbo (in modern Nigeria), a term for a rich man was "Give Me Something". Those who were too successful were liable to be accused of witchcraft. In this way, power remained dispersed and classes were prevented from forming.

A Patriarchal Political Structure

The political model tended to be the patriarchal family in which age confers authority. Women and young people had their recognized place in society, but it was below that of the old men. Marriage was used as a means of social control. The older men apportioned out the marriageable young women as wives for themselves or for appropriate young men. Such societies were not, therefore, egalitarian. Although there were no kings or aristocracies, and social differentiation by wealth was prevented, the men dominated the women, and the old dominated the young.

Over the generations, power was regularly transferred from older to younger. Where the basic unit was the age-group, children were initiated together into an age-grade. This determined their place in society for the rest of their lives. The young age-grades had no authority. Every few years, however, at a formal ceremony, the age-grade above them handed over new responsibilities, and they moved up to a higher status.

Those in the prime of life held the dominant grade, although older people were still given respect and high status.

In other communities, power was vested in "secret societies"—societies, that is, whose members claimed to have secret, supernatural knowledge. (See the feature *Holding Society Together*.) Boys were initiated at an early age, and decisions were made in secret conclaves. The decision-makers were concealed behind body masks that gave them a supernatural sanction, enforceable, if need be, as a death sentence. Women were excluded. Although women sometimes had their own powerful societies, with their own secret knowledge, the decisions of these societies were usually binding on women only.

All these political activities were validated by supernatural sanctions, which also guided people in their everyday lives—hunting, farming, child-rearing. These sanctions were reinforced by communal rituals, performed with special music, dances, and costumes. All members of the community were thus constantly made aware of the bonds that united them.

These loose, flexible political structures could hold large numbers of people together. An estimate made in the mid-twentieth century suggested that in West Africa alone at that time, there were something like 35 million people living in such communities, let alone those living elsewhere in Africa. One cannot, therefore, just write these communities off as "primitive" or "vestigial", or leave them out of African history altogether.

M. & A. KIRTLEY/ANA

◄○ Constructed out of plaited straw, this mask reveals the wearer's arms and legs but conceals his identity. It was made for use in a society in the Baule country, in modern-day Côte d'Ivoire.

♀ These rock paintings, too, in the Tassili N'Ajjer mountains, now in the middle of the Sahara, in modern-day Algeria, were painted by people living within a loosely organized political community.

PICTUREPOINT LTD

☝ A terracotta portrait head of a queen of Ife, from the Yoruba country, modern Nigeria.
ANCIENT ART & ARCHITECTURE COLLECTION

♀ A Benin bronze plaque, showing a royal or noble figure with subordinate attendants. Hundreds of such plaques were formerly fixed to the walls of the royal palace in Benin, modern Nigeria.
BRITISH MUSEUM/WERNER FORMAN ARCHIVE

The Rise of African Kingdoms

The forces that united these loosely organized polities often broke down. One group, or one powerful individual, came to dominate the rest and established a centralized structure of government. This process of centralization is customarily presented as progress into a "higher stage" of social organization. Yet, when one recalls that many people today are perturbed by trends towards centralized authority and bureaucratization, one has to question whether the change is to be applauded unthinkingly. It is a question some Africans seem to have asked themselves. There is evidence that the Igbo people gave up centralized, monarchical rule and reverted to decentralization.

The oral traditions that record the histories of African kingdoms usually start with a male founder who persuaded or forced people to accept his rule. Often he is presented as a stranger endowed with a supernatural power, such as being able to make rain or to work iron. There are many traditions in which the founder-king was a blacksmith. Armed with a supernatural sanction, rulers could enforce their authority. Sometimes, it

was enforced peaceably. Some traditions record that the new ruler was welcomed gladly by his people (although this may well be no more than royal propaganda). Or a ruler and his followers might simply have seized power and ruled by force, subjecting the people to the authority of an alien monarchy and aristocracy.

Sometimes, economic changes generated political change. As long-distance trade developed, markets were established along the trade routes. Organizing a market offered political opportunities to enterprising individuals. Controlling the market meant controlling the people who used it. In Africa, as in other parts of the world, large states thus grew up round market centers, notably the kingdoms of the western Sudan that exploited the wealth of the trans-Saharan trade, and the kingdoms of south central Africa that controlled trade down the Zambezi to the Indian Ocean.

Vestiges of the previously loosely organized structures often survived. The local economies were usually still organized on the familiar small-group pattern, though now under rulers who appropriated the surplus product as taxes. Royal power was still limited by practices surviving from the old community-based days. African kingdoms were constitutional monarchies, where kings were subjected to checks and balances. Their authority was restricted by their councilors, whose opinions they could not ignore. Sometimes, secret societies survived as a check on royal power.

Outwardly, and in view of their lesser subjects, kings may have seemed to be absolute monarchs. The trappings of majesty invested many of them with what appeared to be supernatural authority (like the "divine right of kings" claimed by many European sovereigns). People acted out allegiance to their rulers in gestures of abasement. In the kingdom of Ancient Ghana, they fell on their knees and sprinkled their heads with dust when they approached the king. Indeed, physical prostration of inferiors before superiors, wives before husbands, juniors before seniors—the visual, day-to-day enactment of the rules of a hierarchical society—was widespread. Every day, every hour, people were reminded of their political and social status.

Some kings lived invisibly, secluded in their palaces, seen only on state occasions with their faces veiled. Yet, although they might appear to have been absolute, in practice, African kings were controlled by their councils. The council members might have had to approach their sovereign groveling on the ground, but once they reached his ear, he had to listen to them. When policy was decided, their voices were decisive. In some kingdoms—for example, among the Yoruba (in modern-day Nigeria) and in some of the East African Great Lakes' kingdoms—a king's council could even make him commit suicide if they had had enough of him.

HOLDING SOCIETY TOGETHER

CHRISTOPHER FYFE

Many African political communities chose to retain a loosely organized political system rather than accept the constraints of centralized kingship. Each had its own constitution and laws. There were no monarchs, hereditary nobles, or permanent officials. Yet these loose forms of government held together large numbers of people. Historians and political scientists must, therefore, take them seriously.

JEAN M. BORGATTI

⚱ This spirit mask from the Dafing people of Burkina covers the whole body ("mask" including not only the face mask but the full costume), making the male wearer invisible and his appearance mysterious. The wooden headpiece gives him extra, domineering height. Altogether, the mask presents an alarming image of supernatural authority.

Performance as Social Control

Whatever form the constitutions took, they had to be made comprehensible and acceptable to their constituent members. In societies where people did not read and write, constitutions could not be written down. If the law was to be enforced and maintained, people had to be made aware of its authority, and of the sanctions that upheld it, by visual means, in performance. It had to be publicly enacted in ceremonies in which everyone participated, with songs and dances that gave them meaning for the participants, and these ceremonies thus acted as political controls.

The illustrations have been chosen to show some of the ways in which political control was enforced. They are all photographs taken recently, and do not, therefore, illustrate what was done in the remote past. Styles changed over time. But even if the styles have changed, the photographs indicate how such African political communities functioned. The visual record illustrates the constitutional mechanisms.

Law and custom were given supernatural sanction by reference to some outside force or spirit that, when presented visually, seemed to be overpowering and beyond human control or questioning.

Secret Societies

Many political communities were controlled by a secret society. The Ngbe society, open only to men, gave political solidarity to the Ejagham people of the Cross River, Nigeria. A figure wearing a mask represents the society in public, for the existence of the society is not secret, only its esoteric knowledge. The mask hides everything but the wearer's hands, and the face has no mouth (as befits a society with secrets).

Women, too, had their secret societies. Members of the women's Bondo society (in Sierra Leone and Liberia), where girl initiates received their education as women, were

MARILYN HOULBERG

genitally mutilated as a mark of womanhood. It is believed to be the only African society in which a spirit mask is worn by a woman.

The Edo peoples (in Nigeria) had an age-grade political structure. Every five to seven years, a masquerade marked the admission of an age-grade into its new, higher status. The specially designed masks worn were destroyed before the next admission ceremony.

The Power of Dead Ancestors

Continuity in government could be maintained by appeal to dead ancestors, whose opinions had to be respected. The community was seen as a community of the living and the dead, still bound together politically. Hence, some proposed political innovation could be rejected on the grounds that the ancestors had never known it.

These few illustrations do no more than indicate the inventiveness and creativity that underlay the exercise of political power in Africa over thousands of years.

⚱ The Yoruba people (in Nigeria) had royal governments, but this Yoruba mask is a spectacular example of an ancestral presence. The dead ancestors were believed to parade in the annual Egungun masquerade—fully hidden under their elaborate masks—whereby they exerted their moral influence as guardians of the community.

FREDERICK LAMP/BALTIMORE MUSEUM OF ART

⚱ These boys are being prepared by a masked instructor for admission into the Rabai society, one of the secret societies of the Temne people, in Sierra Leone. They were instructed in the ways of manhood, taught the society's secrets, and circumcised.

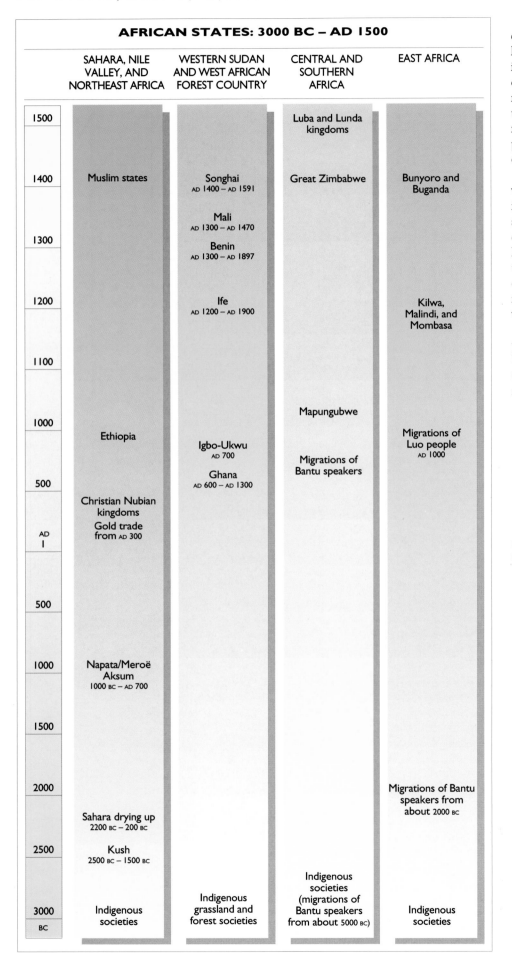

AFRICAN STATES: 3000 BC – AD 1500

	SAHARA, NILE VALLEY, AND NORTHEAST AFRICA	WESTERN SUDAN AND WEST AFRICAN FOREST COUNTRY	CENTRAL AND SOUTHERN AFRICA	EAST AFRICA
1500	Muslim states	Songhai AD 1400 – AD 1591	Luba and Lunda kingdoms	
1400		Mali AD 1300 – AD 1470	Great Zimbabwe	Bunyoro and Buganda
1300		Benin AD 1300 – AD 1897		
1200		Ife AD 1200 – AD 1900		Kilwa, Malindi, and Mombasa
1100				
1000	Ethiopia	Igbo-Ukwu AD 700	Mapungubwe	Migrations of Luo people AD 1000
500		Ghana AD 600 – AD 1300	Migrations of Bantu speakers	
AD 1	Christian Nubian kingdoms / Gold trade from AD 300			
500				
1000	Napata/Meroë Aksum 1000 BC – AD 700			
1500				
2000	Sahara drying up 2200 BC – 200 BC			Migrations of Bantu speakers from about 2000 BC
2500	Kush 2500 BC – 1500 BC			
3000 BC	Indigenous societies	Indigenous grassland and forest societies	Indigenous societies (migrations of Bantu speakers from about 5000 BC)	Indigenous societies

When a king died, his successor was usually chosen by "kingmakers", often after armed conflict known as "The Choice of Spears". Anarchic though it may seem to regularly make a king's death an occasion for civil war, this acted as a constitutional mechanism. The balance of power that shifted to the king in his lifetime, shifted back to the king-making nobles on his death. Thus, kings were prevented from accumulating new powers to pass on to their eldest sons or other chosen successors.

Similarly, restrictions on accumulating private wealth remained. Although kings and private individuals could grow rich, they were still under strong pressure to redistribute their wealth. People demanded, and expected to receive, rewards. Kings who failed to give lost popular support. In the kingdoms, as in the loosely organized polities, capital formation was restricted, and class formation based on the accumulation of private wealth was kept firmly in check.

In some kingdoms, queen mothers were powerful. Women occasionally reigned as queens, but this was a rarity. In Africa, as in most parts of the world, male rule was the norm, and female rule, the exception.

⚚ A glazed stone animal from Meroë, in modern-day Sudan.
KHARTOUM MUSEUM/WERNER FORMAN ARCHIVE

The Kingdom of Kush–Meroë

The first African kingdoms, founded in the Nile Valley by the peoples of Upper Egypt and the Nile delta, coalesced into the kingdom of Ancient Egypt. The peoples living south of the Egyptian frontier, in what the Egyptians called Kush (the northern part of the modern Republic of the Sudan), organized regular trade down the Nile with Egypt. About 2500 BC, they united as one kingdom, with its capital at Kerma.

Kerma was plainly a large city: the cemetery contains tens of thousands of graves. Its kings were buried in vast, brick-built tombs surmounted by a domed mound of earth. The largest to have been excavated is more than 90 meters (295 feet) wide. At royal funerals, hundreds of victims were sacrificed. About 1500 BC, however, the Egyptians, in a period of imperial expansion, advanced up the Nile and conquered Kush. Kerma was then abandoned, until archaeologists found it in the twentieth century.

The Egyptians ruled Kush as a province of Egypt. By at least the ninth century BC, however, it had once again become an independent kingdom. During the period of Egyptian rule, Kushite culture had become Egyptianized. The kings adopted the royal Egyptian religious cults. Early in the eighth century BC, Pi-ankhi, King of Kush, invaded and conquered Egypt, and for the next 70 years he and his successors ruled the Nile Valley from Kush to the Mediterranean as pharaohs. Eventually, the Kushites were driven back up the Nile, although their kings still considered themselves to be the kings of Egypt. For about another thousand years, ruling first from Napata, near the Egyptian frontier, and then from Meroë, higher up the Nile, they maintained the ancient Egyptian traditions long after Egypt itself had been conquered, first by the Greeks and then by the Romans. (See the feature *Meroë: Capital of a Prosperous Kingdom*.) Temples and palaces were built in the Egyptian style, with inscriptions in the Egyptian hieroglyphic script and figures depicted according to the traditional Egyptian canon of proportion. When the kings died, they were buried in pyramid tombs.

As in Egypt, queen mothers had great power. Moreover, there were at least five ruling queens of Meroë. One of them is depicted on a stone monument wearing the double crown of Egypt, originally designed some 3,000 years earlier. As the years passed, however, the culture became more distinctively Meroitic, with locally devised styles of sculpture and handicrafts. Lion-headed Meroitic gods appeared. Queens were depicted with wide hips instead of in the slim Egyptian style. Eventually, Egyptian hieroglyphs were superseded by a Meroitic script, which reproduced the local language.

Meroë was situated within the rainfall belt, surrounded by fertile land that was suitable for growing grain and pasturing cattle to feed a large urban population. Here, as in other parts of Africa in this period, iron was mined and worked. Archaeologists have still not determined when or where iron was first mined in Africa. Nor are they sure whether the technique of iron-working was an imported skill or invented locally in a number of different places.

Meroë's prosperity was maintained by regular trade with Roman Egypt, with exports of gold, ivory, wine, and slaves and imports of luxury goods. As Roman power slackened, however, the neighboring peoples began raiding the Nile Valley, eventually cutting Meroë off from Egypt and thus undermining its prosperity. These invaders founded their own state, Ballana, between Meroë and Egypt, where royal burial sites full of imported luxury goods have been discovered. Eventually, during the fourth century AD, the kingdom of Meroë came to an end, presumably as a result of pressures from these peoples (but the evidence is uncertain).

UNDERLINED NAMES refer to peoples

PEOPLES AND STATES IN AFRICA: 3000 BC TO AD 1500

Most Africans lived in small, loosely organized political communities throughout the long period from 3000 BC to AD 1500. An estimate made in the mid-twentieth century suggested that in West Africa alone at that time, there were about 35 million people living in such communities.
CARTOGRAPHY: RAY SIM

◄ A stone pillar at Meroë bearing an inscription in the Meroitic script. This script can be read (in the sense that individual characters can be identified) but has not yet been deciphered.

⬆ Only a few of the pillars built at Aksum, in present-day Ethiopia, to commemorate kings survive today.

♀ A worshiper emerges from one of the rock-face churches of Lalibela, in modern-day Ethiopia.

The Kingdom of Aksum-Ethiopia

During the last centuries BC, the peoples in the upland country along the Red Sea coast (in modern-day Ethiopia) created the kingdom of Aksum. Aksum was an inland city on the Red Sea, with its own seaport at Adulis. By the first century AD, it had become a major trade center, trading with the other Red Sea ports and India, its main export being African ivory.

Temples and royal palaces were built in Aksum. The kings were commemorated by tall, flat-sided pillars up to 30 meters (100 feet) high, a few of which survive today. In the mid-fourth century AD, at about the time Emperor Constantine made the Roman Empire Christian, a Greek from Alexandria converted King Ezana of Aksum to Christianity. His coinage is evidence of his conversion: the early coins bear non-Christian symbols; the later, Christian. Aksum became a Christian kingdom, owing religious allegiance

to the Coptic Church of Egypt (as the Ethiopian Church still does today).

The kings of Aksum progressively conquered an empire in southwestern Arabia. In the seventh century AD, however, the tide turned. When Mohammed converted the Arab peoples to Islam, he inaugurated a great period of Arab conquest. Arabs crossed the Red Sea and took over the coastal regions, gaining control of the Red Sea trade. Aksum became an inland kingdom. Its kings gradually moved their power base southwards, through the high mountainous plateau around and beyond Lake Tana, the source of the Blue Nile, creating the kingdom of Ethiopia (sometimes referred to as Abyssinia).

As the Askum kings moved inland, the peoples they conquered were converted to Christianity. In the tenth century AD, their advance was stalled by protracted opposition led by a non-Christian queen (whose name has not been recorded). Distinctive styles of Christian worship and practice developed. Theological debates generated civil wars. The nominal head of the Ethiopian Church, the Abuna, was an Egyptian, sent from

⚲ One of the Lalibela churches, showing how the building has been carved out of the surrounding rock.

↔ Lalibela is famous for its churches hewn directly out of huge rock faces in the tenth century AD. The interiors are decorated with paintings.

⚲ The church of St George at Lalibela. St George is an important saint in the Ethiopian Church. Here, in accordance with local custom, a worshiper places his forehead against the wall and kisses it, as a mark of reverence.

Alexandria, but in practice, the king controlled the church and used it as an instrument of government. Richly endowed churches and monasteries, their walls decorated with paintings and jeweled plaques, were built throughout the country as guardians of state authority. Some, like the famous churches of Lalibela, were hewn out of rock. The Aksum kings themselves claimed descent from the biblical King Solomon and the Queen of Sheba, giving the royal family a mystical status that was officially asserted until the fall of the Ethiopian monarchy in 1974.

The precipitous mountain countryside made it easy for dissident nobles to defy the king from their isolated fortresses. So royal discipline was harsh, and rebellion was punished ruthlessly. Moreover, to reinforce royal authority, the king, once he had been crowned at Aksum, moved around the country continuously instead of ruling from the capital. A Portuguese priest who visited Ethiopia in the early sixteenth century was amazed by the vast royal court of about 150,000 people, accommodated in tents and always on the move, and by the enormous number of richly

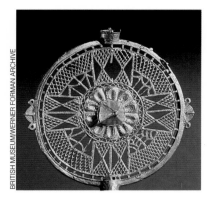

BRITISH MUSEUM/WERNER FORMAN ARCHIVE

This ornament worked in gold was worn by a senior official at the court of Asante, in modern-day Ghana, in the eighteenth or nineteenth century.

PETER CARMICHAEL/ASPECT PICTURE LIBRARY

Blocks of salt, mined in the central Sahara, were a regular commodity in trans-Saharan trade. They were carried on camelback to the trading cities of the Niger to be exchanged for gold or slaves. These blocks are from Bilma, in modern-day Niger.

decorated churches and monasteries. This was a high point for the Ethiopian monarchy, to be followed by two and a half centuries of invasion and civil war.

The Kingdoms of Nubia

After the fall of Meroë, the mid-Nile peoples regrouped into three new states. These were the kingdoms of Nubia: Nobatia, Makuria, and Alwa. In the sixth century AD, Christian missionaries converted the Nubian kings. Nubia, like Ethiopia, owed allegiance to the Coptic Church in Alexandria. As in Meroë, there was regular import–export trade with Egypt. When, in the seventh century, the Muslim Arabs conquered Egypt and then the whole North African coast, they tried without success to invade Nubia. Defeated, they made a trade treaty with the Nubian kings instead, and henceforth goods were regularly exchanged between the Christian and Muslim countries.

For another 600 or 700 years, the Christian kingdoms flourished, their densely built-up towns and villages ranged round cathedrals and churches (now being excavated by archaeologists). They coexisted peacefully with their Muslim neighbors, and tolerated any who chose to settle among them, particularly Arab pastoralists who came to pasture their cattle in the Nile Valley grasslands.

In the thirteenth century AD, a Nubian king unwisely sent an army to help the European Christian crusaders who were trying to conquer Palestine. The Muslim Egyptian army retaliated and invaded northern Nubia. Although the Egyptians were driven out, Muslim rulers took over the northern kingdom. The royal cathedral became a mosque. In the south, too, Muslims gained power, until by the end of the fifteenth century, all the kingdoms were ruled by Muslims.

The new Muslim governments made no attempts to forcibly convert the Christians to Islam. Christians were tolerated in Nubia as they were in Egypt (where, after 1,300 years of Muslim rule, there are still four million Coptic Christians). Deprived of their Christian governments, however, and remote from Alexandria, the center of their church, these peoples gradually became Muslims and the Christian Church faded away. Today, few Sudanese realize that their country was Christian for nearly a thousand years.

The Western Sudan

For about 6,000 years, the Sahara was well watered, and substantial communities lived alongside its rivers and lakes. From about the third millennium BC, it began to dry up. Increasingly, it became uninhabitable, although people continued to live around the surviving oases.

The art of domesticating camels—first practiced in Arabia—spread across the Red Sea to inland Africa, and by the early years of the Christian era, had reached the Sahara. The introduction of camel

ANGEL MARTINEZ BERMEJO/SYGMA/AUSTRAL

transport revolutionized the economy. Camels could carry heavy loads over long distances, covering 30 to 40 kilometers (20 to 25 miles) a day without food or water. They could cross the desert without needing artificially constructed roads. Although there is archaeological evidence to suggest that there may perhaps have been trade across the Sahara at earlier periods, camel transport introduced regular, efficient long-distance trading of a completely new kind.

In the forest country of West Africa, there were large mineral deposits, and people here had been mining and working copper and iron for at least 500 years. Now, with camel transport available, they began extracting gold to exchange with traders who carried it northwards across the

MUSEUM OF MANKIND, LONDON/THE BRIDGEMAN ART LIBRARY

⦿ The main mosque at Jenne, in present-day Mali, has been rebuilt over the centuries, but it probably originally dates from the introduction of Islam, about the twelfth century AD.

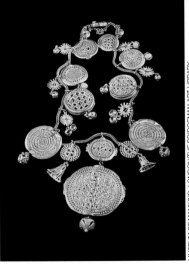

✪ Known as a *kuduo*, this brass container from the Asante kingdom, in modern-day Ghana, was used to hold valuables. *Kuduos* were sometimes buried with their owner after death.
MUSÉE ROYAL DE L'AFRIQUE CENTRALE/
WERNER FORMAN ARCHIVE

✪ This gold necklace, also from the Asante kingdom and now mounted on a European chain, was made using a method of casting known as the lost-wax technique.

Sahara. There is evidence of gold coins being minted in Roman North Africa in the third century AD, presumably from West African gold, and within three or four centuries, substantial quantities were being minted there.

When the Arabs conquered North Africa, there was a demand for an additional commodity: slaves, captured in the sub-Saharan countries and exported across the desert to supplement the traditional supply of slaves to the Mediterranean area from eastern Europe and central Asia. Much of the gold was re-exported from Muslim North Africa to Europe, which received most of its gold supply from West Africa until the sixteenth century. The slaves worked chiefly in North African households. Manufactured luxury goods were imported into West Africa in exchange for exports of mineral and slaves. Horses, too, were imported. Because disease makes them difficult to breed in West Africa, they were in great demand, revolutionizing warfare in the grassland countries. The volume of trans-Saharan trade increased steadily. Although often referred to as an "Arab trade", it was mostly conducted by Africans, particularly by Berber, Tuareg, and related Saharan peoples, and by the Mandinke peoples of the mid-Niger region.

The country south of the desert, stretching from the Nile to the Atlantic, was called in Arabic "Bilad-es-Sudan"—"The Land of the Blacks". Already, in the western Sudan, in the mid-region of the Niger Valley and westwards, people had

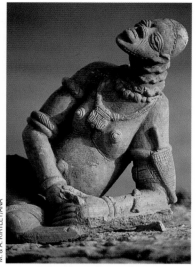

⚜ One of several terracotta figures of great beauty and complexity that have been excavated at Jenne, in present-day Mali. They cannot be properly studied by scholars, most of them having been smuggled out of Mali into private collections in Europe, but plainly, they date from before the period when Islam became the dominant religion.

⚜ Shaped like a horse and rider, this brass weight from the Asante kingdom, in modern-day Ghana, was used to weigh gold dust. Millions of these gold weights survive in museums and private collections around the world.

BRITISH MUSEUM/WERNER FORMAN ARCHIVE

M. & A. KIRTLEY/ANA

started living together in small, stone-built towns. With long-distance trade established, these towns could develop into market centers. Powerful individuals took control of the markets and turned the towns into kingdoms. Sometimes intruders from the desert took over, sometimes local people. In Ghana, the first kingdom to attract international attention, there was, according to tradition, at first a white (light-skinned, desert-based) ruling family, which was then superseded by a black ruling family.

Kumbi Saleh, identified as the capital of Ghana, was in what is now a desert region of modern-day Senegal (well north of modern-day Ghana). We have a description of this kingdom from an eighth-century AD Arab geographer. The king (by this period, black) presided in state in a palace within a walled city. He and his attendants, his horses, and even his dogs were decorated with gold ornaments. His revenue was drawn from customs duties on imports and exports, including salt, mined in the central Sahara and transported in blocks. He controlled the gold trade, deliberately restricting production to prevent inflation.

Ghana declined during the twelfth century AD, possibly as a result of warfare, but more likely because of the environmental deterioration of its heartland. The political and economic center shifted east to the market cities of the mid-Niger—Jenne, Timbuktu, and Gao—where the Mandinke people created the state of Mali. From this period, historians have narrative records they can turn to in the form of oral histories, both those translated into Arabic and written down by historians working in Timbuktu in the seventeenth century, and those still being recited in the twentieth century. Sunjata, the founder of Mali, was the hero of great epics. By the fourteenth century, Mali had become the dominant power, controlling territory southwards into the gold-producing forest country and westwards to the Atlantic, making it larger than any state in fourteenth-century Europe.

Through trade, Islam spread into the western Sudan. The long-distance traders were usually Muslims, finding in their religion a useful bond of commercial solidarity. The kings of Ghana kept their own religion. In Mali, however, they adopted Islam. Mansa Musa, the most famous king of Mali, made a spectacular pilgrimage to Mecca, traveling with a vast train of attendants and lavishing presents of gold on his way. But kings who became Muslims risked cutting themselves off from their subjects, whose daily way of life was closely tied to their religious observances. However unwillingly, kings had to go on performing the old rituals in order to retain their people's allegiance, and Islam remained the religion of a small minority.

Holding together an empire such as Mali (for so it may properly be called) depended very much on the personality of the rulers. If their power slackened, provinces would secede under new leaders, or the people would simply revert to their own community-based forms of government. By the fifteenth century, Mali was in decline, eclipsed by Songhai, a breakaway province, centered at Gao. Like Mali, Songhai had a great conquering hero, Sunni Ali. In his case, however, the historical record diverges. He alienated Muslim scholars and was remembered in their writings as a man of evil, but in popular epic he was a great warrior and a mighty magician.

The rulers of Songhai waged wars against the grassland peoples to the south, who grouped together into kingdoms of their own, including Mossi and Dagomba. Mossi horsemen raided the Niger cities and even sacked Timbuktu. The Songhai empire had also to be defended against attacks from the desert Tuareg. It remained the dominant power, however, until the end of the sixteenth century.

Southeast of the Niger bend, the walled cities built by the Hausa people (of modern-day Nigeria) attracted long-distance traders and grew into commercial centers. By the fifteenth century, they had developed into (by tradition) seven kingdoms. Eastwards, around Lake Chad, was the kingdom of Kanem (later enlarged as Borno), founded in the eleventh century by a member of the Sefuwa family. This family reigned until it was displaced by a usurping ruler in 1846—one of the longest-reigning royal dynasties in the world.

West African Forest Country

Much of what we know of the early history of the West African forest kingdoms comes from archaeological work concentrated on Nigeria, which began intensively only in the 1940s. The most spectacular find has been a royal burial dated to the ninth century AD at Igbo-Ukwu, west of the Niger, in Igbo country. The burial contained regalia worked with sculptural techniques of greater sophistication than anything found in ninth-century Europe. Locally mined metal alloys were used, showing that the people had their own way of processing metals as well as sculpting them. The burial also contained thousands of imported glass beads, indicating that the kingdom was linked to the trans-Sahara trade network. Nothing more is known of it. Today, the Igbo peoples have no tradition of centralized monarchy—although the Igbo language contains many words that describe its trappings. One might infer that, at some later period, they renounced their kings and returned to their former loosely organized political systems, which they retained until the twentieth century.

West of the Niger, in Yoruba country, kingdoms were established by about 1000 AD. Yoruba history has been confused by myths invented in the nineteenth century to confer prestige, alleging ancestral migration from Arabia or Egypt. The archaeological and linguistic

Central and Southern Africa

Most of Africa south of the equator is inhabited by peoples who speak one of the many Bantu languages. Linguists and archaeologists have pieced together the story of their movements. From a homeland in the country between the Benue River and Lake Chad (in modern-day Nigeria and Cameroon), they began moving out in small groups about 3,000 years ago and gradually expanded over the continent, reaching the Indian Ocean coast of the present-day Republic of South Africa about the fourth century AD.

They used iron tools and lived by farming. They also kept cattle when the environment was suitable. They settled in small, scattered villages, and when a village grew too large, some inhabitants would move away to form a new village. There was a pattern of dispersed settlement, unlike the heavy urban conglomerations of West Africa, where the soil and vegetation allowed more intensive cultivation and high population densities. Even when kingdoms formed, the royal capitals were smaller and less permanent than the West African capital cities.

Individuals as well as communities moved about. Many royal traditions relate how a stranger arrived, alone or with followers, and persuaded or forced people to accept his rule. Or a cluster of adjacent villages might come together for protection and eventually be formed into one unit by a powerful leader. The traditions of the Kuba people of modern-day Zaire relate how two rival contestants and their followers strove for power, the victor founding the Kuba kingdom. Here, later on in the eighteenth century, sculptors carved a series of wooden portrait statues to commemorate their founder kings.

NATIONAL MUSEUM OF DENMARK

⚜ A decorated ivory cup from Sierra Leone, carved from an elephant's tusk in the fifteenth century AD.

evidence, however, points to long, continuous occupation by the same peoples. Tradition gives primacy among the Yoruba kings to the *oni* (king) of Ife. Archaeologists working at Ife have discovered a magnificent series of royal portrait busts, dating from the eleventh or twelfth century, which bear witness to an elaborate court life. In these Yoruba kingdoms, a powerful secret society (*ogboni*) survived, a relic of the pre-royal past.

In Benin, in the Niger delta, royal tradition dates the present royal family back to the fourteenth century, when it was said to have superseded an earlier family. Archaeologists date the first urban occupation of Benin to about a century earlier. A great period of building followed in the fifteenth century, when the city was rebuilt with a new street plan and a city wall enclosing about 1,400 square kilometers (540 square miles). Here, as at Ife, bronze-casters worked at the royal court, making portrait busts of the kings and queens. Sculptors also worked in ivory. During the British occupation of 1897, much of the vast royal treasure was looted and scattered over museums in Europe and America.

West of the Yoruba kingdoms, in the gold-producing forest country of present-day Ghana, the Akan peoples were linked to the Niger cities through regular trading routes. Here, too, small states arose. East of the Niger River, in the inland grassland country of modern Cameroon—an area of great linguistic diversity, which suggests long occupation by the same peoples—kingdoms developed among the Bamenda and Bamilike peoples.

⚜ This bronze portrait head of an *oni* (king) of Ife, is one of a magnificent series from the eleventh or twelfth century discovered in Yoruba country, in modern-day Nigeria.

ANCIENT ART & ARCHITECTURE COLLECTION

♀ Of intricate design, this velvet pile cloth was woven from raffia in Kuba country, in modern-day Zaire. Such cloths were worn by important people and were highly cherished. Traders carried them over long distances.

E. ANSPACH COLLECTION, NEW YORK/WERNER FORMAN ARCHIVE

⮡ "Great Zimbabwe" is the most famous and extensive of the stone palaces called "zimbabwes", which were built from about the tenth century AD.

TOM NEBBIA/ASPECT PICTURE LIBRARY

⚲ The doorway of "Great Zimbabwe". The palace walls were built using a dry-stone technique, the granite blocks shaped and laid without the use of mortar.

ROBERT HARDING PICTURE LIBRARY

As elsewhere, mineral resources provided an exploitable base for royal wealth. In the coastal forest kingdom of Loango (in modern-day Zaire), and in the Kongo kingdom southeast of it, copper was mined and exported over long distances with other commodities, including sea salt and a special kind of cloth woven from fiber. Long-distance trade brought wealth to rulers. The Luba and Lunda kingdoms of the central grassland country around the headwaters of the Zaire and Zambezi rivers grew powerful through controlling trade.

There were vast deposits of copper under the grasslands (later known as the Copperbelt), and also gold. Here, royal burials dating from the sixth to the tenth centuries AD have been found, containing fine copper ornaments. Copper, which can be burnished to a beautiful surface, tended to be used for personal body decoration. At Mapungubwe, in the Transvaal, just over the border of the present-day Republic of South Africa, small gold sculptures have been found in royal graves.

There was also an export market for gold. In central Africa, mined gold and alluvial gold washed from the riverbeds was transported down the Zambezi River for export to countries along the Indian Ocean coast. Sofala, on the seacoast (in modern-day Mozambique), became the main export emporium. Eastern commodities, including Chinese porcelain and Asian beads, were imported in exchange, and are found in royal burials. Thus, there were two unconnected gold trade routes from Africa: from the West African deposits northwards across the Sahara to Europe, and from the south central African deposits eastwards to the countries of the Indian Ocean.

Much of the central African gold lay far below the surface, inaccessible to miners working with iron picks. So the rulers here derived far less wealth from gold than those in West Africa. The real wealth of those who ruled the grassland plateau country around the Zambezi lay in cattle. Cattle were a political as well as an economic asset; those who had power distributed cattle to their dependants. But cattle-based states tend to be unstable, since herds can easily be rustled away by rivals, and a long series of successive kingdoms rose and fell in the Zambezi region.

From about the tenth century AD, people began building large stone buildings called "zimbabwes" for their kings, siting them away from land where the tsetse fly, which infects cattle fatally with trypanosomiasis, breeds. About 150 survive today as ruins (many having been demolished in the nineteenth and twentieth centuries by Europeans looking for gold). Over the centuries, the building styles became more sophisticated. The most famous and extensive of these palaces is "Great Zimbabwe", from which the Republic of Zimbabwe took its name. It was built over a period of 200 years and formed a vast elliptical enclosure, with high granite walls ornamented with soapstone sculptures. People no longer lived there after the middle of the fifteenth century, probably because the soil had become eroded by overintensive cultivation for the royal court, but it continued to be used as a religious shrine. Other "zimbabwes" continued to be built elsewhere over succeeding centuries, notably at Khami, although none on the scale of "Great Zimbabwe".

East African Kingdoms

Peoples who spoke Bantu languages settled around the Great Lakes. Here, the development of kingdoms has often been seen as part of a regular pattern, as warlike cattle-keeping peoples from the vast swampy region to the north (the Sudd) invaded and, as conquerors, lorded it over the sedentary lakeside farmers. This is a misleading oversimplification, however. While some of the first state-builders were invaders from the north, notably the Luo people, others were of local origin. Pastoralists did not necessarily wield power over those who cultivated crops. The Luo, originally a cattle people, eventually settled down and cultivated the soil. Historians have studied the oral genealogies of the Great Lakes kingdoms, which record the names of the successive kings. By assigning notional life-spans, they have constructed a rough chronology, which indicates that most of the states were founded in the thirteenth and fourteenth centuries AD. One date is more precise. The traditions of the Nyoro kingdom record that during the reign of the fifth *mukama* (king), the sun was darkened. This solar eclipse would have been visible in the region in 1520. Moving five reigns back gives a probable date for the first *mukama* in the fifteenth century.

As elsewhere, powerful individuals and their followers took power by persuasion or force. In some, notably the Nyoro and Nkore kingdoms (in modern-day Uganda), the kings and ruling families formed a hereditary elite, marrying only among themselves. They maintained a strict social distance from their subordinates, whose lower status was deliberately emphasized and acted out in daily living. In neighboring Buganda, social relations were rather more relaxed. There, the *kabaka* (king) took a wife from each clan, integrating the monarchy into the lineage system and making his subjects his relatives.

East of the Great Lakes, people retained their loosely organized political systems. Towards the coast, the land turns to arid semidesert, called the Nyika, which forms a wide barrier between the lakeside country and the sea. Although people ventured across it from the interior to the coast, there is evidence to show that no coastal traders traveled inland. No imported goods are found in the royal burials in the lakeside kingdoms before the eighteenth century.

The Bantu-speaking peoples who settled along the Indian Ocean coast had opportunities for overseas trade with seaborne traders from Arabia and the Persian Gulf. The trading towns that developed there are often described inaccurately as "Arab colonies". This is a misnomer, because there was no colonizing power in Arabia at this time. Arabs came in as individual traders, and although they were allowed to settle in the coastal towns and marry (since they did not usually bring their own wives), they lived there under the rule

of the existing governments. In time, the two populations merged, helped by the diffusion of Islam, which had become the prevailing religion by at least the fourteenth century AD. A distinctive coastal language developed in the form of Swahili, a Bantu language strongly influenced by Arabic.

About 40 city-states grew up along the East African coast, including Malindi, Mombasa, Kilwa, and Zanzibar. They were filled with mosques of a distinctive local style, palaces, and merchants' houses, built of locally worked coral. Their wealth came from trade—exports of ivory, which was in great demand in India and China, and other local commodities, and also gold shipped north from Sofala. They stretched out along a thousand or so kilometers of coast, each politically independent and in commercial rivalry with the others. So when the Portuguese invaded in 1498, there was no concerted resistance, and one after another, they were looted and conquered.

African Kingdoms by AD 1500

By AD 1500, much of Africa was under the control of centralized, royal governments, although large numbers of people still chose to live under their own noncentralized form of government. The kingdoms had some common features—for instance, constitutional checks on royal power and social mechanisms to restrict the accumulation of individual wealth. Each kingdom had evolved in its own distinctive way, however, with its own particular political constitution and rituals, its own forms of economic and financial organization and policy, and its own characteristic styles of art and music.

GEOFF TOMPKINSON/ASPECT PICTURE LIBRARY

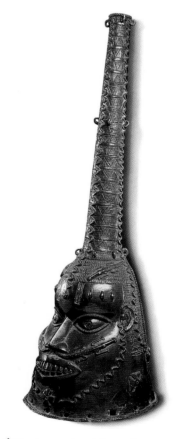

In common with other cities on the East African coast, the ancient port of Suakin has buildings constructed from blocks of coral.

The bronze headpiece of a ceremonial mask from the Benin kingdom, in modern-day Nigeria.
BRITISH MUSEUM/THE BRIDGEMAN ART LIBRARY

⚘ The royal cemetery at Meroë was in use from about 300 BC until the fourth century AD. Some chapels and small pyramids have been restored in recent times.

MEROË: CAPITAL OF A PROSPEROUS KINGDOM

ROBERT G. MORKOT

Meroë flourished for more than a thousand years as one of the two major centers of a state that at its greatest extent (between 710 BC and 664 BC) stretched from the Mediterranean to the south of modern-day Khartoum, in the Sudan. It was well placed to control the fertile savanna land of the central Sudan, and the routes by which its precious commodities—notably ivory, ebony, and incense—traveled north to Egypt.

The name Meroë first occurs in the second half of the fifth century BC, in

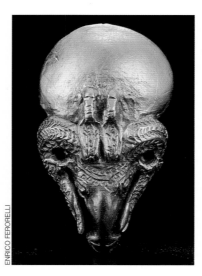

⚘ An earring from Meroë depicting a ram's head with a solar disk.

both indigenous Kushite texts and the writings of the Greek historian Herodotus. Archaeological remains, however, have been dated to as early as the seventh century BC, and there may have been a major center here, or in the vicinity, as early as the second millennium BC. The town and cemeteries were in continuous use until the fourth century AD, the town flourishing particularly in the third century BC and first century AD, when economic contacts with Egypt were strong.

The Town Site

The town site of Meroë covers an
area of approximately 1,000 meters
by 1,000 meters (3,300 feet by
3,300 feet). It remains largely
unexcavated, with the exception of
the royal compound, a large, stone-
walled enclosure. This "Royal
City", with the adjacent religious
center, may have been separated
from northern and southern
"suburbs" by branches of the river.
The stone wall encloses an area of
about 200 meters by 400 meters
(650 feet by 1,300 feet) and was
probably built in the third century
BC, since the excavators noted
Greek masons' marks.

Some of the buildings may be
considerably older. Two-story
buildings lined a broad street on the
north-south axis, and there were
signs of rebuilding over a long
period. An extraordinary structure
in the southwest of the enclosure

THE KINGDOM OF MEROË

At its greatest extent, between 710 BC
and 664 BC, the kingdom of Meroë
stretched from the Mediterranean to
the south of modern-day Khartoum,
in the Sudan.
CARTOGRAPHY: RAY SIM

This gold sheath, with its delicate
engravings of winged goddesses and
relief decoration of sacred cobras,
ram's heads, and papyrus plants,
probably held a rolled papyrus bearing
protective spells.
ENRICO FERORELLI

The so-called "Roman kiosk" at
Naqa, an important royal and religious
city south of Meroë, was a resting
place for statues carried in procession.
The style of the kiosk shows the
influence in Egypt of Alexandria's
Hellenistic architecture. It was probably
built in the late first century AD, but the
date is uncertain.

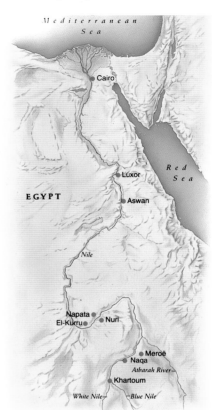

ENRICO FERORELLI

ENRICO FERORELLI

⊛ A painted decoration in the tomb of a king's mother in the earliest of the royal cemeteries, el-Kurru, dating from about 660 BC. The scene is from Egyptian funerary literature.

♀ This bronze head of the Roman emperor Augustus was taken from a statue in the Egyptian frontier town of Aswan, which was attacked by the Meroitic armies about 24 BC, during a war with Rome. It was discovered buried beneath a victory temple in the city of Meroë.

WERNER FORMAN ARCHIVE

⊛ The lion-headed god Apedemak was the most important indigenous god of the Meroitic pantheon, standing alongside the Egyptian god Amun. Apedemak was a solar and warrior god—here depicted carrying a military standard. He was also a god of vegetation.

♀ This pair of gold tweezers is one of three from the grave of King Aspelta, who was buried about 580 BC.
ENRICO FERORELLI

ROBERT CAPUTO/AURORA

was almost certainly a water sanctuary. Called "The Roman Bath" by the excavators, it featured a deep, open water tank, fed by a complex of pipes. Painted scenes and glazed tiles decorated the walls of the room, and stuccoed and painted sculptures lined the edges of the tank. The architecture and decoration were derived from Egyptian, Hellenistic, and Roman models, as well as typically Meroitic styles, pointing to influences on the court culture of the first century BC and first century AD. There was also a small chapel with painted walls within the "Royal City". Beneath its floor was a magnificent, larger than life-size head of the Roman emperor Augustus, probably buried ceremonially after being brought from the Aswan region during the conflict between Meroë and the Romans about 20 BC.

The main temple at Meroë, dedicated to the Egyptian god Amun, adjoined the palace enclosure. Built on an east-west axis, it was a massive building of brick and stone, 120 meters (400 feet) long. Little survives of the scenes depicted in the relief sculpture, painted columns, and tiled floors that originally decorated the temple. A ceremonial way extended to the east from the main entrance. This was lined with granite rams as far as a small, pillared resting place for the processional statues, and continued eastwards, flanked by other temples. There is some reason to think that the Amun temple originally (in the seventh to sixth centuries BC) faced a branch of the Nile, and was enlarged—the processional way extended, and new temples built—at a time when the river channel had dried up (perhaps in the first century AD).

Although the main religious district was in the center of the town, other temples have been located, the most important being the "Sun Temple", so named by the excavators after Herodotus's description of a "Table of the Sun" outside the city walls. Probably built by King Aspelta in the early sixth century BC, it was rebuilt in the late first century BC. The temple itself consists of a chapel with a towered gateway standing on a platform in the center of a colonnaded court. Some fragmentary remains of relief sculpture show that the original decoration was largely military, possibly connected with the royal cult. Blue-glazed tiles cover the floor and walls of the sanctuary itself.

PICTUREPOINT LTD

The colonnade of the temple of Musawwarat es-Sufra, an important Meroitic temple in the savanna of the central Sudan. Musawwarat seems to have been a place where the king was crowned and also, perhaps, hunted elephants. Although elaborately decorated, the columns carry no royal names. The temple was probably built about 300 BC.

ROBERT CAPUTO/AURORA

The flat-topped sacred mountain of Gebel Barkal rises 90 meters (300 feet) high, near the fourth Nile cataract. An enormous temple to the ram-god Amun was built here about 700 BC.

This gold ewer was found in the tomb of King Aspelta, who ruled in the early sixth century BC at Nuri, on the opposite bank of the Nile to Gebel Barkal. Nuri was the main royal cemetery from the mid-seventh century BC until about 300 BC, when it was superseded by Meroë.

ENRICO FERORELLI

Cemeteries for the Elite

Three elite cemeteries lie to the east of the town: the northern and southern cemeteries are situated on sandstone ridges; the western one, on the plain.

The southern cemetery contains more than 200 graves. The earliest, from the twenty-fifth dynasty (seventh to sixth centuries BC), are mainly pit burials, but there are also mastaba tombs (with sloping sides and a flat roof) and pyramid tombs. Some members of the royal family were buried here, although at this early date, the kings and major royal women were buried near Napata, at el-Kurru, and Nuri.

The west cemetery, consisting of about 500 graves, contains some pyramid tombs, but none of these appears to belong to a ruler.

The north cemetery was the main burial place of rulers from the mid-third century BC. These pyramid tombs have small funerary chapels attached and are mostly built of local sandstone, although some of the latest are of mudbrick. The body was buried in a rock-cut chamber beneath the pyramid.

The pyramids have rather steep angles, resembling the pyramids of private tombs in Egypt rather than the royal pyramids of the Old and Middle Kingdoms. Styles changed at different periods, some being smooth-faced and others slightly stepped. Although badly plundered, the cemeteries have yielded large quantities of objects, including many fine pieces imported from the Mediterranean world.

acropolis
The citadel of an ancient Greek city. The best-known example is the citadel of Athens (the Acropolis), where a number of temples were erected in the fifth century BC.

agora
The public square and marketplace in an ancient Greek city.

Amphora

amphora
A pottery jar used to hold liquids, especially wine, and to store other substances, such as resin. Amphoras were made in various ovoid shapes throughout the Aegean and eastern Mediterranean regions.

archaeozoology
The study of animal remains, often bones, from the past and of the impact of animals on past economies. Also called zooarchaeology.

aryballos
A small, one-handled pottery flask, about 5 to 8 centimeters (2 to 3 inches) high, used for scented oil and perfume, and also for some condiments. Originally made at Corinth from about 575 BC, such jars with painted patterns on them were typical for the period until about 550 BC.

Austronesian language family
Austronesian is a major language family to which the languages of Taiwan, the islands of Southeast Asia, the Pacific (excluding much of New Guinea), Madagascar, and parts of the Southeast Asian mainland belong. Although all Austronesian languages are related, they are not necessarily mutually understandable.

barbican
An outer defense to a fort or settlement, often built as a tower over a gateway.

boat grave
A type of burial during the Late Iron Age in which the body or cremated remains were

placed in a boat, which was then covered by a mound of earth. Boat graves are found in Scandinavia, and in East Anglia, in Britain. They were particularly common between AD 550 and AD 800.

bracteate
A thin, ornamental dish or plate made of gold or silver.

Brahmin
A member of the highest, or priestly, caste in the Hindu caste system.

Bronze Age
A prehistoric period in the Old World, defined by the use of bronze as a new material for tools, weapons, and ornaments. In Europe, the Bronze Age proper spans the second and early first millennia BC.

caliphate
An Islamic empire ruled by a caliph. The title "caliph" means successor, and was adopted by the rulers of the Islamic world, who were seen as the successors of Mohammed. The caliph was the leader of all Muslims in both spiritual and civic matters.

Canopic vase

canopic vase
A container with a lid in the shape of an animal-headed god, used in ancient Egypt to hold the entrails of an embalmed body.

carnelian
A reddish variety of the semiprecious gemstone chalcedony, much favored in antiquity for jewelry. Carnelian is usually found in volcanic rocks, such as the Deccan Traps of western India (where it is particularly common). Heating improves the color.

Cham
An Austronesian language, closely related to the languages of island Southeast Asia, that was formerly widely spoken in central Vietnam and is still spoken in parts of the Southeast Asian mainland. Cham was probably spoken by the people of Vietnam's Sa-Huynh culture, a late prehistoric Iron

Age culture, which formed a series of powerful kingdoms until it was overthrown by the Vietnamese in the fifteenth century AD.

chamber tomb
A type of tomb found in the Aegean region in which the burial place, consisting of one or more room-sized chambers, was at the end of a horizontal or sloping passage cut into the ground, usually into a hillside. Chamber tombs were usually family tombs, and were reused over the generations.

chape
The mounting at the upper end of a scabbard, which has a ring for attaching the scabbard to a belt.

cist grave
A burial place made of large slabs of rock, especially slate, schist, or granite. The name comes from the Greek word *kiste*, meaning chest or box.

city-state
An independent, self-governing city. The city-state usually incorporated the territory surrounding the city, as well as smaller towns and villages. In ancient Greece, the city-state was called a polis.

Classical Age
The period in history that encompasses the Greek and Roman civilizations.

composite bow
An archer's bow in which the wood of the bow was reinforced on one side by layers of animal sinew and on the other side by animal horn. It was more powerful than a simple bow made of a single piece of wood only.

Confucianism
A system of ethics that follows the teachings of the Chinese philosopher Confucius (Kung Fu-tzu). It emphasizes an idealized human society governed by worthy, educated leaders, in which individuals are loyal to their family and friends, and treat each other as they would like to be treated.

Coptic language
The most recent stage of the language of ancient Egypt. It was used by the Egyptian Christians, and was written in the Greek alphabet with the addition of six letters derived from the Demotic script (the most recent and cursive of the scripts of ancient Egypt).

crater
A large bowl made of pottery or metal. In ancient Greece, craters were used to serve wine, mixed with water in varying proportions, into individual drinking cups—for example, at the all-male drinking parties known as symposia.

crucible smelting
A technique of separating copper from ore by heating the ore in an open vessel (designed to withstand very high temperatures) rather than in a closed furnace.

cuneiform script
A system of writing that developed in Mesopotamia. By means of a square-ended reed, wedge-shaped pictograms were impressed into the smooth surface of wet clay tablets, which were then baked. Cuneiform scripts were used in particular for the Sumerian, Akkadian, Elamite, and Old Persian languages. The oldest examples of developed cuneiform script date from about 2500 BC. The name comes from the Latin word *cuneus*, meaning wedge.

Dasas
The inhabitants of northwestern India at the time of the Indo-European migrations. They are described in the Rig-Veda as having dark faces and snub noses, unintelligible speech, and no religion, but living in fortified cities and being very rich. The Dasas are often identified with the inhabitants of the towns of the Indus Valley culture.

Delphic Oracle
A seer at the Temple of Apollo at Delphi, in Greece. The oracle played an important political role, particularly during the period of Greek colonization from the eighth to sixth century BC.

diadem
A crown or band of metal worn as a badge of status or office.

dolmen
The French term for a megalithic tomb with a single capstone carried by orthostats (or standing stones).

Dongson drum

Dongson drum
A type of cast-bronze drum, usually large, made in northern Vietnam and southern China in the first millennium BC and used for warfare and rain-making ceremonies. The drums are named after the site of Dongson, in Than Hoa province, Vietnam, where they were first found in an archaeological context.

Doric order
One of the architectural orders of ancient Greece, characterized in particular by simple columns and a frieze of triglyphs and metopes.

Dravidian language family
Dravidian is a language family spoken in southern India to which the Tamil, Telegu, Malayalam, and Karmada languages belong. It is thought to have been spoken in northern India before the spread of Indo-European languages in the second millennium BC, and was probably the main language of the Harappans.

einkorn
A variety of wheat with pale red kernels, *Triticum monococcum*, which was cultivated in Neolithic times. It probably originated in southeastern Europe and southwestern Asia, and is still grown in mountainous parts of southern Europe as grain for horses.

emmer
A variety of wheat, *Triticum dicoccum*, which has been cultivated in the Mediterranean region since Neolithic times, and is still grown in mountainous parts of southern Europe as a cereal crop and livestock food. It is thought to be the ancestor of many other varieties of wheat.

faience
Bronze Age faience is a primitive form of glass. It is made by baking a mixture of sand and clay to a temperature at which the surface fuses into blue or green glass. Faience beads of Aegean and southwestern Asian origin were traded widely in eastern and central Europe, Italy, and the British Isles in the second millennium BC.

feudal system
A hierarchical social system in which the peasantry was ruled by a class of landowners.

Fibula

ILLUSTRATIONS: KEN RINKEL

fibula
A metal fastener or brooch, used much like a modern safety-pin by many Iron Age and later Europeans, including the Greeks, Etruscans, and Romans. Although primarily functional, fibulas were often also highly decorated items of personal adornment.

freeholders
Members of the peasantry who owned the small plots of land they farmed. Italian freeholders were the main source of recruitment to the Roman army during the period of the Roman Republic.

funerary cult
The ongoing rituals, with their associated offerings, performed for the benefit of the deceased at the tomb or in a funerary temple, by relatives or specially appointed priests.

garrison state
A fortified state established in a strategic position. The garrison states of the Zhou feudalistic network were protected by walled cities, and ruled by the kinsmen and allies through marriage of the Zhou royal house.

Geometric period
A period in Greece between 900 BC and 700 BC, named after a distinctive style of pottery decorated solely with geometric designs, including circles, squares, triangles, meandering lines, zigzags, and rhombic shapes.

greave
A piece of armor designed to protect the lower part of the leg.

Hallstatt period
A cultural period of the Late Bronze Age and Early Iron Age in central Europe, divided into four phases, Hallstatt A, B, C, and D. The period of Hallstatt A and B (from about 1200 BC to about 800 BC), also known as the Urnfield period, was characterized by the burial practice of placing the cremated remains of the dead in clay urns, which were then buried. Hallstatt C (from about 800 BC to 600 BC) marks the beginning of the transition from the Bronze Age to the Iron Age. The Hallstatt period is named after a site in Austria. It precedes the La Tène period.

Helladic culture
The culture of central and southern mainland Greece in the Bronze Age (3000 BC to 1100 BC).

Hellenistic period
The era between the death of Alexander the Great (323 BC) and the rise of the Roman Empire (27 BC), when a single, uniform civilization, based on Greek traditions, prevailed all over the ancient world, from India, in the east, to Spain, in the west.

helot
A serf or slave in ancient Sparta.

hero cult
In ancient Greece, the worship of a god of partly human and partly divine origin, such as the worship of the hero Hercules. Hero-cult worship was the forerunner of the worship of living rulers, a feature of Hellenistic and Roman times.

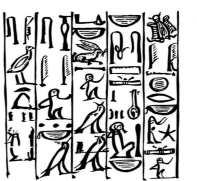
Hieroglyphs

hieroglyphs
The pictographic script used in ancient Egypt. Many of the symbols consist of a conventionalized picture of the idea or object they represent.

hypostyle
A building in which the roof or ceiling is supported by columns.

iconography
The art of representing or illustrating by means of pictures, images, or figures.

ideogram
A pictorial symbol representing a concept or idea directly, rather than standing for its name or the sequence of sounds that make up its name. Ideograms were often used in early writing systems.

intaglio
Incised carving (as opposed to relief carving), in which the design is sunk below the surface of hard stone or metal.

Ionic order
One of the architectural orders of ancient Greece, characterized in particular by column heads with spiral coils on each side.

Iron Age
A late prehistoric period in the Old World, defined by the use of iron as the main material for tools and weapons.

iron-making, direct process
The technique of smelting iron ore in a furnace with charcoal and limestone to produce a spongy, low-carbon form of iron known as a bloom. This is a ductile material, which can then be forged into tools and weapons.

iron-making, indirect process
The technique of smelting iron ore in a furnace at a very high temperature to yield a molten, high-carbon form of iron. Because the high-carbon content makes this material too brittle for most direct uses, it must undergo a secondary process, oxidization, to make it more ductile. It can then be forged into weapons and tools. The indirect process of iron-making was developed in China early in the first millennium BC.

Jainism
An ascetic sect founded in northern India in the sixth century BC in reaction to the rigid Vedic Hindu caste system. Jainism developed alongside Buddhism, with similar doctrines, but emphasized withdrawal from the world.

***Karoshti* script**
One of the two main early Indian scripts, used from the fourth century BC to between the third and fourth centuries AD. It may have developed from the Aramaic used by the Achaemenid rulers of northwestern India and was particularly common in that region and along the Ganges Valley as far as Bengal. The name *Karoshti* literally means asses' lips, and is said to refer to the similarity of the highly curvilinear script to the movement of asses' lips.

Khmer
An ethnolinguistic group who speak a language that is part of the Mon–Khmer group of Austro-Asiatic languages. The Khmer are best known for the art and architecture of the ancient city of Angkor, dating from the ninth to the fourteenth centuries AD. Today, the Khmer are found mostly in Cambodia, and in northeastern Thailand and southern Vietnam.

knapping
A technique of striking flakes or blades from a hard, brittle rock, such as flint or obsidian, by means of short, sharp blows delivered with a hammer of stone, bone, or wood. Knapping was used to fashion stone tools and weapons, such as blades and arrowheads, and in the Harappan culture of the Indus Valley was also applied to making beads from agate and carnelian.

kurgan
The Russian term for a burial mound, most often used in connection with the nomad cultures of southern Russia and the Ukraine from the fourth millennium BC onwards.

La Tène period
A cultural period of the Iron Age in central Europe lasting from about 500 BC until the Roman conquest of Gaul, in about 50 BC. It is named after a site in Switzerland.

lapis lazuli
A semiprecious stone much prized by the Sumerians and other ancient peoples for use in jewelry and other decorative items. It is found in northern Afghanistan and Iran.

latifundia
Large agricultural estates owned by the Roman upper classes and usually worked by slaves. The first *latifundia* were created in Italy towards the end of the Roman Republic. They were common throughout the western part of the empire in the early centuries of the first millennium AD.

Linear A script

The system of writing used in Minoan Crete from the early palace period (1900 BC to 1700 BC) until about 1400 BC. A syllabic script, it is found most often inscribed on clay tablets (in the form of economic records) and on religious vessels made of stone.

Linear B script

The system of writing used in Mycenaean Greece. Like Linear A, it is a syllabic script and was probably created in Crete in the late fifteenth century BC by adding many signs to the existing Linear A signs. It is known chiefly from Knossos, on Crete, from Pylos, in Mycenae, and from Tiryns and Thebes, on the Greek mainland. The script is found most often inscribed on clay tablets, but also on terracotta jars that were traded throughout the Aegean region. Linear B was the writing system used for the economic administration of the Mycenaean kingdoms.

loess

A loamy deposit consisting of fine particles of windblown soil, laid down during the Ice Age. Loess forms a fertile and easily worked soil.

lost-wax casting

A method of casting complex forms, such as statuary. The object is modeled in wax and then surrounded by a clay mold. When the clay is heated, the wax melts and drains away, leaving a hollow space that can be filled with molten metal.

Mahavamsa

The most important historical and religious book of Sri Lanka. Written between the second century BC and the first century AD, it records the arrival of the Indo-European-speaking Sihalas in the fifth century BC and the conversion of Sri Lanka to Buddhism in the third century BC.

mandala

In Tantric Hinduism and Buddhism, a design, usually circular, symbolizing the universe and used as an aid to religious meditation. Although mandalas are commonly two-dimensional, such as the Tibetan *tanka* (cloth scroll painting), three-dimensional examples also exist, notably the monument of Borobudur, in Indonesia, dating from the ninth century AD .

Mandala

mastaba

In ancient Egypt during the Old Kingdom, a flat-roofed, rectangular structure, housing an offering chapel, built over a deep shaft that contained a burial chamber or burial chambers. The word comes from the Arabic for bench, and was used by Egyptian workers during mid-nineteenth-century excavations because of the similarity in appearance of the mastabas to oblong benches.

mausoleum

The original mausoleum was the gigantic tomb of Maussollos, ruler of Caria, in Southwest Asia Minor, from 377 BC to 353 BC. It was considered one of the seven wonders of the ancient world. The word later came to be used for any tomb built on a monumental scale.

megalithic monument

A funerary or commemorative monument built from exceptionally large stones. Its name comes from the Greek words *megas* (large) and *lithos* (stone).

megaron

The architectural unit that forms the main hall of a Mycenaean house or the central block of a Mycenaean palace. It is rectangular in plan and comprises a main room, sometimes with a central circular hearth, that is accessed through one or two outer rooms.

Menhirs

menhir

A standing stone, most often referred to in a megalithic context.

metope

In the Doric architectural order, the square panel between the triglyphs of the frieze.

mobile

The settlement pattern of social groups who move from place to place within a given territory, building camps at each site.

Mon kingdom

The name often applied to the area of distribution in Burma (Myanmar) and Thailand of the earliest known examples of images of the Buddha. The images, in stone, terracotta, and stucco, date from between the sixth century AD and the thirteenth century AD and share a common style, called Dvaravati. There is little evidence, however, of a unified kingdom corresponding to the geographical spread of Dvaravati objects.

Mongol

The Mongol, or Yuan, dynasty (AD 1279 to AD 1368) was established by Kublai Khan, the grandson of Genghis Khan. Its rule was short, but powerful. In the early years of the dynasty, in the course of a military campaign aimed at bringing southern China under their control, Mongol armies invaded and sacked the Burmese capital at Pagan.

monotheism

The belief or doctrine that there is only one god.

nation-state

A political unit consisting of a number diverse cities and their hinterlands, organized into a single state with a unified set of laws and system of government.

necropolis

A burial site or cemetery, often near a town.

Neolithic

Literally, the "New Stone Age". The term refers to the final phase of the Stone Age, when farming became an essential part of the economy.

nomadic

A term used by ethnographers to describe the movements of whole social groups of pastoralists who utilize different parts of a given territory in different seasons, usually summer and winter pastures, and build camps for those periods.

nomarch

In ancient Egypt, a provincial governor.

obsidian

A black, glassy volcanic rock often used to make sharp-edged tools.

oligarchy

A system of government in which the state is ruled by a small clique of wealthy people.

oppidum

A fortified Celtic town that had residential, industrial, market, and administrative functions.

oracle-bone inscriptions

During the Shang dynasty, inscriptions recording predictions, made on dried turtle shell or animal bone. The shells or bones were heated with burning grass to produce patterns of cracks, which were interpreted by a diviner, and the prediction revealed by each pattern inscribed beside it. The writing system used for oracle-bone inscriptions is a prototype of modern written Chinese.

paleobotany

The study of ancient plants from fossil remains and other evidence, such as vegetable materials, preserved by charring, desiccation, or in waterlogged deposits. Paleobotany provides information about the climate and environment and about materials available for food, fuel, tools, and shelter.

Paleolithic

Literally, the "Old Stone Age". It began some two million to three million years ago with the emergence of humans and the earliest forms of chipped stone tools, and continued through the Pleistocene Ice Age until the retreat of the glaciers some 12,000 years ago. The Paleolithic is equivalent to the Stone Age in sub-Saharan Africa.

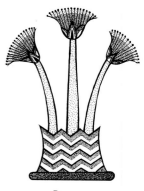

Papyrus

papyrus

A reed, *Cyperus papyrus*, found in the Mediterranean region and northern Africa, especially Egypt. Its stems, when split open, flattened out, and pasted together in two layers, formed a writing material that was easily made, flexible, and portable. The stems were also bound together to make lightweight fishing skiffs. The fan-shaped flower spray of the papyrus was a popular decorative motif in the art of ancient Egypt.

patrician

A member of the highest level of the hereditary aristocracy during the time of the Roman Republic.

pictogram

A picture or symbol that represents a word or group of words. Also called pictograph.

plebeian

A member of the freeborn, commoner class during the time of the Roman Republic.

polis

A city-state in ancient Greece.

Ptolemaic Egypt

Egypt during the Hellenistic era, when it was ruled by the dynasty of the Macedonian general Ptolemy I (323 BC to 283 BC) and his descendants.

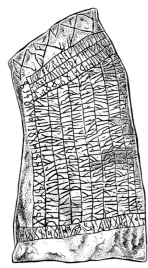
Rune stone

rune stone
A memorial stone with inscriptions of runes, a northern European script believed to have been developed in the fourth century AD. Rune stones from the Viking period are found throughout Scandinavia.

saddle quern
The earliest-known example of milling equipment, invented in Neolithic times. It consisted of a large, slightly concave, lower stone and a smaller upper stone. Grain spread on the surface of the lower stone was ground by being rubbed over with the upper stone.

Sanskrit
The most important early Indo-European language of northern India. For several centuries, it was the medium for much Hindu and Buddhist religious writing. Sanskrit is related to Greek and Latin.

Sed festival
In ancient Egypt, a festival marking the first 30 years of a king's reign, when the gods of the land, in the form of their cult images, came together in the capital to perform a ritual renewal of the powers of the king. Some elements of the ceremony repeat those of the coronation, others are a test of the king's physical strength.

Seleucid
A dynasty of Greek rulers descended from Seleucus I, a general under Alexander the Great, who lived from about 358 BC to 281 BC. From the fourth century BC to the first century BC, the Seleucid dynasty ruled over an area extending from Asia Minor to the Indus River, in present-day Pakistan.

Semite
A set of related languages assumed to be associated with an ethnic group who has inhabited portions of Southwest Asia since the time of the first cities. Arabic and Hebrew are surviving examples of Semitic languages.

shaft tomb
A tomb in the form of a rectangular shaft, with a burial chamber at its base. After the burial had been made, the chamber was roofed, and the shaft above it filled in. Elaborate examples, such as the six shaft tombs of Grave Circle A, at Mycenae, consist of stone-lined shafts with stone and wooden roofing covering the burial chambers.

shaman
A person believed to have supernatural powers. In times of sickness, shortage of game, or any other threat to a community's survival, the shaman is called upon to mediate with the spirit world on the community's behalf. The shaman presides over rituals, and may also be responsible for the keeping of laws and the continuity of traditions. Shamanism is the dominant element in the religion of most known arctic and subarctic hunter-gatherers. Most shamans are male.

sherd
A small piece of broken pottery.

situla
A bucket-shaped vessel made of metal, often with a swinging handle across the rim.

stele
An upright slab or column of stone, often decorated with carvings or bearing inscriptions.

Stupa

stupa
A dome-shaped monument of earth, brick, or stone, often elaborately decorated with sculpture and railings, housing a relic of the Buddha or of a Buddhist saint.

stylus
A sharpened wooden implement shaped like a pen with a wedge-shaped tip. It was used for impressing cuneiform writing into wet clay tablets, which were then baked.

Sumerians
The people who occupied southern Mesopotamia from about 3000 BC to 2000 BC. The Sumerians had their own distinct language, and are credited, among many other innovations, with inventing the world's earliest writing system. Some scholars believe that the Sumerians go back much further and may even have been the first sedentary inhabitants of southern Mesopotamia, from about 5500 BC.

Taoism
An ancient Chinese system of philosophy that is based on noninterference with the natural world and the leading of a simple, honest life. In the second century AD, a religion with the same name appeared in China in reaction to the growing popularity of Indian-originated Buddhism.

tholos tomb
A type of tomb, built of stone and set partly underground, associated with the Mycenaean culture of ancient Greece. It consists of a beehive-shaped chamber with a corbeled roof, accessed through a long passage called a *dromos*. The entrance to the passage is a tall doorway topped by a steep-sided gable.

triglyph
In the Doric architectural order, the vertically grooved panel between the two metopes of the frieze.

tuffaceous rock
A soft, porous rock consisting of compacted volcanic ash or dust.

tumulus
A large, circular tomb with an earthen mound on top. Tumuli were used for the burial chambers of Etruscan aristocrats in the Archaic period (from the sixth century BC to the fifth century BC), and the style was later revived by the Roman emperors Augustus and Hadrian.

tussah
A strong, coarse, tan-colored silk obtained from the cocoon of wild silkworms in China. When woven, this silk results in a tougher, shorter-fibered fabric than that made from the silk of the cultivated varieties of silkworm.

'Ubaid period
The period in southern Mesopotamia during which the first villages, and later, the first towns and cities, appeared and many of the characteristics of Sumerian civilization emerged. Objects such as clay tools, a distinctive style of painted pottery, and characteristic buildings help archaeologists identify settlements that were occupied during the 'Ubaid period. It extended for about 2,000 years from about 5500 BC.

Urnfield period
A group of related Late Bronze Age cultures in Europe characterized by the practice of placing the cremated remains of a dead person in a pottery funerary urn, which was then buried in a cemetery of urns. The practice dates from about 1300 BC, when urnfield graves became increasingly common in eastern central Europe; from there, this burial rite spread west, to Italy and Spain, north, across the Rhine to Germany, and east, to the steppes of Russia. Other features of the Urnfield period include copper-mining and sheet-bronze metalworking. The Urnfield period continued until the start of the Iron Age, about 750 BC, when inhumation once again became the dominant form of burial in many areas.

Vedas
The ancient sacred writings of Hinduism, comprising the Rig-Veda, the Yajur-Veda, the Sama-Veda, and the Atharva-Veda. The Rig-Veda records the arrival of Indo-Europeans in India, their struggles with the Dasas, and the establishment of their religious, cultural, and social life. The Vedas are written in Sanskrit and are thought to have been compiled in the late second millennium BC.

Villanova period
An Early Iron Age period in Italy, extending from about 900 BC to about 700 BC, that laid the foundations for the Etruscan culture. It is named after a site near Bologna.

ziggurat
A truncated pyramid of varying height that served as a platform for temples in the early cities of Mesopotamia. The first ziggurats were modest constructions, but by 2000 BC, more imposing examples dominated the great cities of southern Mesopotamia.

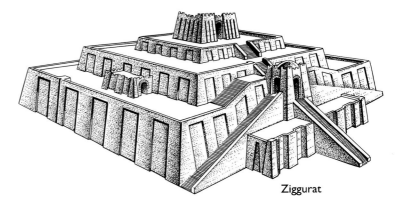
Ziggurat

Göran Burenhult

Göran Burenhult has been Associate Professor of Archaeology at the University of Stockholm, Sweden, since 1981 and is acknowledged internationally as a leading expert on prehistoric rock art and megalithic traditions. Between 1976 and 1981, he was director of the Swedish archaeological excavations at Carrowmore, County Sligo, Ireland, excavating one of the earliest known megalithic cemeteries, and he has undertaken field work on prehistoric rock art throughout the world, including the rock painting areas of the central Sahara Desert. Most recently, he has conducted ethnoarchaeological expeditions to the islands of Sulawesi and Sumba, in Indonesia, to the Trobriand Islands of Papua New Guinea, and to the island of Malekula, in Vanuatu, to study megalithic traditions, social organization, and primitive exchange. He is the author of numerous scholarly and popular books on archaeology and ethnoarchaeology, and has contributed to journals, magazines, and encyclopedic works. Between 1987 and 1991, he produced a series of international television programs about aspects of archaeology.

J.P. Casey

J.P. Casey is Reader in Archaeology at the University of Durham, UK, and is a specialist in Roman numismatics and Roman military history. He is currently working on the coinage and economy of Asia Minor in the Roman and Byzantine periods. He is the author of a number of excavation reports relating to Roman military sites in Wales, and has written numerous papers on the importance of Roman coinage.

Peter Damerow

Peter Damerow is a member of the Center for Development and Socialization at the Max Planck Institute for Human Development and Education in Berlin. There, he conducts research on concept development in the history of science and mathematics. He is currently working in conjunction with the Uruk project in Berlin on the decipherment of the proto-cuneiform writing system of ancient Mesopotamia.

Corinne Duhig

Corinne Duhig is a research student in the Faculty of Oriental Studies at the University of Cambridge, UK, and consultant human skeletal analyst for the Cambridgeshire Archaeology Unit. Her primary research interest is the analysis of human remains in an archaeological context, particularly health and disease in early dynastic Egypt, the use of human bone analysis to interpret mortuary practice in megalithic cemeteries, and the study of trepanation (surgical or ritual removal of skull roundels). Her current projects include the skeletal analysis of a pagan Saxon cemetery in Britain, of megalithic cemeteries in France and Malta, and of a Bronze Age settlement in Greece.

Christopher Fyfe

Christopher Fyfe was Reader in African History at the Centre of African Studies, at the University of Edinburgh, UK, from 1964 to 1991, where he taught a survey course covering African history from the earliest peoples to the present day. His first involvement with Africa, as Government Archivist in Sierra Leone (from 1950 to 1952), led, after a decade of research, to his book *A History of Sierra Leone*. He has also written or edited works on the Atlantic slave trade, African historical demography, and African medicine.

Ian C. Glover

Ian C. Glover is Senior Lecturer in the Department of Prehistoric Archaeology at the Institute of Archaeology, University College London, UK. He has located and excavated archaeological sites in Timor and Sulawesi, in Indonesia, and his field work has also taken him to western Thailand and central Vietnam, where he surveyed and excavated prehistoric, protohistoric, and historic sites.

Helena F. Hamerow

Helena F. Hamerow is Lecturer in Early Medieval Archaeology in the Department of Archaeology at the University of Durham, UK. Her main area of research is Anglo-Saxon archaeology. She has made a particular study of the development and morphology of Mucking, in Essex, the largest Anglo-Saxon settlement excavated to date.

Richard J. Harrison

Richard J. Harrison is Reader in Archaeology in the Department of Classics and Archaeology at the University of Bristol, UK. He is currently researching Bronze Age societies in northern Spain. On a wider scale, his main area of interest is pastoralism in prehistoric Europe. He has spent many years studying the Copper and Bronze Age settlements of western Europe and the development of the Iberian civilization in Spain, and has excavated settlements in the Ebro Valley of northern Spain.

Pontus Hellström

Pontus Hellström is Professor of Classical Archaeology and Ancient History at the University of Uppsala, Sweden. Since 1979, he has been in charge of research and excavations at the fourth-century BC temple site of Labraynda, in the mountains of southwestern Turkey, which has yielded new evidence on the origins of Hellenistic culture. He is the author of numerous books and articles on Mediterranean archaeology, and is a past president of the Swedish Archaeological Society.

Cho-yun Hsu

Cho-yun Hsu is a member of Academia Sinica, Taiwan; University Professor of History at the University of Pittsburgh, USA; and concurrently, Wei-Lun Professor of History at the Chinese University of Hong Kong. His special area of research is the socioeconomic history of early China. He has published several books and numerous articles in both English and Chinese, including *Ancient China in Transition*, *Han Agriculture*, and *The Western Chou Civilization*.

Graham Joyner

Graham Joyner is Lecturer in History and Curator of the Ancient History Teaching Collection at Macquarie University, Sydney, Australia. He teaches Greek language and archaeology, as well as courses in Greek pottery and sculpture, and Greek and Roman numismatics. He studied in Sydney and Athens, and has participated in excavations in Cyprus, Crete, and other parts of Greece. He has published works on Mycenaean Greece and Classical Greek, and has written and presented a television program on writing in antiquity.

Barry Kemp

Barry Kemp is Reader in Egyptology in the Faculty of Oriental Studies at the University of Cambridge, UK. Since 1977, he has been the Field Director of the Egypt Exploration Society's expedition to el-Amarna.

Katheryn M. Linduff

Katheryn M. Lindruff is Professor in the Department of Fine Arts and Professor in the Department of Anthropology at the University of Pittsburgh, USA. Her special area of interest is Chinese art and archaeology. Her publications include *Western Chou Civilization, Art Past/Art Present*, and *Shang and Chou Ritual Arts*. She is currently working on a text on China and its northern neighbors, after undertaking field work in Inner Mongolia.

J.G. Macqueen

J.G. Macqueen retired in 1993 from the position of Reader in Classics and Ancient Middle Eastern Studies at the University of Bristol, UK. His main area of specialization is ancient southwestern Asia, and in particular, Anatolia, where he has conducted field work and excavation. He is also interested in Latin literature, especially satire and Latin poetry of the Renaissance period. He is the author of *Babylon* and *The Hittites*.

Elizabeth H. Moore

Elizabeth H. Moore is Lecturer in the Department of Art and Archaeology in the School of Oriental and African Studies at the University of London, UK. Her special areas of interest are Khmer art in Thailand and Cambodia, and the arts of Burma (Myanmar). In 1989, she conducted preliminary excavations at the protohistoric site of Ban Takhong, Buri Ram province, Thailand. She is currently engaged in joint projects in Cambodia and Burma: in Cambodia, as consultant archaeologist to the UNESCO Zoning and Environmental Management Project (ZEMP) for Angkor; in Burma, she is working with the Department of Archaeology at the University of Yangon on the formulation of a university curriculum in archaeology.

Robert G. Morkot

Robert G. Morkot recently completed a PhD at University College London, UK. He is a specialist in the history of Nubia and the Sudan. He is currently preparing reports of excavations by the Egypt Exploration Society at Sesbi, in the Sudan, and by the University of Oxford in the Meroitic Cemetery at Faras, in the Sudan.

Boyo G. Ockinga

Boyo G. Ockinga is Senior Lecturer in History at Macquarie University, Sydney, Australia, where he teaches ancient Egyptian history, religion, and language (hieroglyphs). He undertakes regular field work in Egypt, and is currently engaged in the excavation of the tomb of Amenemope, the third prophet of Amun, at Thebes.

Susan Pollock

Susan Pollock is Assistant Professor of Anthropology at the State University of New York at Binghamton, USA. Her principal area of interest is the ancient Near East, especially the emergence of state and urban societies in Mesopotamia. From 1985 to 1990, she conducted field work at the Uruk Mound of Abu Salabikh, in southern Iraq, investigating the economic organization of this fourth-millennium town. She has also worked in Iran, Turkey, Europe, and North America. Her theoretical and methodological interests include mortuary analysis, feminist approaches, and political economy.

Himanshu Prabha Ray

Himanshu Prabha Ray is Assistant Professor in the Centre for Historical Studies, at the Jawaharlal Nehru University, New Delhi, India. She has made a particular study of early maritime contacts between South Asia and Southeast Asia, and has participated in a number of archaeological excavations, the most recent being the Thai–Italian project at Tha Kae, Thailand, and the Indo-American project at Arikamedu, Tamil Nadu. She is author of *Monastery and Guild—Commerce under the Satavahanas* and *Buddhism and the Maritime Links of South Asia*.

Charles L. Redman

Charles L. Redman is Professor of Anthropology at Arizona State University, USA, and Principal in Charge of Roosevelt Lake Platform Mound Project (the largest such field project in the country). His major research interests include the development of sedentary societies and improving the effectiveness of archaeological methods. He has directed field work in several countries in southwestern Asia and the Mediterranean, and in New Mexico and Arizona. His publications include *People of the Tonto Rim, Explanation in Archaeology* (co-author), *Research and Theory in Current Archaeology* (editor), *The Rise of Civilization*, and *Qsar Es-Seghir: an Archaeological View of Medieval Life*, and many articles on archaeological methods and early complex societies.

David Ridgway

David Ridgway is Reader in the Department of Classics at the University of Edinburgh, UK. Since 1966, he has worked with Giorgio Buchner, the excavator of Pithekoussai (in the Bay of Naples, Italy), on the definitive publication of this site. His other publications include *The First Western Greeks* and *Italy before the Romans*, co-edited with Francesca R. Ridgway, and he wrote the Etruscan chapters of the new *Cambridge Ancient History*.

Peter Rowley-Conwy

Peter Rowley-Conwy is Lecturer in the Department of Archaeology at the University of Durham, UK. He obtained his PhD with research on the Late Mesolithic and Early Neolithic history of Denmark, and has subsequently researched the European Paleolithic, Mesolithic, and Neolithic periods and the origins of agriculture in Southwest Asia. He has also worked on the economic archaeology of the Nile Valley in the Late and post-Pharaonic periods.

Charlotte Scheffer

Charlotte Scheffer is Senior Lecturer in the Department of Classical Archaeology and Ancient History at the University of Stockholm, Sweden. Her area of specialization is Etruscology and the iconography of vase painting, and she is currently researching concepts of death in Etruscan funerary art. Her field work includes participating in excavations at the Etruscan town of Acquarossa and at Poggio Civitate, near Siena. She has published three books and a number of research articles, and is joint editor of a Swedish periodical on classical antiquity.

Wulf Schiefenhövel

Wulf Schiefenhövel is Research Associate at the Unit for Human Ethology at the Max Planck Society, Andechs, Germany, and Professor of Medical Psychology and Ethnomedicine at the University of Munich. He has conducted field work in Papua New Guinea, Irian Jaya, Bali, East Java, and the Trobriand Islands. His main areas of interest are the evolutionary biology of human behavior, ethnomedicine, and anthropology, especially reproductive strategies, birth behavior, early socialization, nonverbal communication, aggression and aggression control, and cultural diversity and the evolution of culture. He serves on the boards of many publications.

I.M. Stead

I.M. Stead is Deputy Keeper in the Department of Prehistoric and Romano-British Antiquities in the British Museum, London, where he is in charge of the European Iron Age collections. He has supervised many field excavations: initially, in the position of Inspector of Ancient Monuments, during the 1960s, when he worked first on Roman villas and then on Iron Age burials. He coordinated work on the Lindow Man bog body (from 1984 to 1986), and initiated excavations at Snettisham, in Norfolk, where hoards of gold torques were found. He has written many articles on excavations, artifacts, and Celtic art.

David Hurst Thomas

David Hurst Thomas is Curator of Anthropology at the American Museum of Natural History, New York, USA. He is a specialist in the archaeology of the American Indian. He discovered and excavated the Gatecliff Shelter, in Nevada, the deepest rock shelter known in the Americas, with tightly stratified deposits spanning the past 8,000 years. He is the author or editor of many distinguished publications, has written more than 60 monographs and scientific articles, is on the editorial board of several journals, and is a founding trustee of the National Museum of the American Indian. In 1989, in recognition of his services to American archaeology, he was elected to the National Academy of Science.

Håkan Wahlquist

Håkan Wahlquist is Curator of Asian Anthropology at the National Museum of Ethnography in Stockholm, Sweden, and Keeper of the Sven Hedin Foundation. His area of specialization is the anthropology and cultural history of Asia, especially southern, central, and eastern Asia. He has undertaken social anthropological field work in northeastern Nepal.

Peter Warren

Peter Warren is Professor of Ancient History and Classical Archaeology at the University of Bristol, UK. His area of specialization is Aegean prehistory, and in particular, the Minoan civilization of Crete, and he has directed excavations in Crete at Myrtos, Debla, and Knossos. He is also interested in the historical botany and use of plants on Crete, in the archaeology of the Cycladic island of Thera (Santorini), and in Aegean chronology. He has written numerous articles and five books on aspects of Aegean prehistory.

J. Peter White

J. Peter White is Reader in Prehistoric Archaeology in the School of Archaeology, Classics and Ancient History at the University of Sydney, Australia. He has a special interest in the prehistory of Australia and the Pacific, especially Melanesia. He began research work in New Guinea in 1963, excavating for prehistory and studying the technology of Highlanders who grew up in the Stone Age. More recently, he has worked in New Ireland and undertaken taphonomic studies in the Flinders Ranges, Australia. He is co-author, with Professor J. O'Connell, of *A Prehistory of Australia, New Guinea and Sahul*, and has edited the journal *Archeology in Oceania* since 1981.

Charlotte Wikander

Charlotte Wikander is Lecturer in the Department of Classical Archaeology and Ancient History at the University of Gothenburg, Sweden. She is currently working on a publication of Etruscan inscriptions. She participated in the excavation of the Etruscan town of Acquarossa, and wrote her doctoral dissertation on terracottas from the site.

Örjan Wikander

Örjan Wikander is Associate Professor in the Department of Classics at Lund University, Sweden. His main areas of research are Greek and Italic architectural terracottas, Roman watermills, and the use of water power in ancient times. He is also interested in Etruscan and Roman bronzes, and Etruscan inscriptions. He has taken part in excavations at Etruria and Rome, and has published four books and numerous articles on classical archaeology and ancient history.

⟜ This Egyptian cosmetic spoon, fashioned in the form of a woman swimming with a duck, is made of wood and ivory and dates from the eighteenth dynasty (1540 BC to 1295 BC).
THE LOUVRE/LAUROS-GIRAUDON

I N D E X